POEMS OF NATION, ANTHEMS OF EMPIRE

Winner of the Walker Cowen Memorial Prize
for an outstanding work of scholarship
in eighteenth-century studies

Suvir Kaul

POEMS OF NATION,
ANTHEMS OF EMPIRE

*English Verse
in the Long
Eighteenth Century*

UNIVERSITY PRESS OF VIRGINIA

CHARLOTTESVILLE AND LONDON

The University Press of Virginia
© 2000 by the Rector and Visitors of the University of Virginia
All rights reserved
Printed in the United States of America
First published in 2000

LIBRARY OF CONGRESS CATALOGING-IN-PUBLICATION DATA

Kaul, Suvir.
 Poems of nation, anthems of empire: English verse in the long eighteenth century/
Suvir Kaul
 p. cm.
 Includes bibliographical references (p.) and index.
 ISBN 0-8139-1967-3 (cloth: alk. paper)—ISBN 0-8139-1968-1 (pbk.: alk. paper)
 1. English poetry—18th century—History and criticism. 2. Nationalism and
literature—Great Britain—History—18th century. 3. Imperialism—History—18th century.
4. Nationalism in literature. 5. Imperialism in literature. 6. Colonies in literature. I. Title.

PR555.N27 K38 2000
811'.509358—dc21

00-027526

CONTENTS

ACKNOWLEDGMENTS

Writing this page is the equivalent of heaving a sigh of relief: there is, finally, a book in prospect, and it is time to look back and to thank those whose suggestions and complaints made the task of writing it easier, more rewarding, and considerably more difficult. As library acquisition budgets shrink and academic publishing becomes more and more demanding, it takes the combined efforts of a great many people to produce a manuscript that is considered acceptable by editors in the humanities, and I am very glad to thank Bradin Cormack, Jonathan Lamb, Ania Loomba, and Felicity Nussbaum for their wonderful readings of the manuscript and for their many suggestions for revision. This project also benefited from the attentions of a larger reserve army of occasional readers: Srinivas Aravamudan, John Bender, Laura Brown, Martin Evans, Jay Fliegelman, Seth Lerer, Marty Wechselblatt. For conversations and support in flourishing and in difficult times, I thank Sam Otter and Caverlee Cary, Ben Crow and Deborah Gordon, Shalini Advani, Amanda Anderson, Henry Abelove, Neeladri Bhattacharya, Anston Bosman, Walter Cohen, Simon Dickie, Chris Gabbard, Maureen Harkin, Geraldine Heng, Scott Herring, Sharon Holland, Robert Kaufman, Annette Keogh, Sean Keilen, Margaret Kelley, Paula Moya, Donna Landry, Andrew Parker, Adela Pinch, Helen Tartar, and Robert Warrior. Dennis Marshall's copyediting skills granted my writing more precision and accuracy; for this I am grateful. Finally, I would like to thank David Shields and David Konig, the judges for the Walker Cowen Award, for their vote of confidence in my manuscript.

The travails of any manuscript are shared by family as well as friends— my parents, Kaushalya and Bhavanesh Kaul, anxiously followed its progress, as did Urvi and Anal Puri, Kalpana, N. G., and Tia Kaul. They celebrated with me the Walker Cowen Award, as did Primla Loomba and Bindia Thapar, Vineet and Suneet Puri, and Tahira Thapar. And then there is Tariq, whose skepticism about 'lit-crit speak' is as unbounded as his affection, and I am grateful for both.

This book is for Ania, and for her unswerving faith that the life of ideas is one worth living.

POEMS OF NATION, ANTHEMS OF EMPIRE

INTRODUCTION

POETRY, NATIONAL PRIDE, AND
THE CALL TO EMPIRE

To begin, I make a large claim of a small poem: the aggressive nationalism of James Thomson's ode "Rule, Britannia!" (1740) is the condition to which much English poetry on public themes written in the late seventeenth and eighteenth centuries aspires. The formal features and thematic concerns of this ode repeat many of the poetic forms and topics central to the practice of poetry in this period; they also summarize recurrent concerns in Thomson's own literary career. Domestic agricultural prosperity (unencumbered with any sense of agrarian strife), a social and political order anchored in a constitutional balance between Parliament and the monarchy, commercial success abroad ensured by a dominance of naval power—these are the prospects Thomson and his fellow poets delighted in (and worried about). That "Rule, Britannia!" became as well known and beloved as it did, till it functioned virtually as the anthem of British nationalism and imperialism, has much to do with the practiced ease with which Thomson orchestrates these topoi within his poem, but it is also a product of features specific to this ode: its pithy jingoism, the fervor of its patriotic sentiment, its prophetic, yet curiously defensive tone, the jaunty simplicity of its rhymes, the choric character of the refrain, and the sheer scope of the theological, political, cultural, and even civilizational authority it orchestrates. In this ode, quite remarkably, Thomson is able to invoke all these themes in a way that combines their ideological potency, and to do so in verses that are populist in their ballad-like ease.[1] He enables a weighty world-picture here and does so in a form and vocabulary that naturalizes, assimilates, renders popular.

Appearing as it did at the end of a public performance (of *Alfred: A Masque,* a work by Thomson and David Mallet) "Rule, Britannia!" enacts fully the desire of British poets for a cultural power that would be more than literary—that would declaim to a rapt audience the coming to global power of a puissant Britain, divinely ordained inheritor of the imperial and civilizational traditions of classical Europe. In the masque, the ode is sung by a "venerable Bard / Aged and blind," a figure whose disability is the conventional marker of vatic power. Each stanza works with an economy of purpose: the first claims divine sanction for this vision of a powerful Britain, an island raised from the ocean in order to rule its surface:

> When Britain first, at Heaven's command,
>   Arose from out the azure main,
> This was the charter of the land,
>   And guardian angels sung this strain—
>   "Rule, Britannia, rule the waves;
>   Britons never will be slaves."[2]

Britain's heavenly origins are enunciated via an odd (but representative) yoking of divine and legal-commercial sanctions: in the beginning was the "charter" (line 3). In the myth of national origins being composed here, British geography and history begin in divine command, which (in a fine instance of the overlapping of religious and commercial discourses in the eighteenth century) takes the form of a contract.

The first four lines exude a confidence that is confirmed in the last couplet, in which the angelic choir (here a trope for communal poetic voice) sings out the refrain of the ode. Britannia is exhorted, somewhat predictably, to rule the waves, but, less predictably, Britons are told that they "never will be slaves." This negative definition of the national self, coming as it does at a time when Britain was fully engaged in slavery and the slave trade, reads oddly. It is, in spite of the blithe and spirited tone of the couplet, an uncomfortable moment, an intimation that the product, and one of the bases, of Britain's power overseas was slavery and the slave trade. The refrain both represses or disavows that knowledge, while serving as a reminder that, in the political and moral economy of mid-eighteenth-century Britain, the obverse of national power is the condition of slaves. This is not an unusual rhetorical coupling; as Robin Blackburn has pointed out, in "the period 1630–1750 the British Empire witnessed an increasingly clamorous, and even obsessive, 'egotistical' revulsion against 'slavery' side by side with an almost uncontested exploitation of African bondage."[3]

In Thomson's poem, we might think of this couplet as the surfacing of a poetic or indeed national bad conscience, or we might ask if such negative self-definition derives from a contemporary cultural anxiety about Britishness: who, after all, was a Briton, and who (for Thomson and Mallet were both Scots) would know that question more intimately than Scotsmen?[4] Given that the making of "Great Britain" involved the effective colonization of parts of Ireland and the suppression of local institutions and political autonomies in Scotland (and, going back still further, in Wales), the forging of this island-nation was itself a reminder of the military, political, and economic processes whose most brutal, and most visibly racist, contemporary form was slavery.[5] Considerably more than three hundred thousand Irish and Scots poor were forced into indentured servitude in British America during the course of the eighteenth century, and while they were not slaves, their lives suggested the profound gaps between "British" liberty and provincial reality. Within the dynamic of the poem, then, the reference to slavery functions as an unexpected impediment to the buoyant, upbeat tone of the stanza. The couplet, sung, as is the rest of the strain, by an angelic choir, yokes together the optative and the prophetic: the waves/slaves rhyme, emphatic in its end-stopped closure, is certain that Britain's command of the oceans gives it control over the slave trade. However, contained in the couplet are historical tensions—"Britons" might themselves be enslaved, now or in the future—that threaten to destabilize this slogan of commercial and imperial dominance.

There is of course one more important way to read the reference to slavery here, and indeed to explain the centrality Thomson gives this sentiment by locating it in the refrain. Christine Gerrard has recently pointed out that the poem "began life as a potent piece of opposition propaganda," and that Thomson wrote as one of the Whig supporters of Frederick, Prince of Wales, who styled themselves Patriots.[6] Thus, the ringing refrain that Britons never will be slaves is conceivably a pointed slogan of dissidence directed at Robert Walpole, one that derives its buoyance from Admiral Vernon's naval victory over the Spanish at Porto Bello in November 1739.[7] Yet for Gerrard, "Rule, Britannia!" which she thinks of as "an apparently straightforward expression of patriotism—proves resistant to analysis." She argues that this is because the "Walpole era witnessed not one, but a number of complex, interrelated forms of patriotism," which means that propagandists opposed to each other often share a "patriotic" vocabulary and icons. Gerrard notes the internal inconsistencies and contradictions that characterize positions taken by contributors to these debates about national policy, as also the contention surrounding each claim to a politically nonpartisan defence of the realm (one party's patriotism being another party's factionalism).[8] That is, any expression of patriotic sentiment (including Thomson's poem) must not be taken at face value, for neither its motives nor its title to the nationalist high ground it stakes out for itself turn out to be as clear as first imagined.

And yet the terms of Thomson's nationalism in "Rule, Britannia!" are clarified, not clouded, by its location in the masque, which closes in a blaze

of triumphalist prophecy (this time as the vision of a hermit who exhorts
Alfred to confident action):

> I see thy Commerce, *Britain*, grasp the world:
> All nations serve thee; every foreign flood
> Subjected, pays his tribute to the *Thames.*
> Thither the golden South obedient pours
> His sunny treasures: thither the soft East
> Her spices, delicacies, gentle gifts:
> And thither his rough trade the stormy North.
>
> . . . .
>
> Shores, yet unfound, arise! in youthful prime,
> With towering forests, mighty rivers crown'd!
> These stoop to *Britain's* thunder. This new world
> Shook to its centre, trembles at her name:
> And there, her sons, with aim exalted, sow
> The seeds of rising empire, arts, and arms.
>
> > *Britons*, proceed, the subject Deep command,
> > Awe with your navies every hostile land.
> > In vain their threats, their armies all in vain:
> > They rule the balanc'd world, who rule the main.[9]

While it is true that the aggressive commercial and naval expansionism of
these lines, like that of "Rule, Britannia!" itself, must necessarily be understood
with reference to the political positions taken by City of London trading
interests (which Walpole slighted and Frederick flattered), there can be no
doubt that Thomson and Mallet are here articulating nationalist sentiments
and icons that we, in historical hindsight at least, can recognize as the
dominant tropology of nation in eighteenth-century Britain, and indeed in
the century and a half after. Political partisans they may have been, but
Thomson and Mallet are here working with the very stuff of nation, of the
making of "Great Britain" in an international frame in the long eighteenth
century.

If, then, "Rule, Britannia!" proves resistant to analysis, it does so because
in reading it we deal with, in some powerful ways, the problem of colonial
modernity itself, and of the role literature and, more particularly, poetry
played in its articulation. Stuart Hall has an eloquent comment on this
problem: "We know the words to the song, 'Rule Britannia' but we are
'unconscious' of the deep structure—the notions of nation, the great slabs
and slices of imperialist history, the assumptions about global dominance
and supremacy, the necessary Other of other people's subordination—which
are richly impacted in its simple celebratory resonances."[10] The poem, that
is, can be returned to its precise domestic political location, but what we

also need to do, in a postcolonial critical moment, is to pay attention to precisely those commonplaces of history and nation that have been so naturalized as the language and rhetorical forms of English poetry itself, that we take for granted their imaginative consistency without recognizing that such cultural coherence—which is a subset of the larger articulation of a Great Britain—was achieved in the face of resistant lands (or rather, in the language of the poem, of those found and as yet unfound nations and shores that would stoop to British thunder). Thus "Rule, Britannia!" is not simply evidence of the centrality of the nationalist concerns of contemporary poets; it is testimonial to the fact that poets in the long eighteenth century imagined poetry to be a unique and privileged literary form for the enunciation of a puissant (and plastic) vocabulary of nation, particularly one appropriate to a Britain proving itself (in fits and starts, to be sure) great at home and abroad. That in a nutshell is the claim of this book, but before I describe that argument in greater detail, I will conclude this reading of "Rule, Britannia!" in order to point to congruent themes that will also be addressed later.

To return to the matter of slavery: the second stanza brings the reference home, as it were, by claiming that Britain is blessed with the absence of domestic tyranny:

> The nations, not so blest as thee,
>   Must in their turns to tyrants fall;
> While thou shalt flourish great and free,
>   The dread and envy of them all.
>   "Rule," &c.
>
> *(lines 7–11)*

Britain's constitutional monarchy ensures national freedom and enables international strength, which is the claim that the next two stanzas elaborate:[11]

> Still more majestic shalt thou rise,
>   More dreadful from each foreign stroke;
> As the loud blast that tears the skies
>   Serves but to root thy native oak.
>   "Rule," &c.
>
> Thee haughty tyrants ne'er shall tame;
>   All their attempts to bend thee down
> Will but arouse thy generous flame,
>   But work their woe and thy renown.
>   "Rule," &c.
>
> *(lines 12–21)*

Thomson's method here combines a prophetic insistence on British power with the awareness, impossible to lose in the eighteenth century, that such power would always have to be earned in war. Britain, after all, fought successive wars, most often against France, throughout the century. Warfare, as any citizen of Britain then knew from the nation's recent experiences, includes reverses, and Thomson's vision includes that possibility in lines 12 and 13, subsuming them into a promise of inevitable recovery and even greater national strength. But this acknowledgment of defeat and hesitation before the nation rises "more dreadful" and renowned than before is also manifested in the curious combination of prophetic and wishful tones that define these stanzas: the repetition of "shall" or "will," for instance, paradoxically confirms the mood as optative rather than imperative. Prophecy and the "wished-for" are of course not separate, but their combination certainly qualifies the hortatory tones of this poem.

As does another feature that I will comment upon here before returning to Thomson's depiction of the nation recovering powerfully from adversity. The first line of the refrain, "Rule, Britannia, rule the waves," meant as a divine decree to command the oceans (and other lands), succeeds also in expressing a more computational ambition, to measure and chart the seas.[12] Absolute authority of the first sort contains within itself, and is predicated upon, this other sort of authority, which is the development of precise geometrical and navigational techniques. There is an important reason to treat the word *Rule* as more than an unintentional pun in the poem, albeit one that is made resonant by what we know of the emphasis on measuring, chart making, and calculation in the making of British naval supremacy in the eighteenth century. For the poem is itself an attempt to impose an impossible mensurational linearity on the ebbs and flows of national fortune—here suggested by the metaphoric disorder of the oceans, of the rise and fall of waves—for the poet's vision of Britain's coming to power, and *staying* in power, is dependent upon such control over the vicissitudes of time and the recalcitrant lessons of history. I am not suggesting that the poet should be seen as an eighteenth-century Canute, here ordering the waves to obey his will, but arguing that the measured orderliness and repetitions characteristic of "Rule, Britannia!" express, at the level of form, the poet's desire for a well-regulated and forward-moving vision of history. Thematically and formally, the poem seeks to master the oceans, to claim the same success perhaps that developments in the instrumental sciences allowed British mariners. But poetry is not science, and the dynamic of this poem suggests not so much the linear progress of history into a British future, with the poem as a map or chart of that progress, as it does the apprehensions, hesitations, and reversals that necessarily interrupt the nation's rise to overseas power.

Typically, Thomson's analogy for recovery from national defeat features a contemporary symbol for Britain's naval and commercial might made famous by its poets: the "native oak" (line 15).[13] In this instance, Thomson's oak remains rooted (rather than sailing off down the Thames) as an expression of the power of the majestic state to revive itself when confronted by foreign challenges. As a symbol of domestic and natural strength, though, the oak also stands in for precisely those agrarian and commercial virtues that Thomson suggests anchor Britain's power overseas:

> To thee belongs the rural reign;
>   Thy cities shall with commerce shine;
> All thine shall be the subject main,
>   And every shore it circles thine.
>   "Rule," &c.
>
> *(lines 22–26)*

These lines identify the social and economic continuum that the oak signifies: the majesty of the nation-state, the agrarian practices of rural Britain, the commerce that was transforming its cities (and indeed reaching into its countryside) and its burgeoning naval and imperial power, master of the "subject main" and of other territories.

The last stanza of "Rule, Britannia!" invokes another topos that Thomson and a great many of his compatriots found irresistible in their meditations on the rise and fall of empires and civilizations. If the poem opens with an account of the divine charter that makes Britain a contemporary commercial and imperial power, then this last stanza invokes the cultural presence of what Thomson called the Muses in order to confirm the appropriateness of Britain's authority:

> The Muses, still with freedom found,
>   Shall to thy happy coast repair:
> Blest isle! with matchless beauty crowned.
>   And manly hearts to guard the fair.
>   "Rule, Britannia, rule the waves;
>   Britons never will be slaves."

As John Crider has shown, the idea that "the arts move in liberty's train" is a "great commonplace of Augustan poets."[14] As Crider also suggests, it is not only the medieval and Renaissance convention of *translatio studii* that is referred to at such moments, but also the "underlying . . . idea . . . of *translatio imperii*, the westward movement of empire."[15] Thomson's linking of the Muses and British "freedom" (line 27) is thus a comment on national destiny within an international—and more particularly, imperial—framework. The transitions of history—here figured in the movement of the Muses—are predicated upon national distinction. As the entire poem argues, the Muses will settle in Britain not only because its constitutional politics differentiates it from other nations but because it now lays claim to the mantle of past European empires and their cultures. Of interest, then, is the poem's celebration of the "manly hearts" that guard the fair (the Muses—British women): this sentiment is of course fueled by the naturalization of the Muses, but also looks forward to a less classical usage.[16]

One last note before I move away from "Rule, Britannia!" Earlier, I had mentioned Thomson's Scots origins as a possible source of one rhetorical oddity in the poem; now I would like to point out just how historically apposite it is that a Scotsman composed the anthem of British imperial culture. In *Devolving English Literature*, Robert Crawford argues that, after the 1707 Act of Union, Scottish "improvers" began the work of producing an English(ed) language and culture that would allow Scottish people to "play a full part" in the new Britain. In doing so, they produced not so much an improved Scottish culture, but the culture of the nation itself—including, Crawford suggests, the idea of an "English Literature" central to that culture.[17] Crawford's insight has recently been extended to argue that the very category of *culture* that was demarcated in this period (and that is so important a marker of the rise of the social and disciplinary formations that constitute eighteenth-century British modernity) is itself "tied to the status of Scotland in the Union: the reorganizations of knowledge and of nation go hand in hand."[18] The work of culture is to articulate the provinces and the center into a new whole; the work of the poet is part of that process: that is crucial to the history of eighteenth-century Britain. We should notice, though, not only internal subordination and its sublimation, but also that other constitutive element that *enables* and *justifies* such sublimation, the vision of Britannia, mistress of the empire of the sea.

To analyze the vocabulary and concerns of "Rule, Britannia!" is to come to understand many of the economic, political, cultural and aesthetic values Thomson took seriously throughout his poetic career. It is also to recognize that Thomson, like many of his contemporary poets, thought of poetry as a useful—indeed, recommended—vehicle for commentaries on issues of great public significance for the nation and for society. Poetry, including its lyrical forms, is not an exercise in inwardness for Thomson, but a viable and even vital way of intervening in, and molding, public discourse. This is of course not a new idea for students of poetry (particularly of the work of male poets) in this period.[19] Even though some critics have emphasized the midcentury turn toward the self-conscious inscription of inwardness, whether it be the embattled neurasthenia of Gray or Collins, the more disassociated hysteria of Chatterton or Smart, the melancholy sensibility-on-display of Young's *Night Thoughts* or of the other graveyard poets, it is worth remembering just how *worldly* this inwardness actually is, how compounded of a intensely felt (sometimes too intensely felt) sense of the materiality of nature and history. And this inward turn is more noticeable largely in comparison with poetic practices that came before, and those that continued alongside: the engagement of Milton, Marvell, and Dryden with the turbulent politics of their time; Pope's will to legislate over the "republic of letters" then coming into being as part of the larger public sphere demarcated by print culture and its conversational analogue, the coffeehouse; Stephen Duck's and Mary Collier's public debate on the nature and gender of rural labor; Johnson's professional struggles, which resolved themselves in part via a dictionary of the national tongue and literary biographies that stabilized a national canon; James MacPherson's forging of a Celtic prehistory for Britain; Goldsmith's concern with enclosure, depopulation, and the state of the nation (and Crabbe's response to him and to other pressing agrarian issues); or even Blake's visionary conception of history as a record of the war between "natural innocence" and culture. The point is, quite simply, that eighteenth-century British poetry—even in its images of retirement and retreat—brought itself into being as part of the larger cultural conversation of the nation.[20]

And this brief list names only those poets who have been incorporated into literary-critical memory; in fact, the public face of poetry in the late seventeenth century and the eighteenth century might well be that of the near-anonymous (and now forgotten) propagandist who writes satire or polemical poems on urgent sociopolitical issues. This model of poetic intervention in debates about national priorities or governmental policies is formative of the poems I will examine; even when these poems are not couched in the genres or forms considered popular for public intervention (satire, lampoon, burlesque, panegyric, Pindaric) they are still shaped by the search for forms and idioms appropriate to weighty or inspired meditations upon the state of the nation. This book is thus about the quest for poetic confidence, with one important proviso: such confidence is not seamless even in those poems we might think of as anthems, by which I mean lyrics or songs that enunciate a confident collectivity and direct it into the future. Even such poems are rarely secure from internal inconsistencies and betray, if nothing else, the rhetorical *effort* required to forge a collectivity in the language of poetry. I will emphasize, that is, the formulaic or innovative ways in which poets were able to mobilize a rhetoric of (national) collectivity in their poetry only by repressing vital cultural, social, and economic contradictions. Indeed, the poems reveal such repression, or, more often than not, *manage* such contradictions by thematizing them, with the plastic, expansive dynamic of each poem providing a formal structure for the expression of, and the reconciliation or sublimation of, such contradictions.[21]

The model of contradiction I invoke here proposes that the primary task of a political criticism is to decode the largely unconscious resolutions supplied by the narrative search for ideological closure or coherence. This is of course the most powerful form of the critique of ideology as it has been developed by literary and critical theorists in the last two decades, and its arguments and methods are presumed by much that follows in this book.[22] In addition however, the peculiarly *public* nature of the literary materials I deal with here, and in particular the historical fact that these poets were engaged in debates whose opposing positions, arguments, and rhetorical forms they knew well and needed to counter, leads to their producing a whole series of more conscious oppositions—contradictions at the surface, so to speak; contradictions that structure the movement of the poem—in order to manage these tensions and to achieve (not always successfully) an overall dynamic that is the stronger for having supplanted or sublimated its own weaknesses or inadequacies. I do not want to suggest that these poems are the equivalent of the point-and-rebuttal format cherished by debating clubs, but they contain elements of such techniques, and are energized, in conception and in formal progress, by the desire to use both the affective and cognitive, the emotive and the critical, resources of poetry to intervene in public processes. Thus, Dryden's *Annus Mirabilis* arrives at its celebration of the monarch and the nation by superseding contemporary arguments that dramatic events in London—the fire, the plague—were portents of an impending republican revolution.[23] Similarly, if Hannah More sings the praises of English "Liberty" in "The Slave Trade" (a poem written to mobilize parliamentary opinion in favor of abolition), she is quick to differentiate it from that "mad liberty" espoused by the London mobs who had taken to the streets in 1780 during the Gordon riots. In each case, we are dealing with poets who have a precise sense of all they write on behalf of, but also a sharp awareness of what they are up against. Therefore, my analyses of this body of poetry will pay attention to the interplay between conscious and unconscious contradictions, those thematized and those more latent, those that ripple the formal surface and those whose powerful undertow remains submerged.

Why poetry, we might ask? Why should poetry become so manifestly the literary and imaginative space for such cultural and ideological work? One way to address that question is briefly to follow the movement of similar ideas in eighteenth-century British prose fiction, and to notice the changing ways in which that genre thematized considerations of the nation in its international frame, expressed cultural and geographical difference, and constructed historical genealogies for Great Britain and its empire. After all, if we take Behn's *Oroonoko* (1688), Defoe's *Robinson Crusoe* (1719) or *Moll Flanders* (1722) and even *Roxana* (1724), and Swift's *Gulliver's Travels* (1726) to be important milestones in the early progress of the novel in eighteenth-century Britain, we might expect to see far more novels in which the world beyond Britain's borders provides the spaces and the experiences, and indeed the pressing concerns and issues, considered by novelists. These are traveling novels, novels whose narrative energy and creativity is inextricable from the horizons of contemporary mercantilist and colonial expansion. In each case, the British subject—and indeed subjectivity itself—is constituted in a process of overseas discovery, its often uncomfortable lessons brought home in the dislocations of Gulliver or the tragedy of Moll. But this is not the world of Richardson and Fielding, whose novels achieve their density precisely by restricting their scope to interior spaces and landscapes: even the latter's chosen mode of discovery is a traveling at home rather than in strange and hostile territories abroad.[24] Felons, not the novels themselves, are now transported overseas—to that extent, the domestic resolutions of the bourgeois novel represent a withdrawal from the ethnographic curiosity and exploratory risks taken by Behn, Defoe, and Swift.

In this account, then, one of the features of the "rise of the novel" is a partial retraction from its colonial origins, or at least a reassertion of the proper relation of center and margins in the imagination of the nation.[25] The itinerary might be simply described as the movement from the violent centrality of the sugar plantations of Surinam to *Oroonoko* to the discreet necessity of Caribbean plantations in Jane Austen's *Mansfield Park* or to Brontë's *Jane Eyre*. The process by which this proper relation between English center and colonial periphery is *re*established in the novel also suggests to me a formal and generic evacuation: of the sheer *messiness* of Behn's narrative (its epistemological and anthropological uncertainties, its cultural dislocations, its obsessive and hyperbolic representation of violence and the breaking of slave bodies, its desire for, and fear of, miscegenation), of the great *difficulty* of making sense of the new worlds being created by colonial expansion. Both *Robinson Crusoe* and *Gulliver's Travels* are wracked by the same sort of libidinal excitement and terror: these are narratives within which writers articulated the quickened desires of displaced Royalists, shipwrecked sailors, and adventuring merchants, or charted the fanciful and perverse reaches of the colonizer's imagination; these are the narratives in which they, in short, crafted the rapidly changing geographical and historical axes of the nation in the late seventeenth and eighteenth centuries.[26]

The thematics of exploration and empire do not disappear, not in a British century defined by its energetic, uneven, and often destructive engagement with cultures and lives at the periphery of the island-nation and in its territories overseas. As Felicity Nussbaum demonstrates, feminist attention to the figuration of women (or of proper femininity) in fiction makes clear the importance of models of geographical, cultural, racial, and sexual difference to the making of the later-eighteenth-century novel in Britain.[27] Via comparative commentary on peoples and customs elsewhere, the histories, romances, and conduct books work toward a model of Christian bourgeois domesticity that defines the nation as much as the family, and indeed suggests that the nation-in-the-making is a family, united under a patriarchy whose norms are iterable in Edinburgh and in Dublin as much as in London. As this turn to the family and the domestic becomes the definitive feature of novels, their exploration of the constitutive relation between subjectivity, nation, and empire becomes less overt, even while these connections retain a symbolic or ideological centrality. There are of course exceptions to this trend: Nussbaum points to the vogue in oriental tales, examples of which are Johnson's *Rasselas* (1759) and Frances Sheridan's *History of Nourjahad* (1767), and calls attention to Phebe Gibbes's *Hartley House, Calcutta* (1789), and Markman Ellis has pointed to several sentimental novels, particularly those that engage in the late-eighteenth-century debates about slavery and the slave trade, as texts in which the activities of Britons overseas define or contest British self-conception in general.[28]

To some extent this story can be repeated in the history of the theater: while the Restoration stage is full of stories of the violence and mayhem of colonial warfare and of competing nations, theater in the eighteenth century becomes much more circumspect, much more domestic, in its themes, characters, and locations, even if it never loses its awareness of people and places overseas. Davenant's *The Siege of Rhodes* (1656/1661) or *The Cruelty of the Spaniards in Peru* (1658); Dryden's *The Indian Emperor, or, The Conquest of Mexico by the Spaniards* (1665) or the two parts of *The Conquest of Granada* (1670) or *Aureng-zebe* (1675/76) and Otway's *Venice Preserved* (1682) are good examples of the way in which "foreign" locations enabled English playwrights to refine both a geopolitical vocabulary and the idiom of tragedy.[29] Heroic tragedies in this period did not simply exercise the royalist prerogatives (and illusions) that accompanied Charles II home; they provided English culture an opportunity to reflect upon the costs and requirements of international warfare and colonial competition.[30] We might note also (though this is not the place to develop this idea at the length it deserves) that it is the tragedy (that is, the tragic form) that allows for such exploration: the overwhelming emphasis on territorial greed, intercultural and interracial cruelty, and the violent codes of heroism (here leadership in the name of a national collectivity) are all stabilized ultimately by the bloodletting and catharsis that define the form. Important, too, is the way in which scenes of colonial torture (that of Montezuma and the Indian high priest in act 5, scene 2 of *The Indian Emperor*, for instance) become occasions for the staging of debates on cultural and religious values and differences, in much the same way as the torture of Oroonoko (and the death of Imoinda) make more pointed the meditations on national and racial difference that characterize Behn's novella.

But as heroic tragedy loses its favor on the London stage, the staging of colonial violence and cruelty largely disappears, too, as does the opportunity for a playwright like Dryden to say that he brings Montezuma back to life because Montezuma is safer under the aegis of the English monarchy than he was under the Spanish "in his Native *Indies*."[31] The reflection upon, and the crafting of, the vocabularies of national difference (the Indians as victims of the Spanish, the English as better because less violent in the colonial theater than the Spanish) is a crucial feature of such playwrighting. As is, to be sure, a more generalized concern with the seductions of colonial power, a concern articulated in surprisingly nuanced forms in some plays. I am here thinking particularly of a play far removed from the blood and gore of these plays of colonial savagery, but one that achieves extraordinary discursive complexity in its staging of the cultural and psychological coordinates of colonial domination. This is Addison's *Cato* (1713), in which Juba, the Numidian prince who worships Cato and "Roman values," and Syphax, his older adviser, debate the ideological hegemony of the conqueror. Juba believes that

> A Roman soul is bent on higher views:
> To civilize the rude, unpolished world,
> And lay it under the restraint of laws;
> To make man mild and sociable to man;
> To cultivate the wild, licentious savage
> With wisdom, discipline, and lib'ral arts.
>   *(1.4.30–35)*[32]

Syphax on the other hand, as resistant rather than colonized subject, argues strenuously that "these wondrous civilizing arts, / This Roman polish and this smooth behaviour" (1.4.40–41) are hypocritical and dissembling, the public face of the conquerors' "pride, rank pride and haughtiness of soul" ("I think," he says bitingly, "the Romans call it stoicism") (1.4.83–84). In its full form, this debate is even more nuanced, but this brief exchange suggests its flavor, and indicates just how important such plays were at providing a forum, as it were, for the expression of colonial anxieties and concerns. Cato's famed Stoicism—the psychology and ideology of the colonizer here— is under investigation as much as Juba's colonized consciousness, and the play itself a displaced analysis of the play of racial and cultural difference in models of benevolent, "civilizing" empire.

As opposed to these studies in the dislocations of culture and subjectivity—for both colonizers and colonized—attendant upon colonial contact, we have the more self-assured, Gallophobic nationalist hero of Susanna Centlivre's *A Bold Stroke for a Wife* (1718).[33] The hero Fainwell describes himself at the end of the play as someone who detests the beau monde as much as he does the "enemies of my religion" (Quakers in this case), but really as a man who has "had the honour to serve his Majesty and headed a regiment of the bravest fellows that ever pushed bayonet in the throat of a Frenchman; and notwithstanding the fortune this lady brings me [he has wooed and won the heiress Ann Lovely], whenever my country wants my aid, this sword and arm are at her service" (5.1.547–55).[34] In order to win Ann Lovely, Fainwell has successively duped her guardians, the aristocratic dandy Modelove, the pseudo-scholarly "virtuoso" Periwinkle, the avaricious merchant Tradelove and the hypocritical Quaker, Prim; in each case he does so by masquerading as the beau, the antiquarian, the international trader and the religious zealot in a way that fools the appropriate other into believing that he, Fainwell, is the real thing. In Centlivre's play, the narrative of romance (the knight Fainwell coming to the aid of the lovely lady in distress) enables the crafting of the new national subject (the patriotic and warrior-like Colonel) who is shown to be a composite of, or at least adept at, the codes of behavior representative of varied and opposed social constituencies in early-eighteenth-century Britain. The theater of self-determination has changed, though, away from foreign lands and back home to London, even if the vocabulary of colonial competition is pervasive: Fainwell gulls Tradelove by playing Jan van Timtamtirelereletta Heer van Fainwell, a rich Dutch merchant, and his closing speech emphasizes the centrality of anti-French feeling to his very English being.

Perhaps the signal instance of the process by which these early texts of colonial cruelty and victimage, of interracial desire and its punishments, were replaced by more banal and safe versions of intercultural contact like that of Centlivre's *Bold Stroke* is Thomas Southerne's 1695 redaction, for the stage, of Behn's *Oroonoko*. Southerne's play contains none of the distressing eyewitness accounts of colonial torture that are featured in Behn's story, and his Oroonoko goes to a dignified, Othello-like death, rather than suffer the mutilation and dismemberment detailed in the former account. The critique of contemporary plantation slavery unavoidable in Behn is muted into the individual tragedy of a natural aristocrat brought to his death by uncomprehending lesser mortals.[35] The violence of the colonial periphery that both captivated and disfigured the earlier narrative is returned to the margins in Southerne's play, and a more acceptable "literary" model of interracial love and suffering (the Othello precedent) takes its place at the affective center of the text. We witness the sublime suicide of Othello, not the dismemberment of Oroonoko. In this resolution we can see a crucial step in the historical and ideological process I trace here—the process, that is, that I have earlier described as part of the work of literature (in particular the work of poetry) in this period: the articulation of a formal structure for the expression of, and the reconciliation or sublimation of, the contradictions between any (benevolist or humanitarian or even providentialist) account of nationalist aspirations overseas and the embattled realities of disputed territories, trading posts, and plantation colonies.

Even as the worlds of the novel and the stage seem to look homeward in this period, the horizons of the British nation were constantly expanding. The focus on domesticity that is a feature of the novel and in particular of sentimental comedy (which becomes the dominant genre of the stage) does not disavow concern with the world overseas, but does displace or sublimate those concerns. There is no question that, in the form of commodities and markets, professional and semiprofessional avenues of employment, or stories of war and settlement abroad, this world continues to impinge upon and shape domestic concerns. Indeed, the fearful and excited exploration of the prospects and practices of colony and empire, or the sense in which adventuring abroad allowed the writer free and different range, or the palpable importance of reshaping the discourse of national belonging and identity in response to the imperatives of mercantile competition and colonial expansion find expression also in other species of writing and become the disciplinary project of travelogues, or take less fanciful form in bureaucratic correspondence, journalism (in newspapers and periodicals), and parliamentary debate.[36] The discourse of nation formation becomes a part of (is ceded to?) the quasi-scientific conversation of historians and political economists, the philosophizing of aestheticians and critics of a comparativist bent, and the deliberations of polemicists and policymakers of one political stripe or the other. And there is another important factor to be taken note of: as more and more women write poetry or the novel or plays, they distance themselves from the literary practices and dubious reputations of Behn (or even Montagu) or from the scandal, in 1709, of Delarivier Manley's *The New Atalantis.*[37] As new writing, by men and women, takes seriously both women and domestic concerns, the world of imaginative literature is enriched and has limiting boundaries drawn around it. This, in short, is the dual process by which literature, along with other cultural forms, becomes the appropriate object for bourgeois consumption, and the bourgeois subject is elevated into properly "literary" status.

But what of poetry in this process: why do poets feel entitled to continue the kinds of poetic explorations of places and persons that they had begun in the seventeenth century? Why are the poets I discuss in this book not similarly moved to retreat from the expression of colonial desires, from the exploration of newly found lands made available by accounts of "discovery" and conquest, from the calculus of wealth and power always on the horizons of the nation? Perhaps, quite simply, because of the history of poetic practice itself, because of the status of poetry as the sublime form of imaginative or literary utterance. In practice, of course, poetry is far from homogeneous, having finely differentiated internal models of enunciation (the ode might perform, for instance, a transcendence not available to the more earthbound georgic), but poetry always preserves its claims to utterance above and beyond the mundane and the everyday. Indeed, at its most expansive, in the form of the epic, poetry speaks to and of nations and the even larger "collectivities" that result from international conflict. To that extent, poetry was historically the most elite of forms, and it stands to reason that, as English prose in this period functionally democratized its ambit and vernacularized its vocabularies, the practice of poetry did not follow suit, or at least not to the same extent. Thus, even if the poetic idiom created by Duck and Collier, or by Gray or Thomson or Cowper or George Crabbe, represents a shift toward vernacular rhythms and speech, the poetry produced by these writers is marked by Milton's Latinate sublimities, or the romantic archaisms of Spenser, or simply by the formal and metrical codes by which poets conducted their business. The famed intertextuality of such poetry is not to be found only in allusions and verbal echoes, but in each choice of formal discipline: to write the pastoral is to rewrite Virgil or Milton, as it is to write the georgic or to translate the epic. The burden of the past, that is, might well be the special nature of poetry itself.

I am not arguing here that these poets are haunted shadows of former poetic fathers, condemned to repeat their achievements, only in more enervated ways; rather, that the formal imperative in poetry is strong enough to both support and limit the exploration of conflictual themes in social or cultural history, including those made pressing by England's forays into empire. Thus, as shown in chapter 1, Marvell's "Bermudas" rewrites the providentialist argument for the "discovery" of the islands (a claim disturbed by the interspecies violence depicted in Waller's "The Battle of the Summer Islands") precisely by reimagining its form: in place of the mixed form of Waller's poem, which literally includes too much, Marvell writes a hymn of celebration and thanksgiving, and returns the discourse of discovery to its proper spiritual anchor. But Marvell's poem is not, in the argument of this book, representative of poetic practices in the long eighteenth century: I am here concerned particularly with poems of mixed form and genre, with combinations of pastoral and georgic elements (in the loco-descriptive poem for instance), or those that combine the celebratory transports of ode with the didacticism of the georgic, or those that weave together the imperial ambitions of epic and the more banal details of the care of British sheep and the global wool trade. In each case, the poems shift between or negotiate varying generic codes in an effort to craft the most effective combination of elements with which to explore the great themes of nation building and empire. The poetry of mixed form is particularly important, I will argue, for the expression and *sublimation* of the ideological contradictions of nationalist aspiration, and thus for the expression of such aspiration itself.

There is now a critical consensus that the category *Literature* came into being as a result of the more general proliferation of writing in this period, and indeed in order to create a hierarchy of cultural value that would separate "special kinds of deeply imaginative writing" from the everyday world of writing as work.[38] The historical and disciplinary trends I have charted here certainly contributed to this understanding of literature. If the work of the literary writer was in part to generate self-reflexive accounts of all that makes the text "literary," then poetry was particularly suited to this exercise, as each poem confirmed itself as part of a specialized history of formal practice, and key poems thematized, in agonistic and celebratory ways, their own poetical genealogy (I am thinking here of the "progress of poesy" elements built into many poems written in this period). To see the self-reflexive, self-authorizing rhetoric of these poems as constitutive is to understand better a profound historical irony: even as the poems examined in this book were certain of their need to contribute to, and of their place within, public culture, few of them have remained alive in any of the canonical forms of "literary memory" (anthologies, curricula, critical commentary). I do not claim that these poets thought of their poems in the same way as a political philosopher or a spokesman for an economic interest might have thought about writing, but there was certainly an overlap in that all of them wrote to intervene in the public sphere, to sway influential minds, and to mold opinions more generally. Perhaps these poems are, to that extent, embarrassments to the idea that Poetry and Literature demarcate the privileged realm of the operations of a noninstrumentalist conception and performance of writing. These poems do not, as romantic poems often do, call attention to the world only to disavow its noise and clutter and enlarge into explorations of poetic subjectivity and the growth of the poet's mind. They are of their world and their nation, and if they must sing its sheep, they do so. The georgic, after all, authorizes such concern, and the historical moment demands the song: the subject is finally not the poet but the nation.

Since this is a book about the centrality of ideas and fantasies of nation and empire to the poetic imagination, I attend to poems that energize themselves via meditations on the history and prospects of the nation. They do so most often in a comparative mode, seeking solace and warning from nations and states in the past, and, more competitively, arguing Britain's distinction from contemporary European powers and from the overseas lands and peoples that one or other of the European states had colonized or were colonizing. These poems—and the myriad others from this period I do not engage with here—reveal the extent to which British poets labored to bring into being the imperial nation (they were far from, of course, the only, or even the most important, contributors to this monumental task, even though their writing, at its most overblown, claims for itself such vatic prerogative). These poets act locally—they take sides on topical matters, argue domestic agendas—but think globally. They wrote the poetry of contemporary globalization, tracing its contours in a paranoid or celebratory vein, or usually in a combination of both. These are large claims, and for the purposes of this book they can be qualified into a more pointed literary-historical claim: I am arguing, that is, that the history of English poetry in the long eighteenth century is best written as a history of poets' attempts to endow the nation with literary, cultural, and iconic capital adequate to its burgeoning status as a global power.[39]

The title of this book—*Poems of Nation, Anthems of Empire*—derives both from the thematic preoccupations of the poems it examines and from a key formal feature shared by many of them, which is their polemical repetition of ideas, positions, or sentiments. These poems construct their arguments by accretion and reiteration; their progress is replete with digressions and looping returns to well-established positions and views. The commentary on geography, culture, and politics, even as it explores the world, often comes home to the safe harbor of nationalist celebration; equally, historical analysis and comparison, a staple of these poems, offers repeated lessons for the present and future of Britain. The canvas is often vast and cluttered: cultural and political terms are debated, as are moral and ethical values; the boundaries of nation, state, and citizenship are demarcated, new worlds surveyed and apportioned, and systems of overseas trading and colonization explored; historical genealogies are crafted; providentialist explanations of human progress or decline are emphasized or ignored in favor of more secular accounts of the history of empires and nations; domestic concerns and constituencies are assuaged or condemned, nationalist or sectarian icons celebrated or debunked, and poetic and philosophical inheritances traced; the role and ambition of the poet is examined and redefined, and the themes, vocabulary, and formal qualities of poetic genres are reevaluated and "improved" upon. Of course not every poem I consider addresses all these issues, and most, rather than call attention to them separately, attempt to weave a seamless fabric of description, narrative, and meditation that incorporates such discussions as motifs within a larger pattern. Such design-work is not always successful though, and the poems are rife with contradictions in historical opinions and ethical positions. In each poem, however, repetition, albeit with significant variation, is very much the principle of organization, and the primary formal and ideological method of reinforcing the continuity of argument and self-conception they offer their readers.

The second, equally striking feature of these poems is that they are molded by their contemplative or more aggressive concerns for the shape of the British-nation-in-the-making, whose values and institutions are defined vis-à-vis the expansion and consolidation of overseas naval, commercial, and colonial power. They are thus self-conscious, motivated exercises in the production of images of the nation, of the culture and ideology of the "Great Britain" that is presumed to follow upon (though not always in the right ways) the formation of a British Empire.[40] Thus, these poems explore domestic concerns—whether large issues like the uneven amalgamation of Scotland (or any of the other geographically and culturally "outlying" areas of England) into the entity of Great Britain, or the transformation of the nation from a predominantly agricultural to a mercantile and colonial power, or narrower questions about the practice of science, technology, or poetry most appropriate to the changing culture of the nation—within a larger exploration of the globe, or, rather, those parts of it that were being incorporated into European or British spheres of influence. Hence, *Poems of Nation, Anthems of Empire.*

In recent years, the histories and processes of nation formation in countries across the globe have received much critical attention. The breakup of global empires has fueled the intellectual urgency of such analyses, for decolonization calls renewed attention to the coercive and consensual structures of power and authority that go into the creation and the fracturing of nations. That the newly independent nations would find themselves grappling with questions of national identity or the sharing of power or resources is to be expected, but such questions apply equally to those nations that had controlled vast colonial territories but now were left to come to terms with different material and social-psychological realities (I wished to write that they were left to their own resources, but that is far from the case, for neocolonial political and economic relations successfully perpetuate many previous forms of more direct control). In colonized countries, the struggle against imperialism mobilized constituencies marginalized both by colonial and more local systems of domination; these constituencies—women, marginal peasants and landless laborers, indigenous peoples, the urbanized industrial working classes— continued their activism in the aftermath of decolonization, insisting that the political, social, and cultural forms of independent nationhood be receptive to their aspirations and needs. Much of this is true of the formerly imperial countries, too: to take the instance of Britain, the aftermath of the loss of empire has seen a resurgence of domestic cultural and political tensions, with successful movements for the devolution of authority in Ireland, Scotland, and Wales; with minority populations insisting on their right to equal citizenship; with the loss of legitimacy of a number of the icons of imperial status, including that of the monarchy.

The intellectual and political priorities of a "postcolonial" world have thus led to a renewed interest in the formation of imperial nations, and, importantly, of imperial mentalities. There have been many answers to the overriding question: what allowed a handful of countries in Europe (and one just off its shores) to arrogate to themselves the confidence and authority to conquer and rule most of the world? Political economists have supplied partial answers, which have been complemented by others provided by historians of science and technology or by military historians. Such materialist histories have now more or less supplanted the older forms of political history that described the growth of empire as an expression of the desire and "will to power" of great male imperialists. One important way in which materialist historiography has become more descriptively and analytically convincing is that it has inscribed (however uncertainly and unevenly) cultural processes into its investigative paradigms. Thus, critical attention has been paid to the development of the ideology of imperialism, or at least the working consensus forged in the face of military campaigns overseas and the promise of national wealth and personal profit in the colonization of lands across the globe. These analyses have also broken away from imperial forms of historical storytelling, from the narratives of manifest destiny, in which each episode in imperial history is understood as a separate unfolding of a providential or even historical telos. Imperial success, of course, had bred historiographical blindness to the relentlessly contingent, tentative, and even stumbling means by which territories were subjugated and empires consolidated: the drama of empire was given a more finished form than its actual performance warranted. A great many texts and other evidence that attest to the misgivings, anxieties, and brutalities of colonial power were sidelined in order to tell these tales of historical inevitability.

A similar conceptual shift has informed the study of modern nation formation, too, which, as Benedict Anderson has argued, must see the rise of nationalist consciousness (for both colonizers and the colonized) as inextricable from the imaginative geographies yielded by imperialism and empire.[41] Today, for instance, any history of the formation of "Great Britain"—that is, any history of the idea and the nation after the seventeenth century—must take into consideration the powerful shaping force of mercantilist and colonial expansion (and the former always contains visions of the latter, as is shown by the poems here, or indeed by many early modern literary texts). Linda Colley, whose recent work on the forging of the British nation has done much to emphasize the role played by enemies without (the continental powers, especially France, and various embattled people native to overseas colonies) and "enemies" within (Roman Catholics; Jacobites; the "outlandish" cultures of the Celtic margins), argues that "what enabled Great Britain to emerge as an artificial nation, and to be super-imposed on older alignments and loyalties, was a series of massive wars between 1689 and 1815 that allowed its diverse inhabitants sometimes to focus on what they had in common rather than on what divided them, and that forged an overseas empire from which all parts of Britain could secure real as well as psychic profits."[42]

Historians like John Brewer and Christopher Bayly have described the development of the commercial and state machinery necessary to this consolidation of the nation;[43] Gerald Newman and Kathleen Wilson have written compellingly on texts and events that contributed to the making of a shared national and imperial culture;[44] and Stephen Greenblatt and Richard Helgerson have provided us with a complementary version of late-sixteenth- and early-seventeenth-century England, work that, too, has emphasized the many ways in which the sense of nation in early modern England was caught up with overseas exploration, trade, and territorial control.[45] Such critical studies of early modern colonial and nationalist discourse in Britain have made it seem as if many of the seeds of later colonization and imperialism were contained in the texts and documents they examine. In historical hindsight, and in the aftermath of the colonization of the globe, these texts seem almost prophetic, if only because they often put on display the colonial ambitions, commercial desires, cultural pathologies, and neurotic anxieties that fueled the imperial temper of later years.[46]

This is not to claim that England's trading agendas and territorial aspirations in the seventeenth century were identical with those of the nineteenth, but it is indeed possible to trace, amid many policy disagreements at home and failures abroad, a discursive and ideological continuum between the voyages of Raleigh and the exploits of Kitchener. Thus Shakespeare's *Tempest* has been read as a compelling allegory of colonization and its discontents, with the antagonism between Prospero and Caliban providing a model of colonial authority and the resistance of colonized peoples. The later poetry of mercantilism and national ambition is no less proleptic in the claims it makes for a global future for Britain, but it is far less dialogic in its representation of the relationships between colonizers and colonized. Individuated native characters are rare in these poems, though the native communities of the Caribbean or of the Americas are often referred to as victims of Spanish imperialism who would benefit from the benevolence of British rule.[47] But even more important (and this has to do with the differences between the imaginative maps enabled by English exploration in the late sixteenth and the early seventeenth centuries and those that accompanied English and British colonization a century later), the poems I consider here meditated upon the now highly visible processes of mercantile and colonial expansion as part of a larger effort to intervene in these processes, to inform and to mold them.[48]

This is not a particularly extravagant idea, nor to be written off as a symptom of poetic self-aggrandizement or mania. The structures of patronage—the financial and cultural affiliations—that structured the writing of poetry on public themes in the seventeenth century are well known, and poets were linked with politicians and public figures well before Robert Walpole made it state policy to suborn as many of them as possible.[49] Thus when poets wrote on the "nation" in the thirties, they most often do so on behalf of, or to discredit, Walpole's government or economic policies. This results in a poetry extremely supple in its understanding of the motivated connections between the ostensibly nonpartisan, generalized discourse of nationalism and the particular agendas of opposed political and economic interests. (And even when poets imagined themselves to be outside the circuit of aristocratic or public favor, they understood their writing of poetry to be crucial to their endeavor for personal preferment and cultural centrality). The point is simply that when Waller or Marvell or Dryden wrote poetry, they had the ear of influential people, and even when this circuit of literary production and reception widened considerably during the eighteenth century (which is the process that we think of as the making of the modern public sphere in Britain), poets like Pope or Addison or Young or Dyer or Thomson still retained a clear sense that they addressed both particular persons in public authority as they did a more amorphous and anonymous reading public. Later in the century, when Lady Balgoni asked Cowper to write ballads that could be sung by street activists of the antislavery movement (Cowper's earlier antislavery writing was also part of the larger Evangelical crusade to end the slave trade),

or the Committee for the Abolition of the Slave Trade commissioned Hannah
More to write antislavery verse with which to lobby parliamentarians, they
did so in continuing acknowledgment of the role played by poets in crafting
the imagination, and at least some of the public debate, of the nation.

And precisely because they enact the claim to such cultural and even
moral authority, these poems provide valuable evidence for the anxieties and
hesitations inherent in any vision of expansion: their obsessive retrospection
about the rise and fall of previous empires, their fears for what commercial
and colonial success might do to the traditional arrangements of economic
and social power at home, their sustained fear that overseas power might not
last because of imperfections in the national "character," their knowledge that
the policies they advocated, or the national "heroes" they spoke on behalf of,
faced articulate opposition at home.[50] These poems contain passages that are
belligerent and jingoistic in their patriotism, for they are aware of another
form of resistance: that offered to British trading and plantation interests by
competing European states. The poems are thus replete with celebrations of
nationalist icons and ethical exemplars, for these figures are meant to guarantee
British distinction from their competitors, and thus the long-term vitality of
Britain's power. And since these are poems written as interventions in public
debate and conversation, they are often self-conscious about the place and
function of poetry, and about the forms and idiom adequate to the poetic
conception of a Britannia regnant over greater and greater territories abroad.

Poetry, National Pride, and the Example of Rome

Pope's "An Essay on Criticism" (1711) is a poem cluttered with observations
on "Nature," history, culture, literary practices (including those that define
national traditions), human behavior, and a host of similar topics, all of which
it seeks to orchestrate into a cohesive critical argument. In this spirit of
wide-ranging observation, Pope claims an equivalence between the growth
of empire and of learning, and he offers these lines as an exemplary insight
into the appropriate milieu of criticism:

> *Learning* and *Rome* alike in Empire grew,
> And *Arts* still *follow'd* where her *Eagles flew*;
> From the same foes, at last, both felt their Doom,
> And the same Age saw *Learning* fall, and *Rome*.
> *(lines 684–86)[51]*

Pope's historical observation and imperial iconography are part of a much
wider cultural phenomenon: in the eighteenth century, in a far more systematic
and categoric way than before, English theoreticians and legislators of culture,
aesthetics, and poetics considered the connections between histories of imperial

and cultural progress and came to the conclusion that they might be parallel. Not all of them thought such a conclusion, however qualified, an entirely happy one, and we will consider why that might be, but it is important first to ask why it was that the literary figures of this period so consistently defined themselves vis-à-vis the classical, more specifically the Augustan, tradition in art and literature. Literary historians have argued about the validity or usefulness of labeling this period the Augustan or the neoclassical in English literature, but it is in any case clear that writers like Dryden, Pope, and Swift, not to mention a whole host of less-read poets, styled themselves after Virgil, Horace, and Juvenal and laid claim to that cultural inheritance.

One simple and convincing explanation has been the seemingly obvious advantages of such a cultural identification: Virgil, Horace, and Ovid were celebrated poets (as Livy was a great historian); indeed, their work set the standards against which all subsequent writing must be judged, and therefore there were many advantages to claiming that one's work followed upon their principles and models. One of the problems with this explanation, as has been pointed out by literary historians, is that it takes at face value, and repeats as convincing, similar claims made for their own work by many seventeenth- and eighteenth-century poets. Howard Weinbrot has pointed out, for instance, the very qualified, ambivalent, conflicted identification between our poets and their Augustan (or classical) fathers—one that does not allow us, as it did not them, to rest content with any claim to seamless cultural inheritance.[52] I use the word *fathers* here quite deliberately, to call brief attention to the fact that a critic like Harold Bloom has proposed a largely oedipal scenario to explain all such agonistic and anxious literary identifications, but such a paradigm can help us understand the historical specificity of any cultural moment only if it is grounded in that specificity; that is, it must help us answer the question, Why do these eighteenth-century poets choose the Augustan poets to identify with, differ from, and generally stand up to?[53] Margaret Anne Doody has also emphasized this element of choice; these poets were no "schoolboys doing Latin exercises" imposed on them, she reminds us, but craftsmen in search of "congenial literary models."[54]

The partial answer offered by some of the poems I examine in the chapters ahead emphasizes the fact that Augustan Rome was the high point of the Roman Empire, and resulted from a consolidation of Augustus's supreme power. Rome had been a republic for some years before Julius Caesar, and for a brief while after, but under Augustus the absolute authority of the emperor was confirmed, especially as the empire had never been as extensive, and the imperial identity never stronger.[55] One of the features of the Augustan imperial identity was the emperor's patronage of the arts: following upon his lead, powerful and wealthy aristocrats like Maecenas (whose name became synonymous with *patron*) made it possible for writers like Virgil to, as it were, gain an audience. (Paul Alpers, among others, has read Virgil's first *Eclogue* as providing a dramatized version of such royal patronage, and of its obverse, absolutist dispossession.)[56] What I am describing in this brief summary is the creation of a set of relationships, a social and cultural structure, that seemed to have encouraged a remarkable literary productivity. This then, is one of the bases for the attraction that many early-eighteenth-century poets felt for Augustan literary culture. They were still close to the primary cultural process within which most seventeenth-century poetry had been produced, by and for the aristocracy and its client groups, with most writers achieving a source of income and social recognition within a structure of patronage. So as a model of a superior literary support system, Augustan Rome seemed appropriate. A quick instance of this might be Dryden's note to John Sheffield (to whom *Aureng-zebe* [1676] is dedicated) that he admires Virgil's times "because he had an Augustus for his patron. And to draw the allegory nearer you, I am sure I shall not want a Maecenas with him. 'Tis for your Lordship to stir up that remembrance in his Majesty."[57]

In addition, a particularly powerful reason for poets in this period to have thought of themselves, their culture, and their history vis-à-vis the poetry and culture of Augustan Rome is that they were becoming increasingly conscious that the socioeconomic and material bases of a likely British empire were being put into place, and that this historic development would generate new cultural and literary possibilities and challenges, ones for which the Augustan empire and its literary culture could provide fruitful parallels. Weinbrot has suggested that Gibbon (among others) would have argued "that the only appropriate 'Augustan age' for his nation would have been the interregnum of Oliver Cromwell, for he too violated the constitution and brought all power into his own hands."[58] This is true, but Cromwell is also in some senses appropriately "Augustan" because it was his aggressive military and foreign policy that enabled the mercantile and imperialist state that England was to become in the next century and more (I discuss this in chapter 1). While this is not the place for an extended account of the steady successes (and some spectacular failures) of the various British trading companies, especially the East India Company, in the late-seventeenth and eighteenth centuries, we should be quite clear that the discursive coordinates of contemporary mercantilism included an awareness that trading practices and strategies were often a prelude to colonization and the setting up of exclusive monopolies and administrative controls. Portugal and Spain provided recent examples of monarchs financing and authorizing trading voyages in order to extend their territories, especially in lands unknown.[59] The imperial vision seemed always latent in the ideological schema of mercantile expansion, and this is what our poets recognized, examined, celebrated, looked forward to, worried about, and, in a sense, demanded and made possible.[60]

In literary-historical terms it is by, and in, the work of such purveyors of culture that the practical and strategic sense of imperial possibility that accompanies mercantile expansion was translated into a consensual vision of a manifest national destiny, as poet after poet, writer after writer added his voice to the massed chorus singing hallelujahs of praise to trade and empire. I quote a well-known instance from Pope's *Windsor-Forest* (1713):

> Thy Trees, fair *Windsor!* now shall leave their Woods,
> And half thy Forests rush into my Floods,
> Bear *Britain's* Thunder and her Cross display,
> To the bright Regions of the rising Day;
> Tempt Icy Seas, where scarce the Waters roll,
> Where clearer Flames glow around the frozen Pole;
> Or under Southern Skies exalt their Sails,
> Led by new Stars, and born by spicy Gales!
> For me the Balm shall bleed, and Amber flow,
> The Coral redden, and the Ruby glow,
> The Pearly Shell its lucid Globe infold,
> And *Phoebus* warm the ripening Ore to Gold.
> The Time shall come, when free as Seas or Wind
> Unbounded *Thames* shall flow for Mankind,
> Whole Nations enter with each swelling Tyde,
> And Seas but join the Regions they divide;
> Earth's distant Ends our Glory shall behold,
> And the new World launch forth to seek the Old.
>
> *(lines 385–402)*

This is poetry that expresses imperial ambition, poetry in the service of the historic national and international project that became British imperialism (here in an aspect as benign as the *Pax Britannica* that was meant to follow upon the Treaty of Utrecht).[61] It is also, as I claimed above, the characteristic cultural tone and temper developed by poets in eighteenth-century Britain.[62]

Thus, when they thought of Augustan Rome, these poets warmed, in a loosely jingoistic or occasionally belligerent way, to the prospect of empire, but were also excited by the possibility that great poetry might follow upon, perhaps even contribute to (and certainly be a marker of) great national power, as seemed to have been the case with Virgil, Horace, and even Ovid. Imperial strength seemed to them to be the very condition of possibility of cultural advance, and cultural achievement in turn a definitive index of the status of empire. At the very least, it seemed to some, it would be possible to sing of imperial progress in forms and vocabularies conventionally associated with heroic or otherwise elevated poetry, with lots of stirring invocations and apostrophes to gods and heroes thrown in, and with lots of scope for the poet to claim a public status befitting a chronicler and celebrant of the national destiny. That is, they were committed (albeit at times less surely than at others) to creating a poetic and cultural identity that would accommodate itself to an imperial destiny. Thus, in aspiration if not always in performance, these poets had an important role to play in the consolidation of the ideology of imperialism: they provided many of its cultural attributes, as also rhetorical and iconographical models that allowed its circulation and assimilation as the dominant, indeed hegemonic, national culture of Britain.

However, as I remarked earlier about such identification with the cultural achievements of the Augustans, none of this came entirely easily for these poets. Notwithstanding the general attractions of imperial destinies and cultures, they belonged to different classes, oppositional political parties, divergent literary persuasions. When they looked into the mirror of Augustan Rome, they learnt varied lessons. For instance, the fact that Octavian Caesar, the strategic republican, had transformed himself into Augustus the absolute ruler was no small embarrassment for those poets who swore by a limited monarchy for Britain, and whose sense of the evolution of British constitutional history included the central idea that this history had come to fruition in the Glorious Revolution of 1688.[63] They were willing to learn from the Augustan literary culture, to identify with Augustan imperial strength, but they were certainly not willing to celebrate the virtues of what they could only call tyranny. Thus, when they laid claim to an Augustan inheritance, they had to strenuously disqualify its political organization, or at least portray Augustus in ways that would qualify his status as tyrant. John Dyer, in "The Ruins of Rome" (1740), takes this escape route at one point. He describes Virgil (Maro) in his humble rural tenement, occasionally walking and conversing with Horace and Augustus—here Augustus becomes a dyed-in-the-wool Platonic ruler, an image that is an incongruous testimonial to dire poetic and ideological need (lines 370–86).

In fact, as Weinbrot shows, there was no shortage of writers who condemned both Augustus and those poets who sang his praises.[64] Sir John Harrington's translation (1591) of Ariosto's *Orlando Furioso* is part of this anti-Augustanism: "*Augustus Caesar* was not such a Saint, / As *Virgil* maketh him by his description," (canto 35, verse 26). Harrington goes on to write that, but for the grace of Virgil, Augustus would have seemed another Nero (and that Nero might have had a different historical reputation if he had been kinder to poets). The sense of Augustan absolutism also led to attempts to suggest that the appropriate political, and hence social and cultural, model for Britain was not the Rome of Augustus, but in fact the republican Rome that the caesars subverted. This is Shaftesbury in his *Characteristicks of Men, Manners, Opinions, Times* (1711): "We are now in an age when Liberty is once again on its Ascendant. And we are ourselves the happy Nation, who not only enjoy it at home, but by our Greatness and Power give Life and Vigour to it abroad; and are the Head and chief of the European League, founded on this Common Cause. . . . 'Tis with us at present, as with the Roman People in those early Days, when they wanted only repose from Arms to apply themselves to the Improvement of Arts and Studys." And this is Susannah Centlivre in *The Wonder: A Woman Keeps a Secret* (1714): "The English are by nature, what the Ancient Romans were by discipline—courageous, bold, hardy, and in love with liberty. Liberty is the idol of the British, under whose banner all the nation lists; give but the word for liberty, and straight more armed legions wou'd appear, than France and Philip keep in constant pay." Thus, when contemporary commentators wrote about the appropriate context for cultural achievement, they credited the overarching achievement of Roman literature to the energy and relative political freedoms of the republic, and argued that the great Augustans were in fact the last manifestation of such creativity.[65]

Many poets of this age of constitutional monarchy, however, including Dyer at some moments, responded to the "political problem" of Augustanism with a fine ingenuity, one whose logic was so compelling that it became one of the staple arguments for those who would claim an empire of arms and arts for England and retain an Augustan cultural genealogy for this imperial destiny. Rather than ignore or wish away the fact that Augustan absolutism rendered this genealogy suspect, writers began to call attention to this problem, in part by emphasizing the importance of "Liberty" to British success. Leonard Welsted, for instance, in his "An Epistle to Mr. Steele, on the King's Accession to the Crown, 1714," begins by comparing the accession of George Augustus to the promised coming of "Augustus the divine," but then, in a long passage prophesying the triumph of Protestantism, of overseas trade, and the rise of domestic prosperity, makes clear that the motive force for national success is the goddess Liberty:

> Thy charms
> Politeness give to Peace, and fame to Arms:
> Great Patroness of arts! thy ripening fire
> Instructs each waking genius to aspire.
> *(lines 85–88).[66]*

Indeed, English poets argued the absence of absolutism as the major reason why the would-be British empire was different from the Augustan, and claimed—here is the ideological power of this solution—that this was the precise reason why the British empire would flourish and survive for ever even as the Roman (and a host of others) had declined and fallen. British "Liberty" (identified loosely with constitutional monarchy and a sturdy record of public dissent and even local insurrections) would guard against the abuses that Roman tyranny had encouraged, and this would mean that no matter how rich trade and empire made the British, they would not fall prey to dreaded "Luxury," as the Romans had; that they would not go soft and allow the contemporary equivalent of the Goths to vandalize them. They concentrated, that is, on representing Rome not only as a model for imperial and cultural strength, but as a paradigm for the decline of this strength, from which obvious political, social, and moral lessons needed to be learned so that Britain could avoid the same fate.

Their poems, then, insistently allegorized the *ruins* of ancient Rome, and read in them evidence both of its grandeur and its inevitable decay. As long as Britain could learn—or, rather, as long as these poets could teach Britain how to deal with the social and moral impact of imperial expansion—the inevitability of decline, as demonstrated in the history of Rome or any other empire, could be reversed. The usefulness of this solution is borne out by the number of poets who saw fit to incorporate it into their poems—Whigs and Tories, bullish expansionists and more cautious "moralists," aristocrats and bourgeois, writers of epics, georgics and odes—all wrote about the politically enabling power of "Liberty" and the socially and morally corrosive threat of "Luxury," though they had different ideas about what that meant in terms of state or commercial transactions and policies. Once this vocabulary was in place, poets echoed and manipulated it ceaselessly, together orchestrating the eighteenth-century rhetoric and iconography of the British imperial destiny. As a paradigmatic instance, I quote from the address to Britain in Thomson's *Britannia* (a poem I examine at great length in chapter 3):

> A State, alone, where Liberty should live,
> In these late times, this evening of mankind,
> When Athens, Rome, and Carthage are no more,
> The world almost in slavish sloth dissolved.
> For this these rocks around your coast were thrown;
> For this, your oaks, peculiar hardened, shoot
> Strong into sturdy growth: for this, your hearts
> Swell with a sullen courage, growing still
> As danger grows; and strength, and toil for this
> Are liberal poured o'er all the fervent land.
>
> *(lines 195–204)*

So far I have outlined a set of themes upon which there are, of course, many variations. One common form is for the poet to examine diagnostically not only the past (the ruins of Rome and of other imperial states) but also the present condition of other European nations in order to prevent Britain from being infected by their political, social, and cultural diseases.[67] This is not to suggest, however, that these comparative histories were being read only as warnings for the future; quite the contrary. They also served a compelling present need, to convince Britain and Britons that even as they were the deserving inheritors of the imperial and cultural traditions of Europe, it was their political system, their enshrining of "Reason," and the benevolence of a more or less Whiggish and Protestant God, that made sure that their destiny would be distinct from that of other states. This led to a quasi-anthropological, quasi-historical comparative technique, one whose twists and turns, and occasionally startling conclusions, can be read today only as evidence of the national chauvinism these poets sought to encourage. As O. H. K. Spate suggests, these poems weld together a number of disparate topics in their argument for British supremacy: "Liberty, Property 'that Goddess heavenly-bright,' the Power of Trade, the empire of thought in Newton, all were interwoven, all added up to Britannia's Manifest Destiny."[68]

Poems in this period thus flaunt various tropes and images of poetic inspiration or achievement that show Poetry and Culture following triumphantly where mercantile and military ships sail. Or sometimes, more self-aggrandisingly for the poet, they enact the process by which the Muses use their powers to inspire and show the way, the whole process adding up to that overly grand and much abused term *civilization*. Older models of the movement of culture *(translatio studii)* are now increasingly mapped onto those of the transition of empires *(translatio imperii)*: the Muses are represented as following the westward flight of the imperial eagle, settling where it does, confirming empires, one state taking over where the other leaves off. George Berkeley's "On the Prospect of Planting Arts and Learning in America" (written in 1726) is a good instance of this sentiment:

> The Muse, disgusted at an age and clime
> Barren of every glorious theme,
> In distant lands now waits a better time,
> Producing subjects worthy fame.
> *(lines 1–4)*

Berkeley promises "another golden age, / The rise of empire and of the arts," but not "such as Europe breeds in her decay; / Such as she bred when fresh and young" (lines 13–18). Poets will have the opportunity to sing this future empire in America, an empire whose genesis is mandated by the laws of history:

Westward the course of empire takes its way;
    The first four acts already past,
A fifth shall close the drama with the day;
    Time's noblest offspring is the last.

(lines 21–24)[69]

In such poems, the operative term is *Progress:* of Empire, of Poesy, of Commerce, and of the Muses. In his comment on those eighteenth-century British poets who invoked "The Muse of Mercantilism," Spate writes that the "game was played according to strict rules and a standard form; announcement of subject, invocation to Muse, apostrophe to Patron, and then the technical body-work, interlarded with picturesque description and touching moral anecdotes."[70] I wish to add certain literary-historical questions to Spate's accurate description of the form of these poems: where does the predictability of this format come from, and what are its effects? How hard, or how easy, is it for poets to put together poems that seem ideologically and formally programmatic but that address changing economic, social, and cultural concerns, and often do so from politically opposed points of view? These long poems traversed a vast canvas, and painted pictures so full of details, so full of impressionistic or more considered movements between topics and issues, that the "strict rules" and "standard form" Spate mentions might have been not simply a principle of organization but a source of some reassurance: even as the poem meandered through its "technical body-work," heaping example upon example, offering comparison after comparison, mounting digression upon digression, the fact was that the poem followed a recognizable format, and offered comfortable conclusions about the authority to be exercised by Britain and by British ways in the world of commerce and colony.[71]

In addition to the poems I consider here, elaborate instances of such themes are to be found in poems by John Dennis, Matthew Prior, and Thomas Tickell and in anonymous poems printed in collections of occasional verse or as flattering gifts to men in high places.[72] These themes also shape poems by Pope, William Collins's "Ode to Liberty (1746), Thomas Gray's "The Progress of Poesy: A Pindaric Ode" (1754), and Oliver Goldsmith's "The Traveller, or A Prospect of Society" (1764), to list a few poems by poets who have lingered more forcefully in literary-critical memory. It is worth pointing out that a search of any CD-ROM-based database of seventeenth- and eighteenth-century British poetry, using terms like *Britannia, Liberty, empire* (terms central to this book), throws up an astonishingly large number of now forgotten *published* poems whose themes and forms parallel those described here. Reading even a sample of these poems, with their insistent repetition of idiom and sentiment, provides a cautionary gloss on the ease with which we have attributed originality or even individual achievement to a number of canonical poets and poems. (A list of poets—excluding those dealt with in this book—who wrote on these themes will include Samuel Cobb, William Congreve, Laurence Eusden, John Hughes, Matthew Prior, Nicholas Amhurst, George Jeffreys, John Oldmixon, Isaac Watts, Richard Savage, John Gay, Thomas Tickell, Cornelius Arnold, Mark Akenside, Mary Barber, James Grainger, Stephen Duck, Samuel Boyce, William Dodd, Robert Dodsley, Thomas Fitzgerald, James Grahame, Richard Jago, William Mason, William Julius Mickle, Thomas Parnell, Henry James Pye, John Mayne, Percival Stockdale, Anna Seward, Joseph Warton, and both Thomas Warton the Elder and Thomas Warton the Younger).

Such a catalog of poets (and there are at least as many not listed here) begs the question, Why did so many poets write poems so similar in theme and execution? My use of the metaphor of a chorus—a national chorus—is an attempt to provide a way of modeling this phenomenon, but it is also certain that such a long-drawn-out and consequential poetic and cultural consensus (even with individual variations and political disagreements) could be driven only by the ideological power of national expansion. As commercial and colonial success provided the material circumstances for the imagining of a "Great Britain," poets helped provide its idealized representations, crafted for it cultural and historical genealogies, and offered it hyperbolic visions of the future. Could such insistent repetitions also have been driven by the poets' sense that poetry was in fact losing its literary primacy in the face of the public sphere being generated via prose culture? This seems entirely likely, for, even as many of these poems include self-reflexive moments that assert the age-old poetic claim to vatic power, or to the right to comment critically on more mundane community affairs, they also always suggest the historical ebb (for a variety of real and fanciful reasons) of such power.

In the poems examined in this book we see how very different eighteenth-century poets responded to the idea that the growth and decline of the arts was intrinsically connected to the rise and fall of empires. What is often particularly revealing is the need for these poets to define new forms of poetry, or strategically revive some in disuse, in order to create an idiom that will serve a particular ideological function (as in Young's discussion, in *Imperium Pelagi*, of the reasons the Pindaric is a form particularly suited to the celebration of the noble subject of Trade). At stake in each case, it seems to me, was the desire for a poetic and cultural identity that would complement the contemporary discourses of mercantilism and imperialism. With the hindsight of history there is of course a great deal we might read into this congruence of poetic and imperial desire: in another context, I have tried to show how such a poetics finds expression not only in poems

on public themes, but also in private, "occasional" poems.[73] All such verse
drew strength from, and facilitated, the larger historical and sociopolitical
discourses of mercantile and imperial expansion, and bears eloquent witness
to the influence of empire on the poetic imagination.

Indeed, it is not an overstatement to say that there is scarcely a poet in
the period who did not, in public or in private verse, treat (or indirectly
represent) the conjunction of the patriotic, the poetic, and the imperial.
The study of these poems reminds us that the history of British cultural
nationalism is constituted by a retrospective and prospective internationalism
(only a seeming paradox, for no nationalism is constructed without an
enabling *international* genealogy and vision of the future). This is an insight
that has taken on a transformatory power in literary-cultural studies of the
English Renaissance, as it has in studies of romanticism and nineteenth-
century culture. For instance, in the case of the latter, Nigel Leask has
(following Raymond Schwab) argued that the "anxieties and transports of
Romanticism . . . are as much the products of geopolitics as of metaphysics,
and an ideological analysis which stops short at metropolitan social relations
is only telling half the story."[74] Except for a few important exceptions
(referred to in this introduction's notes), critics have not paid such systematic
attention to the history of eighteenth-century British poetry. As I will show,
the "internationalism" of late-seventeenth- and eighteenth-century poetry
took various forms: visions of past and future empires; grave debates on
cultural and racial difference; less-considered (indeed, throwaway) observations
on other peoples' labor and land; and engaged, spirited arguments for the
supremacy of British values and interests globally. This spirit of religious
and rational—technological and scientific—enlightenment was the motor
force, and the alibi, for empire as it was for so much poetry, and its blindnesses
and triumphs fueled equivalent poetic aporia and euphoria.

In this introduction, I have for the most part described both the period and
the poems I write about in broad terms; in some ways this is necessary in
order to provide a summary (and occasionally polemical) account of this
project, one that will later be further defined and qualified. I have briefly
called attention to historical analyses of the cultural and ethical issues raised
by, or the idiom and iconography characteristic of, the making of the modern
British mercantile, colonial, and imperial nation. For the most part, historians
and literary critics who have commented upon these issues have focused
on cultural and political documents other than poetry; this book, on the
other hand, is primarily an exercise in the history and interpretation of
English poetry in the late seventeenth and eighteenth centuries, one that
takes seriously the sustained interest poems written in the period had in

matters related to trade, colonies, and empire. In general terms, my enquiry is into the discourse of empire; but the particular form it takes is the analysis of the repeated formulae, and the innovative practices, of poetry in this period.[75] Reading these poems, I believe, allows us to sharpen our understanding of some of the constituent features of colonial and imperial discourse, and to do so by following a specialized form of its enunciation. I am making the case, that is, for the particular importance of the specific form of this poetry—its internal movement, particularly the dynamic of the long (or even ambitious) poem in this period—that reminds us about the halting, uncertain, but always willful and aggressive craft of those who imagined Britain as a power dominant in the world.

This emphasis on the interrelations between poetics and ideology adds a further (and often neglected) dimension to the study of historical and cultural change. While literary texts, including poems, are often read as providing evidence for larger arguments about social change, particular attention to their dynamic or formal qualities allows us a nuanced sense of the many (and often contradictory) ways in which definable constituencies in any historical moment imagine and motivate themselves. In keeping with this concern, the method of this book is, for the most part, answerable also to the disciplinary concerns of critics and historians of poetry, and to questions developed by those interested in the intersection of poetics and ideology in different historical periods. Thus, when I offer revisionary readings of poems, or call attention to poems that have dropped out of literary-critical circulation, I also want to suggest different (and perhaps "postcolonial") ways of thinking about the performance and practice of poetry in the period of British mercantile and colonial ascendancy. But a book of this length cannot presume to be a systematic literary history; I do not, for instance, work my way through representative poets to comment generally on the evolution of poetic trends in the long eighteenth century. Some commentary along these lines is of course inevitable, particularly since I believe that the corpus of most poets in this period shows their direct or more mediated concern with nationalism and empire, if only at the level of an enabling cultural vocabulary. These are writers conscious of the task at hand, which is to produce cultural documents that motivate, guide, make richer the project of Great Britain.

Margaret Anne Doody has argued for the "unconscious presence in poetry (and poetics) of the same qualities or mental dispositions that made, in the practical or historical sphere, for England's expansion and domination of trade." Her observations on style are equally pertinent: "The stylistic qualities of 'Augustan' poetry are metaphorically and more than metaphorically related to the qualities and activities of that energetic and greedy time, and the qualities of appetite and expansiveness can be seen in the poetry of the period, along with the desire to mix, to import, to remake and remodel. The vices and virtues of Augustan poetry are the vices and virtues of buccaneering millionaires, intelligent, ingenious and insatiable."[76] While I do not wish to detract from Doody's emphases, as I believe they represent a welcome shift in the critical paradigms governing our understanding of late-seventeenth- and eighteenth-century poetry, I should point out that many of the poems I consider exhibit not only these appetites but also symptoms of the social and ethical indigestion that often accompany such surfeit. The energy of the "buccaneering millionaires," that is, is often qualified by a poetics of nationalist fear, of the salutary sense that the empire of the sea drowned sailors and even nations, and that the winds that favored the buccaneer and the ship of state also brought great storms in their wake. This is bound to be the case, for these poems negotiate not just the political unconscious of British expansion, but engage self-consciously with its energies and difficulties.

In doing so, the practice of poetry begins to play both a conceptual and material role in the making of commodity and consumer culture in this period. Poems in the late seventeenth and eighteenth centuries grow large with their catalogs of circulating commodities and their accounts of overseas riches; they also themselves enter into the market circulation attendant upon the development of print culture in London (and increasingly in provincial cities). As manuscript circulation (usually a marker of aristocratic or elite cultural practices) gives way to the wider audiences enabled by publishers and booksellers, and poems are reified, via subscription lists and book publication, into cultural commodities, they embody (for poets) and evoke (in readers) both the excitement and the moral anxieties that greeted the full flow of imported goods into Britain. To the psychic and ideological comforts (however tenuous or short-lived) poetry offered its writers and readers must now be added the reassurance provided by the production and possession of a volume of poems—the possession, that is, of a materialized form of cultural capital. Precisely because it is a commodity to be purchased, while being different from other goods in the market, a volume of poems serves as a mark of distinction, one that is engendered by, but does not subscribe to, market values. This, too, is the work poetry does in fostering some of the conversational and literary emphases of the British public sphere, for its proliferation in the form of books, its new *volumes,* suggests the ability of the most rarefied forms of cultural practice to draw imaginative energy from, comment upon, but also to contain within recognizable moral and discursive limits, the flood of imported finished goods and raw materials that were transforming daily life in uncertain and unpredictable ways.

However, it is not containment but exuberance that we first notice: there

is no question about the cultural power of the vocabulary of import and
transport, of desire and domination, of commodities and consumption.[77] Poets
who explore the contours of "virgin" territories in the bodies of their lovers,
or those who posit a faraway land of romance that they can colonize with
their spouses, find in the geographical "discoveries" of their age the *frisson*
that energizes their rhetoric, if not their love. The same sense of far-reaching
ambition guides those poets who believe that the time is right to claim a
British literary achievement that is the equal of any continental tradition
(classical or contemporary); they respond confidently to the urgencies of a
cultural nationalism, which itself derives from material and ideological
competition with other would-be European empires. This is true also of those
poets who write the "progress" of historical and literary figures into their
poems, and thus construct cultural genealogies for the nation. Similarly, poets
who believe that the time is ripe for formal experimentation (which might
take the shape of a renewal of poetic conventions in disuse) because changes
in the icons of British heroism overseas demand new modes of panegyric or
celebratory verse, complement those who argue more strenuously that British
heroism, in its contemporary variant, authorizes their nation to rule the waves
(or other territories that the waves wash ashore on). Even that quintessentially
English poetic form, the loco-descriptive poem or celebration of local
topography and nature, is rewritten in the eighteenth century just as surely,
and in response to the same imperatives, as the imagination of the country
and the city is rewritten by empire.

I invoke the title of Raymond William's book in homage to what still
remains the most humane and moving enquiry into transitions in the writing
of "country literature," which he describes as "a prepared and persuasive
cultural history" of the nation. He finds this history "active and continuous"
and argues that it describes the relations "not only of ideas and experiences,
but of rent and interest, of situation and power; a wider system."[78] *The Country
and the City* is thus a powerful argument about the place of literary texts
in—as mystifications of or as witness against—the transformation of the
English countryside and nation that followed upon systematic enclosure,
the capitalization of agriculture, and the onset of the industrial revolution.
What Williams does not do, however, is take into account the role played
by trade and conquest overseas in this transformation, a role he himself
points to: "In the imperialist phase of our history the nature of the rural
economy, in Britain and in its colonies, was again transformed very early";
and (when he writes of the developing contrast between country and city)
"as the processes of the city become self-generating, and especially in the
course of foreign conquest and trade, there is a new basis for the contrast
between one 'order' and another."[79] Thus the story Williams tells is in some

crucial ways incomplete, and not simply because he leaves that part of the tale to someone else. For his account of the poetry of domestic transitions can be arrived at only by not paying attention to those large sections of verse in which poets in the seventeenth and eighteenth centuries engaged with ideas of their nation in the world. Williams notes that Drayton sets his version of the Golden Age and of Paradise in an overseas colony (in "To the New Virginia Voyage"), but makes little of that detail. Nor does he register the fact that, for instance, Thomson arrives at his worldview, which includes his systematic meditations on the state of nature and of the nation, by comparing both with what he knows (or thinks he knows) of the rest of the globe.[80] Instances like this could be multiplied, and not only with Williams; indeed, in some ways the argument of this book derives from much that literary critics have ignored in their readings of late-seventeenth- and eighteenth-century poetry.[81]

In this book I read many poems, my purpose being to examine different ways in which poets in the late seventeenth and eighteenth centuries commented upon material, intellectual, and ethical issues urgent to their nation. In chapter 1, I read poems by Waller, Marvell, and Dryden; in chapter 2 poems by Defoe, Henry Needler, Addison, Lyttelton, Pope, Dyer, and Anna Letitia Barbauld; in chapter 3, James Thomson; in chapter 4, Young, Richard Glover, and Dyer; in chapter 5, Cowper, Hannah More, Elizabeth Bentley, and Barbauld.

Chapter 1 begins with a study of Marvell's "Bermudas" and Waller's "The Battle of the Summer Islands," to show the contrast between the pacific tones of the hymn to territorial expansion and the violent interspecies battle fought in the same island utopia in the latter. I suggest that Marvell, who shares some of Waller's idiom, rewrites the earlier poet's more expansive poem by staying within the narrower boundaries of the celebration of divine providence formalized in the hymn. I then move to poems that engage with the recent history of the successful projection of English power across its borders (Cromwell's campaigns in Scotland and Ireland, for instance), and those that follow the development of English trade and colonial power. Chapter 1 also underlines the transition from providentialist explanations of England's prowess to those that emphasize its scientific and technological advance. Chapter 2 examines poems that offer comparative evaluations of nations and empires in the past and the present. I comment briefly on the heterodox model of porous national frontiers that Defoe offers as the history of England in his *The True-Born Englishman*, then move to poems that meditate on the ruins of Rome in order, I argue, to comment on the desirable and undesirable features of Britain as an empire.

Chapter 3 analyzes some of Thomson's major poems to argue that their encyclopedic form and concerns are products of a desire to create verse capable of representing the nation as dominant within an international frame. Thomson's search for forms (the seasonal cycle that is at once pastoral, georgic, and historical poem) or for a myth of history (the Spenserian conception of *The Castle of Indolence*) is impelled by a world of observation and imagination that expands into a poetry whose fissured and baggy forms, whose twists and turns of argument, become a fine instance of the power of commercial and colonial expansion to both enable and warp the work of the poet in the mid-eighteenth century. Chapter 4 features poems that explore definitions of heroism appropriate to an age of mercantilist and colonial expansion: in two odes, Young celebrates the ocean as the new medium of British power and self-consciously develops a poetics of the expansionist nation.[82] I close with two oddly parallel poems, one by Glover, who crafts a mythology for commerce, and the other by Dyer, who does much the same for the British wool trade.

Chapter 5 addresses a key development—antislavery activism—that transformed the discourse of British "civilization," and that, among other important developments, allowed women, as writers and poets, and as key players in the movement itself, to stake a claim to the public sphere. Britain, they argued, was not as repressive as Roman Catholic continental empires, and should take the lead in abolishing the slave trade and slavery. As they mobilized against slavery, they enacted the ethical and religious concerns that they believed should define their nation. Their vision featured the humane glory that would accrue to Britain, and that would confirm it as a nation greater than any other. This argument was a crucial component of the justificatory logic of nineteenth-century imperial ideology and its claim that it was Britain's necessary and manifest destiny to share its enlightened values with its subjects all over the world, including those it would free from slavery and other sorts of bondage into the freedoms guaranteed by British sovereignty.

These topics weave in and out of, and highlight specific features of, the broad themes summarized in the preceding sections of the introduction. Perhaps a comment on the choice of poets and poems is in order, for there are a great many poems not listed whose vocabularies and ideological concerns parallel those of the poems examined here. It might even be possible, for the purposes of this study, to replace these poems with others like them (which would only confirm the argument that these poems represent the contemporary practice of poetry), for my concern is with shared poetic aims and ambitions in the period rather than with distinctive achievement. This book moves between poems that are still read and discussed in specialist circles to others that have virtually dropped out of even academic circulation. If these poems share anything, it is that overlap of themes and images that adds up to the less-critically-acknowledged concerns of the practice of poetry in this period. Although literary critics have often derived models of English society and "sociability" from their representation in eighteenth-century poetry, it has not been felt necessary to connect this sociability (in any of its poetic variants—the company of like-minded souls in rural retirement or the exuberant, vital conversation of gatherings in the city, or any other) with larger systems of intercourse: those of international commerce, of the varied comings and goings of merchants and colonists, of the speculations and ethnography of travellers and scientists.[83] And yet when we read these poems it is impossible not to be aware that the world they represent is criss-crossed by ideas and experiences that originate far beyond British shores, and that their very sense of what it might mean to be a Briton is derived from rapidly changing, and increasingly global, cultural, economic, and political coordinates.

There is one other link between most of these poems—they are all about, or they take very seriously, the oceans (and the Thames that flows out into them). If the English topographical poem is primarily a celebration of features local and terrestrial, of the genius loci, the poem of empire claims for itself the global flows of the oceans, and all that they make available. Historically, the oceans were of course the medium of modern European colonialism and imperialism, but the epic memory of the Greeks and their seafaring ways is much longer than that, and often surfaces in these odes to ocean. The Homeric highways of the sea are here the sea lanes that are the basis of British mercantile and colonial success, over which the British fought what now seem like an unending round of battles with—at various times in the seventeenth and eighteenth century—the Dutch, the Spanish, the French, and then with the breakaway United States. The control of the oceans became, in this period, the new nomos of British political and commercial life. Culturally, the oceans made feasible a new internationalism, albeit one in which (in these poems at least) crucial emblems and technologies of modernity radiate *outward* from the island center of Britain (this ranges from Dryden's celebration of English shipbuilding techniques to Dyer's circulation of high-quality wool to Hannah More's export of Evangelical humanism in the service of antislavery). In these poems, oceans are venerated not only as the material basis for British expansion but also because they provide a fecund, mythopoeic medium, rich in the symbolic lore that could be deployed in the generation of new myths of the island-nation and of its manifest global destiny.

I substantiate the claims of this book not so much by staging a confrontation, as it were, between texts—that of the poet and that of the traveler, for instance, or that of a contemporary philosopher or economist— but by reading through poems, following their twists and turns, analyzing their thematic and formal concerns and difficulties. This might be construed a departure from the critical protocols popularized by at least two important and revisionary recent critical tendencies—those of cultural materialism and new historicism, but I believe such close readings are an extension of their political means and ends. My method here is in part dictated by a desire for cogency of *literary* argument: since poetry is a specialized form of writing, with its own internal logic and dialogic history (which is what is indicated when critics write of intertextuality or quotation or allusion or formal discipline and innovation), much of the power of explanation here is derived from such details. This is not a rejection of the claims of cultural history; nor should it be thought of as an unacceptable narrowing of the scope of enquiries into the historicity of literature or poetry. Quite the reverse, for I would argue that such narrowing can be extremely productive, and allow us a precision of description and detail that inescapably rewrites the history of poetry (or literature), a not inconsiderable or unimportant task. A literary history of poetic forms, that is, is not a denial of other crucial narratives or accounts of history; it is a particular instantiation of the cultural dialectic through which the poet reworks the world. In the case of this book, my readings of poems will show that the history of English poetry in the long eighteenth century is inextricable from our historical accounts of "discovery," trade, seaborne power, plantations and colonies, slavery and the slave trade, and the concomitant rise to power of Great Britain. These are, after all, the terms of nationalist inspiration in the period: poets drew breath in this heady (and occasionally fetid) atmosphere, and derived from it the expanding frontiers of their aspiration.

Thus, the point is not only to see where these poets got their ideas from but to see what use they made, as *poets* (and, to be sure, as men and women of their world) of issues and arguments crucial to its "newness." It seems to me that one of the sources of poetic reaction or innovation is the shock of the new, of the need to come to terms with, to *domesticate*, phenomena like the "Feather'd People," the "naked Youths and painted Chiefs" who appear in Pope's *Windsor-Forest* (404–5), or the "various offerings of the world" that appear on Belinda's toilette and enable her to "call forth all the wonders of her face" (*The Rape of the Lock*, 1.130, 142). In the first case, the rhythmic control of the heroic couplet stabilizes the poem as it, like the Thames, flows out into uncharted expanses and reports on the world; in *The Rape of the Lock*, the mock-heroic normalizes unstable perspectives and values by rewriting as trivial—the making of a coquette—the historically transformatory force of imported commodities. Pope is not the only English poet (nor was he the first) to grapple with the power of mercantile and colonial modernity to reshape individuals and nations; if Johnson is moved to survey "Mankind, from China to Peru," he is motivated in part by his unhappiness that Britons were staining "with Blood the *Danube* or the *Rhine*" in pursuit of empire, as Alexander and the Romans had done before them.[84] Certainly all the poets I consider in this book, and many others in this period, were concerned with analogous issues. This poetic enclosure of newness, then, is another important reason to pay close attention to form, for ideological closure (the domestication of discomfort or difference) is often achieved with difficulty.

Formal irresolution and resolutions are thus important indices of ideological contradictions. In each case I take seriously the need felt by these poets to offer compelling, expansive narratives of history, nations, and cultures, subjectivities and cultural formations, even as they craft local variations on classical or neoclassical topoi and poetic conventions. The formal stresses, fissures, and occasional innovative precision that result are easier to trace in longer poems, and my arguments are often based on a strain-by-strain analysis of these meandering poems. This has also meant that I have often had to follow the development of particular themes, or transitions between them, in these poems; such thematic analysis is performed alongside more engaged readings of local details—I trace, that is, the contours and geography of each poem. I have summarized sections of poems on occasion, but I have also quoted at length, largely because I believe it unlikely that these poems will be fresh in the reader's memory, to say the least. And I do call attention to similar moments in poems without reading through each of them (a pragmatic procedure for which even sympathetic readers might be grateful). In my reading of most poems, I have found useful Marshall Brown's suggestion that some "problems of interpretation are eased or even dispelled as soon as we take movement rather than coherence to be the constitutive impulse of literary structures."[85] The troubled or smooth internal dynamic of poems, their ability to move, can tell us a great deal not simply about ideas poets took seriously but also about how they wished to be taken seriously by their readers. Since the poems examined here were written as interventions (to use a term made feasible by developments in the eighteenth-century British public sphere) into public discussion, their creativity is tied up with that desire to convince and persuade.

And it is of course a particular form of persuasion and conviction we are dealing with here, one that follows from the decision to write in verse. Almost all the poets considered here also wrote prose—prefaces, aesthetic treatises, political pamphlets, chapbooks or tracts, novels, drama—and often chose to address similar issues in such writing. But there is no doubt that

their decision to write poetry enacted a certain distinction not available to
them in prose (even as they were aware of the new cultural power of the
latter) and this is almost as true of the poets of the later eighteenth century
as it is of those of the later seventeenth. The difference might be that Marvell
and Dryden took for granted the cultural power of poetry to exalt subject
and poet, whereas Cowper or Hannah More wrote more defensively, with
a sense of the diminishing prestige of the form. Yet for them, too, the
conventions of poetry tapped into a history resonant enough to make poems
fit vehicles for public appeals across the social spectrum, from fundamentally
illiterate workers (Cowper's ballads) to aristocratic parliamentarians (More's
poems on behalf of the Committee for the Abolition of the Slave Trade).
And in any case, for Young or for Thomson, the reinvigoration or expansion
of poetic forms (that of the Pindaric or the seasonal cycle) suggested the
possibility of rejuvenating the practice of poetry itself, for creating cultural
documents adequate to the ambition of the poet. These ambitions and
struggles are thematized in the poems, for (as I have argued in a study of
Thomas Gray) eighteenth-century poets constantly work with a sense of
vocational vulnerability—a sense that the new public sphere (and the "republic"
of letters it spawned) was marginalizing their work and their sociocultural
aspirations.[86] Thus, professional neuroses almost inevitably surface in such
poetry, and intersect with and intensify other intellectual, cultural or political
anxieties.

For readers today, these poems can also offer evidence from the eighteenth
century for so many of the rhetorical and psychological features that came
to define nineteenth-century British imperialism, and indeed imperialism
itself: the development of codes of hypermasculinity; of the image of modern
man as the servant of the expanding nation, working at the behest of the
state; the insistence on racial, cultural, and religious hierarchy; the development
of philosophical and historical justifications for inhumanity and, as Ashis
Nandy puts it, the bringing into being of those parts of "British political
culture which were least tender and humane."[87] Is it, then, only a coincidence
that the poets who wrote these poems were men? Is it coincidence that the
first powerful instance of the discourse of humanitarian sympathy in the
service of a national ideal came from Cowper—that "stricken deer"—or
from Hannah More and the other women active in antislavery?[88] Having
said that, I want to emphasize once again that the lesson of these poems is
precisely the creative and imaginative *work* that is required to craft a credible
imperial manner. The flag-waving pieties of nationalism, especially a
nationalism forged in the service of empire, do not come "naturally" or
even seamlessly to these male poets. Their poems work to construct the
argument for empire, but the more ambitious they grow, the more they

have to come to terms with historical, political, and human contradictions. These poems, much more than any comparable literary or nonliterary contributions to the making of colonial discourse, reveal to us that no one, perhaps least of all poets, is born to the arrogant assumption that the world is created in order to make large sections of it available to the control and exploitation of a single people. But they can be taught that, which is the task of the belligerent forms of nationalism. And that, in the long eighteenth century in Britain, was also the ideological work performed in the development of the supple forms of a poetics of empire.

A final word on what I do not do here: this book is not much concerned with that staple of literary criticism, the evaluation of a poem or a poet's corpus based on predefined "aesthetic" criteria. This is not because I am unable to see a well-wrought poem when I read one, or recognize the precision of particular constellations of words or rhymes, or know when the metrical scheme of a line detracts rather than adds to its meaning, but because such details of craft and local organization lead me not to conclusions about the "organic" achievement of the poem but to an examination of the effectivity of its presentation or of its self-conception. And in that line of argument, as in any narrative of the self, it is the fissures and the ruptures, the hesitations and the contradictions, that offer the more credible analysis of creativity and its discontents. On one occasion later in the book I refer to the "loose, baggy monsters" that populate the world of eighteenth-century poetry—I use Henry James's phrase to describe rather than dismiss, particularly since I believe that it is precisely this shapelessness (which is as self-conscious and volitional as any attempt at a tightly crafted poem) that allows these poems to best engage with the new worlds that attracted their attention. And it is a similar encyclopedic desire to incorporate new experiences, visions, and values that makes these poems, for us, such fine guides to the world of the poet in the long years in which "Great Britain" was consolidated as an empire, at home and abroad. Poetry, in these readings, participates in the public discourse of its time; like all vital and contested public discourses, it tells us a great deal about not only the great issues of the day but about the quieter—and sometimes even more intense—musings, fears, and aspirations of those who put pen to paper in the service of their ideals.

1

THE POETRY OF NATION

The Ode is bolder, and has greater force;
Mounting to Heav'n in her Ambitious flight,
Amongst the Gods and Heroes takes delight;
Of Pisa's Wrestlers tells the Sin'ewy force,
And sings the dusty Conqueror's glorious course:
To Simois streams does fierce Achilles bring,
And makes the Ganges bow to Britan's King.

— John Dryden, "The Art of Poetry"

Others may use the ocean as their road,
Only the English make it their abode,
Our oaks secure, as if they there took root,
We tread on billows with a steady foot.

— Edmund Waller, "Of a War with Spain, and a Fight at Sea"

If there is a single utopian moment in the poetry of travel, "discovery," and colonization produced in early modern England, it is surely Andrew Marvell's lyric "Bermudas." Probably written during or after Marvell lived at the Eton home of John Oxenbridge in 1653, this poem stages the thanksgiving of Puritan exiles, who voyage to Bermuda for the same reason that Oxenbridge himself had first gone there in 1635, to escape persecution by Archbishop Laud in England. "Bermudas" is suffused with a divine grace, with the assurance that it is a providential wind that speeds the exiles to their earthly paradise. Its idiom combines the joyful simplicity of hymnody with a sense of island riches derived from travelogues and from the promoters of trade and colonial settlement in the seventeenth century. As it looks back to the 1630s in England, and finds in religious persecution at home the justification for travel and settlement abroad, it invokes an older frame of spiritual explanation and justification, one soon to be added to, if not supplanted, by more material arguments for the necessity and the success of English trade and colonization overseas. Those arguments, as in other poems by Marvell, Waller, and Dryden, emphasize naval and military strength, economic necessity or benefit, and scientific advance in their looking forward to English dominance of the seas (and thus the globe).

This is not to suggest that religious faith, and the social and cultural rationales it enabled, lost their hold on the popular or elite imagination in seventeenth-century England. There is a transition, however, one that is well described by Philip Corrigan and Derek Sayer as the "partial displacement of religion as a dominant legitimating code for and within the state, towards solid bourgeois values of law, property, 'liberty' and civility."[1] What we witness, they go on to say, "is less the demise of religion as a 'moral technology' than a shift in its forms, from the visible coercion of Church courts and public penances to internalized disciplines of conscience and sect; a shift thoroughly consonant with a wider embourgeoisement of social relations and identities."[2] Thus, while much of the analysis that follows deals with the rhetoric of divine revelation and providential destiny that is an inescapable feature of seventeenth- and eighteenth-century poetry on public themes, it also charts a variety of more "secular" arguments about the necessity of state support for particular economic and political formations and for mercantile and colonial adventuring. In doing so, the analysis also outlines the role claimed for poetry in the construction of a consensual public culture adequate to the demands of an ascendant commercial and imperial nation.

In "Bermudas," though, the nation is not an operative category, even if the singers are described, toward the end of the poem, as being in "the English Boat" (line 37). In fact, they are refugees from the nation, cast out of its definition of good citizens, traveling toward shelter and sustenance. However, poets—including Marvell in some of his other poems—were never far from attempting to define England (and later, in the eighteenth century, Britain) as a land of enterprising merchants, hardy sailors, and powerful leaders committed to the expansion of national power, in peace and through war. There were yet other poets (and, sometimes, the same poets who celebrated overseas expansion) who had qualms or more serious political and economic objections to the effects mercantilism and colonization had on the fabric of domestic life, and more occasionally for the impact of the European presence on the lives and lands of the people they came in contact with, and some of the poems considered below suggest such concerns.[3] Marvell's "Bermudas," however, betrays no such anxieties, and depicts in the new islands only the rewards of faith.

The context for this is, of course, religious persecution at home, which makes "an isle so long unknown, / . . . far kinder than our own" (lines 7–8). This sense of a community in exile is emphasized in the opening of the poem, in the image of "a small boat" rowing along, approaching the "remote Bermudas," which themselves "ride / In th' ocean's bosom unespied" (lines 1–3). The remoteness of the islands (their protective isolation) and the size of the boat suggest the guiding winds of providence, which have

sheltered the voyagers on their long journey; a theme that begins the hymn
of thanksgiving:

> "What should we do but sing his praise
> That led us through the wat'ry maze,
>
> . . . .
>
> He lands us on a grassy stage;
> Safe from the storms, and prelate's rage."
>
> *(lines 5–12)*

This sense of divine protection, and indeed intervention, here invoked by
Marvell in the face of religious persecution was, as Peter Hulme shows, a
recurrent feature of the early-seventeenth-century discourse surrounding
these islands (not only the Bermudas, of course; parallel instances could be
cited from the colonial settlement of Virginia and the Plymouth Plantation).
However, the issue of God's will in making the Bermudas available for English
occupation had been much debated because of a series of events in the
early English colonial history of the Bermudas. In May 1609, nine ships of
colonists sailed from Plymouth to Virginia, and one—the *Sea Venture,* which
carried the leaders of the expedition—was blown off course to the Bermudas,
where the colonists survived and built two ships in which they sailed to
Jamestown in 1610 (and "saved" that colony). The presumed loss of the *Sea
Venture* had been read by detractors of the Virginia Company as providential
condemnation of the colonial enterprise; the survival of the colonists provided
proof to the contrary. In a discussion of William Strachey's *True Reportory of
the Wracke* (1610), Hulme points out that Strachey's report suggests an
"allegorical conclusion," that these misadventures were part of a divine plan:
"God had kept those islands secret from everyone else and protected them
by their reputation for tempest and thunder so that they could be bestowed
upon the people of England." Via such providentialist writing and thinking,
Hulme argues, "England was beginning to discover its manifest destiny."[4]

In Marvell's poem, the pastoral abundance and self-sufficiency of the
island provides further evidence of this destiny. The poem contains a catalog
of food, fruit, and commodities whose ornamental richness condenses a
biblical vocabulary of God's bounty with the newer acquisition promised
by travel and trading to lands both to the east and west of England:

> "He gave us this eternal spring,
> Which here enamels everything;
> And sends the fowl to us in care,
> On daily visits through the air.
> He hangs in shade the orange bright,
> Like golden lamps in a green night;

And does in the pom'granates close
Jewels more rich than Ormus shows.
He makes the figs our mouths to meet;
And throws the melons at our feet:
But apples plants of such a price,
No tree could ever bear them twice.
With cedars, chosen by his hand,
From Lebanon, he stores the land;
And makes the hollow seas, that roar,
Proclaim the ambergris on shore.
He cast (of which we rather boast)
The gospel's pearl upon our coast."

(lines 13–30)

Michael McKeon, responding to the "tone of cheerful self-satisfaction" in this passage, writes that it "forces one to linger over the image of God as an improving landlord, to be valued for the 'price' of his natural commodities."[5] This translation of colonial nature into commodity, or rather, this definition of a supposedly pastoral, Edenic nature by the tokens of contemporary mercantilist expansion, might also suggest a divine trader and prospector, making available to his fellow English merchants the bounty of faraway lands.[6] If the reference to Lebanese cedars can be understood as proceeding from biblical notions of wealth and splendor, "Ormus" calls attention to an important contemporary entrepôt.[7] Hormuz was the large trading center that controlled entry into the Persian Gulf. In 1622, the East India Company assisted the shah of Persia in capturing Hormuz from the Portuguese, an event that K. N. Chaudhuri suggests marks "the entry of the English and the Dutch to the Middle Eastern markets through the back door of the Indian Ocean."[8] Whether or not Marvell was aware of this fact, or indeed of its historical significance, the comparison of Bermudan pomegranates to jewels from Hormuz marks both the contrast, and the likeness, between commercial commodity and colonial nature—these are the twin poles of the adventuring imagination (or that of the poets of such adventure) in the seventeenth century. Even as the Puritans in "Bermudas" row resolutely toward their faraway island, the poem itself suggests a world much larger than their own, a world (and its riches) made available by trading and by settlement. This, in combination with the poem's faith in a divine providence that makes these new worlds available, might mark, as McKeon suggests, that "religiosity . . . of which was born, in the very decades through which Marvell was living, the manifest destiny of modern imperialism."[9]

Over the next century and more, this manifest destiny was translated into reality through battle, largely on the seas and usually involving the capture or exchange of colonial territories.[10] This history has led Linda Colley, in her recent account of the "evolution of Britishness," to argue that the British were far from being a conventionally insular people: "For most of their early modern and modern history, they have had more contact with more parts of the world than almost any other nation—it is just that this contact has regularly taken the form of aggressive military and commercial enterprise. . . . This is a culture that is used to fighting and has largely defined itself through fighting."[11] When poets celebrated military or naval victories and heroes, as they often did, or wrote satires or diatribes against the enemy, they contributed to this definition of the English nation-state. The praise of individual heroism or more general valor yielded a fine harvest of attributes that could be seen as characteristic of Englishness, just as the celebration of victories abroad led to the greater legitimation of the state apparatuses that made such victories possible (in the same way, significant military or territorial losses overseas provided the grounds for criticism of ministers, generals, and other functionaries of the state). All this did not of course happen for the first time in the mid seventeenth century: Shakespeare's *Henry V* (1599) is perhaps the locus classicus of such nationalist mythmaking, but as Britain expanded its overseas spheres of influence and control in the next century, such themes became cultural staples. Historians of poetry are now paying increasing attention to the very large number of poems on public themes, and there are a great many poets whose work can be fruitfully examined by students of literature interested in the vocabulary and iconography of the early modern English nation.

Violence at Sea: Waller's "The Battle of the Summer Islands"

Before I move to that discussion, though, a detour through Edmund Waller's "The Battle of the Summer Islands" (1638) might help us balance the image of beatific territorial expansion sans violence that characterizes Marvell's "Bermudas." Indeed, it helps us see precisely how Marvell's poem rewrites the complex dynamic of territorial expansion that structures Waller's poem, producing a hymn of thanksgiving from a more conflicted sense of the lack of fit between pastoral visions and colonial realities. Waller's poem, which is also about Bermuda, is not directly about the use of force in the taking and holding of overseas territories (in this case the islands were not populated), but it does make the "Summer Islands" the scene of an near-epic battle waged against two stranded whales. Nature is itself the opponent here, and in this quasi-allegorical depiction of warfare in Edenic circumstances, Waller's poem provides an exemplary instance of the myriad ways in which cultural documents of this period are compendiums of territorial desire and colonial anxiety, of Edenic fantasy and of dystopian fear. "The Battle of the Summer Islands" is divided into three cantos, the first of which is a pastoral celebration of the natural fecundity of the island, while the second describes the coming of the whales and the preparations made to kill them, and the last portrays the battle itself. As the title suggests, the poem is meant primarily to describe the "battle," and this is indeed how the poem opens, with the first four lines invoking the Roman "Bellona" as aid to the telling of this tale of "the dreadful fight / Betwixt a nation and two whales" (1.1–2).

However, the rest of this canto is a lavish account of the riches contained on the island, an elaborate catalog of food and commodities that Marvell drew upon in his "Bermudas":

> Bermudas, walled with rocks, who does not know?
> That happy island where huge lemons grow,
> And orange trees, which golden fruit do bear,
> The Hesperian garden boasts of none so fair;
> Where shining pearl, coral, and many a pound,
> On the rich shore, of ambergris is found.
> That lofty cedar, which to heaven aspires,
> The prince of trees! is fuel for their fires.
>
> (1.5–12)[12]

Waller continues in this vein for the next thirty lines, with his account of climatic perfection and Edenic fertility ("Heaven sure has kept this spot of earth uncursed, / To show how all things were created first" lines 46–47), punctuated just twice by references to more historical concerns.[13] When Waller writes of the figs on the islands, he invokes "fierce Cato," who offered this "rare fruit" as evidence of Carthaginian riches (and hence of extravagance and luxury) when he invited his fellow Romans to sack Carthage (lines 21–24). This memory of the despoliation of cities and the wars of competing empires sits oddly with the celebration of divine and natural bounty, but preserves, within that celebration, the imperial contours of Waller's fantasy of colonial exploitation.

Waller does take into account the fact that Bermuda has now been incorporated into the colonial plantation economy and grows tobacco and cotton, but in each case these cash crops are accommodated into the effortless productivity of nature:

> Tobacco is the worst of things, which they
> To English landlords, as their tribute, pay.
> Such is the mould, that the blessed tenant feeds
> On precious fruits, and pays his rent in weeds.
>
> (lines 29–32)

Similarly, cotton is part of the bounty that a "coarser" England "tastes of," and returns to the island as cloth, "Which not for warmth, but for ornament is worn" (lines 36–39), since Bermuda always enjoys a "kind spring" (line 40). This acknowledgment of Bermuda as a producer of raw materials and as a market for finished goods produced in England—which is the circuit of production and consumption that defines colonial economic systems—is woven into the pastoral fabric of this canto with a finesse that does not disrupt, but only adds to, its profusion of natural patterns and motifs.

Toward the end of the canto, the poet's immersion in this idyll is so complete that there is no denying the seductive signature trope of the pastoral, the recumbent *poeta*. Here, he longs to escape from the "unripe and ill-constrained notes" that he produces in England ("this northern tract") and to lay "his careless limbs . . . / Under the plantain's shade, and all the day / With amorous airs my fancy entertain" (lines 58–64). This fantasy includes a faith that his repetition of "the sweet sound of Sacharissa's name" will "make the listening savages grow tame" (lines 70–71)—a faith he shares with (and perhaps derives from) Prospero in the *Tempest*. In this canto, as Waller describes Bermuda first as providential gift and then as pastoral idyll, he fuses biblical and classical vocabularies into a song of colonial celebration. But, as the concluding couplet of the first canto reminds us, the theme of the poem is battle, not "pleasing dreams," and the poet returns to his appointed task (lines 72–73).

Canto 2 begins by reemphasizing the natural impregnability of the islands (which was taken as a sure sign that a benign providence had made them to be discovered and kept by their English inhabitants): "rocks so high about this island rise, / That well they may the numerous Turk despise" (lines 1–2). These rocky defences are however breached by nature itself in the form of "Two mighty whales! which swelling seas had tossed, / And left them prisoners on the rocky coast" (lines 11–12). Nature in fact turns out to be an agent of great destruction, the "wild fury" of tempests responsible not only for beached or dead whales ("So there, sometimes, the raging ocean fails, / And her own brood exposes" lines 23–24), but also for "the fate of ships, and shipwrecked men" (line 20). Waller's lines suggest some of the human cost of territorial expansion, but for the inhabitants of the island, the plight of the whales is not this poetic reminder of the power of the oceans to destroy shipping; they see in them only "a certain prey" (line 34), and arm themselves with "Pikes, halberts, spits, darts" and other "instruments of war" (lines 42–43). The battle is to be joined, yet the uniqueness of this encounter—the whales are more prey than worthy antagonists—casts the heroism of the "young men" in a somewhat sardonic light. This is so particularly as these heroes think as merchants do, and

> Dispose already of the untaken spoil,
> And, as the purchase of their future toil,
> These share the bones, and they divide the oil.
>
> *(lines 35–37)*

This reminder of the commercial instincts of these contemporary heroes taints their would-be heroism, a taint that Waller's verse records in its turn to burlesque: the "vigorous lads" prepare to show off, before their assembled elders and "lovely lasses," all that "love, or honour, could invite them to" (lines 44–47). This ironic, mock-heroic tone is caught, too, by the diction of the closing couplet, and in its rhyme (which plays out the fluctuation between elevation and limitation): "But how they fought, and what their valour gained, / Shall in another Canto be contained" (lines 56–57).

Canto 3 describes the "battle," in which the whales use their tails as battering rams to counter the men in their boats. The narration is largely sympathetic to the whales, who, though described as monstrous, are shown as fighting back only in response to being attacked. The younger ("cub") whale has his side "rudely gored" (line 3), and his tortured struggle is compared to that of a "bream" who, "to please some curious taste," is cast live into boiling water (lines 5–8). This sense of the whales as victims continues into the description of the mother's travails, and the struggle of the whales to escape death takes on heroic proportions, with the cub compared to Aeneas, who risks his own life to save that of Creusa. Their loyalty puts the men who attack them to shame: "The men, amazed, blush to see the seed / Of monsters human piety exceed" (lines 65–66). At this point, and particularly because their weapons are lost to them, being embedded in the bleeding sides of the whales, the men wish for "composition with the unconquered fish" (line 70), but go on to fire muskets at the whales. This discharge does not kill them either, and before the men can send off for larger weapons (the cannon that defend the island-fort), great Neptune intercedes and sends a "tide so high" that the whales are floated out to sea: "And thus they parted with exchange of harms; / Much blood the monsters lost, and they their arms" (lines 89–90). This uneasy truce, if it can be called that, with the bloody and gored whales escaping into the ocean and the men left without some of their weapons, seems an apt closing for this parable of colonial encounter. The "exchange of harms" staged here plays out an inequality of violence and suffering that cannot but interrogate the long celebration of divine and natural bounty in the first canto. By the end of the poem, that is, the pastoral and Edenic motifs of the poem are abandoned almost entirely, and the "Summer Islands" become the theater of cruelty and of battle.

In reading Waller's poem, we can plot one way in which the discourse of divinely sanctioned discovery confronts, and comes to terms with, the

limitations imposed upon it by historical conditions. The lyrical simplicity of
Waller's first canto gives way, in the descriptions of the fears of the inhabitants
about invasion, or indeed of nature in its less benign garb (the storms that
wreck ships, the inexplicable, terrifying noise that turns out to be the cries of
the trapped whales), to a different idiom, that of violence and warfare. Waller's
couplets, whose formal regularity is often commented upon, are in fact flexible
enough to accommodate not only the elements of mock-heroic that surface
in the second canto, but also the more serious, more bloody, descriptions of
the attack on the whales in the third. In this process, the enclosed, safe space
of the pastoral gives way to the heavily defended, violence-prone borders of
the colonial territory, as Waller's poem turns into a contemporary beast-fable,
one whose allegorical coordinates are defined by the conflicted histories of
seventeenth-century English expansion into North America and the Caribbean.
The "battle" with the whales in this poem (here understood, as the title tells
us, as "The Battle of the Summer Islands") is particularly interesting in that
these islands were uninhabited, and hence not an arena for the warfare and
bloodshed that marked the taking of equivalent territories in the New World.
And yet there is no denying the poem's sense that the battle it recounts, the
emotions it describes, and the motivations it questions, are all representative
of the processes of contemporary colonial expansion.

Perhaps the couplet that most captures this relation between Englishmen
and their colonial circumstances is one whose oppositions refuse the
naturalized equivalence between consumers and commodities in the pastoral
landscape emphasized by the first canto. In the third canto, when the sailors
recognize the courage and loyalty that characterizes the whales, they wish
they could disengage from the attack, and even help the whales find their
way out to sea. But this wish is only momentary, for there can be, in this
scheme of things, no empathy between sailor and whale, "hero" and "monster,"
hunter-trader and prey: "But how instructed in each other's mind? / Or what
commerce can men with monsters find?" (lines 73–74). The sailors fire their
muskets, and Waller's allegory of colonial oppositions and violence is complete.

Marvell on European Competitors

Most contemporary poems did not in fact feature the manifest opposition
between colonizer and territories or people, but concentrated on defining
the rights and interests of Englishmen by contrasting them, and their nation,
to competing Europeans and their states. In this section, I analyze two poems
by Marvell ("The Character of Holland" and "On the Victory obtained by
Blake over the Spaniards in the Bay of Santa Cruz, in the Island of Tenerife,
1657") on nations and on national power, both of which are, in different

ways, part of the ideological project of nation building in the middle of the seventeenth century. "The Character of Holland" was probably written in early 1653, during the first Anglo-Dutch war (1652–54) and is part of the large mass of Hollandophobic travelogues and caricatures produced in the later seventeenth century, some of which responded to particular events, such as the Dutch destruction of an English settlement at Amboyna in 1623.[14] Most, however, can be traced to the continuing mercantile and naval rivalries that resulted in three wars in the century (the second in 1665–67 and the third in 1672–74). In fact, England's ambition to become the dominant mercantile power in Europe was achieved at the cost of Dutch shipping and commerce, which, in the first half of the seventeenth century, was quite the most successful of the rival nations. For the English, the United Provinces (a loose federation of seven provinces) provided a model of the flourishing mercantilist state, in that many of its financial and political policies emphasized the conduct of overseas trade, whether that meant the carrying of goods between European markets, the development of trading centers in the East and in the West Indies, or the setting-up, through force or purchase, captive colonies.[15] As far as the English were concerned, there was much to emulate, and therefore much to distance themselves from and to despise, in the conduct of the Dutch.[16]

In Marvell's satire, Dutch claims to national power and sovereignty are swamped by their lack of defined boundaries and territories, in that their coastal lands are constantly fighting to maintain their integrity against the encroaching sea.[17] The opening lines turn the fragility of the coastline into a claim that Holland "scarce deserves the name of land" as it is "but the off-scouring of the British sand," or the product of the leavings of the ocean, the "indigested vomit of the sea" (lines 1–8). The Dutch hunger for land, and their efforts to reclaim and preserve it, are compared with the desire of miners for ore, divers for ambergris, and the labor of swallows building nests and beetles transfusing dunghills (in that order). While Dutch commerce is also ridiculed in the association of gold and ambergris with the pickings of swallows and beetles, it is by no means clear that these images do not taint the activities of commerce in general. Insofar as Marvell's commentary on Holland, and the particular targets he chooses to attack, are inevitably meant to distinguish its people and its policies from the English, this poem, too, suffers from a possible porosity of rhetorical and satiric reference—if the Dutch grub for their land and their trade, do the English do otherwise? While the poem does not explicitly address this problem, it does go on to connect the inundation of the Dutch coast with a very specific maritime quarrel between England and Holland that had to do with the English claim to the sovereignty of the English Channel, a claim contrary to the

freedom of the seas espoused by the Dutch lawyer Hugo Grotius in his
Mare Liberum (first published anonymously in 1608):

> Yet still his claim the injured ocean laid,
> And oft at leap-frog o'er their steeples played:
> As if on purpose it on land had come
> To show them what's their *Mare Liberum*.
>
> *(lines 23–26)*

In this clever twist, the "injured," avenging ocean reclaims its freedom and
its sovereignty from the Dutch, its natural power standing in for the English
and their equally "natural" claim.

Marvell next attacks the Dutch system of government, which he derides
as loose and lacking in defined authority. It is "Something like a government"
(line 38), in which anyone with any expertise at land reclamation qualifies for
leadership: "Who best could know to pump an earth so leak / Him they
their Lord and country's Father speak" (lines 45–46). In Marvell's depiction,
Holland's geography defines its political collectivity and mocks its attempts to
create a state apparatus adequate to the needs of a would-be nation; it leaves a
people searching for a viable form of governance: "For these Half-anders, half
wet, and half dry, / Nor bear strict service, nor pure liberty" (lines 53–54).
This last line in particular resonates powerfully in an England that had only
very recently emerged from internecine warfare brought on, in part, by crises
in its systems of governance and authority; between the Royalists and the
Levellers, both "strict service" and "pure liberty" had been argued for and
fought over. Once again in this poem, the representation of Dutch traits touches
upon, and perhaps helps distance, English anxieties. This logic continues into
the next object of satire, which is the overly tolerant nature of religious life in
Holland, so much so that the Dutch seem, to an Englishman concerned about
the disruptive role that religious affiliations play in his own country, to be
schismatic to the point of incoherence:

> Hence Amsterdam, Turk—Christian—Pagan—Jew,
> Staple of sects and mint of schism grew,
> That bank of conscience, where not one so strange
> Opinion but finds credit, and exchange.
> In vain for catholics ourselves we bear;
> The Universal Church is only there.
>
> *(lines 71–76)*

In the 1650s, Amsterdam was the richest and most prominent trading center
in Europe—the gathering place of merchants from Asia, the Persian Gulf, and
Europe. Marvell's metaphor of the "bank of conscience" is meant to discredit

that financial and economic achievement, but it also functions as a reminder that trading success is often linked to ecumenical latitude. Amsterdam's religious excess suggests a more appropriate English norm, but buried within this example is a somewhat different economic lesson for English traders and policymakers.

As this reading of the poem suggests, in key passages Holland functions as a sort of perverse mirror in which we can trace the contours of economic, political, and religious issues important to English self-conception. There are of course other objects of satire in the poem, including misogynist and scatological portrayals of the Dutch, but they are framed within this concern for the nation and its objectionable aspects.[18] In fact, in a central passage, Dutch women embody, and render more immediate and grotesque, the porosity that characterizes the geography of their nation, as Marvell describes them as mermaids, half fish and half women, with bodily secretions that pollute the churches they attend:

> See but their mermaids with their tails of fish,
> Reeking at church over the chafing dish:
> . . . .
> While the fat steam of female sacrifice
> Fills the priests nostrils and puts out his eyes.
>
> *(lines 85–92)*

Dutch stealth and slipperiness are once again emphasized when their ingratitude for past English support is condemned (lines 101–12), particularly their belligerence at a time of great turmoil for "Our sore new circumcised Commonwealth" (line 118). However, in a show of energetic masculinity, the commonwealth strikes back, as "our armed *Bucentore* / Doth yearly their sea nuptials restore" (lines 135–36). The ambiguity in line 136 (which yearly "sea nuptials" are restored by the armed English ship of state? or is it simply that Britain reduces Holland to its proper status of wife?) is perhaps of less consequence than the clear sexual politics of the historical analogy. The *Bucentore* was the Doge's ship that was central to the annual ceremonies in which Venice married the sea, and it provides Marvell a useful analogy for the nautical and commercial mastery that he wishes for his English bridegroom.

In its conclusion, "The Character of Holland" returns to the military antagonism that prompted it, and to the sense of mercantile and colonial competition that causes the poem to both identify with, and to revile, the Dutch:

> And now the hydra of seven provinces
> Is strangled by our infant Hercules.
> Their tortoise wants its vainly stretched neck;
> Their navy all our conquest or our wreck;

> Or, what is left, their Carthage overcome
> Would render fain unto our better Rome,
> Unless our Senate, lest their youth disuse
> The war, (but who would?) peace, if begged, refuse.
>   For now of nothing may our state despair,
> Darling of heaven, and of men the care;
> Provided that they be what they have been,
> Watchful abroad, and honest still within.
>
> *(lines 137–48)*

In Marvell's vision, a triumphant England will be a successor to Holland's empire, a "better Rome" to "their Carthage" (this comparison is to be found in Dryden's *Annus Mirabilis*, too). Typically, the language of providential approval ("Darling of heaven") is invoked to guarantee this transition, in which England will build upon the gains of the Dutch and supplant Holland as the dominant European mercantilist and colonial power. To that extent, Richard Todd is surely right in arguing that, in "The Character of Holland," Marvell "argues nothing less than his sense of what it was to be English in 1653 at a providentially unique historical moment during the Interregnum."[19] To write the character of a competing nation at this time is to delineate, in one way or another, the characteristics of one's own.

These characteristics though, as "The Character of Holland" makes clear, are of consequence particularly in that they enable or further arguments for English action, especially overseas. In "On the Victory obtained by Blake . . . ," the second of Marvell's topical poems against a competing trading and colonial power, Spanish colonialism is repeatedly and inescapably associated with gold, and thus defined as different from English rule.[20] The Spanish fleet is "Freighted with acted guilt, and guilt to come: / For this rich load, of which so proud they are, / Was raised by tyranny, and raised for war" (lines 4–6). The *guilt/gilt* pun allows Spanish expropriation of colonial wealth to be seen as morally dubious, a dubiety that is emphasized during the course of the poem, in passages that castigate the corrupting power of gold:

> fatal gold, for still where that does grow,
> Neither the soil, nor people, quiet know.
> Which troubles men to raise it when 'tis ore,
> And when 'tis raised, does trouble them much more.
>
> *(lines 57–60)*

> Their galleons sunk, their wealth the sea does fill—
> The only place where it can cause no ill.
>
> *(lines 151–52)*

The English fleet, and the English presence in the Canary Islands generally, is seen as a force that can destroy the tyranny of the Spanish and of gold, which has no place in that idyllic, pastoral world (lines 24–66):

> The jarring elements no discord know,
> Fuel and rain together kindly grow;
> And coolness there, with heat doth never fight,
> This only rules by day, and that by night.
>
> *(lines 35–38)*

> There the indulgent soil that rich grape breeds,
> Which of the gods the fancied drink exceeds;
> They still do yield, such is their precious mould,
> All that is good, and are not cursed with gold.
>
> *(lines 53–56)*

The poem, which is addressed to Cromwell, walks a fine ideological line in its argument for the supplanting of Spanish, gold-driven tyranny by English "pastoral" benevolence in the Canary Islands. The natural fertility and beauty of the islands can only be enhanced by, and thus invites, English (Cromwell's) rule:

> Your worth to all these isles, a just right brings,
> The best of lands should have the best of kings.[21]
> And these want nothing heaven can afford,
> Unless it be—the having you their lord;
> But this great want will not a long one prove,
> Your conquering sword will soon that want remove.
>
> *(lines 39–44)*

Yet Cromwell's "conquering sword" cannot be seen as the source of war: that must be the Spanish—or, rather, the gold that is their emblem. In a disingenuous move—and here the full force of the pun comes into play—the "guilty" Spanish are at fault, as their unwarranted presence in the islands brings war in its wake:

> Ah, why was thither brought that cause of war,
> Kind Nature had from thence removed so far?
> In vain does she those islands free from ill,
> If fortune can make guilty what she will.
>
> *(lines 61–64)*

In this equation, the Spanish (fortune-hunting?) presence is a crime against nature. By this point, the earlier jingoistic characterization of Cromwell's "conquering sword" and the claim that "peace" had made the islands Spanish property, "but war will make them" English (lines 51–52), is rewritten into a providentialist and moral scenario where Blake's fleet will rid the paradisiacal Islands of a "guilty" Spanish imperialism.

The bulk of the poem is then given over to a description of the naval hostilities between the Spanish galleons and the English fleet (lines 67–152). The engagement is so intense that "War turned the temperate into the torrid zone." At this point, in one of those rhetorical flourishes that historical hindsight makes prophetic, Marvell describes the battle as a struggle for the globe, for the temperate and the torrid zones: "Fate these two fleets between both worlds had brought, / Who fight, as if for both those worlds they fought" (lines 125–26). The English victory is hard-won, and then, in a surprising passage in an otherwise jingoistic and belligerent poem, the sinking of the Spanish galleons and their cargo of gold leads to an emotional plea against the seductions of the "Indies":

> Ah, would those treasures which both Indies have,
> Were buried in as large, and deep a grave,
> Wars' chief support with them would buried be,
> And the land owe her peace unto the sea.
> Ages to come your conquering arms will bless,
> There they destroy what had destroyed their peace.
> And in one war the present age may boast
> The certain seeds of many wars are lost.
>
> *(lines 153–60)*

And yet these lines are not as surprising as they first may seem. First, because the blame for colonial and imperial warfare is shifted onto the feminized "Indies" and their "treasures," rather than onto those who wish to expropriate them. Thus, the "Indies" can only be grateful to anyone who will either rid them of their treasures or whose control will be so total that no wars can ensue. Secondly, these lines in fact argue, in the name of a fervent moralism, the same geopolitical schema as the rest of the poem: Cromwell's "conquering arms" will destroy the Spanish treasure-ships, thus ridding the area of a source of tension. This logic, when extended to both the Indies and their treasures, is effectively a plea for English "peace-keeping" and control, which is the propagandistic point of the poem as a whole. Blake's victory then, becomes a model for victories elsewhere, in which a moral English power replaces "guilty" Spanish colonialism. As an ideological model for the legitimation and extension of English power across the globe, this argument grew from strength to strength throughout the seventeenth century until it became one of the key tokens of British imperialism. Particularly in the late seventeenth and the eighteenth centuries, the export of British patriarchal morality, enlightened constitutionalism, religious toleration (especially when opposed to Roman Catholic fanaticism), technology and science, and administrative systems—broadly speaking, the apparatus of British imperial modernity—became the powerful alibi for aggressive British trading, warfare, and colonial settlement. In Marvell's celebration of Blake's victory over the Spaniards as a supplanting of bad colonialism by good—the land now owes her peace to the conquering embrace of a new master—the poet became part of a longer and more consequential rhetorical and ideological tradition than he might have imagined.

As both "Bermudas" and this poem show, Marvell's tropology of nature— his celebrated "pastoralism"—provides him compelling rhetorical and ideological schemas within which to write his providentialist and propagandistic verse. If a divine will makes available to the Puritans, as reward and as earthly salvation, the Bermudas, and if the fertility and paradisiacal nature of the Canary Islands demands Cromwell's rule (as a protection against the corrupting presence of Spanish gold), then we can see precisely how Marvell's masterful use of poetic conventions strengthens the scenario of English expansion that he imagines. In these poems, the pastoral moment does not mark the Edenic time before (the fall into) history; rather, it is achieved as the telos of a providentialist English history.[22] Further, as the "Character of Holland" makes clear, trading and colonial rivalries and wars create a need for direct nationalist propaganda or, less overt but nonetheless effective, apologias and alibis for expansionism. All such writing, as I have suggested from the examples above, is to be understood as part of the process of national imagining and understanding, such that a view of England powerful abroad becomes central to the self-conception of Englishmen. Cromwell's military triumphs in Ireland and Scotland, and the reorientation of European power forced by such success, was the domestic counterpart to English belligerence on the oceans, both in the conduct of trade and in the taking of rival ships and colonial territories.[23] Cromwell's reputation and power were in fact very important to the polemicists of English ascendancy in Europe and in the colonial theaters.

What Cromwell Wrought: Waller, Marvell, Dryden

In 1650, Andrew Marvell had, in his "An Horatian Ode upon Cromwell's Return from Ireland," incorporated just such sentiments in his qualified, ambivalent, celebration of Cromwell's ascension to power, the general's very brutal and successful campaign in Ireland, and his taking over of the army to launch a preemptive strike against Scotland (in place of Fairfax, who resigned rather than lead such a campaign):[24]

What may not then our isle presume
While victory his crest does plume!
    What may not others fear
    If thus he crowns each year!
A Caesar he ere long to Gaul,
To Italy a Hannibal,
    And to all states not free
    Shall climacteric be.
The Pict no shelter now shall find
Within his parti-coloured mind;
    But from this valour sad
    Shrink underneath the plaid:
Happy if in the tufted brake
The English hunter him mistake.

(lines 97–110)

The comparison of Cromwell and a caesar is not of course as straightforward as panegyric would demand: in lines 23–24, Marvell has already compared Charles I to Julius Caesar, precisely to suggest that even a caesar's laurels are no protection from an irresistible power like that of Cromwell. The reference to a conquering Hannibal, too, is complicated in the close of the poem, with its oft-quoted warning that those who live by the sword might die by it: "The same arts that did *gain* / A power must it *maintain* (line 119–20). But Cromwell did provide English poets with a powerful instance of a military (and, later, political) leader able to project English power across its borders, be it into Ireland (lines 73–74) or Scotland, and perhaps even onto the Continent (lines 99–100), and Marvell is clearly enthused by that ability.

Such enthusiasm is the staple of Waller's tribute to Cromwell, "A Panegyric to my Lord Protector, of the Present Greatness, and Joint Interest, of His Highness, and this Nation" (1655). Waller's poem was written in the middle of the period that David Armitage has identified as the "imperial moment of the English republic [that] extends from the peace settlement which concluded the first Anglo-Dutch War in 1654 to the second Protectoral Parliament in 1656, and it comprehends Cromwell's Western Design, [and] the beginnings of the Anglo-Spanish War."[25] Waller celebrates Cromwell's ability to "bridle faction," (line 2), and thus to "Make us unite, and make us conquer too" (line 4). The next few stanzas emphasize England's rise to international power: Cromwell is compared to Neptune as he calms the "storms of ambition" that were tossing the ship of state, a comparison whose logic is made clear as sections of the poem go on to detail England's sea-based power. Cromwell's England is

> The seat of empire, where the Irish come,
> And the unwilling Scotch, to fetch their doom.
>
> The sea's our own; and now all nations greet,
> With bending sails, each vessel of our fleet;
> Your power extends as far as winds can blow,
> Or swelling sails upon the globe may go.
>
> *(lines 15–20)*

Since, as the title suggests, Cromwell's Neptune-like greatness and "Interest" are identical with that of the nation,[26] Waller, as an Englishman, can claim the expansive benefits of such an identity:

> Lords of the world's great waste, the ocean, we
> Whole forests send to reign upon the sea,
> And every coast may trouble, or relieve;
> But none can visit us without your leave.
>
> *(lines 41–44)*

This domination of the seas allows the English to "harvest" commodities not available in England, and to do so without suffering climatic inconvenience or putting in the labor required to produce them:

> The taste of hot Arabia's spice we know,
> Free from the scorching sun that makes it grow;
> Without the worm, in Persian silks we shine;
> And, without planting, drink of every vine.
>
> To dig for wealth we weary not our limbs;
> Gold, though the heaviest metal, hither swims;
> Ours in the harvest where the Indians mow;
> We plough the deep, and reap what others sow.
>
> *(lines 57–64)*

Waller's verse weaves a complex fantasy here: other people in foreign lands do the work, and the English benefit because they control the seas. Mercantilism becomes a dream of accessible commodities detached from the labor that produces them; pastoral fecundity and laborless ease provide the model for the easy circulation of trade goods. Gold, long regarded as symbolic of the ethically tainted practices of (particularly Spanish) colonialism, is here detached from its moorings in forced labor and colonial cruelty and transmuted into shoals of fish swarming to England. The rhetorical sleight of hand that produces these gold fish does not extend quite so flawlessly into the last two lines here: the shift to a georgic vocabulary (the English plough, reap, and harvest the sea) might be read as the crafting of an exculpatory frame for the extraction of colonial labor (the Indians who mow, or the others who sow, their lands). The English work for their riches, too, these lines now suggest, only in a different medium.

Waller's view of the inevitability of Britain's rise to global dominance emphasizes a divine mandate: "Heaven, (that has placed this island to give law, / To balance Europe, and her states to awe)" (lines 21–22); Cromwell's leadership (which is itself a sign of that mandate); and the nature of the English soil that "breeds" stout men and warlike steeds (lines 65–66). His extended account of Cromwell's conquest of the "Caledonians" compares him to Alexander, but suggests that the Roman emperors might be a more fruitful comparison because they allowed their "vanquished foes" to be "free citizens of Rome" (lines 95–96), which is the privilege Cromwell allows the defeated Scots and Irish. The Roman analogy is developed to argue that Cromwell is particularly important to England because he has stilled the "tempest" (line 155) of civil war that threatened to engulf the country:

> As the vexed world, to find repose, at last
> Itself into Augustus' arms did cast;
> So England now does, with like toil oppressed,
> Her weary head upon your bosom rest.
>
> *(lines 169–73)*[27]

None of this poetic-historical iconography is unexpected; if anything, Waller's "Panegyric" is a compendium of the images and vocabulary that contemporary poets used to celebrate Cromwell's accession to, and consolidation of, power. Cromwell may be responsible for the stilling of forces threatening the domestic fabric of England, but he is, most importantly, the guarantor of England's power beyond its borders. This is the note on which Waller ends his poem— Cromwell as conqueror, with English poets mouthing his praise:

> Here, in low strains, your milder deeds we sing;
> But there, my lord; we'll bays and olive bring
>
> To crown your head; while you in triumph ride
> O'er vanquished nations, and the sea beside;
> While all your neighbor-princes unto you,
> Like Joseph's sheaves, pay reverence, and bow.[28]
>
> *(lines 183–88)*

Cromwell's military successes certainly provided all his panegyrists with materials appropriate to various forms of heroic verse. However, not all the poets who wrote poems to or about Cromwell extended their celebration of his power into a vision of English might being projected overseas. Milton, for instance, in his 1652 sonnet (number 16, which bears the manuscript title "To the Lord General Cromwell, May 1652, on the proposals of certain ministers at the Committee for the Propagation of the Gospel") begins with Cromwell's victories but turns that compliment into an injunction to look inward and rectify the problems of peace:

> While Darwen stream, with blood of Scots imbrued,
> And Dunbar field resounds thy praises loud,
> And Worcester's laureate wreath; yet much remains
> To conquer still: peace hath her victories
> No less renowned than war; new foes arise
> Threat'ning to bind our souls with secular chains.
> Help us to save free conscience from the paw
> Of hireling wolves whose gospel is their maw.
>
> *(lines 7–14)*

Milton wrote this poem to address a specific socioreligious issue: the possibility that a parliamentary committee would propose the imposition of "a kind of state-controlled Congregationalism—which Milton the individualist saw as a new Established Church."[29] The poem objects to such an institution. While Milton had objections to some forms of statism and the centralization of power, he had fewer qualms about the projection of state power abroad (particularly into Ireland). However, he certainly wrote no poetry demanding action abroad in the same way as he asks for intervention at home here.[30]

In fact, as David Quint argues, in *Paradise Lost* Milton's recasting of some of the events of Camões's *Lusíadas* "into Satan's journey, suggests that the voyages are the work of the devil. As da Gama opened up a route to the Indies for the trade and imperialism of Europe—particularly Catholic Europe— so Satan blazes a trail for Sin and Death." For Quint, it is "not surprising that the Puritan poet Milton should reject the providential interpretations of the exploits of Renaissance discovery advanced by Catholic epic poets such as Camões and Tasso. His criticism is in keeping with a general rejection in *Paradise Lost* both of imperialism and of the Virgilian epic of empire." Milton objects to both martial heroism, the subject of the epic tradition, and mercantile activity, newly elevated in narratives about voyages of discovery: "The focus of Milton's criticism constantly shifts between a revision of an earlier epic tradition and an indictment of European expansion and colonialism that includes his own countrymen and contemporaries." Quint explains Milton's rejection of "epic nationhood" as a response to the restoration of Charles II, and adds that within this "resistance of the defeated republican to the restored monarchy there appears to lie a second strain of resistance to statism, to centralizing projects—such as Cromwell's Triers—that intruded on individual and local liberty."[31]

The importance of Cromwell's rise to supremacy, and the concomitant strengthening of the state, can scarcely be overstated. Even within the British Isles, Cromwell's campaign in Scotland (which ended in 1653) meant that the republic in England could claim greater territories that obeyed its writ than any monarch who had come before. This power, in part, enabled it to take far more aggressive positions against European powers and their possessions abroad. As T. O. Lloyd puts it, republican rule

transformed the way that the English dealt with the world outside Europe; even though Charles's son came back to the throne as Charles II in 1660, the Republic changed the direction of English imperial policy and set a pattern followed at least until the death in 1714 of the last direct descendant of Charles I to sit on the throne. Queen Anne died after the signing of the treaty of Utrecht, which had brought to an end a cycle of wars which, while primarily concerned with the balance of power in Europe, had given English governments an opportunity to take colonies away from other European countries and increase their empire by annexation as well as by settlement. Annexation showed that the English government had much more power to take action outside Europe than it had possessed in the first half of the century.[32]

Lloyd points to several events as key in the confirmation of English power overseas: the success, in 1650, of the government fleet in imposing its authority over the colonists and traders in Virginia and the West Indies (who for reasons of royalism or for greater profits from trading with the Dutch, had sought to distance themselves from the republic);[33] the 1651 Navigation Act (which sought to protect English trade by "laying down that imports could be taken to the ports of England or of English colonies only by English ships or by those of the country that produced the goods"—and precipitated a war with the Dutch); and the 1655 capture of Jamaica and the 1657 reorganization of the East India Company.[34]

Thus, in 1655, when Marvell published his poem on "The First Anniversary of the Government Under His Highness the Lord Protector," he paid tribute to Cromwell's dominance in domestic affairs but also called attention to the development of English naval power. A "foreign prince," awestruck and fearful, asks can this be

> "the nation that we read
> Spent with both wars, under a captain dead?
> Yet rig a navy while we dress us late;
> And ere we dine, raze and rebuild their state.
> What oaken forests, and what golden mines!
> What mints of men, what union of designs!
> . . . .

> Theirs are not ships, but rather arks of war,
> And beaked promontories sailed from far;
> Of floating islands a new hatched nest;
> A fleet of worlds, of other worlds in quest;
>
> . . . .
>
> What refuge to escape them can be found,
> Whose watr'y leaguers all the world surround?
> Needs must we all their tributaries be,
> Whose navies hold the sluices of the sea.
> The ocean is the fountain of command,
> But that once took, we captives are on land.
> And those that have the waters for their share,
> Can quickly leave us neither earth nor air."
>
> *(lines 349–72)*

The poem then returns to Cromwell, with the foreign prince saying that he fears "That one man . . . / More than all men, all navies, and all arms" (lines 375–76).

This passage does more than make that compliment credible—the entire poem is structured, as Steven Zwicker has argued, by Marvell's representations of not only "the singularity of Cromwell's rule, but the isolation and distance of the great captain from all societies: sociable, libertarian, radical, or patriarchal and monarchical. . . . In the powerful dialectic of this poem, Cromwell is finally unlike any other figure, distinguished in the form of his governance not only from foreign princes but from his nation as well."[35] While this is certainly the case, it seems to me that the poem does provide one frame within which Cromwell's military and administrative singularity expresses the will of the nation, and that is his encouragement of a navy powerful enough to project English power overseas. This fusion of captain and seafaring nation— "The nation had been ours, but his one soul / Moves the great bulk, and animates the whole" (lines 379–80)—is in fact the primary ideological work performed by the long speech of the foreign prince (lines 349–94).

This passage is also a fine example of the hold that armed conquest overseas was beginning to take on the English imagination. Indeed, in their emphasis on the role of oceans in the projection and consolidation of imperial control, lines 365 to 372 anticipate the economic and political restructuring of European power, and the globe, over the next two hundred years. In 1660, the restoration of Charles II may have brought back to England the aristocratic culture of late dressing and dining marked here as foreign (lines 351–52), but there was to be no contrast between that royal culture and the growth of English trade and empire. Marvell's vivid picture of the English navy as "A fleet of worlds, of other worlds in quest," within an account of the irresistible might of these "arks of war," reminds us that, by the middle of the seventeenth century, exploration and "discovery" were seen as a prelude to colonization.[36] In this tribute to Cromwell, Marvell's expression of national power and imperial desire allows us to recognize an uncanny prolepsis: what Marvell imagines here is in fact the foundational role played by belligerent mercantilism and colonization in the making of the modern British nation-state.[37]

That Dryden, too, was committed to the idea of a nation whose power is derived, at least in part, from its strength internationally is clear from his first major poem, also on Cromwell: "Heroique Stanza's, Consecrated to the Glorious Memory of his most Serene and Renowned Highnesse OLIVER Late *lord protector* of this Common-Wealth, &c. *Written after the Celebration of his Funerall*" (1659).[38] After praising Cromwell's personal qualities, Dryden sings of Cromwell's military might. Cromwell is made out to be a reluctant entrant into the civil war, who "fought to end our fighting, and assaid / To stanch the blood by breathing of the vein" (lines 47–48). If this image of Cromwell as a bloodletting physician functions as a metaphoric exculpation of his role in military and political turmoil, the verses that follow make no attempt to play down Cromwell's military victories, especially those that took him beyond the boundaries of England. Indeed, Dryden suggests the speed of Cromwell's triumphs over the domestic opposition by comparing them to Alexander's imperial campaigns, and then goes on to describe his role in the making of the modern nation:

> Swift and resistlesse through the Land he past
> Like that bold *Greek* who did the East subdue;
> And made to battails such Heroick haste
> As if on wings of victory he flew.
>
> He fought secure of fortune as of fame,
> Till by *new maps* the Island might be shown,
> Of Conquests which he strew'd where e'er he came
> Thick as the *Galaxy* with starr's is sown.
>
> . . . .
>
> Peace was the Prize of all his toyles and care,
> Which Warre had banisht and did now restore;
> *Bolognia's* Walls thus mounted in the Ayre
> To seat themselves more surely then before.
>
> Her safety rescu'd *Ireland* to him owes;
> And Treacherous *Scotland* to no int'rest true,
> Yet blest that fate which did his Armes dispose
> Her Land to Civilize as to subdue.[39]
>
> *(lines 49–68)*

Cromwell is also commended for his peacetime foreign-policy successes, which feature his negotiations with those continental powers that had colonial and mercantile interests. He makes peace with a "suppliant *Holland* . . . / Our once bold Rivall in the *British Main*" (lines 81–82), and his support of France in its struggle against Spain tilts the balance of power in its favor (lines 85–92). In each case, English power is enhanced, and its citizens, traders, and sailors made beneficiaries:

> From this high-spring our forraign-Conquests flow
> Which yet more glorious triumphs do portend,
> Since their Commencement to his Armes they owe,
> If Springs as high as Fountaines may ascend.
>
> He made us *Freemen* of the *Continent*
> Whom Nature did like Captives treat before,
> To nobler prey's the *English Lyon* sent,
> And taught him first in *Belgian walks* to rore.
>
> That old unquestion'd Pirate of the Land
> Proud *Rome*, with dread, the fate of *Dunkirk* har'd;
> And trembling wish't behind more *Alpes* to stand,
> Although an *Alexander* were her guard.
>
> By his command we boldly crost the Line
> And bravely fought where *Southern Starrs* arise,
> We trac'd the farre-fetchd Gold unto the mine
> And that which brib'd our fathers made our prize.
>
> *(lines 109–24)*

A good one-third of the poem is devoted to Cromwell's spectacular military successes at home and abroad, and to the resurgence of English power overseas. For Dryden, Cromwell made available a new definition and understanding of the nation, and that is what, for the most part, makes him a fit subject for commemoration.[40]

Cromwell's government made possible a vocabulary of English state and naval might that also shaped the poetic celebration that accompanied the restoration of Charles II.[41] When Dryden wrote "Astrea Redux. A POEM on the Happy Restoration and Return Of His Sacred Majesty Charles the Second," in 1660, he needed to publicly reverse the political affiliation and admiration detailed so eloquently in his memorial verses on Cromwell.[42] He preserves elements of that earlier celebration though, for they belong to the discourse of national power, and are not easily dispensed with in the writing of panegyric. Thus, the coming of Charles II is a warning to competing nations that the English "Lyon" is not to be trifled with (compare lines 115–16 of Dryden's "Heroique Stanza's" quoted above):

Tremble ye Nations who secure before
Laught at those Armes that 'gainst our selves we bore;
Rous'd by the lash of his own stubborn tail
Our Lyon now will forraign Foes assail.

(lines 115–18)

The benediction that closes the poem develops this theme of English power overseas, and brings into conjunction a great many of the motifs and images characteristic of the contemporary language of national greatness, in particular that of its international frame. I therefore quote it at some length before examining its constituent elements:

Our Nation with united Int'rest blest
Not now content to poize, shall sway the rest.
Abroad your Empire shall no limits know,
But like the Sea in boundless Circles flow.
Your much lov'd Fleet shall with a wide Command
Besiege the petty Monarchs of the Land:
And as Old Time his Off-spring swallow'd down
Our Ocean in its depths all Seas shall drown.
Their wealthy Trade from Pyrates Rapine free
Our Merchants shall no more Advent'rers be:
Nor in the farthest East those Dangers fear
Which humble *Holland* must dissemble here.
Spain to your Gift alone her *Indies* owes;
For what the Pow'rful takes not he bestowes.
And *France* that did an Exiles presence fear
May justly apprehend you still too near.
. . . .
Oh Happy Age! Oh times like those alone
By Fate reserv'd for Great *Augustus* Throne!
When the joint growth of Armes and Arts foreshew
The World a Monarch, and that Monarch *You.*

(lines 296–323)

Whether Dryden writes to commemorate Cromwell or to celebrate Charles II, the idea of the nation that he invokes is the same—an England settled at home and powerful abroad. (In the development of this ideal of domestic order and international strength, one was often thought to lead to the other. In this case, in lines 296–97, the "united Int'rest" of the nation leads to its power over others; in lines 141–44 of the "Heroique Stanza's," Cromwell's successes abroad ensure the absence of domestic discord even after his death). Time, nature, the circularity of the oceans, all provide poetic and prophetic reassurance of the growth of English mercantilism and of the spread of its colonies.[43] The plastic strength of this political-historical discourse comes from the fact that, in each case (Cromwell, Charles II) Dryden resolves bitter partisan ambivalences and memories in a celebration of the nation-state. Memories of the extraordinarily divisive internecine warfare that led to Cromwell's accession, or even of the complicated political struggle that led to the Restoration, are dissolved into a heady cocktail of pride, belligerence, and mercantile possibility.[44] The formulae of nationalist panegyric in this period, as Dryden here shows, are at their most persuasive when the poet projects his imagination, and that of the nation, abroad, and finds in trade and colonialism a confirmation of present, and a promise of future, greatness.[45] Further, the imperial future is imagined as the working out of a divinely sanctioned teleology, in which the riches of the globe are laid out for English taking and control.

The resolution of domestic discord or fear via an appeal to a predestined imperial future is not only produced by rhetorical sleight of hand, as it were. Dryden closes "Threnodia Augustalis" by explicitly asking heaven to unfold its "adamantine Book" in order to encourage the "wondering *Senate*," stunned by the death of Charles II, to take appropriate political and fiscal action. The combination of divine prophecy and imperial promise is meant to reassure English policymakers in a time of potential historical turmoil and irresolution; this form of poetic closure, that is, is designed to address and allay national political anxieties:

> Let them, with glad amazement, look
> On what their happiness may be:
> . . . .
> The long retinue of a Prosperous Raign,
> A Series of Successful years,
> In Orderly Array, a Martial, manly Train.
> Behold ev'n to remoter Shores
> A Conquering Navy proudly spread;
> The *British* Cannon formidably roars,
> While starting from his Oozy Bed,
> Th' asserted Ocean rears his reverend Head;
> To View and Recognize his ancient Lord again:
> And with a willing hand, restores
> The *Fasces* of the Main.
>
> *(lines 496–517)*

This reference to a Roman symbol of public authority, the "Fasces," might take us back to the close of "Astrea Redux," and its comparison of Charles II to Augustus. Such late-seventeenth-century (and indeed early-eighteenth-century) comparisons of England to the empire of Augustus made a strong (if never simple or unambivalent) claim to an imperial culture.[46] The "joint growth of Armes and Arts" (line 322) as a sign of imperial domination owes much to the weight of classical cultural and literary achievement during the rule of Augustus, but it is also a tribute to the fact that the Roman Empire was at its zenith at the time. For would-be empires like Britain, and for the spokesmen (and critics) of mercantile and colonial expansion, Augustan Rome thus provided a compelling historical example of the making of empires (but also their worrisome devolution—a theme I take up later). Here, Golden Age mythology is brought together with Augustan history to suggest the efflorescence of military and cultural triumphs that the Restoration promises. Such comparisons are not always made in any detailed way, but they became a staple in the poetic prospect of empire. In fact, as Howard Weinbrot and Howard Erskine-Hill have shown, incidental comparisons with, or extended debates about, the political and cultural features of the Roman Empire were an important part of contemporary discussions about the present and future state of the kingdom. In some crucial ways, meditations upon Rome (and its ruins) threw into relief the excitement and the anxieties attendant upon the expansion of trade, plantations, and colonies abroad and resulted in a series of rich literary and cultural contributions to the emerging discourse of English nationalism.[47]

The Science of Nationalism: Dryden Looks Ahead

As I have suggested earlier, the discourse of national and state power in late-seventeenth-century England is not derived simply from the celebration of military and naval power, nor of victories overseas, but derives its intensity, ideological suppleness, and formal consistency from its inclusion of a wide variety of arguments that specify English scientific, technological, or even antiquarian achievement. Dryden's poetry provides good examples of such argumentation, as I will now detail in an analysis of "To My Honour'd Friend, Dr Charleton, on his learned and useful Works; and more particularly this of Stone-Heng, by him Restored to the true Founders" (1663).[48] The poem's celebration of science and of an English scientific community is part of a larger shift in Restoration attitudes toward history, politics, the conditions of knowledge and the role of the poet. In a perceptive account of the poem, Richard Kroll argues that it describes the "construction of a new ideal of science, a new scientific community, and the terms under which the reader in Dryden's text becomes a corollary to participating in this new cultural milieu."[49] The reader is invited, that is, to recognize the powerful intellectual and historiographical claims being made on behalf of English science, and to see in such power an England newly coming to terms with, and improving upon, its classical inheritance in philosophy and culture.[50]

The historical and philosophical transition mapped by the poem is vast, and sweeps between the "Tyranny" of Aristotelian thought and the "free Reason" of Englishmen such as Bacon, Gilbert, Boyle, Harvey, Ent, and Charleton:

> The longest Tyranny that ever sway'd,
> Was that wherein our Ancestors betray'd
> Their free-born *Reason* to the *Stagirite*,
> And made his Torch their universal Light.
> So *Truth*, while onely one suppli'd the State,
> Grew scarce, and dear, and yet sophisticate,
> Until 'twas bought, like Emp'rique Wares, or Charms,
> Hard words seal'd up with *Aristotle's* Armes.
>
> *(lines 1–8)*

In these lines, the intellectual power of Aristotelian philosophy is described in terms that make it a corollary of the political power of the state, such that the word "Armes" in line 8 inevitably suggests both the coercive sanction of Aristotle's imprimatur as it does that of the military strength of a tyrannical state. As opposed to this long history of "pre-scientific" philosophy ("Emp'rique Wares, or Charms"), Dryden lists the English scientists whose work suggests the proper development of "free-born *Reason*":

> Among th' *Assertors* of free Reason's claim,
> Th' *English* are not the least in Worth, or Fame.
> The World to *Bacon* does not onely owe
> Its *present* Knowledge, but its *future* too.
> *Gilbert* shall live, till *Load-stones* cease to draw,
> Or *British* Fleets the boundless Ocean awe.
> And noble *Boyle*, not less in *Nature* seen,
> Than his great *Brother* read in *States* and *Men*.
> The *Circling* streams, once thought but pools, of blood
> (Whether life's fewel, or the Bodie's food)
> From dark Oblivion *Harvey's* name shall save;
> While *Ent* keeps all the honour that he gave.[51]
>
> *(lines 21–32)*

This is the august company to which Charleton belongs, in particular because of his investigations into the origins of Stonehenge, which he argued was a Danish coronation site (as opposed to, for instance, Inigo Jones's argument that it was the site of a Roman temple).[52] Dryden's royalist verse celebrates Charleton's *Chorea Gigantum* (1662) not only because its account of the historical meaning of Stonehenge is the product of modern investigation but because this meaning is easily accommodated to the mythology of the

Restoration, even if there is no clear link between Charles II and the Danish rulers who were perhaps crowned at Stonehenge:

> These Ruines sheltred once *His* Sacred Head,
> Then when from *Wor'sters* fatal Field *He* fled;
> Watch'd by the Genius of this Royal place,
> And mighty Visions of the *Danish* race.
> His *Refuge* then was for a *Temple* shown:
> But, *He* Restor'd, 'tis now become a *Throne.*
>
> *(lines 53–58)*

Charleton's science (and the closing turn in Dryden's poem) suggests that the true meaning of Stonehenge is fully realized in the restoration of the monarchy, particularly in that what would appear to be the contingencies of history (Charles II having sheltered at Stonehenge) are now shown to be the performance of a royalist script of travail and final triumph.[53]

This symbolic restoration of a non-Roman prehistory for Stonehenge parallels, within the revisionary logic of the poem, the freeing of English reason from its confinement by Aristotle's "Charms." Both in the distancing of Aristotle and of Rome, the automatic priority of the "ancients," those classical—Greek and Roman—intellectual, cultural, and political authorities, is denied.[54] The community of British "moderns," the scientists, offer, quite literally, a different view of the world. Their view (and this passage marks the conceptual center of the poem) follows upon Columbus's revision of the map of the world, a revision that challenges Aristotelian geography:

> *Columbus* was the first that shook his Throne;
> And found a *Temp'rate* in a *Torrid* Zone:
> The fevrish aire fann'd by a cooling breez,
> The fruitful Vales set round with shady Trees;
> And guiltless *Men,* who danc'd away their time,
> *Fresh* as their *Groves,* and *Happy* as their *Clime.*
> Had we still paid that homage to a *Name,*
> Which onely *God* and *Nature* justly claim;
> The *Western* Seas had been our utmost bound,
> Where *Poets* still might dream the *Sun* was drown'd:
> And all the *Starrs,* that shine in *Southern* Skies,
> Had been admir'd by none but *Salvage* Eyes.
>
> *(lines 9–20)*

Columbus's voyage, and the lands and people he made available to the fertile European imagination, mark, in the poem, the advent of modernity. For Dryden, the break with the classical, or rather, the salutary reminder of the limited horizons of Aristotelian thought, comes via an act of navigational and cartographic daring. The discourse of travel and "discovery," with its accounts of Edenic landscapes and "guiltless" people who do not labor, makes available new worlds for consideration, and it is these new worlds that stimulate modern poetry (line 18) and modern science (lines 21–42).[55]

Yet it is not simply "modern" poetry and science that Dryden is interested in here. His is a more specific and nationalistic investment in the progress and achievement of late-sixteenth- and seventeenth-century English science, and in the view of the world it encourages. A global belligerence is not separate from this investment—indeed, the perceived longevity of Britain's control of the seas assures the continued fame of English scientists ("*Gilbert* shall live, till *Load-stones* cease to draw, / Or *British* Fleets the boundless Ocean awe." lines 25–26). What seems now a historical commonplace—the prospect of Britain's domination over the oceans—is important to the structure of the poem. It allows Dryden to claim Columbus as a progenitor of English science (not a claim that can be made credibly otherwise); it links technological and scientific achievement with the projection of national power overseas; and it suggests a dynamic conception of historical and cultural progress that leads from the reconsideration of classical learning to a view of new worlds to be explored. Put less instrumentally, we might say that the argument and development of Dryden's poem—the movement from the dethroning of "the Stagirite" to the enthroning of Charles II—makes sense only within the larger cultural discourses of discovery, colonization, and chauvinist nationalism that energized late-seventeenth-century Britain. To that extent, even the restoration of Charles II that closes the poem becomes an episode—a signal one, perhaps—in the evolution of these themes in nationalist self-conception.

For the larger purposes of this book, it is worth emphasizing the fuzzy, but nonetheless very significant, political logic put into play in the transition from Aristotelian "tyranny" to (ostensibly) a more balanced view of power at the close of the poem, in that the institutions of modernity (science; the restored monarchy) are meant to embody the exercise of "free-born *Reason*." Particularly after 1688, this sense of England as the home of constitutional liberties and institutions not available in any Continental kingdom, and thus as the home of liberty and its various cultural and intellectual attributes, became central to the definition of Britain as a nation. In his "THRENODIA AUGUSTALIS. A Funeral-Pindarique POEM Sacred to the Happy Memory of King CHARLES II" (1685), Dryden makes a similar claim for the Restoration. He thanks Charles

> For numerous Blessings yearly shour'd,
> And Property with Plenty crown'd;
> For Freedom, still maintain'd alive;
> Freedom which in no other Land will thrive,

> Freedom an *English* Subject's sole Prerogative,
> Without whose Charms ev'n Peace wou'd be
> But a dull quiet Slavery.
>
> *(lines 297–303)*

The argument of British political progressivism became a remarkably potent ideological weapon in the hands of the enthusiasts of colonial and imperial expansion, who claimed that Britain's domination of other lands and peoples often freed them from systems of local or foreign oppression, and that Britain had a bounden civilizational duty to export its "freedoms."

Dryden's Epic of the Nation-State: *Annus Mirabilis*

Dryden's most ambitious and encyclopedic poetic contribution to the forging of national identity is of course *annus mirabilis. The Year of Wonders, 1666. an historical poem*, to which I now turn. Born out of a series of crises, this poem is Dryden's attempt to "dissolve class, party, and sectarian distinctions by defining 'things as they are' to be in the national interest or according to the benign will of God—the outcome, that is, of political or providential necessity."[56] This means that the poem works hard to forge a language of nation—of people brought together by a commonalty of interest (in this case mercantilism and the riches of overseas trade) and united (under a deserving royal leadership) in the face of adversity. Typically, this sense of nation, and of cohesive, evident national priorities, emerges from the staging of international rivalries, especially those that result in warfare and naval battles.[57] *Annus Mirabilis* opens with Dryden's justification of the Anglo-Dutch war—Holland has restricted the activities of English merchants and has garnered for itself trade that should rightfully belong to them:

> Trade, which like bloud should circularly flow,
>   Stop'd in their Channels, found its freedom lost
> Thither the wealth of all the world did go,
>   And seem'd but shipwrack'd on so base a Coast.
>
> For them alone the Heav'ns had kindly heat,
>   In Eastern Quarries ripening precious Dew:
> For them the *Idumæn* Balm did sweat,
>   And in hot *Ceilon* Spicy Forrests grew.
>
> *(lines 5–12)*

The "unnatural" blockage of trade and the manifest imbalance in imports is to be redressed, and stanza 5 provides a historical analogy for such redressal: Holland is compared to Carthage and England to Rome, and the war to the Second Punick War. Like all useful historical parallels, this one, too, offers a comforting moral, which is the general triumph of Rome.

Before we continue this discussion of the military antagonisms between England and its rival states, it is interesting to note that the poem does qualify the bullish, expansionist view of trade and commerce that accompanies the celebration of English might and victories in the poem. First, products representative of mercantile trade are described in a way that suggests an unstable, even dangerous, relationship between commodities and merchants and sailors. The connection between imports and warfare is emphasized in stanza 24 where the Dutch fleet from India is described as "fraught / With all the riches of the rising Sun" and also as carrying "precious Sand from Southern Climates," which are the "fatal Regions where the War begun" (lines 93–96). Just how fraught their cargo of spices is for the Dutch is spelt out in stanza 26, where the Dutch fleet, hiding from pursuing English ships off the coast of Norway, is nevertheless hunted down by the latter: "By the rich scent we found our perfum'd prey" (line 101). In this vision, commodities can betray; in fact, in stanza 29, the Dutch die by the riches stored in their holds:

> Amidst whole heaps of Spices lights a Ball,
>   And now their Odours arm'd against them flie:
> Some preciously by shatter'd Porc'lain fall,
>   And some by Aromatick splinters die.
>
> *(lines 113–16)*[58]

Second, Dryden concludes this account of the destruction and part-capture (stanza 31) of the Dutch trading fleet by the English with a meditation upon the human costs of trading (stanzas 32–35). It is true that Dryden's vocabulary here blunts the potential force of his own observation, for it oscillates between the specificity of ships and men lost in battles and storms to lines where such losses become metaphors for the human condition, in which "we suffer Shipwrack every where" (line 138). In any case, however, this general meditation upon the lives of merchant sailors reminds us that the celebration of nation and trade in this period is almost always marked by an awareness that success extracts its own price, and at least lip service is paid to the memory of sailors killed in battle and merchants drowned at sea.

But the call of the moment in *Annus Mirabilis* is the account of English naval strength against the combined forces of its opponent nations: Holland, France, Denmark (stanzas 39–42). Dryden's rhetorical and ideological priority is the construction of a heroic image of the English nation, which means that Dryden's descriptions of the battle scenes, and of the inspirational authority of the duke of Albemarle and Prince Rupert, emphasize the aristocratic heroism and military honor embodied in the protagonists of national epics. Notwithstanding the mercantilist priorities of the opening of the poem, stanzas 47 to 138 resolutely suggest the importance of aristocrats and royalty (and of warlike qualities) in the leadership of the nation. The caliber of aristocratic leadership not only anchors the victories that are the subject of Dryden's poem, but also augurs a great future for England. The battle scenes, then, via their individual and collective acts of valor, and their depiction of English victories won at great cost, argue a national singularity, a strength in arms that balances the more mundane ship repairing and shipbuilding abilities that are the subject of stanzas 142 to 166. Dryden's representation of England as the rightful ruler of the seas thus combines the rights guaranteed by military might with those bestowed by the superiority of English shipbuilding and navigational techniques.

In the "Digression concerning Shipping and Navigation" and in the "Apostrophe to the Royal Society" (stanzas 155–66), Dryden provides a synoptic history of the development of shipbuilding and navigation that begins with the rudimentary origins of canoes (which are based upon the observation of nature), of which "the *Irish Kern*" and the hollowed, "floating troughs" of the "untaught *Indian*" are examples (617–28). The addition of sails marks the advent of commercial shipping—this is also the point where Dryden's description turns into a *translatio studii*:

> Adde but a Sail, and *Saturn* so appear'd
> > When, from lost Empire, he to Exile went,
> And with the Golden age to *Tyber* steer'd
> > Where Coin and first Commerce he did invent.
>
> Rude as their Ships was Navigation, then;
> > No useful Compass or Meridian known:
> Coasting, they kept the Land within their ken,
> > And knew no North but when the Pole-star shone.
>
> *(lines 629–36)*

English scientific knowledge changes that: navigation "Shall in this Age to *Britain* first be shown, / And hence be to admiring Nations taught" (lines 643–44). Studies of ocean tides and more precise measures of longitude will allow the seaways to become as familiar as mapped paths on land (lines 645–48), and all this will be toward the greater glory of international commerce:

> Instructed ships shall sail to quick Commerce;
> > By which remotest Regions are alli'd:
> Which makes one City of the Universe,
> > Where some may gain, and all may be suppli'd.
>
> *(lines 649–52)*

The Royal Society is praised for its projects and its patronage of ideas that will "fit the levell'd use of humane kind" (line 664), and for providing the nonmilitary basis for English superiority in a world where shipping and commercial skills lead to national strength and glory.[59] Indeed, the "Apostrophe to the Royal Society" and the elements of historical and prophetic reading in the text are, as McKeon has shown, crucial to the political schema of *Annus Mirabilis:* "The power of knowledge guarantees that England, once having learned to read the future, will be able to create it. Dryden prophesies that the *translatio studii* of navigational arts will become a *translatio imperii* at the point when England makes the technological breakthrough which inaugurates the coming age" (in stanza 161).[60] That is, in many ways, the ideological center of the poem, the point at which we recognize that Dryden's construction of a united, puissant nation represents not only the defeat of rival European powers but the mercantile and (at least potentially) imperial subordination of other regions of the globe.

This combination of commercial and imperial desire structures the close of the poem, too, which locates, in a revived and rebuilt (*faux* Elizabethan?) London, the center of English power. London rises from the flames "New deifi'd" as Augusta (lines 177–78), as Dryden develops, via this personification, the seductive drama of feminized city and masculine trade:

> Before, she like some Shepherdess did show,
>   Who sate to bathe her by a River's side:
> Not answering to her fame, but rude and low,
>   Not taught the beauteous Arts of Modern pride.
>
> Now, like a Maiden Queen, she will behold,
>   From her high Turrets, hourly Sutors come:
> The East with Incense, and the West with Gold,
>   Will stand, like Suppliants, to receive her doom.
>
> The silver *Thames*, her own domestick Floud,
>   Shall bear her Vessels, like a sweeping Train;
> And often wind (as of his Mistress proud)
>   With longing eyes to meet her face again.
>
> *(lines 1181–92)*

Conventional representations of seductive femininity prepare us for the transformation of pastoral shepherdess—simple, not yet possessed of "the beauteous Arts of Modern pride"—into the heroine of romance. The gender dynamic at work here naturalizes the unusual fact that *trade* is the engine of this elevation in genres. Romance conventions also underwrite Dryden's refiguration of merchants into chivalric suitors, and even the wind pays court to his royal mistress. Augusta as Maiden Queen thus puts into play romance notions (high turrets and all) that retain some of the comforting iconography of aristocratic culture, and offer the nation a future in symbolic continuity with its past. This melding of mercantile achievement and aristocratic apparatus is, as I suggest later in a discussion of Dryden's preface to the poem, one of the important features of *Annus Mirabilis*.[61]

In the scenario of a glorious future that is sketched here, the "silver *Thames*" will supplant other European rivers as the bearer of global shipping, as London ("fam'd Emporium") will attract merchants and merchandise away from competing European ports: "The *British* Ocean shall such triumphs boast" (stanzas 298–301).[62] In keeping with this tone, the last stanza of the poem reimagines—and updates—Eden, transforming pastoral idyll into a mercantilist's paradise (there can perhaps be no greater tribute to the transformatory power of mercantile and imperial desire than such refigurations of Edenic peace). Dryden marries mercantile promise with millenarian prophecy, assuring his readers not only of a national recovery from war, fire, and other signs of political and economic disaster, but of a rich future secured from the difficulties faced by mercantile voyages and not subject to the vicissitudes of historical time:

> Thus to the Eastern wealth through storms we go;
> But now, the Cape once doubled, fear no more:
> A constant Trade-wind will securely blow,
> And gently lay us on the Spicy shore.
>
> *(lines 1213–16)*

This rewriting of the events and portents of a momentous year completes Dryden's project, whose point and methods he had spelled out in his dedication of *Annus Mirabilis* to the City of London and its representatives: he cannot imagine, Dryden writes, that "Providence" has "resolv'd the ruine of that people at home, which it has blessed abroad with such successes. I am therefore to conclude, that your sufferings are at an end; and that one part of my Poem has not been more an History of your destruction, than the other a Prophecy of your restoration."[63] This restoration, Dryden goes on to say, is the "wish of all true *Englishmen*," as it is that of the poet. As political propaganda, as an intervention in public discourse, the poem is meant to be inclusive, and is designed to voice an unassailable consensus via its depiction of the naval valor of Englishmen and their ability to recover quickly from national disaster. But if there is one primary act of bringing-together this poem performs, it is that of fusing aristocratic action with mercantile consequences, of writing a national epic whose heroes are gentlemen-warriors and traders, both of whom act to further the same national interest.[64]

In his "account of the ensuing Poem" (in the prefatory letter to Sir Robert

Howard), Dryden writes about his project, about his choice of form, his aesthetic values, and his poetic influences. He is at pains to establish the generic weight, as it were, of his poem: "I have chosen the most heroick Subject which any Poet could desire: I have taken upon me to describe the motives, the beginning, progress and successes of a most just and necessary War; in it, the care, management and prudence of our King; the conduct and valour of a Royal Admiral, and of two incomparable Generals; the invincible courage of our Captains and Sea-men, and three glorious Victories, the result of all." Dryden goes on to list the Fire, the King's role in combating it, and the "courage, loyalty and magnanimity of the City" as his next subject. He nowhere lists the celebration of merchants and of trade in this prospectus, though the poem opens, as we have seen, with an account of the commercial rivalry between England and Holland and closes with a vision of a mercantilist paradise. This rivalry might perhaps be subsumed in the "motives" for the war that Dryden says he will describe, but there is no independent acknowledgment that *Annus Mirabilis* will, particularly in its digression on the Royal Society and in its emphasis on the renewal of London as the emporium of the world, link the contemporary forms of national greatness to mercantile success.

Dryden is quite clear about the epic theme, if not the scope, of his poem: "I have call'd my Poem *Historical*, not *Epick*, though both the Actions and Actors are as much Heroick, as any Poem can contain. But since the Action is not properly one, nor that accomplish'd in the last success, I have judg'd it too bold a Title for a few *Stanza's*, which are little more in number then a single *Iliad*, or the longest of the *Aeneids*." The action is not properly that of epic, not only because the poem shifts between the narration of naval battles and a description of the great fire of London, but also because its framing theme is that of English mercantile rivalries and hoped-for ascendancy. *Annus Mirabilis*, with its "broken action, ti'd too severely to the Laws of History," is to that extent like the work of Lucan, who Dryden thinks of as "among Historians in Verse, than Epique Poets." Dryden, always acute about the burdens of literary convention, calls attention to the disjuncture between epic requirement— heroic actions and actors—and his local need, which is to offer a (partisan) reading of contemporary historical events. Further, Dryden writes at a point in European history when it was clear that national greatness would follow from the development of mercantile power, which is a sociohistorical development outside of the ambit of the traditional epic.

Dryden's embarrassment about—or, more accurately, self-consciousness about—the lack of fit between martial valor and mercantile values results in a reiteration of the aristocratic allegiances of the poem at some unexpected moments in his "Letter" to Howard. For instance, when he explains that he had to learn nautical terms ("for my own part, if I had little knowledge of the Sea, yet I have thought it no shame to learn") so that he could describe naval battles "in the proper terms which are us'd at Sea," he ends his explanation by claiming that his labors were lightened by the fact that he was writing about great men and their victories, as if the invocation of these personages will rid him of the taint of an ungainly, though sought after, realism:[65]

> Yet, though the trouble I had in writing it was great, it was more than recompens'd by the pleasure; I found my self so warm in celebrating the praises of military men, two such especially as the *Prince* and *General*, that it is no wonder if they inspir'd me with thoughts above my ordinary level. And I am well satisfi'd, that as they are incomparably the best subject I have ever had, excepting onely the *Royal Family*; so also, that this I have written of them is much better then what I have perform'd on any other. . . . All other greatness in subjects is onely counterfeit, it will not endure the test of danger; the greatness of Arms is onely real: other greatness burdens a Nation with its weight, this supports it with its strength."[66]

And yet the images of national greatness that the poem ends with are, at the very least, equivocal in this regard: we have seen that London's revival, represented as the transformation of a "Shepherdess" (line 1181) into a "Maiden Queen," also involves "Sutors" who are contemporary merchants, and come from the east with incense and from the west with gold (lines 1185–88). The last ten stanzas, in fact, emphasize London's transformation into a "fam'd Emporium" (line 1205), one whose economic attractions will dispense with the need for armed coercion: "The beauty of this Town, without a Fleet, / From all the world shall vindicate her Trade" (lines 1203–4). And while there is a continuing commitment to a "pow'rful Navy" (line 1201) and oceanic triumphs (line 1206), the Edenic close of the poem emphasizes a future defined by successful trade, not by "greatness of Arms."[67]

As Dryden makes clear, he finds in Virgil's *Georgics* a literary and formal rationale that will allow *Annus Mirabilis* to detail aristocratic military exploits, elaborate on the loyalty and resilience of the "people" (of London during the fire), and mark the transfer of national power, as it were, to the merchants of the city.[68] In doing so, the poem becomes a prototype of the patriotic-historical poem that replaces, in ideological function if not in scope, the epic. The triumphalism and bellicosity of these poems follow from their demonstration of providential sanction for national greatness, particularly via successes abroad. They highlight scientific and technological advance, particularly those techniques that made English ships, navigation, and weapons more effective than those of their rivals. But alongside this celebration of the utilitarian, poets also developed a vocabulary of civic virtues and argued that the English had developed a public culture superior to all others. In doing so, they were enabled by their faith that their writing contributed to the definition and education of that same public culture. To that extent, in writing *Annus Mirabilis*, Dryden also enacts the conjunction of arms and arts that his contemporaries took to be a fulsome indicator of civilization, particularly one considered in reference to the cultural and imperial achievement represented by Virgil and by Augustan Rome.

In 1684, in his "To the Earl of *Roscomon*, on his Excellent *Essay* on *Translated Verse*," Dryden returned to the theme of *translatio studii* in order to describe Britain's inheritance of the empire of the classical muse.[69] His compliment to Roscomon begins with a schematic account of the westward movement of the arts. With translation as the governing trope of such movement, Dryden tracks the shift of the arts from their possible origins in Egypt or Tyre to their flowering in Greece, their adoption by imperial Rome, and their mixed fortunes in the intervening period before they arrive in Britain. "Conquering Rome / With *Grecian* Spoils" brings "*Grecian* Numbers home" (lines 7–8), but then barbarous nations reduce "the majesty of Verse to Rhymes," until Renaissance Italy once again makes "Rhyme an Art" (lines 11–19). Dante, Petrarch, and the French improve matters further, but

> *Brittain*, last
> In Manly sweetness all the rest surpass'd.
> The Wit of *Greece*, the Gravity of *Rome*
> Appear exalted in the *Brittish* Loome;
> The Muses Empire is restor'd agen,
> In *Charles* his Reign, and by *Roscomon's* Pen.[70]
>
> *(lines 24–29)*

Thanks to Roscomon, Dryden writes, the British may now

> On equal terms with ancient Wit ingage,
> Nor mighty *Homer* fear, nor sacred *Virgil's* page:
> Our *English* Palace opens wide in state;
> And without stooping they may pass the Gate.[71]
>
> *(lines 75–78)*

But it is perhaps inappropriate to end this discussion of Dryden with this image of him as the poet of national consensus, speaking on behalf of—and creating the cultural grounds for—an England sure of its national and international destiny. Late in his career, because of his sympathies for Roman Catholicism, and because of the changes in the nation's political climate that led to the accession of William and Mary in 1688, Dryden found himself marginalized from the centers of cultural power (he lost the laureateship to Thomas Shadwell in 1689). In *The Hind and the Panther*, perhaps because he wished to argue the priority of his religious view of the world, or perhaps because his Catholicism suggested to him a more sympathetic view of those European nations who had colonized lands abroad in the name of their faith, Dryden wrote, in a tone reminiscent of Marvell's "Bermudas," of a time when

> The Gospel-sound diffus'd from Pole to Pole,
> Where winds can carry, and where waves can roll.
> The self same doctrine of the Sacred page
> Convey'd to ev'ry clime in ev'ry age.
>
> *(2.552–55)*

In contrast, he offers a picture of immoral English trade and settlement:

> Our sayling ships like common shoars we use,
> And through our distant colonies diffuse
> The draughts of Dungeons, and the stench of stews.
> Whom, when their home-bred honesty is lost,
> We disembogue on some far *Indian* coast:
> Thieves, Pandars, Palliards, sins of ev'ry sort,
> Those are the manufactures we export;
> And these the Missionaires our zeal has made:
> For, with my countrey's pardon be it said,
> Religion is the least of all our trade.
>
> *(2.558–67)*

We may or may not take seriously the religious basis of Dryden's critique, but there is no denying the embattled view of English mercantilism and penal settlements that these lines decry.[72]

In reading these samples of Dryden's poetry on public themes, I have called attention to those passages that engage themselves, overtly or less directly, with question of national identity, the dynamics of mercantile expansion, the science and technology that would support the projection of state power overseas, the proper culture of a would-be empire, and the place of poetry in the creation of a consensual public culture (the restoration of the "Muses Empire," this time in England)—and, indeed, to a continuing anxiety about the impact of such "progress." In each case, the point has been to show not simply that Dryden, along with his contemporaries, was alive to the prospects (and embattled difficulties) of an English or British empire, but that such issues are often key to the worldview and the meanings generated by the poem. Marvell's "Bermudas," for instance, details contemporary mercantile and colonial desire for the Bermudas and other similar islands, but is located in a time of religious persecution and Puritan exile so that such desire is dissolved into the culturally and morally authoritative vocabulary of divine reward for religious faith. Dryden's lines from *The Hind and the Panther* invert, as it were, this religious viewpoint and attack a colonialism that forgets its divine mandate in favor of more mercenary rewards. If such providentialist explanations provide one way of justifying (or castigating) the ways of English merchants and settlers, then the more secular axioms of a bellicose nationalism, in tandem with a largely pragmatic understanding that the domination of international maritime trade is the key to national power, provide another, as we have seen in "The Character of Holland," in "On the Victory obtained by Blake," or in Waller's verse.

In the Cromwell poems of Waller, Marvell, and Dryden, and in *Annus Mirabilis*, the imagery of English nationalism is constructed in contrast to that of competing European states, but because this competition is for lands and resources spread out across the globe, these poets (and so many others like them) actively frame their picture of the nation within a fretwork of overseas trading and colonial interests and experiences. As I have pointed out here (and will continue to do throughout this argument), Augustan Rome provided important icons and standards against which the evolution of a culture of arts and arms in England was measured. Most poets were classicists by education and even temperament, and Dryden was one of the most learned. The changing complexity of his relation to classical culture is, of course, best tracked in a study of his translations and his criticism, but, as we have seen, his poems, too, provide us examples of the use to which cultural memories of an empire of "arms and arts" could be put in definitions of late-seventeenth-century England.[73] Whether they looked back into history for examples or prophesied a providentially inspired future (or did both), English poets in this period projected images of naval belligerence and power, of a state and a people united in the pursuit of a common mercantile interest, and of a developing public culture adequate to this accession to global power.

2

THE EBB AND FLOW OF NATIONS
AND EMPIRES

When he [the Thames] to boast, or to disperse his stores
Full of the tributes of his grateful shores,
Visits the world, and in his flying towers
Brings home to us, and makes both Indies *ours;*
Finds wealth where 'tis, bestows it where it wants
Cities in deserts, woods in cities plants.
So that to us no thing, no place is strange,
While his fair bosom is the worlds exchange.
O could I flow like thee, and make thy stream
My great example, as it is my theme!
Though deep, yet clear, though gentle, yet not dull,
Strong without rage, without ore-flowing full.

—*John Denham*, Cooper's Hill

England *unknown as yet, unpeopled lay;*
Happy, had she remain'd so to this day,
And not to ev'ry Nation been a Prey.
Her Open Harbours, and her Fertile Plains,
The Merchants Glory these, and those the Swains,
To ev'ry Barbarous Nation have betray'd her,
Who conquer her as oft as they Invade her.
So Beauty guarded but by Innocence,
That ruins her which should be her Defence.

—*Defoe*, The True-Born Englishman

As cultural historians rewrite the history of eighteenth-century England to incorporate their growing sense of the centrality of contemporary debates about the state of the nation, we realize that, far from being a record of unambiguous celebration or even of controlled enthusiasm, literary performance in this period suggests a much more ambivalent response to the possibilities and events of mercantile or colonial expansion. While there is certainly a great deal of evidence to suggest the excitement and ferment of a burgeoning commodity culture, or the sense of a nation coming to commercial and naval power, what is also clear is that even the most bellicose and hortatory of literary texts arrives at its conclusions only after registering symptomatically or negotiating overtly a variety of misgivings about the shape of the new worlds in the making, at home and abroad. In a period of unprecedented expansion, when imported commodities were changing the very texture of daily life, and when such overseas trade (including colonial, plantation, and slave-trading ventures) was proving to be the basis of a revolution in the political economy of the nation, poets and propagandists took on the task of crafting suitable narratives, and a new ethical and historical vocabulary, with which to express adequately the hopes, and assuage the anxieties, particular to the making of a Great Britain.[1]

While my focus in this chapter, and elsewhere in the book, is on the role played by overseas activity, both commercial and military, in the making of "Great Britain," it should be clear that, particularly in the last decade of the seventeenth century and the first two decades of the eighteenth, the "greatness" of Britain followed equally from the consolidation of its borders, both in Ireland and, later, with the union, in Scotland. In the two years after William came to power, in spite of some early Jacobite successes in Ireland, he was able to assert his military power there, in campaigns that culminated in the defeat of the Roman Catholic armies at the Battle of the Boyne in July 1690. The Treaty of Limerick in October 1691 set the stage for the "Protestant Ascendancy," and effectively transformed Ireland into a colony of England (which is in any case how a great many English writers had thought of it for almost a century). The incorporation of Scotland took longer, though once James fled to France in December 1688, and men loyal to William assumed positions of power, the process was under way. However, there continued to be Scottish resistance (and not only by Jacobites) to William's armies and to the imposition of English parliamentary control for many years to come. Eventually, the economic benefits of union, particularly those available from overseas trade, moved the Scottish Parliament to agree to its own dissolution. (The disastrous failure of the Darien Scheme in 1700, which wiped out hundreds of Scottish stockholders of the Company of Scotland for Trading with Africa and the Indies, and a large percentage of available Scottish capital, played no small role in preparing the ground for this decision.)[2]

This extension of English control over the British Isles was part and parcel of the military and foreign policies that William's accession brought to the fore, as he first went to war against Catholic France to in order to protect both his throne against James II and his continental interests, and then to protect British commercial, economic, and colonial stakes.[3] After 1689, in fact, the theater of war and control was no longer contained within the European continent, and every continental diplomatic or military maneuver stemmed from, or held firmly in view, control of trade routes, plantations, and colonies in North America and elsewhere. The Nine Years War (1688–97) and the War of the Spanish Succession (1702–13) inaugurated more than a century of intermittent warfare against France, and Britain's commercial ambitions took center stage. Indeed, historians have widely understood the Treaty of Utrecht, by which Britain made peace with France in 1713, as cementing its rise to European power. Britain gained bases in Gibraltar and Minorca, established greater territorial and maritime control in the Caribbean (and thus in North America), and gained the *Asiento*, the right to trade—including in slaves—with Spanish colonies in South America for thirty years. For the next four decades (as indeed over the course of the century), Britain's navies were able to protect and enhance its ocean lanes, its trading interests, and the colonial possessions that consolidated its mercantile strength.

This emerging sense of Britain and its changing relation to the Continent (or England and the Continent, if we do not wish too quickly to suggest the consolidation of a British "identity") finds odd expression in Defoe's *The True-Born Englishman* (1701), a poem that will delay us briefly on our way to a consideration of poems that meditate upon, or offer models of, the difficult making of Britain as a commercial power or empire. I begin with Defoe to point out how a poem written to serve a very specific and partisan purpose—to defend a foreign-born king against attacks on his foreignness—incorporates into its defence materials that we can see deriving from the expanding horizons of English culture, or more specifically from the more worldly idea of England that its spokesmen were now articulating. But I also begin with this poem because its attack on xenophobic nationalism has the poet turning a comparative gaze on the origins, boundaries, and people of England (thus reversing the priorities of description that were to provide the bulk of nationalist commentary in the century to come) and leading to what now seem some quite startling formulations about culture and history.

By Defoe's account, he wrote *The True-Born Englishman* as an intervention against antiroyalism couched in xenophobic terms. In August 1700, he writes,

there came out a vile abhor'd Pamphlet, in very ill Verse, written by one Mr. *Tutchin,* and call'd THE FOREIGNERS: In which the Author, *who he was I then knew not,* fell personally upon the King himself, and then upon the *Dutch* Nation; and after having reproach'd his Majesty with Crimes, that his worst enemy could not think of without

Horror, he sums up all in the odious name of FOREIGNER. This fill'd me with a kind of Rage against the Book, and gave birth to a Trifle which I never could hope should have met with so general an Acceptation as it did, I mean, *The True-Born Englishman*.[4]

Defoe's response, as he makes clear, is to show that "from a Mixture of all Kinds began, / That Het'rogeneous Thing, *An Englishman*" (lines 334–35), which he does by listing the many "races"—Romans, Gauls, Greeks, Lombards, Saxons, Danes, Scots, Picts, Irish, Welsh, Normans, Dutch—who have intermingled to produce "your *True-Born Englishmen*" (line 244). Defoe produces a catalog of conquerors and colonizers, a history of England that is punctuated by the invasion of groups who live beyond the geographical borders of the island-nation, each of which contributes to the making of England and Englishmen. Defoe's satiric method, his historical and cultural polemic, are obviously dictated by his need to defend a Protestant, though foreign-born, king, but his model of porous borders and inviting natural features and of an England ravished by her conquerors is surprising and somewhat incongruous. By 1700, the vocabulary of conquest and colonization (as we have seen in chapter 1) is more usually one that features England as dominant. In fact, in an ironic reversal, the very geographical properties ("Her Open Harbours, and her Fertile Plains") that English topographical poets celebrate as the source of England's strength at home and abroad, here "To ev'ry Barbarous Nation have betray'd her." In this reversal, England is feminized in the terms usually reserved for the regions "discovered" by English merchants and sailors; like some of those lands, it is imagined as "unknown" and "unpeopled."

Such a reversal of viewpoint portrays England, now embarking on an aggressive mercantile and colonial agenda, as the historical victim and creation of invasions. It demands that Englishmen recognize their hybrid and polygenetic origins even as the discourses of racial and national difference—fostered by adventuring abroad (including in the Celtic periphery), Gallophobia, or even the seventeenth-century history of anti-Dutch invective that crested during the Anglo-Dutch wars—were gaining new and nation-defining power. It calls attention to, if only for a brief satiric moment, the material basis of contemporary xenophobia: as European tribes and nations once went to war over England, they now compete for trading rights in, and dominance over, different parts of the globe, giving rise to the belligerent vocabularies of a militant nationalism. There are other surprises in this poem, as England is imagined as the virgin land raped by the violence of competing conquerors. Further, in another reversal, this time of the providentialist discourse usually invoked to sanctify exploration and settlement, Defoe's model for imperial expansion and rule is Satan's empire (here he follows Milton's example in *Paradise Lost*):

The List of his Viceregents and Commanders,
Outdoes your *Caesars*, or your *Alexanders*.
. . . .
Through all the World they spread his vast Command,
And death's Eternal Empire's maintain'd.

(lines 72–77)

Via his "Deputies," Satan "plants the distant Colonies of Hell," and "*binds the World in his Infernal Chains*" (lines 131–34). At the heart of Defoe's attack against the contemporary forms of insular nationalism and antiroyalism is this inversion of the rhetoric of invasion and empire. England becomes, as it were, the image of lands in the Caribbean, or in Asia, once "Happy" and protected by their isolation but now the "Prey" of "ev'ry Nation" (lines 150–52).

If the extremity of Defoe's reversals are surprising, his comparative method, indeed his focus on the origins of the nation in conquests by the Romans and the Anglo-Normans (among others), is not unique. As Nicholas Canny points out, "all educated Europeans were conscious that colonization was a method that had been employed in ancient times by the Romans to advance their authority and civility throughout much of Europe, and in medieval times by the Anglo-Normans to extend their influence, including their involvement with England, Scotland, Wales and Ireland."[5] Thus, "colonial methods" were understood to be part of the "historic civilizing mission" and part of the inheritance of English culture, and appropriate to the extension of that culture into Scotland and Ireland. However, there is also a more contemporary concern behind Defoe's inversion, whereby England itself becomes the focus of an evaluative gaze that is trained elsewhere, and the subject of cultural and historical comparison with other lands and nations. Such an inversion is to be found in a number of late seventeenth- and early-eighteenth-century texts, and I will mention two instances.

In *Oroonoko* (1688), which contains fine instances of early Eurocentric ethnographic description, Behn stages a moment of what we might think of as reverse ethnography, as the narrator and her party become the subjects of examination by a village of Indians in Surinam.[6] The straightforward polarities of the narrative are reversed—briefly—in much the same way as when Pope, in *Windsor-Forest* (1713), brings Behn's Indians home. The poem looks forward to a time when travelers from the new world "launch forth to seek the old," and "naked youths and painted chiefs admire, / Our speech, our colour, and our strange attire!" (lines 402–6).[7] Critics have argued that such a reversal of viewpoint is crucial to eighteenth-century satire; here, we might notice its place in texts that subject Englishness (or Britain) to a comparative historical or ethnographic examination. And this is not an idle coincidence, for, as this chapter shows, the turn to Augustan Rome for classic models of satire (to Horace and Juvenal, for instance) provided also the historical and geographical vantage point from which Britain could be seen in comparative perspective.

Such examinations of or meditations upon England or Britain characteristically result in portraits—serious or satiric—of the nation as enriched and/or threatened by the trading goods or the people that breach its amphibious boundaries. Britain is most often represented as at the threshold of empire, and the concern is with the pitfalls of expansion and power. The poet turns historical allegorist, reading the past with twofold purpose, to exhort and to warn. Thus, the comparison with the history of an empire (or empires) now known only in its ruins, locates Britain within an older European history both to establish a sense of continuity and cultural inheritance, but also to emphasize (depending on polemical need) religious and political differences from these continental (and occasionally Mediterranean) histories. The legacy of Rome provides, in particular, the starting point for discussions of contemporary Britain, and this is the frame within which I now discuss Addison's "A Letter from Italy" (1704), George Lyttelton's "An Epistle to Mr. Pope" (1730), and John Dyer's *The Ruins of Rome* (1740).

In the case of these three poems, I focus my argument upon the theories of imperial history that they generate, and point to a singular feature they share, which is the fear of national collapse. Meditations upon empires past often confirm the transience, rather than the encouraging permanence, of international power. These poems are haunted by the ruins of Rome, not to the point where they can see nothing but decline, but certainly in a way that qualifies their visions of future grandeur. At the end of this chapter, I suggest that the iconography of decline retained its compelling power for poets well into the century, and into the next. Goldsmith's *The Deserted Village* caps its account of depopulation and forced emigration to the Americas with an account of the Muse, emblem of civilization, forced to make the same journey, a despairing vision that inspired Anna Letitia Barbauld's dystopic meditation on British history *Eighteen Hundred and Eleven, A Poem* (1812), a poem written in the period in which Britain was in the process of establishing its Second Empire.

These poems did not necessarily originate as meditations upon the transformations of nations over historical time, or on the melancholic gap between the will to empire and the record of history (though these are of course central concerns). There is a local opportunism and contingency that births them: indeed, as previous commentators have pointed out, most such poetry was written in the service of identifiable political interests at home. However, no considerable political faction in eighteenth-century

Britain defined its positions without reference to overseas issues (and differences on the proper timing and conduct of warfare and on appropriate commercial and colonial policies determined most political wrangles in Parliament and the ministries), with the result that poets of faction all assumed a far greater theater for their imaginations than their embedded partisan politics might suggest. Poetic imagination, in eighteenth-century Britain as elsewhere (and perhaps as always), derives its inspiration from the furthest reaches of human experience and desire, and even the most instrumental and occasional of these poems shows evidence of having traveled on the busy highways of the seas, and landed upon shores unknown or unfamiliar, if only vicariously. However, it is not the wonder of the world that drives these poems; precisely because they have an instrumental or partisan conception, they massage this wonder into a supple historical poetics with particular ideological implications, and that is the process that I trace in my analyses.

The poems I analyze in this book are not the only ones in this period that comment on nation and empire, and my choice does not imply that these poems represent precisely the range of contemporary responses to these pressing issues. Taken together, however, they do give us a full sense of the key terms and icons, of the jumble of mythological and historical narratives featured by those eighteenth-century English poets who would meditate upon empires past and would-be empires in the present. In these poems, the past offers rich cultural resources to be mined in support of arguments for British expansion, but this engagement with the past and its ruins often compounds the near-obsession with temporality (with the passage of time and with historical change) that characterizes so much of the poetry of this period. The fear that poetry might be a fragile way of engaging with the world and intervening in public discussion leads here to the development of a compensatory formal machinery—Young for instance revives the overblown claims of the Pindaric, and Dyer expands the resources of the georgic into near-epic stretch (I discuss this in the next chapter). For the literary historian, the implications of such poetic experimentation are obvious: we are best able to answer literary-historical and formal questions about the practice of poetry in the period when we pay systematic attention to the way in which these poems articulate their world, and craft their mercantile and imperial visions. No account of the ode (or indeed the apostrophe) or the georgic (or the topoi of idealized country landscapes and labor) in the eighteenth century can be complete without attention to such ideological, indeed instrumental, fashioning. The readings that follow may be taken as suggesting also the contours of such literary history.

The View from Rome: Addison, Lyttelton, Pope, Dyer

The poems I move to now are enquiries into the classical Roman past, whose glories and decline are invoked in a manner that allows them to function as a historical mirror for contemporary British ambition. These poems also read the histories of other nations (and of their own) in order to offer Britons compelling evidence and arguments about future failure or success, and in each case they advocate particular corrective steps. They celebrate the making of empires, of international commerce, and of powerful nations, but they are also deeply aware of the domestic dislocations and changes that follow from these advances. Commerce and colony turn out to be double-edged blessings; the growth of either can paradoxically suggest the decline of national virtues and strengths. As I suggest, such historical retrospection and prognostication also offers an important vocational dividend for these poets: as they make studied comparisons, and forge templates for national social and economic policy (the repeated project of such poetry), they also articulate historical parallels that help define their own practice, and provide cultural authentication for their attempts to speak to, and on behalf of, the "nation."

Historians of the "Augustan" turn in late seventeenth- and early-eighteenth-century British culture have made clear that Virgilian Rome provided historical standards (hotly contested to be sure) against which to measure, as better or as worse, English letters and society. The actual experience of contemporary Italy, however, functioned somewhat differently, and British travelers on the continent responded to Italy as—in Jeremy Black's trenchant phrases—"a theme park of the past, a country de-civilized by a decadent society and culture."[8] The memory of intervening periods—early modern Enlightenment Italy, and of the small Italian republics—receded, and Italy (especially for Britons increasingly conscious of the scientific progress, wealth, and power of their nation) came to stand for a combination of classical ruins and contemporary poverty and ignorance, the latter seen as a confirmation of the decadent ossification of Roman Catholicism. Black emphasizes that the ruins visited by travelers "took on much of their appeal from the degree to which past glory contrasted with a setting of present insignificance, poverty and backwardness. The remains thus served to demonstrate the cyclical nature of history: Italy, particularly Rome, was a *memento mori* of civilisation." This contrast, and the theory of imperial history derived from it, is of particular importance in the poems that follow.

Addison's "A Letter from Italy, to the Right Honourable Charles Lord Halifax" (1704) is one of several poems that address England from the vantage point of Rome. In these poems, Rome is usually the ruins of "Virgil's Italy," which allows the visiting poet to meditate upon both imperial strength and cultural flowering, or rather, to think about the ruins of the former and the continuing power of the latter.[9] Thus, Addison's "Letter" presents the poet surrounded by "Poetic fields"—the landscape he looks upon is one that poets have made available:

> For here the Muse so oft her harp has strung
> That not a mountain rears its head unsung,
> Renowned in verse each shady thicket grows,
> And ev'ry stream in heavenly numbers flows.
>
> *(lines 13–16)*[10]

The first fifty lines of the poem are a fulsome testimonial to the power of poetry to create a sense of, or perpetuate memories of, geographical and historical features:

> Sometimes, misguided by the tuneful throng,
> I look for streams immortalized in song,
> That lost in silence and oblivion lie
> (Dumb are their fountains and their channels dry),
> Yet run for ever by the Muse's skill,
> And in the smooth description murmur still.
>
> *(lines 31–36)*

Here, this praise of the "deathless Muse" (line 43) is not only a trope of poetic immortality. It in fact addresses the problem of historical memory, in particular the memory of natural features so saturated with poetic description that they become symbols of cultures and nations. The Tiber is now "destitute of strength" but because it was "sung so often in poetic lays," it still "With scorn the Danube and the Nile surveys; / So high the deathless Muse exalts her theme!" (lines 37–43). This move from nature to history, or more specifically from the celebration of natural features to the exaltation of nations, is precisely the ideological point of Addison's poem, which pays attention to the rich tradition of poetic representations of the Roman landscape in order to find parallels for Britain. As the Tiber once, the Boyne now: arts and arms lift both from obscurity and make them symbols of national power. The Boyne was once a "poor inglorious stream, / That in Hibernian vales obscurely strayed." Now, Addison's poem says to Halifax, the stream is by "your lines and Nassau's sword renowned," and

> Its rising billows through the world resound,
> Where'er the hero's godlike acts can pierce,
> Or where the fame of an immortal verse.
>
> *(lines 45–50)*

In this poem, the relation between Italy and Britain is one defined by the westward movement of arts and arms; Addison claims grateful inheritance, but also features progress and the desire to supplant Roman achievement. The compliment to Halifax continues into the next few lines as the poet, would-be champion of the British Muse, hopes for victory over the urpoet of nation:

> Oh, could the Muse my ravished breast inspire
> With warmth like yours, and raise an equal fire,
> Unnumbered beauties in my verse should shine,
> And Virgil's Italy should yield to mine!
>
> *(lines 51–54)*

To make such victory feasible, the glories of Rome are enumerated. First, its present-day natural beauty, its fecund, warm seasons (as opposed to the cold "northern air" of Britain, lines 55–68). Next, its historical legacy—its architectural ruins and its statuary (lines 69–92), which move the poet to an awestruck, sublime sense of the wonder that was Rome:

> An amphitheatre's amazing height
> Here fills my eye with terror and delight,
> That on its public shows unpeopled Rome,
> And held uncrowded nations in its womb.
>
> *(lines 73–76)*

This vision of imperial Rome ("here the proud triumphal arches rise"—line 78) inspires the poet to identify with the moral and civic standards that he thinks denoted by the ruins of classical Rome: these ruins are evidence of "the old Romans' deathless acts," and as such they "Their base degenerate progeny upbraid" (lines 79–80). This contrast between old Rome and present-day Italy allows the poet to position Britain as the rightful inheritor of the achievement of classical Rome, which he does by suggesting that Italy cannot any more benefit from its historical and natural riches:

> But what avail . . .
> . . . .
> The smiles of nature and the charms of art,
> While proud Oppression in her valleys reigns,
> And Tyranny usurps her happy plains?
> The poor inhabitant beholds in vain
> The redd'ning orange and the swelling grain.
>
> *(lines 107–14)*

What Italy lacks is "Liberty," which goddess becomes the subject of an apostrophe here:

> Eternal pleasures in thy presence reign,
> And smiling Plenty leads thy wanton train!
> Eased of her load Subjection grows more light,
> And Poverty looks cheerful in thy sight.
>
> *(lines 121–24)*

Typically, this paean of praise for Liberty leads to a celebration of her home, "Britannia's isle," which has "oft in fields of death [its] presence sought," and which reveres liberty above all material wealth, particularly that variety of wealth born of warmer climates. The contrast here is between lush, fertile, politically degenerate "southern" lands and a cold, hardy "northern" climate that nurtures political freedom:

> On foreign mountains may the sun refine
> The grape's soft juice, and mellow it to wine,
> With citron groves adorn a distant soil,
> And the fat olive swell with floods of oil:
> We envy not the warmer clime that lies
> In ten degrees of more indulgent skies,
> Nor at the coarseness of our heav'n repine,
> Though o'er our heads the frozen Pleiads shine:
> 'Tis Liberty that crowns Britannia's isle,
> And makes her barren rocks and her bleak mountains smile.
>
> *(lines 131–40)*

In providing "northern" origins for the British love of liberty, Addison's verse suggests the political and historical values of the "Whig aesthetic," which included, as Samuel Kliger has shown, a theory of British genealogy and psychology based on their being a "branch of the Gothic-Teutonic folk," whose "vigor, hardiness and zeal for liberty" were explained by the "frigid temperature of the Gothic habitat in the northern regions."[11] Britain's Gothic inheritance balances, extends, and restores to civic and imperial manliness the Roman values now lost to modern Italy.

At this point, then, once the opposition between natural riches and political liberty is extended to define the difference between contemporary southern Europe and Britain, the poem feels confident enough to set aside the cultural awe with which it began its descriptions of the poetry, architecture, sculpture, and painting of Italy. The awe makes way for an aggressive political nationalism, which claims for Britain control of the balance of power in Europe:

> Others with towering piles may please the sight,
> And in their proud aspiring domes delight;
> A nicer touch to the stretched canvas give,
> Or teach their animated rocks to live:

> 'Tis Britain's care to watch o'er Europe's fate,
> And hold in balance each contending state,
> To threaten bold presumptuous kings with war,
> And answer her afflicted neighbours' pray'r.
>
> *(lines 141–48)*

Britain's fleets enforce its authority and check "Th' ambitious Gaul" (lines 151–53), whose political machinations are of no avail in the face of "Nassau's arms . . . and counsels" (line 158).

Ironically, having established Britain as the home of liberty and as the arbiter of Europe's destinies, "A Letter from Italy" shrinks away from such patriotic discourse, "struggling" to rein in what we might think of as nationalist poetic ambition: "I bridle in my struggling Muse with pain, / That longs to launch into a bolder strain" (lines 161–62). As we have seen, the poem stages its wonder at the remains and achievement of classical Rome in order to suggest a standard of imperial culture (particularly in the performance of poetry) for contemporary Britain. It then argues that "southern" fertility and natural riches are not the equal of the "barren rocks" and "bleak mountains" of Britain because the latter are home to "Liberty." In the name of Liberty, which is now "Britain's care," the nation stakes its claim to dominance in Europe. However, precisely when the ideological agenda of the poem is most firmly in place, in the ascendancy of Britain and Nassau, the poet checks his desire for "a bolder strain" and retires once more into the felicities of pastoral verse, leaving this "more advent'rous song" to poets like Halifax and Virgil:

> My humble verse demands a softer theme,
> A painted meadow or a purling stream;
> Unfit for heroes, whom immortal lays,
> And lines like Virgil's or like yours, should praise.
>
> *(lines 164–68)*

Some of this turnaround can be explained as the rhetorical convolutions demanded by the poetic compliment Addison pays Halifax in these lines, but the return of Virgil as the touchstone of heroic versifying sits oddly at the end of a poem that has worked hard to portray a Britain now come into its own as the fit subject of transhistorical, Pan-European admiration. Equally, however, this reassertion of Virgil's cultural authority claims it on behalf of nationalist British poets, a company only a "pastoral" modesty prevents Addison from joining.

Addison's "A Letter from Italy" shows us some of the ways in which English poets adapted conventional poetic forms and vocabularies in their search for an idiom flexible enough to accommodate new conceptions of the nation. While definitions of the nation or of some other collectivity have been demonstrably part of poetic practices since their inception, the combination of classical literary-cultural and historical reference and "enlightened" (but undefined) constitutionalism in this poem suggests to us the influence that an aggressive English foreign policy backed by an increasingly powerful navy had on the imagination of nationalist poets. Addison's poem, which begins and ends with images of pastoral retirement (Halifax goes off into Horatian retreat—the poet wishes to write of meadows and streams) is actually a long and complex excursus into the cultural legacy of fallen empires, into climactic theories of national development, and into the special ideological grounds upon which Britain can base its claim to difference from, and dominance over, competing European states. The working vocabulary for this poetics of nationalism is derived from the mythology of *translatio studii, translatio imperii,* and *translatio libertatis.* Thus, even as the poem ends with a genuflection to Virgil, and with a diffident turning away from singing the "immortal lays" of heroes and nations, there is no doubt of its sustained and polished engagement with the power of poetic conventions, with cultural and historical memory, and with the more contemporary bases—material and ideological—of British power. In one way or the other, even as the poet disclaims the song of national power, the poem sings of little else.

The writing of epistles from foreign parts, especially Rome, provided an increasingly familiar format for English poets to comment on contemporary Britain, or on British values and activities, down to, as we will now see, the choice of appropriate poetic genres. Such commentary presumes, as William Dowling puts it, "the idea that the imaginary Republic living on in the *Georgics* and the *Aeneid* and the odes of Horace represents the same moral resource for English poetry that the actual Republic had done for the poets of Augustan Rome."[12] In each case, the lesson to be taught includes a programmatic account of the past genius of Rome, its present political and religious servitude, the coming of Liberty and her various handmaidens to Britain, and the historic responsibility that thus devolves upon Britons. This is a plastic poetic formula, and elements were utilized by poets of different political loyalties—including George Lyttelton, one of the coterie of "Patriot poets" surrounding Frederick, Prince of Wales. Lyttelton's "An Epistle to Mr. Pope, from a Young Gentleman at Rome," (1730) addresses Pope, in explicitly nationalist terms, as the "Immortal Bard" who was "born, our drooping Genius to restore, / When ADDISON and CONGREVE are no more" (lines 1–4).[13] Lyttelton's description of Rome follows Addison's in the poem discussed above; "ancient Wit" is no longer to be found in Italy:

> Fall'n is their Glory, and their Virtue lost:
> From Tyrants and from Priests the Muses fly,
> Daughters of *Reason* and of *Liberty*.
>
> *(lines 10–12)*

The muses have retired to "*Thames's* flow'ry Borders" where they kindle in Pope's "Breast the *Roman* Fire" (lines 15–16). Pope is thus doubly favored— successor to English genius and to that of Rome.

Lyttelton next develops the theme of "unhappy Italy," except that he acknowledges that modern Italy does have its own palaces, cities, and agriculture (lines 23–28). The problem is that Italy's "ancient Spirit is decay'd" (lines 23–32) and thus only the ruins that were emblematic of that spirit can continue to "instruct, and to command Mankind" (line 34). To which the poet, in what is the most purple passage in this largely derivative poem, demonstrates his abject tutelage: "Oft I the Traces you have left explore, / Visit your Ashes, and your Urns adore; / Oft kiss, with Lips devout, some mould'ring Stone," particularly because these "hallow'd Ruins" are better "to see, / Than all the Pomp of modern Luxury" (lines 37–42). His ritual submission is rewarded with a vision of Virgil, who asks him to deliver a message to Pope discouraging the English poet's commitment to satire:

> "Great Bard! whose Numbers I my self inspire,
> "To whom I gave my own harmonius Lyre;
> "If mounted high upon the Throne of Wit,
> "Near Me and HOMER thou aspire to sit;
> "No more let meaner Satire taint thy Bays."
>
> *(lines 51–55)*

Virgil encourages Pope to write the Pindaric (line 57), instead, and to write of national glory:

> "Of Thee more worthy were the Task to raise
> "A lasting Column to thy Country's Praise;
> "To sing the Land, which now alone can boast
> "That LIBERTY unhappy ROME has lost;
> . . . .
> "Such was the Theme for which my Lyre I strung
> "Such was the People whose Exploits I sung;
> "Brave, yet refin'd, for Arms and Arts renown'd,
> "With different Bays by *Mars* and *Phoebus* crown'd,
> "Dauntless Opposers of Tyrannick Sway,
> "But pleas'd a mild AUGUSTUS to obey."
>
> *(lines 63–76)*

If Pope does what Virgil asks for, the closing lines say, he will achieve immortality: "Remotest Times shall consecrate thy Lays, / And join the PATRIOT'S to the POET'S Praise" (lines 81–82).

In its "poetry-by-numbers" approach to the problem of imperial inheritance, Lyttelton's "Epistle from Rome" provides a compact summary of a great many of the political and cultural themes and ideas that motivate this kind of "patriotic" verse. Roman—in particular Virgilian—poetic standards are invoked in order to suggest that English poets and culture are comparable, but in each case the point also is to individuate Britain as a nation possessed of the same combination of "Arms and Arts" that distinguished imperial Rome, except that now Britain is also home to liberty, and is thus in a position to carve out a world-historical place perhaps unknown even to Rome. In this scenario of national grandeur, it is of course a great pity (vide Lyttelton) that Pope insists on performing the pettinesses of satiric verse rather than giving himself over to the elevated sonorities associated with the Pindaric.[14] Pity great enough for Virgil to come alive and to instruct Pope to do his patriotic duty, as Lyttelton does his by kissing moldering stones and conjuring up the spirits of the ancient dead.

A similar archaeology of historical and cultural memory informs a variety of poems, on different topics, in this period. I will briefly examine one more such poem before moving on to John Dyer's substantial *The Ruins of Rome*. Pope's "To Mr. Addison, Occasioned by his Dialogues on Medals,"[15] shows us how the research of eighteenth-century antiquarians and numismatists also provided fodder for the poets of nation. It begins entirely conventionally, and points to the contrast between the magnificence of imperial Rome and its present-day ruins:

> See the wild Waste of all-devouring years!
> How Rome her own sad Sepulchre appears,
> With nodding arches, broken temples spread!
> The very Tombs now vanish'd like their dead!
> Imperial wonders rais'd on Nations spoil'd,
> Where mix'd with Slaves the groaning Martyr toil'd;
> Huge Theatres, that now unpeopled Woods,
> Now drain'd a distant country of her Floods;
> . . . .
> Some felt the silent stroke of mould'ring age,
> Some hostile fury, some religious rage.
>
> *(lines 1–12)*

Pope's poem, as lines 5 to 8 show, is very conscious that the icons of empire are raised on the spoils of conquered nations.[16] Imperial architecture ("Huge

Theatres") is not just symbolic of such power, but is built of materials extracted from subject nations.

But the topic of this poem is not empire as much as its ruins and mementos. Pope describes Ambition as no longer able to "trust" architecture, statuary and even earthworks (line 19–22), since they all collapse into ruin. In what we might think of as a historical conceit, he then describes Ambition's new medium for the perpetuation of her achievements: she

> contracts her vast design,
> And all her Triumphs shrink into a Coin:
> A narrow orb each crouded conquest keeps,
> Beneath her Palm here sad Judæa weeps,
> Here scantier limits the proud Arch confine,
> And scarce are seen the prostrate Nile or Rhine,
> A small Euphrates thro' the piece is roll'd,
> And little Eagles wave their wings in gold.
>
> *(lines 23–30)*

Rome's triumphs, and the subject nations signified by Judaea, the "prostrate" Nile, the Rhine and the Euphrates, are preserved in perpetuity: "The Medal, faithful to its charge of fame, / Thro' climes and ages bears each form and name" (lines 31–32).[17]

Pope's interest in these coins, and in contemporary commentaries on them, is spelled out in two parts, both of which link Roman arts and arms to British aspirations. He pays a compliment to Addison, whose learning allows "Rome's glories" to shine again. Pope assures him that such commentaries on ancient objects are significant, because coins and poetry share a common cultural design and purpose:

> These pleas'd the Fathers of poetic rage;
> The verse and sculpture bore an equal part,
> And Art reflected images to Art.
>
> *(lines 50–52)*

The point here is not simply that cutting a coin and writing a poem are sister arts, but that each includes an important function as memorial, as a reminder of historical glory and the power of imperial nations. Thus even if the Roman Empire contained in these coins and lines is shrunk into memory, it provides powerful inspiration for a contemporary British poet of empire, for, rising up from the surface of coins (in a sort of numismatic prosopopoeia) are the faces of "Patriots"—warriors, philosophers, scientists, poets:

> Oh when shall Britain, conscious of her claim,
> Stand emulous of Greek and Roman fame?

> In living medals see her wars enroll'd,
> And vanquish'd realms supply recording gold?
> Here, rising bold, the Patriot's honest face;
> There Warriors frowning in historic brass:
> Then future ages with delight shall see
> How Plato's, Bacon's, Newton's looks agree;
> Or in fair series laurell'd Bards be shown,
> A Virgil there, and here an Addison.
>
> *(lines 53–62)*

All meditations on history, and on the history of prior (or precursor) empires, include a profound sense of historical passing and loss. The partial, often defaced witness borne by the memorial fragments of imperial conquest—architecture, arches, statues, coins—emphasizes the transience of empires, but also underlines the commemorative power of cultural fragments. This dialectic informs the poetry we are considering here: poems will live in the same way that coins do, as highly compressed, coded records of national glory. Each poem about such transience inevitably makes a case for poetry (and its associated arts) to be thought of as a public and national necessity, as a medium for the articulation and perpetuation of nationalist aspirations. In this case, as in other poems by Pope, those aspirations are manifestly imperialist in their longing for "vanquish'd realms" to supply gold so that a warlike Britain can mint "Greek and Roman fame."[18] This British empire, with "living medals" dedicated to its famous patriots and warriors, is also the necessary prelude to (this is the weight of the "Then" in line 59) the elevation of British philosophy and poetry to Platonic and Virgilian heights. At the close of the poem, all these themes are fused together as Pope writes an encomium to Craggs (his friend and Addison's literary executor) that features a coin imprinted with Craggs's head and with the very lines Pope now writes. Craggs is described, in this address, as "another Pollio" (line 64); that is, as Asinius Pollio, the addressee of Virgil's fourth eclogue. Pope writes here as Virgil once did about the coming of strong gods and empires. It is of course appropriate that he imagines his words engraved on a medal, a token of both the culture and the commodities of an imperial Britain.

In *Ruins and Empire*, Laurence Goldstein comments that in eighteenth-century literature "ruins were a means of mortifying in the public those worldly desires that caused the great empires, like Persepolis and Egypt, to decline and fall." This "ruin sentiment" was ubiquitous in literature and in art and was thought to be "capable of universal application and for that reason a determinant of policy and conduct in a time of expanding empire."[19] Goldstein recognizes also that such meditations upon ruins, and upon the civilizations and people they betoken, create powerful opportunities for poets to claim for themselves a historically sanctioned voice in public debates on empire and nation. Whether they speak with prophetic or vatic vigor, or in the humbler tones authorized by the muse Contemplation, these poets find in the ruins of empires material suitable for both historical and allegorical interpretation. The poems make clear their concern with empires in the past and the present, but they also feature a vocabulary replete with the abstractions that characterize more ahistorical meditations on human and social temporality. This dual method, a combination of historical analysis and ethical and behavioral commentary, is the signature of these texts, and locates them precisely within the discourse of imperial expansion that we are investigating.

John Dyer's *The Ruins of Rome* (1740) is an acknowledged classic in this genre, and a poem that fully instantiates Anne Janowitz's observation that the "paradox of the eighteenth-century ruin was that the figure of decay was at the same time the image used to authorize England's autonomy as a world power."[20] In its opening lines, the poem plots the movement from pastoral to imperial meditation (thus ironically emphasizing the continuities between these forms in English poetry of the later seventeenth and eighteenth centuries). "Enough of Grongar," Dyer begins, setting aside his own earlier topographical poem "Grongar Hill" (1727), as an instance of the kind of poetry he sings "inglorious." It is not only loco-descriptive poetry that he puts aside, but also a particular version of "local" history, one that emphasizes the Celtic prehistory of Britain:

> Enough of Grongar, and the shady dales
> Of winding Towy: Merlin's fabled haunt
> I sing inglorious.
>
> *(lines 1–3)*

It will not serve the purposes he has in mind, for natural features imbued with folk tales and legends do not supply analogues for the contemporary issues that concern him. He must roam further afield, into a different history, led by "the love of arts, / And what in metal or in stone remains / Of proud antiquity" (lines 3–5):

> To Latium's wide champaign, forlorn and waste,
> Where yellow Tiber his neglected wave
> Mournfully rolls. Yet once again, my Muse,
> Yet once again, and soar a loftier flight;
> Lo the resistless theme, imperial Rome.
>
> *(lines 11–15)*

The Muse, no less than imperial Rome, is elevated, irresistible (we note the apostrophic aspiration in the repeated O of "soar," and "loft" and "Lo" and, not incidentally, "Rome"), possessed of an energy that cannot be quelled even by the vision of the "forlorn and waste" plains through which the mournful Tiber now flows.

This paradoxical sense of elevation that follows from an examination of waste and ruin is characteristic: the "throne of nations fall'n" may be "obscur'd in dust," but is "yet majestical." For the poet, to gaze upon ruins is to look into the abyss of history. This is the moment of the sublime, for ruins, poised in that natural and historical limbo that transforms landscapes into allegories of human effort and the limits imposed by temporal change, can also point the way to imaginative and poetic redemption:

> the solemn scene
> Elates the soul, while now the rising Sun
> Flames on the ruins in the purer air
> Towering aloft, upon the glittering plain,
> Like broken rocks, a vast circumference:
> Rent palaces, crush'd columns, rifled moles,
> Fanes roll'd on fanes, and tombs on buried tombs.
>
> *(lines 19–25)*

Irradiated by the flaming god, the "rising Sun" of poetry, the ruins shimmer into new significance, remnants of the imperial past that engender visions of the future.

This sense of sublime, overwhelming power continues into Dyer's description of the natural features he wanders through:

> The sunk ground startles me with dreadful chasm,
> Breathing forth darkness from the vast profound
> Of aisles and halls, within the mountain's womb.
>
> *(lines 57–59)*

The chasms he stares into—here marked as feminine—are in fact man-made: "such the sewers huge, / Whither the great Tarquinian genius dooms / Each wave impure" (lines 64–66). The dreadful chasm, the mountain's womb, turns out to be the channels cut for the swamp-drainage and sewage systems attributed to Tarquinius Priscus, one of the Etruscan rulers of Rome. The fear and exaltation deriving from the poet's experience of the ruins of Rome are brought under control fully only when he returns the public works, stone fragments and statuary he sees to their proper place, which is that of monuments to exemplary Roman civic and military virtue. A calmer, more meditative verse results:

> How doth it please and fill the memory
> With deeds of brave reknown, while on each hand
> Historic urns and breathing statues rise,
> And speaking busts! Sweet Scipio, Marius stern,
> Pompey superb, the spirit-stirring form
> Of Caesar.
>
> *(lines 98–103)*

From this moment on, spiritual turmoil gives way to more reasoned understanding, each encounter with Roman genius encouraging a similar commitment to Britain. The readiness of Roman youth for war, the "virtue" of "Clelia, Cocles, Manlius," the inspiration provided by the Fabii and the Decii, Scipio's valor in battle (lines 120–26)—all teach a single lesson:

> So rose the Roman state. Me now, of these
> Deep musing, high ambitious thoughts inflame
> Greatly to serve my country, distant land,
> And build me virtuous fame.
>
> *(lines 127–30)*

The poet's accounts of Rome's architectural marvels—the Coliseum, the Capitol, the Temple of Concord—all emphasize Roman power and Roman art and point to the presence of symbols that suggest its imperial reach: "tall obelisks from Memphis old, / One stone enormous each, or Thebes convey'd" (lines 199–200). The description of the Temple of Concord, where the senate met in order to act against Catiline's conspiracy (which is treated as an instance of ambition that threatens the republican foundations of the state) leads to a familiar warning for Britain to guard against the loss of "Liberty":

> O Liberty,
> Parent of Happiness, celestial-born;
> . . . .
> —be Britain's care;
> With her, secure, prolong thy lov'd retreat;
> Thence bless mankind.
>
> *(lines 210–15)*

As Goldstein suggests, Dyer's poem here shows an "anxiety about *Caesarism,* ambition either naked or disguised that could effect the same abridgment of liberty and law that weakened Rome."[21] Dyer's Ciceronian espousal of republican liberty here, however, also furthers a different agenda, which is to imagine a Britain at the helm of contemporary nations and power. Britain will have care of liberty and will export it to the world, a sentiment whose ideological roots lie in the vision of the world made possible by Elizabethan courtiers and explorers: the "sacred names / Of Cecil, Raleigh, Walsingham, and Drake" (lines 217–18).

In lines that echo the comparative sentiments espoused by lines 141–48 in Addison's "A Letter from Italy" (quoted above), *The Ruins of Rome* states that while other nations might excel at music, dance, sculpture, architecture, or painting (lines 219–23)—all of which activities give off a whiff of cultural decadence in such cataloging—Britain's genius is sturdily political and mercantile, which makes it the appropriate home of liberty:

> But thou, thy nobler Britons teach to rule;
> To check the ravage of tyrannic sway;
> To quell the proud; to spread the joys of peace,
> And various blessings of ingenious trade.
> Be these our arts; and ever may we guard,
> Ever defend thee with undaunted heart!
>
> *(lines 224–29)*

Liberty also guarantees profound domestic benefits; her "hand benign"

> Teaches unwearied Toil to clothe the fields,
> And on his various fruits inscribes the name
> Of Property.
>
> *(lines 232–35)*

In Dyer's Britain, the magic of (constitutional) liberty smoothes the historical opposition between agricultural labor and the owners of property even as it prepares Britain for (and indeed makes mandatory) expansion abroad.

As we shall see, Dyer's fear of "Caesarism" does not lead him to an equivalent rejection of empire or imperial might. In a somewhat eccentric genealogy or progress of liberty, Dyer lists Judah, "Tyrus and Sidonia," "Libya bright, and all-enchanting Greece," as having heard Liberty's lyre, which also inspired Ausonius to plan "imperial Rome" (lines 235–42). Caesarism is associated with the downfall of the Roman Empire (but not consistently, as we will see in Dyer's portrayal of Augustus as the very model of a Platonic ruler), but Dyer has great admiration for the idea of empire, and his poem is in part a warning about what imperial states and an imperial people need to do to guard against decline. In his analysis of the origins of Roman power, Dyer thus emphasizes manly, martial virtues and pursuits (lines 266–78), his verse breathless with homosocial fantasy:

> There to their daily sports the noble youth
> Rush'd emulous; to fling the pointed lance;
> To vault the steed; or with the kindling wheel
> In dusty whirlwinds sweep the trembling goal;

> Or, wrestling, cope with adverse swelling breasts,
> Strong grappling arms, close heads, and distant feet;
> Or clash the lifted gauntlets: there they form'd
> Their ardent virtues.
>
> *(lines 269–76)*

His analysis also features another important version of manly simplicity: that of the landowner and farmer, the model of republican civic virtue epitomized by Lucius Quinctius Cinncinatus and described in Cato's *De agri cultura:*

> From the plough
> Rose her dictators; fought, o'ercame, return'd,
> Yes, to the plough return'd, and hail'd their peers;
> For them no private pomp, no household state,
> . . . .
> As yet they stood,
> Simple of life; as yet seducing wealth
> Was unexplor'd, and shame of poverty
> Yet unimagined—
>
> *(lines 426–37).*

This is the georgic moment in the eighteenth-century discourse of national power—the claim that working the land is itself a guard against the temptations of enfeebling luxury, which tend to follow upon the expenditure of riches derived from commerce or finance.[22]

This emphasis on the political ethics of Roman republicanism, and on the rhetorical pieties of the georgic, in this "historical" investigation of the foundations of imperial states and rulers renders odd an earlier moment, one that fuses political and poetic wish fulfillment, but confuses Roman political history. Dyer rehabilitates Augustus, who was more usually the target of the Whig (and even Tory) "patriot" opposition to Walpole in the 1730s that claimed for their own the Roman republicans. Such a rendering of a wise and nontyrannical Augustus was by no means unique; even Bolingbroke's *The Idea of a Patriot King* (written in 1738) closes, as his editor David Armitage puts it, by "combining the traditionally incompatible ideas of *imperium* and *libertas*," with the Patriot King as a "new Augustus, at the head of a prosperous and free people, commanding a vast though uncorrupting empire well suited to the maritime capabilities of an island nation."[23]

Dyer's rewriting of Augustus also serves a vocational purpose, for the emperor is described here as patron and confidant of Virgil, and as visiting "Maro's humble tenement," (line 371):

Here oft the meek good man, the lofty bard
Fram'd the celestial song, or social walk'd
With Horace and the ruler of the world:
Happy Augustus! who, so well inspir'd,
Couldst throw thy pomps and royalties aside,
Attentive to the wise, the great of soul,
And dignify thy mind. Thrice glorious days,
Auspicious to the Muses!
. . . .
                    e'en the rugged sons of war,
E'en the rude hinds rever'd the poet's name.

(lines 379–91)

Dyer's fear of "Caesarism" dissolves into this myth of enlightened Augustan patronage, for it allows him to imagine a time, unlike in contemporary Britain—"But now—another age, alas! is ours" (line 392)—when poets were important to the rulers and people of powerful states.

Poets can, after all, offer both historical insight into contemporary problems and propose salutary responses. Accordingly, the last ninety lines of the poem are a description of the decline and fall of Rome, with a specific exhortation to Britons to learn from that story. The poet offers a powerful diagnosis of social and moral pathologies peculiar to the successes of imperial expansion, and in doing so finds an impassioned, oracular voice with which to recount history and point to his nation's future, if only by telling his countrymen what they must guard against. As long as the Roman conquest was motivated by "proud desire / Of boundless sway, and feverish thirst of gold," (lines 455–56) the Romans were invincible. While there was need for battle, Rome remained, literally, fighting fit. Once warfare ceased, however, because of their success against all their enemies, and "the plated greave and corslet hung unbrac'd" (line 468), the Romans become enfeebled and effeminate:

Dissolv'd in ease and soft delights they lie,
Till every sun annoys, and every wind
Has chilling force, and every rain offends:
For now the frame no more is girt with strength
Masculine,
. . . .
                    enfeebling vice
Withers every nerve, and opens every pore
To painful feeling: flowery bowers they seek
(As ether prompts, as the sick sense approves)
Or cold Nymphean grots; or tepid baths
(Taught by the soft Ionians);
. . . .

> while Luxury
> Over their naked limbs with wanton hand,
> Sheds roses, odours, sheds unheeded bane.
>
> *(lines 471–89)*

For Dyer, Roman emasculation follows from its imperial success. The very elements conspire to "dissolve" the once-strong Romans, and "soft Ionians" teach the Romans the joys of "tepid baths" (the OED records one sense in which the Ionian mode was thought of as "soft and effeminate"). Civil society sinks under the weight of mushrooming desires:

> unnumber'd wants,
> Brood of voluptuousness, cry out aloud
> Necessity, and seek the splendid bribe:
> . . . .
> whate'er is known
> Of rarest acquisition; Tyrian garbs,
> Neptunian Albion's high testaceous food,
> And flavor'd Chian wines with incense fum'd
> To slake patrician thirst; for these, their rights
> In the vile streets they prostitute to sale,
> Their ancient rights, their dignities, their laws,
> Their native glorious freedom.
>
> *(lines 490–503)*

Seduced by foreign commodities—clothes, food, wine—the Romans lose their masculinity, militarism, and their political and civic values.

Dyer is of course not interested in just charting the decline of past empires. His object is closer home, and his meditations on the ruins of Rome function as a civilizational allegory for expansionist Britain:

> O Britons, O my countrymen, beware;
> Gird, gird your hearts; the Romans once were free,
> Were brave, were virtuous.—Tyranny, howe'er,
> Deign'd to walk forth a while in pageant state,
> And with licentious pleasures fed the rout.
>
> *(lines 512–16)*

(It is tempting to read the exhortation to Britons to "gird your hearts" as the poet's response to his fear of enfeebled masculinity: what actually needs girding, in this logic, are imperial loins, altogether a more recalcitrant figure for physical prowess and generative strength, as well as the seductive power of "licentious pleasures.") Dyer goes on to give Roman "Tyranny" an imperial face, that of Caesar, elevated to divine status by "the thoughtless many"

THE EBB AND FLOW OF NATIONS AND EMPIRES 109

(lines 517–26). In Dyer's political argument, Caesar's apotheosis is Rome's decline, leaving Romans at the mercy of "the Goth and Vandal," who bring down their "domes, their villas," "their festive piles," "their Parian porches" and "gilded baths" (lines 529–32).

This description of apocalyptic destruction continues, albeit in a more reflexive tone, in the last verse of the poem, which offers a moral-philosophical survey of fallen empires. At the end of its long account of the military and political rise, cultural accomplishments, and degeneration of the Roman Empire, the poem condenses all its diagnoses of the problems faced by "affluent states" into the single, weighty term "Luxury":

> Vain end of human strength, of human skill,
> Conquest, and triumph, and domain, and pomp,
> And ease, and luxury! O Luxury
> Bane of elated life, of affluent states,
> What dreary change, what ruin is not thine?
> How doth thy bowl intoxicate the mind!
> To the soft entrance of thy rosy cave
> How dost thou lure the fortunate and great!
> Dreadful attraction! while behind thee gapes
> Th' unfathomable gulf where Asher lies
> O'erwhelmed, forgotten; and high-boasting Cham;
> And Elam's haughty pomp; and beauteous Greece;
> And the great queen of Earth, imperial Rome.
>
> *(lines 534–46)*

As in all of Dyer's accounts of moral and social degeneration, the agent of change (in this case Luxury) is a highly-charged, sexualized figure. Its seductions unman those who can not resist them; its "soft entrance" leads onto the abyss of history, in whose "unfathomable gulf" lies the detritus of empires long past.

If anything, the close of *The Ruins of Rome* testifies to the seductive ease with which visions of imperial ruin overwhelm the poet of comparative empires and nations. As we have seen, Dyer's poem moves between readings of ruins as evidence of great historical accomplishment and a more traumatized focus on the causes of imperial decline. In the one case, fragments yield appropriate historical and civic examples that can be emulated by successor states, in the other, they turn into vertiginous instances of the "dreadful chasm," the "unfathomable gulf" of history. The poem in turn walks the tightrope between history that can be properly and responsibly allegorized and a past that swallows all such refiguration into an apocalyptic sublimity.[24] Ironically, both modes of registering the passage of time and the dynamic of civilizations are grist for the poet's mill, as he alternates between the tempered tones of comparative historiography and the more unstable, dangerous idiom of prophecy. In this alternation can be glimpsed the polarity between what literary history calls the neoclassical and the romantic tempers, but we can also see the productive affinities between each, and recognize their complementary location in the eighteenth-century discourse of empire. As Dyer looks abroad, or looks back into history, disparate forms of wonder, fear, and excitement mold his poetic historiography: Liberty and Luxury loom large as personified figures of national salvation and destruction; riches abroad beckon, only to turn into commodities whose import saps the physical and moral fibre of the state; past empires point the way forward, but also suggest the seemingly inevitable descent into oblivion.

In his account of Dyer's 1724 trip to Rome, Goldstein quotes a poem Dyer wrote to a friend, Martha Fouke Samson ("known to her admirers as Clio"):

> Nothing, alas, where'er I walk,
> Nothing but fear and sorrow talk;
> Where'er I walk, from bound to bound,
> Nothing but ruin spreads around,
>
> Or busts that seem from graves to rise,
> Or statues stern, with sightless eyes,
> Cold Death's pale people:—Oh! for love,
> Angelic Clio, these remove![25]

Goldstein emphasizes the "fundamental despair" of these lines, which he suggests derives from the encounter between the twenty-four-year-old poet and the ruins of Rome. In them, Dyer saw overwhelming evidence of the decay of all ambition, and of the "extinction of future achievement." This insight, Goldstein argues persuasively, prepared Dyer for religious faith and for the acceptance of any "ideology that promised exaltation of the spirit," be it the "praise of Liberty, Commerce, Rural Virtue."[26] None of these slogans of exaltation, though, seem to have offered proper compensation for Dyer, as his poetry constantly tests them against the evidence of history. *The Ruins of Rome*, as I have suggested above, thus charts both Dyer's desolation in the face of ruin and his attempts to craft a way out of such historical and psychological despair.[27] His engagement with historical themes, both as meditation upon transience and as proof against decay, is figured in this little poem, too, for it is "Angelic Clio," the Muse of History, he calls upon to "remove him" (line 8) from his fearful encounters with the ghosts of the past (here statues are not memorials to a civic past but fantastic specters come to life to remind viewers of "Cold Death"). However, it is precisely the angel of history, as Dyer's little poem shows, who offers but fickle and insubstantial redemption.

In this chapter I have so far tracked the curious and generative tension, in several poems in the first half of the century, between ruins and empire, between the "matter of Rome" and the present and future of Britain. These poems plot continuities and differences between the rise and fall of Rome (and Italy more generally) and the anticipated rise of Britain to imperial power, and develop elaborate mythologies regarding the historical and geographical movement of "Commerce" and of "Liberty" to encourage or discourage certain moral and cultural practices in Britain, and to devise enabling models of national progress. The curious feature of these poems, of course, is their repeated invocation of historical decline, and this is a feature shared, as I have suggested, by poets with different political and cultural affiliation. Such comparative historiography became part of the method and vocabulary of poetry early in the century, and its historical principles— particularly that of the westward movement of empire and civilization— served equally the argument of those who claimed that Britain was the manifest destination of such movement, and those who suggested that corrupt practices in Britain were certain to hasten the drift of power (liberty, the Muses, the arts, empire) further westward.

This comparative method, with its underlying question about the factors that might explain not only the rise and fall of empires in history but the nature of different socioeconomic development in nations and regions in the present, is a crucial feature of the rise of historicist thought in Britain. The poets I consider here helped solidify such historical consciousness, the catalyst and goad to this process being, as these poems make clear, the prospect (and uncertain progress) of a British empire. This is to claim an importance for the method and themes of these poems that, if nothing else, our reluctance to read them has denied. Further, even when critics have read such poems, the tendency is to call attention to the immediate political motivation that precipitates the poem, and not consider the ways in which such incidental writing contributes to the development of historical consciousness and the making of what we today categorize variously as the imperial temper, or as colonial discourse. Indeed, we might wish to consider, from the evidence of such poetry, whether we should think of historicist thought in this period as being synonymous with colonial discourse, or at least recognize that the development of one is not feasible without the intensification of the other.

These poets are thus at best uncertain propagandists for British expansion (with its hesitant progress and fluctuating fortunes) in the first half of the eighteenth century; in this chapter, I have shown how their poems are often deeply suspicious about particular forms of national progress. In fact, it seems clear that the ruin sentiment—its pessimism, its warning, its overwhelming sense of transience—is a mediated expression of the uncertainties that wracked public life in Britain through the century, from military and naval defeats on the Continent and in the colonies, to a more domestic fear about the cultural, social, and economic costs of the expansion of overseas trade. There are, to be sure, passages in these poems that celebrate national mercantile and imperial power, and that celebration is, for the most part, the ideological point of the poem, the hopeful conclusion that they recuperate in the face of storms, sinking fortunes, and—most importantly— the record of history. The remainder of this chapter will follow, in poems by Oliver Goldsmith and one by Anna Letitia Barbauld, the progress of such comparative and historicist observation, and emphasize once again the political and ideological significance of their models of the rise and fall of nations and empires. With both Goldsmith and Barbauld, we notice an increase in concern about the growth of British military and territorial commitments, and a strategic intensification of the historical fear of national decline, and of the westward passage of empire, that we have traced so far.

The Lure and Challenge of Comparative History

In 1767, writing in *The Beauties of English Poesy*, Goldsmith said of Addison's "Letter from Italy" that it contained "a strain of political thinking that was, at that time, new in our poetry."[28] In the intervening five decades, as I have suggested here, other poets deepened this strain of comparative historical and national analysis.[29] Goldsmith himself developed such comparisons at some length in his prose and verse, especially in the 1760s. In "A Comparative View of Races and Nations" (1760), in *The Citizen of the World* (1760–61), and *A History of England in a Series of Letters* (1764), Goldsmith elaborated ideas about the uneven historical development of nations and of regions that were to find prominent place in his *The Traveller, or A Prospect of Society* (1764).[30] Goldsmith's commentaries on the climatic, geographical, and historical factors that enable or retard the rise and fall of nations are part of his more immediate concern with the proper conduct of contemporary British foreign and trade policies. In his journalism, his fiction, and his poetry, Goldsmith argues the case that, as Lien Chi Altangi puts it in Letter 25 of *Citizen of the World*, "extending empire is often diminishing power, that countries are ever strongest which are internally powerful; that colonies by draining away the brave and enterprising, leave the country in the hands of the timid and the avaricious; . . . that too much commerce may injure a nation as well as too little; and that there is wide difference between a conquering and a flourishing empire."[31]

These were not simply philosophical concerns for Goldsmith. While the Seven Years War (1756–63) between England and France, widely understood as a war for trade and territory, particularly in North America, resulted in overwhelming gains for Britain across the globe, its length and costs (both human and financial) did mean that a considerable sentiment for peace developed in its later stages, particularly after the accession of George III, whose administration was not sympathetic to William Pitt's personal power or his increased commitment to the extension of British commerce and colonies. Pitt left office in 1761, but by then Britain had defeated the French in a number of theaters: in 1757, Robert Clive defeated Suraj-ud-Dowla at Plassey, and established control of Bengal; in 1758, the French lost trading posts in West Africa and control over the slave trade; the British took Guadeloupe and Martinique in early 1759, and Canada later that year (Wolfe was victorious in Quebec in September); and between 1760 and 1761, the British established themselves as the dominant power in southeast India. After Britain declared war against Spain in 1762, it won Havana and Manila, and although the Treaty of Paris in February 1763 restored these territories to Spain, and others in the Caribbean (and trading posts in West Africa and India) to the French, Britain's dominance—and the idea of a global commercial and territorial empire—seemed assured.

The war years, and the accompanying discussions about the conduct of military policy and the commitment of human and financial resources, sharpened Goldsmith's critique. In Letter 17 (13 March 1760), Lien Chi Altangi portrays France and Britain as greedy and unthinking, as engaged in a "very destructive war," and "all upon account of one side's desiring to wear greater quantities of *furs* than the other." Goldsmith's irony here extends to Altangi's simplifying incredulity, but there is little that is ironic about the later passage in which Altangi comments on the depopulation of Britain in order to people "the desarts of America": "men who ought to be regarded as the sinews of the people" are to be exchanged for "raw silk, hemp, and tobacco. England, therefore, must make an exchange of her best and bravest subjects for raw silk, hemp and tobacco; her hardy veterans, and honest tradesmen must be truck'd for a box of snuff or a silk petticoat. Strange absurdity!"[32] Goldsmith's suspicions about this expedient exchange of bodies for "commodities" leads to the moving portrayal of a beggar with a wooden leg—indentured into plantation slavery, press-ganged into the army for duty on the Continent, and then, in the service of the East India Company, disabled in wars fought for commercial and territorial benefits he has no share of—still believing in "Liberty, property, and old England, for ever, huzza!"[33]

Goldsmith's refusal to participate in the general enthusiasm for commercial and imperial aggrandizement is anchored in his grave doubts about the domestic consequences of the concentration of wealth that trade made possible. For Goldsmith, the most potent metaphor for these consequences is depopulation, and in "The Revolution in Low Life" (1762), he develops this theme (for which he is perhaps best known), and calls attention to the loss of habitat and livelihood as village and common lands are enclosed into private estates. The new owners are merchants whose "immense fortune" follows from "the encrease of foreign commerce and the extension of our foreign conquests." "Foreign commerce" is blamed for the "accumulation of immense wealth in the hands of a few," for swallowing up liberty in those nations ("Venice, Genoa, Holland") that pursued it with "too much assiduity," for ultimately enfeebling the nation and making it prey to external conquest. The closing historical example, as we have come to expect, is that of Italy before the Gothic conquest, a "garden of pleasure" for those whose villas were replete with imported luxuries, but lacking "the rough peasant and hardy husbandman," who had "been long obliged to seek for liberty and subsistence in Britain or Gaul." The invading Goths find no one to resist them, save the "slaves of the nobility or the effeminate citizens of Rome."[34]

Goldsmith's *The Traveller, or a Prospect of Society* brings together these quasi-ethnographic and historical vocabularies in its survey of the state of affairs in, and national traits of, a number of countries that he imagines "seeing" from his prospect high in the Alps (lines 31–50).[35] The traveler looks, he says, for evidence of happiness in each nation, but understands that happiness is understood differently everywhere, such that the "shudd'ring tenant of the frigid zone" and the "naked Negro, panting at the line," can each claim to be happy precisely where they are (lines 63–74). The traveler says that he is committed to the balanced view (the balance for which critics have often celebrated Goldsmith) that an "equal portion" has been "dealt to all mankind" (lines 75–86). This natural evenness is however, disturbed by art—human effort—which, even as it provides the blessings of "Wealth, commerce, honour, liberty, content," also leads to the development of inequality, as some "favourite good" in each province is "carried to excess" and "begets peculiar pain" (for instance, "honour sinks where commerce long prevails") (lines 87–98).

If this is the theoretical frame with which Goldsmith begins his enquiry, the bulk of the poem offers comments on Italy, Switzerland, France, Holland, and Britain that exemplify and qualify this understanding. I here only sum up, using key phrases from the poem, its account of nations and peoples. Goldsmith's account of Italy repeats many of the geographical, historical, and cultural arguments we are familiar with: the land is blessed in its natural bounty, but that, over time, resulted in a nation that knew only "sensual bliss" and "opulence." Commerce once flourished here, and enabled advances in architecture, art, sculpture, but since commerce is "more unsteady than the southern gale," it slipped away, leaving "towns unmanned and lords without a slave." There are only ruins now, within which, unknowing of the past, the "shelter-seeking peasant builds his shed" (lines 111–64). Switzerland is a land of hardy, cheerful peasants and no great economic disparities, its primary problem being its subsistence economy, which affords few "pleasures" or examples of the "gentler morals, such as play / Through life's more cultured walks and charm the way" (lines 165–238).

France next, "where gentler manners reign," and "honour forms the social temper." Both the Traveller's terms of praise and of condemnation reflect the genteel Gallophobia of his time: it turns out that the French, too sedulous of praise, are led to ostentatious display, "beggar pride," and a petty commitment to shifting fashion (lines 239–80). The Dutch are described as "patient," industrious men who have wrested their nation from the seas, and whose "industry begets a love of gain" that encourages "Convenience, plenty, elegance and arts." However, their love of gain also leads them astray ("liberty itself is bartered here") and converts Holland into a "land of tyrants and a den of slaves" (lines 281–312). At this point, in a turn that completes the geographical and ideological itinerary of the poem, the Traveller's gaze shifts to Britain, and he begins by comparing Britons to the Dutch of old, who, unlike their countrymen now, were warlike and ready to preserve "freedom." What follows is Goldsmith's well-known panegyric to Britain (a nation possessed of "Creation's mildest charms") and Britons—"the lords of human kind"—who are thoughtful, imbued with reason ("intent on high designs"), committed to political liberty (lines 312–34).

The celebration of nation and national traits does not last, however, as Goldsmith moves quickly to the series of warnings that delineate and emphasize his political and economic views of the present course of British affairs. Freedom's blessings turn out to be mixed, for an overemphasis on "independence" among Britons "Keeps man from man, and breaks the social tie; / The self dependent lordlings stand alone" (lines 339–42). These are interesting lines, for they express a complex idea: a political value—independence, or Freedom—is seen to be the source of the loss of social ties, but there is a particular figure to be condemned—the self-dependent lordling—who is a recognizable socioeconomic type, the commercial magnate who lacks the ties of custom that once defined the life of the land. In Goldsmith's model of worrisome socioeconomic change, this figure stands in for an entire "order," whose "disproportioned" growth and power, its "double weight" will "ruin all below" (lines 375–76). A few lines later, the poem makes more clear the nexus it fears:

> Laws grind the poor, and rich men rule the law;
> The wealth of climes, where savage nations roam,
> Pillag'd from slaves, to purchase slaves at home.
>
> *(lines 386–88)*

Roger Lonsdale tells us that Goldsmith probably refers to Clive's recent victories in India here, for in his *History of England* (1771) Goldsmith described the English in India as being "gratified in their avarice to its extremest wish; and that wealth which they had plundered from slaves in India, they were resolved to employ in making slaves at home."[36]

The victories of the Seven Years War had confirmed Britain in its overseas power, but the political aftermath, as ministries and political alliances changed in the years after Pitt's resignation in 1761, suggested to an observer like Goldsmith the dangers of oligarchy, peculation, and the concentration of wealth. Once again, Goldsmith chose to focus on the impact of overseas activities on the countryside: Britain's "useful sons are exchanged for useless ore," and "opulence, her grandeur to maintain," leads "stern depopulation in her train" (lines 398–402). The Traveller specifies a region to which such forced emigration moves, which is North America. Here, he mentions the lands around the Oswego and Niagara Rivers, on the border between British and French possessions, territories that had been fought over in the late 1750s. This model of emigration is far from hopeful—the territories are described as wild, dangerous, and with a hostile "brown Indian" population (lines 413–18). The "pensive exile, bending with his woe," is a reluctant traveler, turning back to cast a "long look where England's glories shine" (lines 419–21)—this last touch the poet's ironic comment on the processes that both enable the rise of national power and result in the immiseration of its vulnerable populations.

Goldsmith's focus on forced emigration to North America is of course based on contemporary observation: that was the destination of the largest number of poor British and Irish people. However, Goldsmith also reverses two crucial poetic and historical topoi here—those that, as we have seen, trace the westward movement of empire and of learning (*translatio imperii* and *translatio studii*) and show how they achieve their proper home in Britain. Or rather, he extends their prophetic and geographic logic to a point at which they no longer serve the ideological ends of British aggrandizement, for there is a further West to which Britain's "useful sons" must move. Depopulation or forced emigration to North America might not seem a particularly apt symptom of the rise of the American colonies, and certainly the poem does not offer these new lands as the welcoming and obvious home for the economic, social, and cultural strengths that Britain, in Goldsmith's argument, was alienating. But there is a prophetic element to his argument, one that surfaced in an earlier essay in which Goldsmith argued that it was "possible for England to have colonies too large for her natural power to manage. Of this we may be very sure, the more powerful her colonies become, the less obedient will they be to another's power."[37]

Before I move on to *The Deserted Village*, the poem that contains Goldsmith's most intense vision of British decline, it is worth asking what advantages accrued to the poet that were not available to the writer—the journalist, translator, reviewer, writer of literary and other lives, and compiler of histories—that Goldsmith had been before the publication of *The Traveller*? As we have seen, there are few ideas in *The Traveller* (and later, in *The Deserted Village*) that Goldsmith had not expressed at greater length in his prose; what was to be gained in writing a poem on public themes and national affairs? To ask this question of Goldsmith's two major poems is to ask it of the practice of poetry in what was increasingly an age of prose, and the answer that Goldsmith's literary career supplies is instructive. Roger Lonsdale tells us that this poem resulted in a "new celebrity," and established "him for the first time as an eminent man of letters." Goldsmith's legendary social clumsiness had contributed to his image as a somewhat learned hack, but the publication of this poem, as Johnson attested, "brought him into high reputation." It literally transformed the public perception of Goldsmith; Lonsdale reports Mrs Cholomondeley's remark to Johnson, "I never more shall think Dr. Goldsmith ugly." Acquaintance with people in high places followed, as did offers of patronage.[38] The writer of a successful poem, even if it reiterated themes and arguments much debated in his prose (or that of others), transformed himself from journalist to poet, from hack to literary celebrity. This was in fact the aspiration that drove much of the writing of poems on public themes throughout the eighteenth century.

Back to images of national decline: Goldsmith's best-known poem remains *The Deserted Village*, a long poem that offers a rambling, cloyingly sentimental evocation of the rural countryside as a prelude to more pointed political and ethical commentary. Not that the romanticized account of Auburn in the first half of the poem lacks purpose: its values—its account of labor and the village community—are derived from the pieties of pastoral and the sunnier moments of georgic, which means that the disruption and loss the rest of the poem mourns is equally the loss of such poetic possibility. This is an idea particularly important to the end of the poem, which features the exile of "sweet Poetry" from contemporary Britain. Goldsmith's method here weaves the "Sweet Auburn" of his observation and memory from a literary topos, the "Sweet smiling village" that such poetry once made possible (which is precisely what George Crabbe objected to thirteen years later in his polemical response *The Village*). In contrast, Goldsmith depiction of depopulation in Auburn and the ruin of the countryside and the village is much sharper, for he is clear about the cause of such devastation. The "bold peasantry, their country's pride" are being uprooted by "trade's unfeeling train" (lines 55–63), and in particular by the estate-building activities of the "man of wealth and pride" who

> Takes up a space that many poor supplied;
> Space for his lake, his park's extended bounds,
> Space for his horses, equipage, and hounds;
> The robe that wraps his limbs in silken sloth,
> Has robbed the neighbouring field of half their growth.
>
> *(lines 275–80)*[39]

Of particular interest here is the vocabulary that Goldsmith uses to further his political argument in the second half of the poem, which includes vignettes of human misery, a condemnation of the people and the socioeconomic practices that cause such sorrow. and—at the height of the poem's denunciatory force—a vision of Poetry ("thou loveliest maid") forced away from her home in Britain, her exile the concluding manifestation of the loss of the arts that legitimate other forms of national power. As before, Goldsmith's diagnosis of Britain's political economy claims that "the rich man's joys increase" is "the poor's decay," that the global circuits of new wealth leave "our useful products still the same," and that enclosure ("the pressure of contiguous pride") drives peasants away from their fields and villages (lines 265–308). His argument extends that of the poem's dedication (to Joshua Reynolds), in which he says: "In regretting the depopulation of the country, I inveigh against the increase of our luxuries; and here also I expect the shout of modern politicians against me. For twenty or thirty years past, it has been the fashion to consider luxury as one of the greatest national advantages; and all the wisdom of antiquity in that particular, as erroneous. Still however, I must remain a professed ancient on that head, and continue to think those luxuries prejudicial to states, by which so many vices are introduced, and so many kingdoms have been undone."

Thus, Goldsmith's insistence on defining the forces that cause the destruction and loss of what he calls the "rural virtues" (line 398) intensifies and makes more real his invocation of the apocalyptic decline to which all states are subject once "Luxury" is on the ascendant. However, as we saw in lines 434–46 of Dyer's *The Ruins of Rome*, Luxury is an abstract agent, a term whose generality is often at odds with any scenario of more precise historical explanation that the poet might offer. Dyer does name many sources of corruption in imperial Rome, and also lists several mercantile and imperial empires in his concluding account of the corrupting, emasculating power of luxury, but what emerges is not a credible historical analysis as much as a nightmarish record of decline. In *The Deserted Village*, however, Goldsmith attempts to anchor his equally horrific vision of decline in a particular socioeconomic argument, one made more pointed by Britain's recent military and territorial successes, and the increase in colonial trade:

> O luxury! thou curst by heaven's decree, . . .
> Kingdoms by thee, to sickly greatness grown,
> Boast of a florid vigour not their own.
> At every draught more large and large they grow,
> A bloated mass of rank unwieldy woe;
> Till sapped their strength and every part unsound,
> Down, down they sink, and spread a ruin around.
>
> Even now the devastation is begun,
> And half the business of destruction done;
> Even now, methinks, as pondering here I stand,
> I see the rural virtues leave the land.
>
> *(lines 385–96)*

The repeated "Even now" underlines what we might call the *real time* of Goldsmith's complaint—the sense that the "wisdom of antiquity" is likely to hold true for Britain because of a particular, identifiable set of political and economic developments in the present.

However, the pull toward ethical abstraction contained in the rhetoric and iconography of "Luxury" developed by eighteenth-century poets proves too strong: as the dislocated rural poor arrive at the point of embarkation, their bodies and identities vaporize into Goldsmith's personifications of "rural virtue." At this point, then, the poem rewrites its socioeconomic critique into the lexicon of ethical exemplarity. The "melancholy band" that pass "from the shore and darken all the strand" are no longer dispossessed peasants, but abstractions: "Contented toil," "hospitable care," "connubial tenderness," "piety," "steady loyalty and faithful love," and, above all, "sweet Poetry" (lines 399–407). While the accumulated force of such ethical and moral categories adds to the poet's denunciation of social evils, there is a distinct shift in idiom away from the particularity featured in some of the other, more diagnostic, sections of the poem. In fact, this shift is important to the vocational and ideological interests of the poem, for it sets the stage for the forced embarkation of Poetry itself.

For poetry is here the final test of both personal probity and national virtue. It offers the poet inspiration and reduces him to vocational distress ("Thou source of all my bliss, and all my woe, / That found'st me poor at first, and keeps't me so" lines 413–14). The "woe" mentioned here is no doubt meant to indicate both the poet's enhanced sensitivity and his lack of advancement (a claim repeated often in the vocational mythology of the eighteenth-century literary professional). Within the same mythology, the service of Poetry—even if thankless—is important because Poetry offers public instruction: "Thou guide by which the nobler arts excel, / Thou nurse of every virtue" (lines 415–16). To worship Poetry is thus to act in the national interest: Goldsmith's metaphors fuse aesthetic convention with nationalist striving, making one inseparable from the other. Poetry is the art that defines the strength of national culture; her loss is therefore an index of imminent national decline—of the translation of civilization away from Britain.

It is this fusion of nation and Muse—in however passive and despairing a manner—that motivates the conclusion of the poem, and allows it (a strained) coherence. Poetry is exiled to the frozen north ("Torno's cliffs" in Sweden) or the "ecquinoctial fervours" of Quito and the Pambamarca River (lines 417–20). This wandering and uncertain exile is a reminder to all right-thinking Britons that they must "spurn the rage of gain" and know (these are Johnson's well-known lines that close the poem):

> That trade's proud empire hastes to swift decay,
> As ocean sweeps the labour'd mole away;
> While self dependent power can time defy,
> As rocks resist the billows and the sky.
>
> *(lines 424–30)*

Johnson's couplets are an odd fit, as they both attempt to restore the pointed socioeconomic moral that is crucial to the argument of Goldsmith's poem, but to so in defensive abstractions that respect the tone and idiom of the thirty lines come before (Johnson had provided similar ballast to the conclusion of *The Traveller* too).[40] The warning Johnson offers in couched in terms and images derived from maritime fears; the storms that disrupted Needler's "A Sea Piece" rage still. The abyss of history is the ocean, a precise irony given that it was control of the shipping lanes that enabled, through the eighteenth century, but particularly in the late 1750s and after, Britain's rise to global power.

In his highly suggestive reading of the concluding lines of *The Deserted Village*, Marshall Brown points to the entirely feminized form of Poetry (a "maid," a "nymph," a "guide," a "nurse," the aid to "slighted truth"), and suggests her mode is understood to be "compliance rather than defiance." What then, he asks, "makes her strong?"[41] His answer is that the poem possesses a "double logic" in which satire joins with ode (as "Johnson's couplets chime with Goldsmith's") to produce a contradictory aesthetic space in which "poetry is *both* a wandering voice and a firm rock," and thus combines social commentary and a deeply personal vision.[42] Another answer might result if we rephrase Brown's question slightly: what, we might ask, makes Poetry an appropriate figure for national self-renewal? The answer that follows comes, as this chapter suggests, from outside the poem, from the long history of *translatio studii* that informed the historical and geographical consciousness of the many poets who sang the westward movement of national power and arts in order to craft a genealogy for Britain's growth to empire. Goldsmith's complication of this model, of course, was to invert its priorities, to read the exile of Poetry as a symptom of the passing of a way of life, and a system of rural order, that he wished to argue central to national health. The muse of celebration is here turned into the muse of decline—a suggestion developed considerably in the poem to which we now turn.

The Poem of History and the Ruins of England: Anna Letitia Barbauld's *Eighteen Hundred and Eleven*

In hindsight, Goldsmith's urgent expression, in prose and poetry, of his concerns regarding the socioeconomic and historical role being played by aggressive British commercial and colonial growth in undermining the traditional strengths of the nation seems misplaced, even quixotic. When we think of the enormous range of British power across the globe in the nineteenth and the first fifty years of the twentieth centuries, it is entirely feasible to minimize the fears of those like Goldsmith or Johnson, whose un-Whiggish politics were realized in a suspicion of the concentration of wealth and power that earlier British overseas expansion made possible.[43] We can trace, as contemporaries surely did, the lineaments of the British Second Empire that was coming into being in this period. But we can also recognize their palpable sense that imperialistic policies, particularly in the 1760s and early 1770s (or, more precisely, protectionist and monopolistic colonial legislation, and taxes that were resisted and could not be collected) were in fact endangering the "benevolent" connections between Britain and its most important colonies in this period, notably those in the Caribbean and in North America. (We remember Goldsmith's warning about an imperial nation: "Of this we may be very sure, the more powerful her colonies become, the less obedient will they be to another's power.")

Four decades separate these poems by Goldsmith and Anna Barbauld's *Eighteen Hundred and Eleven*. Any account of Britain, at home and abroad, in that period must take on board an astonishing scenario of accelerated, epochal change. Just two events, the independence of the American colonies and the revolution in France in 1789, resulted in incalculable changes in transatlantic, European, and indeed global political economy and consciousness. More locally, the ceaseless military activity of these years— the lost War of American Independence (1775–83) and the uneven and long-drawn-out wars against France in the decades following the revolution—toughened the "sinews of power" necessary for Britain's nineteenth-century empire, but also made clear how precarious colonial and imperial dominance could be. The "fratricidal" conflict with, and the loss of, the American colonies was a monumental check to the unlimited commercial and colonial expansion that the Seven Years War had promised. And while the Anglo–French wars that followed finally resulted in the reassertion of British dominance over the oceans and far-flung territories across the globe, the early successes of French armies on the Continent and (under Napoleon) in Italy and Egypt, and the sheer human and economic demands made upon Britain by a war that would not seem to end, often suggested a bleaker scenario.

John Brewer, who wrote the phrase on imperial musculature quoted in the preceding paragraph, has detailed the development of a "fiscal–military state, one dominated by the task of waging war" in eighteenth-century Britain, and it is worth quoting him at greater length on the priorities of state politics (and consequently of their contested nature) at this time:

The frequency of hostilities and the ever-present possibility of renewed warfare meant that even the periods of peace were not properly pacific. Minor skirmishing between the subjects of the great powers was an almost constant feature on the borders of colonial possessions and in areas of trans-oceanic trade. In Europe itself one of the main peacetime activities of the major states was the fiscal consolidation and administrative reform whose chief motive was not so much a desire for financial probity and good governance as a need to be prepared once hostilities renewed. In peacetime it was presumed that war was imminent or, at the very least, that government should act as if it were so.[44]

Brewer's formulations are particularly useful because they remind us that all debates around fiscal policy or "good governance" in this period were inescapably tied up with arguments about the military and imperial state. Thus, when poets or policymakers (and those who would be both) called attention to great social and cultural changes, particularly those they did not approve of, they very often did so at moments charged by public dispute about military adventurism and the conduct of war. Goldsmith's complaint about depopulation is, as we have seen, inseparable from the position he takes on Britain's colonial and commercial policies after the successes of the Seven Years War. Equally, his depiction of the flight of Poetry into exile from Britain is an emphatic extension of the idea that the presence or absence of the Muses (and the arts in general) were crucial indicators of the rise and fall of nations and empires. Britain is not reduced to ruins in his poems, either in *The Traveller* or in *The Deserted Village,* but both poems derive their polemical force from their representation of a country that is losing its fundamental domestic strengths.

This is the context in which Barbauld's *Eighteen Hundred and Eleven* must be read. It is, for a variety of reasons, the logical poem with which to conclude this chapter on the theme of "ruin of nation and empire" in the long eighteenth century. There is first the immediate connection with Goldsmith: Barbauld admired *The Deserted Village,* and in a tribute in verse turned her concluding compliment around the precise image that capped Goldsmith's poem: "Nor can the Muse desert our favoured isle / Till thou desert the Muse and scorn her smile."[45] Barbauld wrote these lines not long after *The Deserted Village* was published; thirty years later, however, the *translatio* motif, the passing of learning and culture further westward from Britain, provided her material for a powerful poem on war, aggressive nationalism, and the ravages of time. Second, *Eighteen Hundred and Eleven* is a reminder, along with the poems considered in this chapter, that, in the long eighteenth century, the poem on historical themes was the prophetic poem—that in these poems, the vatic (or the "fatidick")[46] does not so much repress history as represent its lessons as nightmare or as vision. Third, Barbauld exercises most fully the logic and formulae of the ruin poem, in which prior poets sought to allegorize the ruins of past empires, particularly of Rome, into responsible historical and ethical commentary on contemporary Britain, but in her vision it is the ruins of *London* (and Britain) that haunt the national imaginary, and challenge the collective will to imperial power.

The power of Barbauld's condemnation of the conduct of war and of public policy can in part be understood by keeping in mind that Britain had, since February 1793, been almost continually at war (with time off between October 1801 and May 1803) with the armies of (first, republican, and then, Napoleonic) France. I will not here summarize the different campaigns and stages of these wars, except to say that the *nation* was truly at war, for an astonishing number of men at arms were mobilized, both in domestic militias and in military service overseas (in 1812 there were almost a million men in the army and the navy).[47] Barbauld was not immune to this sense of national urgency: in 1803, invasion fears had swept Britain, and while she was skeptical about their reality, she wrote "Song for the London Volunteers," which supports militia volunteerism, but also claims limited ends for such patriotic and defensive action. Her volunteers are commercial Londoners used to the "buzz of the crowded 'Change," not to the clamor of war:

> They seek not pay or plunder,
> They pray that wars may cease;
> Their joy is not in slaughter,
> For they are sons of peace.[48]
>
> *(lines 12–16)*

Napoleon did not invade (in part because of Nelson's victory at Trafalgar in October 1805), but over the next six years, in a series of victories over the Austrians, the Prussians, and the Russians, he established control over Europe. In these years, French and British policies and naval actions also targeted each other's economic health; Napoleon's Continental System banned trade between France and its allies or dependencies and Britain and its colonies, and Britain responded by blockading all trade, including that by neutrals, with France. By 1811, this conflict had alienated the United States, since it denied their merchants access to the Continent (the Anglo-American war of 1812–14 was to follow), and while there is evidence that the embargoes did greater damage to the French economy, their ill effects were certainly being felt domestically in Britain. Thus, while there seems to be no single or spectacular reason why Barbauld wrote the poem when she did, it seems clear that the fatigue of these war years, and the sense that there was no end in view, prompted her intervention. And an intervention it was meant to be—the title of her poem, *Eighteen Hundred and Eleven*, an index of her topical urgency, a precise updating of the phrase "Even now," whose repetition Goldsmith hoped would call attention to change (for the worse) in the country.

But there is in fact a gap between the precise urgency of Barbauld's title and the idiom of the poem, particularly in the opening lines. The poem begins with the Continent at war, and Napoleon (whose "Colossal Power with overwhelming force / Bears down each fort of Freedom"—lines 7–8) dominant. Napoleon is not named, except as "the Despot" (line 9), and this metaphoric distancing exemplifies the method of the poem at this stage. The war is represented at a remove, both in geography and in poetic idiom. It is in fact fought elsewhere, even as Britain is attentive to the conflict and indeed "Feeds the fierce strife" (line 4). The first thirty-eight lines, written in the "loss-of-rural-fecundity and innocence" vein popularized by *The Deserted Village*, reinforce this geographical distance by representing the ravages of war as the despoliation of a pastoral countryside, one without precise historical or cultural coordinates. Barbauld certainly knew the details of political and military activities at this time, but there is no specificity or topicality to the references. Rather, "Glad Nature" (line 12) is stalked by Famine, Disease, and Rapine here; "blooming youths" go off to die as soldiers far away from home, and their mother, a village "matron," mourns the fact that "Her fallen blossoms strew a foreign strand."

An ahistorical sheen plays over such poetic convention, even if the poem announces itself as engaged with the urgent themes of contemporary history; this is not a poem that names its historical protagonists or events. The Despot holds sway over "the vext nations" (none of which are named; nor is Europe), which nations lose their pastoral innocence in the face of war. The parade of personifications—Famine, Disease, Rapine—lend their abstract quality to "the Soldier," the "helpless Peasant," the village matron, as indeed to the "ensanguined field" of battle. The first interruption of this idiom comes in lines 33 to 38, via the representation of that powerful icon of modern temporality, the daily newspaper. The paper carries both reports of war and detailed maps, and the villagers pore over it to "learn the fate of husbands, brothers, friends" and to learn the precise coordinates—in space and time— of the ravages of war (lines 33–38). No details are in fact provided, but these lines, and the newspaper, are a reminder that Barbauld's poem addresses a specific and precisely historical set of circumstances, and signal the moment when the poem turns its gaze homeward, and closes the gap between continental conflicts and the sense of British distance enacted in the versification so far.

Britain (and Britannia) are addressed directly, in lines that challenge and provoke those who argue that Britain's imperial status ("An island Queen amidst thy subject seas"—line 40) will remain unaffected by the continental wars that it has sponsored, since those wars are not fought on its soil. The transition is rapid, and while Barbauld's commentary on Britain begins in a generalized ethics (Britain's "guilt" in fomenting war will bring retribution home), it moves quickly to quirky socioeconomic insight. Britain is now rife with rumors and "whispered fears," the poet suggests, that create "what they dread" and thus precipitate "Ruin." What seems an odd emphasis on "low murmurs" and rumors as the agents of the Ruin that faces Britain makes sense when we understand the political economy, so to speak, of the figure of Ruin here. It is in fact fleshed out in terms made familiar by Goldsmith and other commentators on the perils of overdependence on overseas trade, vulnerable as it is to news of events far away. As Britain's "princely merchants" watch out fearfully for the "tempest blackening in the distant West," the nation's "baseless wealth dissolves in air away, / Like mists that melt before the morning ray" (lines 39–60). The collapse, in 1810, of some significant London business houses had illustrated the vulnerability of commercial Britain to protracted war, even if those wars are fought elsewhere, and this is the warning Barbauld offers to those who would extend or amplify Britain's participation in them.

At this moment, Barbauld's poem enters the prophetic mode that so many contemporaries found objectionable, and it does so by staging the departure of "the golden tide of Commerce," from Britain's shore to "distant lands." The departure of Commerce leaves in its wake "enfeebling Luxury and ghastly Want" (lines 61–66), all terms we are familiar with from our survey of poems in this chapter. But there is more to come, as Barbauld details, at great length, not only Britain's economic collapse but a total loss of cultural and scientific values in the blighted future. The tone of despair that accompanies this dystopian progress is particularly important, for it is produced by a fatalistic scenario, familiar to us in the historical transitions charted by models of *translatio imperii* and *translatio studii*. Is it "thy fate," the poet asks Britain, "To rank amongst the names that once were great"? The passing of the Ottoman Empire offers a prior model, but Britain's projected decline is more poignant because it is at present revered by surrounding states as the home of constitutional laws and intellectual and artistic achievement (lines 71–78). The British lamp now provides the "streaming radiance" that, along with the British "race," is spread "from Ganges to the pole," and over "half the western world." This then is the particular irony of Britain's decline: the "westward streams" of "the light that leaves thy shores" enables the rise of "Nations beyond the Appalachian hills": "Thy stores of knowledge the new states shall know, / And think thy thoughts, and with thy fancy glow" (lines 87–88).

British philosophers (Locke, William Paley), poets (Milton, Thomson), and playwrights (Joanna Baillie, Shakespeare) will instruct youth in the new world in "their search for truth," and show them how best the "fairer face of Nature to discern," including in the art of dramatic tragedy (lines 89–112). Barbauld produces several lines in praise of Baillie and mentions her historical tragedy *Ethwald,* Baillie's combination of female authorship and historical consciousness being resonant with Barbauld's own project, the full scope of which is revealed in the lines that follow. In them, via the figure of Fancy ("Fond moody Power!") as it meditates upon historical time, Barbauld wonders about a future in which

> Night, Gothic night, again may shade the plains
> Where Power is seated, and where Science reigns;
> England, the seat of arts, be only known
> By the gray ruin and the mouldering stone;
> That Time may tear the garland from her brow,
> And Europe sit in dust, as Asia now.
>
> *(lines 121–26)*

This passage contains material enough to have exposed Barbauld to accusations of lack of patriotism; what follows is in fact a "patriotic" Briton's worst nightmare. Britain's ruins are imagined as providing crash courses in the history of civilizations for young Americans on the new Grand Tour, who walk the banks of the Isis (the Thames at Oxford), the Cam, and the Avon in homage to "the sod / By statesmen, sages, poets, heroes trod" (lines 127–56). As Rome now, London then: the cosmopolitan mart of the world—"Whose merchants (such the state which commerce brings) / Sent forth their mandates to dependant kings" (lines 163–64)—crumbled into ruin. For the tourist, its former glory is signaled by the "untrodden street," the "crumbling turret," and "broken stairs" of what were once "splendid squares," and by the "scattered hamlets" that trace its "antient bound." Barbauld even stages a minireversal of the "prospect" poem, so often (as we have seen) the preferred form for the poet of national expansion: from his precarious perch on the ravaged turret, the tourist's view of "the wide horizon round" reveals only the ruins of London. Even the Thames, proud symbol of national commercial and naval power, is a shadow of its former flow: "choked no more with fleets," the river through "reeds and sedge" pursues its "idle way" (lines 170–76).

If we keep in mind the poetic conventions I have traced in this chapter, we see how Barbauld's poem is a stunning reversal of the aspiration of national expansion, doubly effective in that she reiterates and works within the comparative historical schemas and the poetic idiom constitutive of the poetry of empire. She brings home the ruin sentiment and makes palpable the decline of historical empires, and does so with an uncanny power—one that follows from the repetition of familiar materials and topoi for unfamiliar ends. Her verse, in this section, traces in the future the haunted past—thus, even in the description of Saint Paul's (which still stands), the emphasis is on the memorial function of its "chill sepulchral marbles" (line 181). In fact, the remains of London have their own historically minded guide to show around the visiting Americans (the urban version of Goldsmith's "sad historian of the pensive plain," the "wretched matron" of *The Deserted Village*), and he introduces the visitors to an eclectic catalog of eighteenth-century national heroes: Johnson, John Howard, William Pitt, Charles Fox, Garrick, Nelson, General John Moore, Humphrey Davy, Joseph Priestly (lines 185–204). This mix of writers, scientist-philosophers, parliamentarians, and soldiers replicates the roll call of great men that is a constituent feature of the many progress poems of the preceding century, but here they recede into the dim past rather than point toward a bright future. Perhaps most poignant of all are the "rich remains of antient art" on offer, with Reynolds now as Raphael was before, a monument to historic achievement.

The mercantile and imperial coordinates of Barbauld's vision of London in ruins are spelled out in much the same way as Pope described the place of imperial plunder in the making of Roman grandeur in "To Mr. Addison, Occasioned by his Dialogues on Medals." London despoiled is still a space in which to view the spoils of the world:

> On spoils from every clime their eyes shall gaze,
> Egyptian granites and the Etruscan vase;
> And when midst fallen London, they survey
> The stone where Alexander's ashes lay,

> Shall own with humbled pride the lesson just
> By Time's slow finger written in the dust.
>
> *(lines 209–14)*

In these lines, historic empires cannibalize each other, and these artifacts are memorials to that process; it is therefore difficult to escape the suggestion of a causal connection between imperial plunder and the road to ruin. On display are the remains of imperial glory, and the larger lesson they offer is of "humbled pride" and inevitable decay. The agent of ruin· is time itself, but the poem also traces visible, identifiable patterns and explanations of (historical) decline.

This combination of mythopoeic and historical "explanation" is of course characteristic of these poems on the rise and fall of nations and empires. Here, Barbauld (in phrasing that anticipates Hegelian historicism) embarks on a long account of the translation of commerce, arts, and arms across European and Mediterranean cultures. She writes of "a Spirit" ("Secret his progress is, unknown his birth") who walks the earth, an irresistible force who awakes "the human brute": "He thinks, he reasons, glows with purer fires, / Feels finer wants, and burns with new desires" (lines 221–22). All change follows from the movement of this Spirit—improvements in agriculture, mining, the gifts brought by Commerce, the architecture and luxuries of Babel, Tyre, and Egypt. The "flowers of Genius and Art" flourish, as do "Saints, Heroes, Sages," whose names are recorded with "pen of adamant" by History (lines 215–40). The Spirit is, however, "capricious," and when he comes to hate "what he loved before; / Then empires fall to dust, then arts decay, / And wasted realms enfeebled despots sway" (lines 241–44). Barbauld develops next an extended (and impressionistic) list of regions and city-states that knew their moment of historical ascendancy, and the rapid and unsystematic historical transitions that she traces emphasizes the capricious movement of the Spirit: her verse refers to classical Greece and Rome, Carthage, Troy, Babylon, the Celtic nations, Holland, Venice, Germany, and finally Britain (lines 250–80). In Britain, under the tutelage of the Spirit, Corinthian columns replace the wattled huts that Caesar once saw, and the nation inherits the arts of Rome: "British tongues the fading fame prolong / Of Tully's eloquence and Maro's song" (lines 283–88).

Thus, Barbauld's extension of *translatio* motifs inserts an element of caprice into the otherwise-predictable morality fable of progress poems. The Spirit moves as it pleases, an idea at odds with the political, socioeconomic, and ethical explanations of national decline usually proffered by poets. This tension in explanation (or rather, the tension that suggests the impossibility of credible explanation) is clear in Barbauld's lines on London. The city is described as exultant with plenty, "Gems of the East" adorn her crown, and her example "Holds forth the book of life to distant lands" (lines 305–12). But this moment is temporary: like flowers, Augusta expands "but to decay." If natural processes offer one explanation for urban decline, the next lines provide an interesting fusion of "historical" and "natural" explanation:

> Arts, arms and wealth destroy the fruits they bring;
> Commerce, like beauty, knows no second spring.
> Crime walks thy streets, Fraud earns her unblest bread,
> O'er want and woe thy gorgeous robe is spread.
>
> *(lines 315–18)*

The diagnosis of the state of the nation's capital—Crime, Fraud, luxury ("with grandeur's growth the mass of misery grows")—details a specifiable set of reasons for the decay of the city; the state of nature—Commerce, like the seasonal cycle, knows no second spring—emphasizes transience and the inevitability of change. It seems likely then that Barbauld's readers would have been as disturbed by her representation of the arbitrary movement of her Spirit of history as they were with her denunciation of Britain's protracted wars and the evidence she offered of threats to Britain's future.

In either case, *Eighteen Hundred and Eleven* closes with the flight of this Spirit from Britain (and Europe) to lands west, to the Andean nations of South America (then home to movements for independence from Spanish authority). The call of the Spirit causes a ferment in these nations:

> Ardent, the Genius fans the noble strife,
> And pours through feeble souls a higher life,
> Shouts to the mingled tribes from sea to sea,
> And swears—Thy world, Columbus, shall be free.
>
> *(lines 331–34)*

The historical schema Barbauld develops makes inescapable the understanding that the rise of the American nations spells the doom of Britain; their freedom presumes its decline. There is a mythic finality to this movement, as there was in Goldsmith's *The Deserted Village*, where the flight of Poetry from the shores of Britain is the poet's final comment on the state of the nation. Here, too, the flight of the Spirit ("moody and viewless as the changing wind," line 217) is at once the flight of Fancy ("Fond moody power!" line 115), an announcement that the poet's craft despairs at the future, and can find its proper object only elsewhere, away from its home in Britain.

James Chandler has recently suggested an intellectual location for Barbauld's poem within the discourse of romantic historicism. He calls particular attention to a staple of such historical consciousness: theories of the uneven development of cultures and nations. Chandler argues that these novel theories, as indeed such historical consciousness, follow from an overlapping, *comparative*, awareness of geography and chronology, from an uncertain yet necessary mix of anthropological and historical observation. He also emphasizes the contribution of "the Scottish-Enlightenment discourse of the evolving states of civil society" to romantic historicism, and shows how, within these models of civic evolution, different societies are "theorized as moving stepwise through a series of stages sequenced in an order that is more-or-less autonomous and stable."[49] Barbauld's poem, or indeed the many other poems I have examined in this chapter, reminds us that such theories of evolutionary but uneven development are inextricable from—indeed, enabled by—the vision of the world made available by mercantile and imperial expansion in the eighteenth century. Enlightenment theories of the state of civil society are at root theories of imperial history, anxious attempts to meditate upon the rise and fall of historical empires and nations in order to generate supple new imperial worldviews. And in each case, the narratives of civil, or indeed global, evolution they propose are guided by the ideological and historiographical imperatives of an expansionist nation (and this is true even when the text questions imperialist priorities, as does Barbauld's poem). The idea of uneven development, then as now, is a product of contact between cultures possessed of asymmetrical power. It is perhaps ironic, then, that the poems considered in this chapter offer eloquent testimony that the asymmetries confirmed and exacerbated over the long century of European colonization came at a psychic cost for the poets of empire, who worried obsessively that, for one reason or the other, the "golden tide of Commerce" would abandon their shores.

3

JAMES THOMSON AND
THE "SAGE HISTORIC MUSE"

They contain a Panegyric on Brittain, which may perhaps contribute to make my poem Popular. The English People are not a little vain of Themselves, and their Country. Britannia too includes our native country, Scotland. After this I make an Excursion into Africa, which I intersperse, and conclude with some Reflections.

> —*James Thomson to a fellow Scotsman, David (Malloch) Mallet, on the composition of "Summer"*

I began this book with the claim that analyzing the vocabulary and concerns of "Rule, Britannia!" will allow us to understand crucial aesthetic, cultural, political, and economic values informing the work of Thomson and many of his fellow poets.[1] I have shown that such poets acted upon the belief that their craft played a role in molding social opinions and practices, governmental policies, and the very shape of the nation. In general, Thomson had Whig loyalties, and from the mid 1730s he was of the circle of poets and writers brought together by Lyttelton, whose politics were largely anti-Walpole, and whose prospects were pegged to the coming to power of Frederick, the Prince of Wales.[2] They were often on his payroll, and particular poems can be read as partisan interventions into the political debates that polarized the government and the ("patriot") opposition in the Walpole years. Both Bertrand Goldgar and Christine Gerrard have shown in some detail how these political affiliations and antipathies worked;[3] my project here has been to read these poems as expressions not only of the "patriotic" discourse claimed as their own by Lyttelton and company, but as articulations of a longer-lived, more nonpartisan, "nationalist" discourse. I am arguing, that is, that poetic terms and icons that took on an urgency and a currency because they were deployed in debates about domestic and foreign policy in this period tapped into an older history of usage (which they modified or qualified as necessary), and that they helped define both the forms of national self-identification and the symbolic and ideological formations of colonial and imperial discourse. Thus, one of the aims of critical practice today should be the explication not only of the political circumstances within which these poems originated, but of the lingering contribution they made to the historical conception of a "Great Britain."

Part of the reason for reading these poems in detail, as I have said before, is to develop a different understanding of some important reasons why poets in the long eighteenth century wrote the kinds of poems that they did: both generic innovation and the repeated use of formulaic images and topoi can be better defined if we realize the working difficulties posed by past poetic practices derived from cultures and historical moments whose material and ideological formations were different from the world these English (as some would have it, British) poets worked hard to imagine into being. The prestige of the pastoral, or of the Pindaric, or of the georgic in eighteenth-century Britain was a function not only of their classical origins, but even more so of the relentless reworking of these forms by contemporary poets in their search for poetry adequate to the definition of the nation as an international commercial and colonial power. In the hands of these poets, these forms took on a plasticity that is at once surprising and representative of the period, and that is perhaps the most precise indication of the influence on the poetic imagination of the new horizons of colony and empire.

I have also argued that these details are not to be found only in poems self-consciously weighty in their engagement with social and political issues: the "stuff of the nation," as it were, is *naturalized* into a matter-of-fact, everyday conversational consensus. And it is naturalized in and through the work of poets; it pervades their sense of self and vocation; it becomes an inescapable part of the paraphernalia of their craft. The fundamental figures of poetic self-representation, of the poet's relation with the world, and of the relationship of poetry and its world, are thus also tropes of engagement and intervention. I believe Thomson's vast corpus to be a signal instance of such naturalization, and begin my analysis of his poetry by calling attention to two quick instances that demonstrate just how conventional, how commonplace, such gestures of worldliness had become, even at those formal moments conventionally designated as markers of poetic retirement or retreat.

My first example is Thomson's "Hymn on Solitude" (drafted in 1725 and published in 1729), which begins with an invocation familiar from poetic figurations of the poet as solitary composer: "Hail, mildly pleasing Solitude, / Companion of the wise and good." Later, even as the poem becomes more firmly pastoral in execution, Solitude is confirmed in her *public* function. Surrounded by angels, Innocence, Religion, and Liberty (lines 33–40), the poet feels emboldened to look out from Solitude's "deep recesses" (line 42) and to denounce the corruptions of London. "I just may," he says, "Think of its crimes, its cares, its pain. / Then shield me in the woods again" (lines 47–48). Solitude, like all its other poetic and pastoral synonyms, is here a rhetorical redoubt from which to attack a public (and usually urban) target. We see a similar confirmation of the public role of poetry in "To His Royal Highness The Prince of Wales," which was written for the birth of Princess Augusta on July 31, 1737. In generic terms, of course, there is no more "public" form of poetry than the panegyric, and this poem is one of the mass of occasional panegyrics produced on demand by contemporary poets is search of patronage. The birth of the princess becómes the occasion for urgent commentary on the state of the nation, and particularly its fortunes overseas.

The poem opens with a partisan account of Britain in decline, one derived from Thomson's allegiance to the Prince of Wales, then in the midst of a well-publicized feud with the king:

> While she who wont the restless Gaul to bound,
>   Britannia, drooping, grows an empty form—
> While on our vitals selfish parties prey
> And deep corruption eats our soul away.
>
> *(lines 3–6)*

Thomson offers a prophecy of the return of Britain's glories once the prince's progeny come of age, but also once Robert Walpole's pacific and corrupt administration comes to an end.[4] And then, in a manner typical of the age, Thomson links his muse directly to the projection of British power internationally:

> May fate my fond devoted days extend
>   To sing the promised glories of thy reign!
> What though, by years depressed, my muse might bend?
>   My heart will teach her still a nobler strain:
> How with recovered Britain will she soar,
> When France insults, and Spain shall rob no more.[5]
>
> *(lines 25–30)*

The conventions of panegyric easily accommodate, and are buttressed by, this topical conjunction of poetic inspiration and patriotic aggression. At this moment, for Thomson, the power of poetry is the power of the nation-state, and its proper functions are twofold: the shaping of public opinion and the celebration of national strength.[6]

As this chapter will go on to argue, Thomson's longer poems, including the ones that made his reputation, are also similar exercises in the exploration of nationalist ideas. While *Britannia* and *Liberty* are extended and explicit meditations on British history, on contemporary mercantile, commercial, and political policies, and on the socioeconomic, military, and cultural history of European empires, poems like *The Seasons* and *The Castle of Indolence* also contain substantial passages on these themes. In fact, as I will suggest, even though in these longer poems Thomson's canvas is broader and more varied, the pictures he paints cannot be understood in their fullness without paying systematic attention to these sketches of world history or civilizations. In this analysis of Thomson's poetry, then, I am claiming that Thomson is best understood as a poet of empire, and that the study of his poetry should be part of our larger analysis of the intellectual and cultural history of empire building, of the development and exfoliation of British colonial discourse. Even as I focus upon the importance of Thomson's views of the world, and his energetic interest in mercantilism and empire, I will be drawing on the work of critics like James Sambrook and Ralph Cohen, who have paid careful attention to the philosophical dimensions of the pastoral and agrarian themes and theodicean values of Thomson's poems. Thomson's poems range through historical and geographical explanations for the development and decline of empires, cultures, and civilizations—explanations that provide moral, economic, social, and political lessons for Britain, at home and abroad.

Such an interpretive frame demands that we take the details of the construction and affect of these poems seriously, and not pass over them with a brief comment on their obvious patriotism or jingoism. Apart from the fact that any reading of these poems is only as good as its sustained engagement with their rhetorical and thematic features, at stake are at least three other issues of some consequence. One has been mentioned already, which is that these poems will contribute to our understanding of the efflorescence of mercantilist and imperialist ideas and compulsions in the eighteenth century in England. The second is that we will acknowledge the force of what John Barrell and Harriet Guest have described as the "cognitive functions" of poetry in this period; that is, the powerful sense in which long poems in particular offered descriptions of, and justifications for, different ways of making sense of the world.[7] Finally, we will better come to terms with the fact that partisan politics, nationalist aggression and imperialist desires are in fact the staple of eighteenth-century English poetry; to ignore them, perhaps because they are reminders that the practice of poetry in this period was largely caught up with contentious public debates and discussions and with the production of cultural and ideological values that we find critically embarrassing today, is to arrive at an incomplete and seriously flawed conception of the poetic and literary history of the period. In his account of seventeenth-century landscape poetry, James Turner reminds us that the "contemporary imagination was deeply affected by the spoils of exploration—we can scarcely open a volume of poems without finding some reference to the two Indies of spice and mine."[8] What was true of the seventeenth century is even more so of the eighteenth; if anything, the material benefits (and social and political changes attendant upon them) of trading and colonization were inescapable points of reference for any and all literary and intellectual production at the time.[9]

National Power and Its Pitfalls: *Britannia*

Britannia: A Poem was written in 1727 but published anonymously in 1729, with a misleading legend, "Written in 1719," printed on the title page. The poem is an attack on Walpole's refusal to declare war against Spain in 1727, in spite of Spain's provocative naval actions against British shipping. The legend and the delay in publication might be explained by Thomson's reluctance to make his opposition to the prime minister's policies clear, especially if we keep in mind his earlier dedication to Walpole of the poem on Newton.[10] However, there is no doubt about the poem's political stance, nor is there any ambiguity about its commitment to the idea of an imperial Britain made strong by its control of trading and maritime activities. The poem offers a series of impassioned images, vignettes, reflections on history, and related arguments that add up not simply to an appeal for belligerence against Spain but to a philosophy of history and of the progress (and decline) of empires. The poetic and cultural ambition that underlies this poem is announced in its epigraph, a quotation from Virgil's *Aeneid*.[11] Thomson's poem is not a national epic, but its vision is meant to be as encompassing and uplifting. As Virgil and the practice of poetry were to imperial Rome, so Thomson would be to his version of "great" Britain. It is at these moments that Thomson is most, as Sambrook puts it, "a child of the Union, and perhaps the first important poet to write with a British, as distinct from a Scottish or English, outlook."[12]

The poem opens with a description of a dishevelled, weeping Britannia ("Loose flowed her tresses; rent her azure robe"—line 6), who sits on the seashore mourning "the faded fame" of "her degenerate sons" (line 2). This picture of a ravished Britannia ("Bare was her throbbing bosom to the gale," line 4) is completed when she tears the "laurel" and the "bay" from her "majestic brow" (lines 7–8), a gesture that rids her as much of her imperial identity as of her cultural authority. The political context of such despair is made clear, too. An uneasy peace is no solution when war is in the national interest:

> Peace discontented, nigh departing, stretched
> Her dove-like wings; and War, though greatly roused,
> Yet mourns his fettered hands.
>
> *(lines 11–13)*

From line 16 onward, Britannia speaks: poetic voice is here national and prophetic, even if it is also disturbed. Though Britannia can see "future glory" (line 18) for Britain, and "rising periods yet of bright renown" (line 20), her present rage cannot be soothed

> While, unchastised, the insulting Spaniard dares
> Infest the trading flood, full of vain war
> Despise my navies, and my merchants seize;
> As, trusting to false peace, they fearless roam
> The world of waters wild; made, by the toil,
> And liberal blood of glorious ages, mine.
>
> *(lines 23–28)*

Britannia questions the "meek forbearance, this unnative fear" (line 32) that causes the lack of appropriate British reaction, and mourns the fact that British sailors on duty on "Indian tides" (line 34) are dying of disease rather than going to heroic deaths in naval action (lines 30–46). Merchants suffer because of this inactivity:

> A passenger,
> The violated merchant comes along—
> That far sought wealth, for which the noxious gale
> He drew, and sweat beneath equator suns.
>
> *(lines 46–49)*

Predictably, this account of violated Britons and "the proud Iberian" (line 53) leads to historical retrospection and an invocation of the defeat of the Spanish Armada in 1588. Thomson's interest in images of naval might is so strong that these lines, even as they are meant to suggest the Spanish pride that went before their fall, end up celebrating the Spanish fleet for its "cumbrous pomp" (line 74):

> When all the pride of Spain, in one dread fleet,
> Swelled o'er the labouring surge like a whole heaven
> Of clouds wide-rolled before the boundless breeze.
> Gaily the splendid armament along
> Exultant ploughed, reflecting a red gleam,
> As sunk the sun, o'er all the flaming vast;
> Tall, gorgeous and elate; drunk with the dream
> Of easy conquest; while their bloated war,
> Stretched out from sky to sky, the gathered force
> Of ages held in its capacious womb.
>
> *(lines 64–73)*

The actions of the Britons who defeat the Armada are described in terms that continue to pay homage to the Spanish fleet:

> My dauntless Britons came, a gloomy few,
> With tempests black, the goodly scene deformed,
> And laid their glory waste. The bolts of fate
> Resistless thundered through their yielding sides;
> Fierce o'er their beauty blazed the lurid flame.
>
> *(lines 75–79)*

For herself, Britannia contributed to this victory by raising "confederate winds" (line 84) that scattered the remnants of the armada.

This extended description of the power of the Spanish and the British victory over them allows Britannia to make a precise historical claim about the Elizabethan age: "Such were the dawnings of my liquid reign" (line 90), a reign that led to Europe being "Sustained and balanced by my naval arm" (line 95). The decline of British naval superiority means that the "immortal spirits" (line 96) who made this power possible are ashamed now

> to see their feeble sons
> Shrink from that empire o'er the conquered seas
> For which their wisdom planned, their councils glowed,
> And their veins bled through many a toiling age.
>
> *(lines 102–5)*

These appeals to past victories and historical greatness, while part of the topical agenda of the poem, threaten to present a somewhat skewed view of Thomson's priorities, which are to celebrate the commercial arts of peace and to argue for the necessity of military strength. As the opening of the poem tells us, "Peace discontented" (line 11) has almost abandoned Britain, and in its wake will inevitably follow much else. Accordingly, Thomson provides a long passage on the virtues and possibilities of peace, one important effect of which is to balance the emphasis on battle and bloodthirsty action in the poem so far. This transition between the celebration of war and the catalog of the benefits of peace also suggests to us the method of the poem—that is, the way in which it constructs its particular argument and apologia for Britain's imperial destiny.

Britannia's apostrophe to "Fair Peace" calls her "first of human blessings, and supreme" (lines 106–7). Peace allows all men to live in amity and enjoy the fruits of "honest toil," fruits that "idle, barbarous rapine but usurps" (lines 110–12). These oppositions between peace and warfare mount till they suggest a poetic bad conscience, one that registers in its images and vocabulary the carnage that follows upon military or naval action:

Pure is thy reign; when, unaccursed by blood,
Nought, save the sweetness of indulgent showers,
Trickling distils into the vernant glebe;
Instead of mangled carcasses, sad-seen,
When the blithe sheaves lie scattered o'er the field;
When only shining shares, the crooked knife,
And hooks imprint the vegetable wound;
When the land blushes with the rose alone,
The falling fruitage and the bleeding vine.

(lines 113–21)

In generic or formal terms, the surfacing of the violence associated with conquest signals the difficulty of returning to pastoral forms and conceptions once the iconography and symbolic apparatus of an imperial Britain have been put into place in the early part of the poem. And yet this notion of a settled, orderly, productive countryside, where wine, not blood, flows, is very necessary, indeed central, to the ideological schema of the poem. If *Britannia* is primarily an appeal for the protection and development of shipping, trade, and colonies abroad, it also suggests an awareness that there is a competing landed interest in Britain for whom a set of celebratory images must be deployed. Even if under some strain, the conventions of pastoral felicity and growth, historically associated with the country (particularly in its opposition to the corrupt and commercial city), still remain useful.[13]

This return to the pastoral, then, under the aegis of peace, marks the poem's crucial attempt to create an all-inclusive vision of a prosperous Britain, where country and city are united in sharing the benefits of industry and trade, even as "Science his views enlarges, Art refines, / And swelling Commerce opens all her ports" (124–25). Symptomatically, in a poem that protests the policy of appeasement so closely identified with Walpole, the appeal for a productive peace also focuses on a single agent, and takes the form of a wish for a statesman who would make such peace possible for Britain: "Blest be the man divine" (line 120), who

from the work of death
To grateful industry converting, makes
The country flourish, and the city smile.
Unviolated, him the virgin sings;
And him the smiling mother to her train.
Of him the shepherd in the peaceful dale
Chants; and, the treasures of his labour sure,
The husbandman of him, as at the plough
Or team he toils. With him the sailor soothes,

> Beneath the trembling moon, the midnight wave;
> And the full city, warm from street to street,
> And shop to shop responsive, rings of him.
>
> *(lines 131–42)*

The praise of such a man, and the benefits of the peace he puts into place, knits together (into a fabric we might label the national interest) virgins, mothers, shepherds, plowmen, sailors, and merchants—all those who, presumably, suffer during war. The statesman's presence is felt internationally, and his praise is sung "Till all the happy nations catch the song" (line 146).

That the song of Peace (lines 107–46) in *Britannia* contains as many disruptive images of violence as it does not only suggests a repressed sense of the suffering that inevitably accompanies imperial adventuring, but also reminds us that the purpose of this poem is to demand, and justify, the projection of British naval power. To insist too much on the joys of peace runs counter to the poem's agenda, which is why this passage is followed by a quick turn to the necessity of war, "when ruffian force / Awakes the fury of an injured state" (lines 154–55). War is justified, Britannia suggests, particularly when empire is threatened:

> "And what, my thoughtless sons, should fire you more
> Than when your well-earned empire of the deep
> The least beginning injury receives?
> . . . .
> What better cause, than when your country sees
> The sly destruction at her vitals aimed?
> For oh! it much imports you, 'tis your all,
> To keep your trade entire, entire the force
> And honour of your fleets—
> . . . .
> In intercourse be gentle, generous, just,
> By wisdom polished, and of manners fair;
> But on the sea be terrible, untamed,
> Unconquerable still."
>
> *(lines 166–80)*

Britannia continues in this Polonius-like vein, exhorting Britons to live up to and fulfill their imperial destiny:

> "Make every vessel stoop, make every state
> At once their welfare and their duty know.
> This is your glory, this your wisdom; this
> The native power for which you were designed

> By fate, when fate designed the firmest state
> That e'er was seated on the subject sea."
>
> *(lines 189–94)*

The problem with this last image is, of course, that the sea, however subject, is not a particularly stable medium on which to seat a state, however firm. Nor is this just an instance of the notorious slipperiness of rhetorical figuration. In this poem, which is also a meditation on the genesis, expansion, and devolution of empires in history, the disintegration of past empires once in control of sea trade and traffic is a constant reminder that empires rise and fall; thus any celebration of Britain's imperial future (especially in a poem written explicitly to mourn and warn against the loss of Britain's dominance over Spanish shipping) is haunted by a sense of historical transience. This fear of the dissolution of empire is one that surfaces in all of Thomson's poems (as it does indeed in all the poems written on similar themes in contemporary Britain). Elaborate, and some not so elaborate, explanations for the assured longevity of Britain's empire are devised to counter the destabilizing sense that to think of Britain as the latest in the historical chain of European empires, as inheritor of their economic power and cultural authority, is also to link it to a process of certain decline.

In *Britannia,* anxiety about the rise and inevitable fall of historical empires is dealt with by simultaneously invoking past empires as precedents for Britain and—as we have come to expect—the crucial detail that distinguishes contemporary Britain from such empires: the presence of Liberty. This preserves the chain of European empires so central to Thomson's vision of *translatio imperii,* and also provides a quasi-philosophical explanation of why the westward movement of empire will be arrested in Britain's coming to global power:

> A state, alone, where Liberty should live,
> In these late times, this evening of mankind,
> When Athens, Rome, and Carthage are no more,
> The world almost in slavish sloth dissolved.
> For this, these rocks around your coast were thrown;
> For this, your oaks, peculiar hardened, shoot
> Strong into sturdy growth:
> . . . .
>   strength, and toil for this
> Are liberal poured o'er all the fervent land.
> Then cherish this, this unexpensive power,
> Undangerous to the public, ever prompt,
> By lavish nature thrust into your hand.
>
> *(lines 195–207)*

In this "evening of mankind," Britain is home to Liberty, the undefined political ideal lost to other states. Britain is so favored because of its combination of "lavish nature" and productive industry (line 197), which impose an "unexpensive power / Undangerous to the public" on the nation. What that power might be is explained in the next lines, as Britain is exhorted to empire:

> And, unencumbered with the bulk immense
> Of conquest, whence huge empires rose, and fell
> Self-crushed, extend your reign from shore to shore,
> Where'er the wind your high behests can blow;
> And fix it deep on this eternal base.
>
> *(lines 208–212)*

Britain's empire is distinguished from all the others that came before in that it is not earned through conquest but through trade, whose "high behests" will provide it with an "eternal base." Since in this period, European conquest and trade went hand in hand, or one was often the prelude to the other, Thomson's distinction between the two makes little historical sense. It is nonetheless an ideologically potent distinction though, one that allows him to gloss over the contradiction between the view of Britain as the legitimate successor of past European empires (and thus itself susceptible to the mutations of historical processes) and as the eternal island home of the new British Empire (positioned at the end of imperial history, so to speak).

That this argument is tenuous is demonstrated almost immediately, as these lines are followed by a long passage that begins with a warning that the "eternal base" could easily be a "sliding fabric," which, if it slackens past recovery,

> gathers ruin as it rolls along
> Steep rushing down to that devouring gulf
> Where many a mighty empire buried lies.
>
> *(lines 213–17)*[14]

As these lines suggest, Thomson has a flood in mind, the

> big redundant flood of trade,
> In which ten thousand thousand labours join
> Their several currents, till the boundless tide
> Rolls in a radiant deluge o'er the land.
>
> *(lines 218–21)*

The point about this "bright stream" is that it can, if only lightly inflected, point

> Its course another way, o'er other lands
> The various treasure would resistless pour,
> Ne'er to be won again; its ancient tract
> Left a vile channel, desolate, and dead,
> With all around a miserable waste.
>
> *(lines 222–27)*

Before we go on to examine the full extent of Thomson's dystopian vision of a Britain bereft of the benefits of trade, it is necessary to note that trade here is seen as offering economic coherence ("ten thousand labours join") and as being important also to the political and social fabric of Britain, a fabric then fraying, as John Barrell has argued, under the tensions generated by competing economic interests and occupational specializations.[15] Trade guarantees not only international riches and control but also domestic harmony, which is perhaps why its failure or diversion away from Britain results in an extraordinarily vivid picture of Britain despoiled, economically, socially, spiritually. If Britain is "of her trade deprived," it will turn "wild / Sterile, and void":

> her princes sunk;
> Her high built honour mouldered to the dust;
> Unnerved her force; her spirit vanished quite;
> With rapid wing her riches fled away;
> Her unfrequented ports alone the sign
> Of what she once was; her merchants scattered wide;
> Her hollow shops shut up; and in her streets,
> Her fields, woods, markets, villages, and roads
> The cheerful voice of labour heard no more.
>
> *(lines 237–47)*

The cessation of trade spells here the end of the monarchy, the loss of national power and identity, the death of domestic commerce, and the ruin of agriculture. Far from being the appropriate "eternal base" (lines 211–12) of British power and empire, then, the "bright stream" of trade turns out to be changeable (the "least inflect[ion]" points it elsewhere—lines 222–23) and the consequences of its loss horrific.

It is possible to read such contradiction, and such dystopian visions, as the rhetorical convolutions and hyperbole of a partisan poem Johnson regarded dismissively as "a kind of poetical invective against the Ministry," but to do so would be to miss the centrality of such inconsistency and imaginative excess to the ideological schema of the poem.[16] *Britannia* begins by calling for a military response to Spain's belligerence, but its real interest lies in formulating historical and "civilizational" arguments for the expansion of the British Empire. Trade, rather than conquest, is to be the basis of this empire, and the primary reason that the British Empire will be exempt from the decline suffered by progenitor imperial states like Athens, Rome, and Carthage. However, even as that claim is made, the poem's concern with the histories of past empires makes it impossible to argue that empires gained by trade are immutable in the way that empires won by conquest are not: the elaboration of trade's "resistless" power (line 224) thus includes a powerful sense of the decline that follows upon the loss of trading power. No meditation upon empires, however hopeful and hortatory, can close itself off from a fear of disintegration, and this is the fear that surfaces in the desperate vision of a Britain that has lost its trading prowess.

Britannia does, however, rescue trade, and the present and future British Empire, from such dystopic fear; it does so by invoking one of the staples of the antimaterialistic discourse of the period, the corrosive effects of "luxury":[17]

> "Oh, let not then waste luxury impair
> That manly soul of toil which strings your nerves,
> And your own proper happiness creates!
> Oh, let not the soft penetrating plague
> Creep on the freeborn mind! and working there,
> With the sharp tooth of many a new-formed want,
> Endless, and idle all, eat out the heart
> Of liberty."
>
> *(lines 248–55)*

In this passage, luxury is a combination of sociopolitical evils (which destroy the "freeborn mind" and "liberty") and the culture of commodities (the endless and idle creation of "new-formed" wants). Thomson's representation of luxury as a possibly imported contagion is of a piece with the vocabulary of other eighteenth–century poets (John Dyer and Hannah More, for instance), for whom the creation of consumer desires that accompany, and further engender, trade and commerce was at best a mixed blessing. Luxury, that is, was often shorthand for an excess of trade—for the unsettling effects the riches generated by commerce were having on the class assumptions and social behavior of those traditionally excluded from consideration as consumers in late-seventeenth- and early-eighteenth-century Britain, and on the class anxieties of those traditionally possessed of landed wealth.[18] However, even though the specter of luxury haunts the discourse of expanding trade, Thomson does not specify the link here, leaving the former abstract and undefined. In his poem, Luxury (a moral synonym for too

much trade) now replaces the absence of trade as that feared condition that
weakens the sinews of state and nation:

> Sapping the very frame of government
> And life, a total dissolution comes;
> Sloth, ignorance, dejection, flattery, fear,
> Oppression raging o'er the waste he makes;
> The human being almost quite extinct;
> And the whole state in broad corruption sinks.
> Oh, shun that gulf: that gaping ruin shun!
>
> *(lines 263–69)*

The same devouring gulf ("Where many a mighty empire buried lies")
that had threatened to swallow a Britain uncaring of its trade (lines 216–
17) now opens in front of a Britain ravaged by luxury.

    This analysis of *Britannia* suggests that Thomson's poem is complicated
and internally contradictory in a variety of ways, but that each of these
contradictions is connected to a basic anxiety about the progress and future
of Britain as a trading empire. We have seen how the poem deals with a
series of inconsistencies between its retrospective account of imperial nation-
states and its prospect for Britain, and also how "luxury" supplants declining
trade as the explanation of the poet's dystopian vision of, and warnings
about, Britain. In each case, these convolutions of argument and theme
suggest the difficulties Thomson (and other poets like him) faced in their
efforts to locate Britain within a "civilizational" continuum that reached
back to the great European empires (Greek and Roman in particular) whose
political, cultural, architectural, and philosophical achievements these poets
claimed as the proper inheritance of Britain.[19] Though the awareness of
historical change made it problematic, if not impossible, to argue that the
British Empire in the making would not be subject to a similar historical
mutability, that awareness led also to a search for ideas about economic
planning, and for social and cultural prescriptions and moral-ethical exhortations
that would allow the poet both to imagine a global future for Britain's
empire and to suggest ways of enhancing and safeguarding those prospects.
If Thomson's poem tacks back and forth across an inconsistent variety of
intellectual currents, it does so in order to find the best way of charting an
uncertain, but nevertheless very attractive, imperial future.

    At this point in the poem, then, perhaps to offset the miserable future
promised by the unchecked spread of "luxury," Thomson returns to his other
quasi-philosophical staple, "liberty" (which we will examine at some length
in an analysis of Thomson's long poem of the same name).[20] Britannia now
invokes the blessings of liberty ("The light of life! the sun of humankind! /

Whence heroes, bards, and patriots borrow flame," lines 272–73) upon Britain. While "slavish southern climates beam in vain" (line 276),[21] Britain's possession of liberty will inspire both "public spirit from the throne" (line 277), and a pastoral future (lines 283–85), since it will

> the finer arts inspire;
> Make thoughtful Science raise his pensive head,
> Blow the fresh bay, bid Industry rejoice,
> And the rough sons of lowest labour smile.
>
> *(lines 279–82)*

Then, pleased with this vision of cultural and scientific progress, as with the attendant hope of an industrious future free of class tensions, a revived Britannia invites the poet to hasten to the "active aid" of the country (lines 286, 288) and to inspire British senators to new heights of patriotic oratory and action: she herself will "transformed preside, / And spread the spirit of Britannia around" (lines 291–95). This alliance of poet and nationalist, even imperialist, public muse, then, heralds the future of Britain.

Except that the poem does not close on Britannia's note of renewed vigor and energy but returns to the poet's account of the *disappearance* of his muse:

> This said, her fleeting form and airy train
> Sunk in the gale; and nought but ragged rocks
> Rushed on the broken eye, and nought was heard
> But the rough cadence of the dashing wave.
>
> *(lines 296–99)*

These lines can hardly be construed as suggesting that Britannia actually dematerializes into the spirit of nationalist revival promised in the preceding passage. Britannia sinks into the gale, which, only a few lines before, she has described as the "deaf winds, and waves" that are heedless of her "fruitless plaint" (line 287). The poem ends with both poetic vision ("broken eye") and voice ("nought was heard") impaired and despairing—an extraordinary finale to such a poem. A possible explanation is, of course, that Thomson here emphasizes, once again, the empty future that will result if Walpole's ministerial inaction and general policy of appeasing Spain are allowed to continue, but this pessimism sits uneasily with Britannia's call to rouse senators to patriotic action. In any case, this cessation of poetic voice, and the vanishing of the figure of the imperial muse, echo other moments in the poem where anxieties about the imagined future of Britain surface—as in many other eighteenth-century poems, the loss of voice is a symptom of a loss of public or national confidence. Wittingly or not, *Britannia* encodes in its progress and conclusion an allegory of poetic power that reminds us that the contemporary equation of poetry with public discourse was both enabling and fraught. It encouraged a breadth of concern and speculation but suggested nagging questions about the appropriateness or credibility of poetry as the proper medium for such historical and philosophical exploration. The performative fissures and contradictions of these poems also suggest the uncertainty of poets about the status of their formal contributions to the public sphere. In *Britannia*, Thomson imagines a public role for his poetry, but this role is best spoken in a displaced voice, and via the conventional figure of Britannia. When the vision of Britannia comes to an end, what remains, on the "melancholy shores" (line 286) of the would-be island-empire, are "ragged rocks" and the "rough cadence of the dashing wave."

Before we move to a discussion of similar issues in the form and argument of *The Seasons*, a brief comment on the "invention" of the poetry of mixed genre in the eighteenth century might prove useful. As John Barrell and Harriet Guest have argued, such forms arose as "a response to a pervasive sense that some of the older genres, epic and pastoral in particular, were incapable of representing the nature of the modern world, the diversity, as it was understood to be, of modern European society." Models of epic heroism were hard to come by, and only a sharply muted form of such imagining exists in the literally hundreds of portraits of exemplary figures that populate eighteenth-century panegyrical or commendatory verse. (The literary and cultural power of these genres was of course tainted by the structures of patronage within which much contemporary poetry was composed.) Pastoral was limited, as Barrell and Guest suggest, because the "ideology inscribed within the conventions of pastoral—more or less egalitarian and entirely precommercial—disabled that genre too from describing the divided and ramified forms of commercial society." To accommodate the range and diversity of contemporary topics, poets brought together elements of the epistle, satire, the didactic poem, and, most importantly, the georgic—that "branch of didactic poetry most committed to the representation of economic activity in a positive light . . . to produce the characteristic vehicle of eighteenth-century poetry, the poem of mixed genre."[22]

This literary-historical claim is important for our purposes, particularly as my analytical focus in the following discussion of *The Seasons* (in a fashion similar to the analysis of *Britannia*) will be on contradictions within the progress and arguments of the poem, and on those formal moments where the logic of voice or genre suggests tensions in ideological or poetic resolution. I will suggest that one important source of such contradictions or irresolutions is Thomson's desire to produce an encyclopedic account of the world, and of Britain's dominant place in that world. This involves the poet in a fascinating search for a seamless mercantile and imperial apologetics, and for a corresponding account of ideal socioeconomic, political, and cultural arrangements within England. However, as Thomson's poem looks outward and attempts to maneuver through the historical, civilizational, mercantile, and cultural themes and ideas that suggest themselves, there is little possibility of any kind of thematic and ideological coherence, except for the wish-fulfilling closure available to the theodicean poet. The poet's incompleteness of vision and understanding is revealed to be a product of his humanity: only God knows the overall pattern that reconciles the vicissitudes of human history and the diversity of social arrangements. This final resolution allows the poem to engage with a vast array of issues, and not to be overly concerned with finding explanations for the movement of its constantly changing narratives and descriptions: everything can, after all, be explained away in the invocation and celebration of divine creation. The result is a poem that is a fine example, perhaps the best of its kind, of the poem of mixed genre, especially in that *The Seasons* provides powerful evidence of the dynamic interplay of competing ideas and values whose poetic or critical elaboration (and resolution) are both a symptom of class and other ideological contestation and an attempted concealment of such oppositions.[23] As a corollary of such understanding, we have Barrell and Guest's claim that the formal plasticity and thematic variety of such poems, while not perhaps "invented for the *purpose* of giving utterance to contradiction," actually "*facilitated* the utterance of contradictions."[24]

An Encyclopedia of Nationalist Desire: *The Seasons*

As has been well documented, Thomson revised *The Seasons* repeatedly after he first published it as a complete poem in 1730.[25] As these revisions, except very occasionally, do not materially effect my analysis of the poem, I will treat the poem in its entirety, respecting the internal structure of its final form (*Spring, Summer, Autumn, Winter*) rather than the chronology suggested by the writing and publication of its constituent parts (*Winter, Summer, Spring*). In any case, my interest lies not in providing a comprehensive account of the poem but in pointing out just how crucial the sense of national identity, empire, and the historical translation of imperial cultures and identities is to Thomson's hopes and fears for contemporary Britain.[26] Even when Thomson's vision of past and future empires is not directly a concern, it informs a variety of motifs and formal structures in the poem. And, as I will go on to argue, the proper way to understand the pastoral elements in the poem is to see them as the medium for Thomson's exploration of the imperial vistas opening out for Britain in the eighteenth century. Insofar as *The Seasons* is about the progress of Britain as a nation-state, the scenario of this progress is one that features overseas and "civilizational" dominance.

In the opening of *Spring*, the coming of the season and the creation of the pastoral frame for the poem are both defined with reference to cultural and political icons invoked in the service of a particular, well-considered end for Britain. The poet will sing of the natural effects of the "world-reviving sun," and warns those who live in "luxury and ease, in pomp and pride" that his are not unworthy themes (lines 51–54):

> Such themes as these the rural Maro sung
> To wide-imperial Rome, in the full height
> Of elegance and taste, by Greece refined.
>
> *(lines 55–57)*

"And some" Thomson writes, who "held the scale of empire," returned home to wield the plow: "In ancient times the sacred plough employed / The kings and awful fathers of mankind" (lines 58–66).[27] The literary lesson here—the appropriateness of pastoral and rural concerns to poems on public issues—leads to the important political and socioeconomic analogy that Thomson wishes to draw:

> Ye generous Britons, venerate the plough;
> And o'er your hills and long withdrawing vales
> Let Autumn spread his treasures to the sun,
> Luxuriant and unbounded. As the sea
> Far through his azure turbulent domain
> Your empire owns, and from a thousand shores
> Wafts all the pomp of life into your ports;
> So with superior boon may your rich soil,
> Exuberant, Nature's better blessings pour
> O'er every land, the naked nations clothe,
> And be the exhaustless granary of a world!
>
> *(lines 67–77)*

James Sambrook's suggestion that the "implication of this whole passage is that the local harmony between the husbandman, his team, and his land is the foundation of the larger harmony of a wide mercantile empire which has cultural links with ancient Rome," and that this is one instance of Thomson's search for "all kinds of harmonies—natural, historical, cultural, social, cosmic," is of course correct, but it does not suggest forcefully enough the importance of passages like this to the poem's efforts to craft a national balance of power between the more traditional agrarian, and the newly expanding trading, interests in contemporary Britain.[28] Nor does Sambrook's suggestion allow us to see the role played by the discourse of pastoral in allowing such reconciliation. For that understanding we must notice that it is not the riches of the land but the "pomp" of a sea-based empire that provides the standards for comparison and emulation here (lines 70–73). And even as the "rich soil" and "Nature's better blessings" promise great wealth, they do so only on the assumption of international markets for British wool and produce (lines 74–77). (In passing, we should note the cultural and moral arrogance embedded in nature's mandate to clothe "naked nations" and to be the "exhaustless granary of the world.") In these lines, the future of Britain is clearly imperial and mercantilist, and it is precisely because Thomson so effectively mediates this future via the imagined pastoralism of the heroes and bards of the Roman Empire that he is able to assert the continuing iconic authority of the plow. In fact, in this passage, the role of the poet (Virgil, and by implication Thomson), the form of the pastoral, and the celebration of national power, are all inflected along internationalist, imperial lines.

Pastoral icons and images carry their own accretions of meaning, however, and their logic may not be easily amenable to emendation. Later in *Spring*, in a long passage Thomson retained in all editions of *The Seasons*, from the first to that of 1738, dropping it only in the 1744 edition, Eden, and Edenic social and economic values, are described as precommercial, and pastoral fleece as yet unbloodied by "Tyrian dye":[29]

> This to the Poets gave the Golden Age;
> When, as they sung in allegoric phrase,
> The sailor-pine had not the nations yet
> In commerce mixed; for every country teemed
> With every thing. Spontaneous harvests waved
> . . . .
>   The knotted oak
> Shook from his boughs the long, transparent streams
> Of honey, creeping through the matted grass.
> The uncultivated thorn a ruddy shower
> Of fruitage shed on such as sat below
> In blooming ease and from brown labour free.
> . . . .
> Nor had the spongy full-expanded fleece
> Yet drunk the Tyrian dye. The stately ram
> Shone through the mead in native purple clad.
> . . . .
> Nothing had power to hurt; the savage soul,
> Yet untransfused into the tyger's heart,
> Burned not his bowels, nor his gamesome paw
> Drove on the fleecy partners of his play.
>
>   *(lines 272–97)*[30]

The song of the pastoral poet requires a time—at once imagined and historical—before the operations of seaborne commerce; here, even the oak, that ready signifier of British state and naval power, provides not hardy timber but streams of uncultivated honey. No lambs lose their fleece here, nor their lives to the violence of the hunt; all that is to come later, when pastoral (and the Golden Age) fall into history and the circuit of commerce and commodity suggested by Tyre's mercantile prowess.

The withdrawal of these lines is, however, not the only way for Thomson to dispense with this equation between pastoral/Edenic idiom and a time before history. Later in *Spring*, the fall from the Golden Age into one of Iron is turned to ideological advantage, as it becomes the prelude to the contemporary political and economic resurgence of Britain. The poet, out for a walk with Amanda, points out to her a series of prospects replete with religious, philosophical, and political significance. The last, and perhaps most significant of these, has them climb to "the mountain brow / Where sits the shepherd on the grassy turf, / Inhaling healthful the descending sun." His flock feed and sport around him:

> They start away, and sweep the massy mound
> That runs around the hill—the rampart once
> Of iron war, in ancient barbarous times,
> When disunited Britain ever bled,
> Lost in eternal broil, ere yet she grew
> To this deep-laid indissoluble state
> Where wealth and commerce lift the golden head,
> And o'er our labours liberty and law
> Impartial watch, the wonder of a world!
>
> *(lines 832–48)*

The felicitous return of the pastoral—the ease of the shepherd and the frisking of his carefree lambs—are all guaranteed by the "wealth and commerce" and "liberty and law" of Britain, now the "wonder of a world." In this passage, the historical claim derives from, and supplants, mythology: Britain's prehistory is no longer a lost Golden Age but a past of barbarous disunity and warfare, which the mature nation-state has left behind.

This creation of what Sambrook calls a "pastoral-patriotic symbol" can be seen as part of the poem's larger attempt to forge a nationalist poetics that will offer a distinct set of identities and behavioral codes that can be thought of as uniquely British, and that set off the state and its people from the rest of the world.[31] While we will examine more consequential instances of similar differentiation later in *The Seasons*, a quick instance of such cultural practice is available in *Spring*. The later part of the poem, as is appropriate to the season, contains an extended excursus on love and coupling: the poet and Amanda walk apace; Lyttelton and his Lucinda tour their estate, Hagley Park; a virgin and her lover enact the travails of love and jealousy (lines 963–1112). Then, as Thomson describes the highest form of love, "Where friendship full-exerts her softest power, / Perfect esteem enlivened by desire" (lines 1120–21), he sets such ideal love against the "inhuman" practices of "barbarous nations":

> Let him, ungenerous, who, alone intent
> To bless himself, from sordid parents buys
> The loathing virgin, in eternal care
> Well-merited consume his nights and days;
> Let barbarous nations, whose inhuman love
> Is wild desire, fierce as the suns they feel;
> Let eastern tyrants from the light of heaven
> Seclude their bosom-slaves, meanly possessed
> Of a mere lifeless, violated form:
> While those whom love cements in holy faith
> And equal transport free as nature live,
> Disdaining fear.
>
> (lines 1126–37)

The harem is set against Christian monogamy (love cemented "in holy faith"); more importantly, the harem is explained with reference to climate and geography, and stemming from these, a perverse psychology (lines 1131–32). The temperate English spring here stands for, and makes possible, cultural and moral distinction, and underlies the claim to a superiority of amatory and marital practices. This orientalist reference to "eastern tyrants" and "their bosom-slaves" is also useful in allowing the poet to stabilize his discourse of temperate coupledom and coupling, which has been disordered by the heaving bosoms and "palpitations wild" (lines 968-69) featured in the tale of rural lovers whose sexual appetite leads them astray.[32] Their version of love—the pastoral disturbed by representations of excessive desire—is described, in an overdetermined tableau of exotic corruptions, as tainted by "luxury" (line 1003):

> Even present, in the very lap of love
> Inglorious laid—while music flows around,
> Perfumes, and oils, and wine, and wanton hours.
>
> (lines 996–98)

This species of love, and the disorderly lovers, while useful for the titillating descriptions that energize the sexual and moral allegory Thomson writes, is exorcised only when that form of "wild desire" (line 1131) is fully identified as barbaric and "eastern," as fueled by that fierce sun, as climatically and temperamentally not-British.

The coming of the sun, and particularly of noonday heat, in *Summer*, becomes the occasion for the poet to reflect on the variety of geological, climatic, and natural phenomena to be found across the globe. In each case, as we shall see, these variations are arranged to allow a sense of Britain's specialness to emerge, and to encourage a mercantilist and imperial conception of its national destiny. The sun is, typically, the "Parent of Seasons" (line 113); it is also responsible for subterranean riches (minerals and marble), for the labor that recovers them and the wars they engender, as also for "the nobler works of peace" that "bless mankind," and for the "generous commerce" that "binds / The round of nations in a golden chain" (lines 134–39). The following lines list the precious stones that result from the impregnation of "unfruitful rock" by the sun—the "golden chain" of commerce is inlaid with diamonds, rubies, sapphires, amethysts, topazes, emeralds, opals (lines 140–59). This listing of the fecundity of terrestrial and subterranean riches fathered by the sun is a prelude to suggesting that the international circulation of commodities has divine sanction; the sun is, after all, a stand-in for "Light Himself" (line 176).[33]

Thomson's descriptions of the changing of the seasons, and the coming of summer and the activities typical to it (labor is here rewritten as a species of pastoral play) are of course the primary text of this section of the poem. However, his account of the summer's daily round, and of sheepshearing, leads (as does the passage quoted above) to a claim that looks overseas in order to complete its "pastoral-patriotic" scenario:

> A simple scene! yet hence Britannia sees
> Her solid grandeur rise: hence she commands
> The exalted stores of every brighter clime,
> The treasures of the sun without his rage:
> Hence, fervent all with culture, toil, and arts,
> Wide glows her land: her dreadful thunder hence
> Rides o'er the waves sublime, and now, even now,
> Impending hangs o'er Gallia's humbled coast;
> Hence rules the circling deep, and awes the world.
>
> *(lines 423–31)*

This is a moment typical of Thomson's expansion of the scope of the pastoral-georgic in *The Seasons*: the panegyric to British power argues that rural Britain is the basis of commercial and naval strength overseas. Pastoral themes and images, particularly in this case the sun, are rewritten to accommodate and enable a new, expansive, conception of British national identity and power.

The divine mandate to bring home the "treasures of the sun without his rage" looks forward to a long passage in which the poet, himself in retreat from the full midday sun, asks "bold fancy" to "spread a daring flight / And view the wonders of the torrid zone" (lines 631–34). What follows is a long, exceptionally interesting sequence in which the poet gazes abroad and ranges the globe, offering accounts of differing climates, geographies, natural phenomena, and social and economic development, providing a catalog of all the "wonders of the torrid zone" that so excited the British commercial and imperial imagination:

> Great are the scenes, with dreadful beauty crowned
> And barbarous wealth, that see, each circling year,
> Returning suns and double seasons pass;
> Rocks rich in gems, and mountains big with mines,
> That on the high equator ridgy rise.
>
> *(lines 643–47)*

Even before natural features or geographies are described, equatorial lands are marked as the repositories of "barbarous wealth," of precious stones and mines: such an introduction to the commodities characteristic of this world colors even the catalog of fruit that follows, which is in any case a tribute to the pleasures of *consuming* such fruit and their juice. A familiar goddess, Pomona, is invoked, but her task is to lead the poet to unfamiliar, and faraway, groves and trees: lemon and lime, orange, tamarind, the "Indian fig," palm and coconut, pomegranate, pineapple ("thou best Anana") all offer "ambrosial stores" that are "beyond whate'er / The poets imaged in the golden age" (lines 663–89). In this catalog, the imagined consumption of such fruit allows the poet to claim an advance upon the experiences of earlier pastoral poets, particularly those who wrote before trade had made the riches of the globe available. The frame of reference is resolutely classical—the poet begins the passage with Pomona and ends it feasting with Jove, and Bacchus features in a description of the more "bounteous" juice of the palm—but such conventional familiarity only serves to accentuate the freshness and gustatory joy of exotic fruit. However, even this new and improved Eden is not free of the anxiety engendered by consumption. In a tropical variation on the theme of the recumbent *poeta*, the poet here imagines himself diseased and hot of limb, and asks Pomona to lay him "reclined / Beneath the spreading tamarind, that shakes, / Fanned by the breeze, its fever-cooling fruit" (lines 666–70). This image might mean to emphasize the therapeutic properties of the tamarind, but it becomes one more instance that links the lure of riches abroad with the wasting of the traveler.

The comparative aspect of Thomson's survey continues into his description of vegetation and flowers abroad ("Another Flora there, of bolder hues / And richer sweets beyond our garden's pride, / Plays over the fields," lines 694–96). The crocodile and the hippopotamus attract his attention, as do elephants on the banks of the Niger and the Ganges.[34] Thomson acknowledges that birds and their plumage are at their most colorful in the lands of bright sun, but claims that nature has humbled them in song:

> Nor envy we the gaudy robes they lent
> Proud Montezuma's realm, whose legions cast
> A boundless radiance waving on the sun,
> While Philomel is ours.
>
> *(lines 741–44)*

In these lines, the plumes that mark avian difference are not the feathers of live birds but are desirable possessions, emblems of the power of a native ruler whose defeat by Spanish conquistadors marked an early and crucial moment in European imperialism. The historical and cultural details whose overlay creates this arresting image link together a bloody history with the harmless victory of the nightingale's song. As at other similar moments in Thomson's survey of the globe in *The Seasons*, the natural world, too, is marked by the history of imperial contact.

This surfacing of the imperial unconscious, if we can call it that in a poem that is so consciously concerned with themes of colonial expansion and empire, brings us to a remarkable passage. Thomson invites his muse to range further, to:

> ardent climb
> The Nubian mountains, and the secret bounds
> Of jealous Abyssinia boldly pierce.
>
> *(lines 750–52)*

Poetic and imperial desire fuse here into an expression of arousal so explicit that it leads to a quick assertion of nonviolent intent, one worth quoting at some length because it allows us to see the convolutions in argument and analogy that allow Thomson to invoke the spoils available (in the past) to the merchant or imperial adventurer without committing Britain to the same violent course:

> Thou art no ruffian, who beneath the mask
> Of social commerce coms't to rob their wealth;
> No holy fury thou, blaspheming Heaven,
> With consecrated steel to stab their peace,

> And through the land, yet red from civil wounds,
> To spread the purple tyranny of Rome.
> Thou like a harmless bee, mayst freely range
> From mead to mead bright with exalted flowers.
>
> *(lines 753–760)*

The "thou," we must remember, is the muse invoked in line 747: the return to the pastoral (in lines 759–60 and in the four that follow) in the image of the harmless, flitting (georgic) bee distances Britain from imperial Rome (and perhaps Catholic Spain, as is suggested by lines 755–56) even as it rescues the muse from its earlier posture of aroused aggression as it penetrates the secrets of Nubia and Abyssinia.[35] But what lingers past this recuperation is the sheer difficulty of Thomson's position. The weight of past histories, and the importance of colonial gains in the contemporary moment, ensure that, even in a poem devoted to celebrating the virtues of "social commerce," there is no repressing imperial desire, or the sense that such commerce has so often proved a mask under which colonial possessions are robbed and the tyrannies of empire established.

A. D. McKillop has shown that Thomson was familiar with many travelogues and that passages in *The Seasons* are indebted to such accounts of overseas lands.[36] This is true of Thomson's description of major rivers, which takes him from Egypt to other parts of Africa, to India, Thailand, and the Americas. In each case, he emphasizes the fecundity of the land enabled by the annual flooding of rives: "All, at this bounteous season, ope their urns / And pour untoiling harvest o'er the land" (lines 830–31). The cultural weight of this trope of the "untoiling harvest," of a laborless abundance of natural riches (wasted on the natives), might be gauged from what follows, a long and very specific contrast between (tropical) nature and (British) culture:

> But what avails this wondrous waste of wealth,
> This gay profusion of luxurious bliss,
> This pomp of Nature? what their balmy meads,
> Their powerful herbs, and Ceres void of pain?
> . . . .
>   their toiling insects what,
> Their silky pride and vegetable robes?
> Ah! what avail their fatal treasures, hid
> Deep in the bowels of the pitying earth,
> Golconda's gems, and sad Potosi's mines
> Where dwelt the gentlest children of the Sun?
> What all that Afric's golden rivers roll,
> Her odorous woods, and shining ivory stores?

Ill-fated race! the softening arts of peace,
Whate'er the humanizing muses teach,
The godlike wisdom of the tempered breast,
Progressive truth, the patient force of thought,
Investigation calm whose silent powers
Command the world, the light that leads to Heaven,
Kind equal rule, the government of laws,
And all-protecting freedom which alone
Sustains the name and dignity of man—
These are not theirs.

(lines 860–84)

In the tropics, natural wealth is wasted and mineral riches are "fatal treasures" that invite violence and exploitation; in contrast, Britain has artistic, philosophical, theological, and political achievement on its side, so much so that the phrase "Command the world" (line 880) reads like a cultural imperative rather than an account of philosophy's access to general truths.

But even this contrast between material and more immaterial riches is not stark enough to establish fully the superiority of British culture. The sun, the source of tropical abundance, turns out to be a tyrannical and morally corrupting force there:[37]

The parent sun himself
Seems o'er this world of slaves to tyrranize,
. . . .
                  or worse, to ruthless deeds,
Mad jealousy, blind rage, and fell revenge
Their fervid spirit fires. Love dwells not there,
The soft regards, the tenderness of life,
The heart-shed tear, the ineffable delight
Of sweet humanity: those court the beam
Of milder climes—in selfish fierce desire
And the wild fury of voluptuous sense
There lost. The very brute creation there
This rage partakes, and burns with horrid fire.

(lines 884–97)

The tissue of oppositions—climatic, behavioral, moral—that Thomson weaves serves a simple propagandistic purpose; the pointed use of such oppositions, after all, precedes Thomson and went on after him to become the staple of colonial discourse and the imperial imagination for the next two centuries. In *The Seasons*, Thomson's encyclopedic and global vision encourage a survey of the features of those parts of the world that had become available to the

European imagination via travelogues and similar tales from the "contact zone," but his survey, like those travelogues, works toward the same general purpose, which is to represent the exciting riches of those worlds, to show why European commerce and colonization are justified for economic and other reasons, and to suggest "civilizational" standards that need to be exported in exchange for more material imports.[38]

The questions I am asking of Thomson's poem here are similar to those that Mary Louise Pratt has articulated in her study of travel writing: How has such writing *"produced* 'the rest of the world' for European readerships at particular points in Europe's expansionist trajectory? How has it produced Europe's differentiated conceptions of itself in relation to something it became possible to call "the rest of the world"? How do such signifying practices encode and legitimate the aspirations of economic expansion and empire? How do they betray them?"[39] Thomson's poetry, I have been arguing, is very much of a piece with such writing, and is the product of a time when the possibilities and the dangers of global expansion and empire came to occupy center stage in British culture. The generic eclecticism of his poems (which meld together elements of pastoral, georgic, didactic, and meditative poetry) their expanded canvas, and the scope of his questing gaze are all to be understood as demanded by his poetic ambition and the various possibilities suggested by the historical moment. Equally, the convolutions of argument and image in Thomson's poems suggest how urgently spokesmen for a commercial and colonial culture felt the need to fabricate convincing global explanations and alibis for its policies. I am not of course suggesting that Thomson's poetry should be read only as a species of imperial propaganda. But his poems do contain passages that hold together in tension the promise and the pitfalls of colonial expansion, or play off against each other the excitement of, and moral and cultural proscriptions against, luxurious wealth. Negative historical precedents are set against an aggressive conception of national destiny; the dangers of prospecting for faraway wealth and land are balanced against the knowledge of sea passages and established trade routes; and from this play of imagination and argument emerges a vivid world picture.

Of great consequence for Thomson's mythology of global commercial activity is the fear of alien geographies, and in particular of the ocean, and of the losses their storms precipitate.[40] In a long and animated passage beginning on line 980, Thomson writes of the "roaring winds and flame and rushing floods" (line 996) that wreck ships and drown sailors, but then derives from this scene of dangerous nature a story of the genesis of commerce, and of its European patriarchs:

> With such mad seas the daring Gama fought,
> For many a day and many a dreadful night
> Incessant labouring round the stormy Cape,—
> By bold ambition led, and bolder thirst
> Of gold. For then from ancient gloom emerged
> The rising world of trade: the genius then
> Of navigation, that in hopeless sloth
> Had slumbered on the vast Atlantic deep
> For idle ages, starting, heard at last
> The Lusitanian Prince, who, heaven-inspired,
> To love of useful glory roused mankind,
> And in unbounded commerce mixed the world.
>
> *(lines 1001–12)*

The victories of Vasco da Gama and the patronage of Don Henry of Portugal here ground a renaissance of trade and navigation.[41] In particular, the love of "useful glory" (the phrase a precise combination of bourgeois and feudal codes and values) is the inspiration for explorers and merchants, the new heroes of commercial epic.

And yet, even as this story of origins closes on a note of divinely sanctioned global ascendancy, the passage moves to a fearful coda, where it returns to the "terrors of these storms"—in particular, to the "direful shark" that follows ships. Given the celebration of commerce, Thomson's verse focuses strangely on the slave trade, a violent and corrupt instance of ocean-borne trade. The shark is drawn to the ships not simply because of the possibility of storm-wrecked, drowning sailors, but also by the particular conditions of life on board slaving ships: "Lured by the scent / Of steaming crowds, of rank disease, and death." In an unexpected twist, the shark turns out to be a hidden, coercive beneficiary of the slave trade, but one whose demands serve to equalize slave traders and slaves in a gory commonality of suffering and death:

> And from the partners of that cruel trade
> Which spoils unhappy Guinea of her sons
> Demands his share of prey—demands themselves.
> The stormy fates descend: one death involves
> Tyrants and slaves; when straight, their mangled limbs
> Crashing at once, he dyes the purple seas
> With gore, and riots in the vengeful meal.
>
> *(lines 1013–25)*

The shark is an instrument of equalizing vengeance—whether divine or poetic line 1025 does not specify—but this entire allegory of the violence at the heart of trade serves to qualify radically any notions of the "useful glory" of commerce that came before. As I have suggested earlier, Thomson's verse does primarily create functional mythologies of the power of trade, and in doing so it "encode[s] and legitimate[s] the aspirations of economic expansion and empire."[42] However, it also *betrays* them, enacting, in its dynamic and changing movement, attendant tensions and anxieties.

When Thomson finally recalls his "vagrant muse" (line 1101) from abroad, he does so in order to describe storms at home (lines 1103–68), and also to tell two pastoral tales, that of Celadon and Amelia (lines 1171–1222) and of Damon and Musidora (lines 1244–1370).[43] The return to the pastoral is also a return to the optimistic prospect of Britain, as Amanda and he go on an imaginative walk that overlooks London, Harrow, Windsor, and follows the course of the Thames:

> Heavens! what a goodly prospect spreads around,
> Of hills, and dales, and woods, and lawns and spires,
> . . . .
> Happy Britannia! where the Queen of Arts,
> Inspiring vigour, Liberty, abroad
> Walks unconfined even to thy farthest cots,
> And scatters plenty with unsparing hand.
>
> *(lines 1438–45)*

This panegyric to the rich soil and merciful climate of Britain ends in a pointed lesson on rural class relations:

> On every hand
> Thy villas shine. Thy country teems with wealth;
> And Property assures it to the swain,
> Pleased and unwearied in his guarded toil.
>
> *(lines 1453–56)*

Thomson's own cheerfulness is unwearied here: it leads him to see each city as full with "trade and joy," such that

> even Drudgery himself,
> As at the car he sweats, or, dusty, hews
> The palace stone, looks gay.
>
> *(lines 1458–61)*

Thomson's song of British prowess expands to include sailors and their ships in port; the former are generous, "bold, firm, and graceful," and they scatter "the nations where they go" (lines 1467–69). Lest this be thought somewhat impetuous, the poet hastens to remind us that British policies are presided over by "thoughtful sires" who are

> Sincere, plain-hearted, hospitable, kind,
> Yet like the mustering thunder when provoked,
> The dread of tyrants, and the sole resource
> Of those that under grim oppression groan.
>
> *(lines 1475–78)*

As we know, this theory of British intervention on the side of peace and justice overseas became one of the standard alibis of imperial expansion. In any case, even apart from colonial exigencies, nationalist rhetoric in eighteenth-century England highlighted the constitutional monarchy and parliamentary system in place after 1688 (especially in comparison with various European monarchies) as it did the claim that Britain was the home of freedom and liberty. It is a small step from there to Thomson's boast that Britain was "the sole resource" (even perhaps the "soul" resource) of oppressed people everywhere.

Not surprisingly, then, what follows is a long roll call of national heroes, kings, statesmen, and patriots: Alfred, the Edwards, the Henrys ("the first who deep impressed / On haughty Gaul the terror of thy arms"—lines 1485–86), Thomas More (who was the equal of Cato, Aristides, and Cincinnatus), Walsingham, Drake ("who made thee mistress of the deep, / And bore thy name in thunder around the word"—lines 1495–96), Raleigh ("the scourge of Spain!"—line 1500), Sidney, Hampden, Russel, and Algernon Sidney. This list expands to include scientists, philosophers, and artists: Bacon (who "in one rich soul, / Plato, the Stagyrite, and Tully joined"—lines 1541–42), Shaftesbury, Boyle, Locke, Newton, Shakespeare, Milton, Spenser, and the "ancient master" and "laughing sage" (line 1576) Chaucer. This catalog of great men is of a piece with similar contemporary efforts to draw up lists of famous forefathers, the memory of whose genius implied that Britain was fully prepared, politically, culturally, and philosophically, to assume global dominance. Thomson, unusually, also pays generalized tribute to the beauty and sexual attractiveness of Britannia's daughters (lines 1580–94), all as a prelude to a summing-up of the power of the island-fortress Britain:

> Island of bliss! amid the subject seas
> That thunder around thy rocky coasts, set up,
> At once the wonder, terror and delight,
> Of distant nations, whose remotest shore
> Can soon be shaken by thy naval arm;
> Not to be shook thyself, but all assaults
> Baffling, like thy hoar cliffs the loud sea-wave.
>
> *(lines 1595–1601)*

As *Summer* comes to a close, there are two icons toward whom Thomson genuflects in his prayer for the perpetuation of Britain's global power. The first is traditional, and the prayer an appeal for divine preservation:

> O Thou, by whose almighty nod the scale
> Of empire rises, or alternate falls,
> Send forth the saving Virtues round the land.
>
> *(lines 1602–4)*

The second is unusual and more compelling, for its blessings make possible British cultural and intellectual achievement, which in turn justify imperial dominance. Britain rules by right, a right born of civilizational superiority, especially when compared to subject (or potentially subject) nations. In a paean to "serene Philosophy," Thomson suggests that its power enables all that distinguishes Britain: astronomy (lines 1711–29), the "heights of science" (line 1741), and poetry, "the treasure of mankind, / Their highest honour, and their truest joy!" (lines 1753–57). Without philosophy, "unenlightened man" is "savage, roaming through the woods and wilds / In quest of prey . . . devoid of every finer art / And elegance of life." Such people lack domestic happiness, "moral excellence," "social bliss," and a "guardian law"; they have no agricultural or mechanical skills either (lines 1758–67). In contrast with Britain, they know only "rapine, indolence, and guile," which renders life worse than nonexistence (lines 1771–74). Nor do they possess

> the heaven-conducted prow
> Of Navigation bold, that fearless braves
> The burning line or dares the wintry pole,
> Mother severe of infinite delights!
>
> *(lines 1767–70)*

In this last line, the syntax of the passage allows us to read either Philosophy or Navigation as the "Mother severe of infinite delights," but perhaps it is most in keeping with the spirit of Thomson's verse that we see them as the simultaneous subjects of the sentence. Thomson embellishes this conjunction a few lines later, weaving together, in metaphors of comparative nautical development, the role of divine inspiration and philosophy in allowing Britain its distinction:

> While thus laborious crowds
> Ply the tough oar, Philosophy directs
> The ruling helm; or, like the liberal breath
> Of potent heaven, invisible, the sail
> Swells out, and bears the inferior world around.
>
> *(lines 1777–81)*

There is of course a metaphysical suggestion contained in the last line, in the divine breath that inspires the "inferior world," but in Thomson's comparative schema, the inferior world is that of oar-pulling nations; the sail that swells out belongs to the "ruling helm." Philosophy is an instrumental science here, inspiring, and identical with, navigation; in a crucial sense, this equation is the conceptual center of Thomson's worldview.

In like vein, *Autumn* begins with a long passage in praise of "Industry," whose "rough power" is the "kind source of every gentle art / And all the soft civility of life" (lines 43–46). In Thomson's elaborate schema here, Industry is the "Raiser of human kind" from a barbaric state of nature: it inspired all the "mechanic" arts, as also all science and wisdom, enabling both the development of a political and legal apparatus, and the emergence of cities (lines 47–117). While Thomson appears to be writing a synoptic account of the unfolding of civil society generally, he leaves no doubt that his model is Britain, for, without a change of subject, his verse moves on to talk of the commerce that chokes up "the loaded street / With foreign plenty," and to claim that Industry has chosen the Thames ("Large, gentle, deep, majestic, king of floods!") as "his grand resort" (lines 120–21). Industry builds British shipping, whose belligerent power is made clear: "whence, ribbed with oak / To bear the British thunder, black, and bold, / The roaring vessel rushed into the main" (lines 131–33). Architecture, painting, sculpture— all turn out to be gifts of the same Industry (lines 134–43). It is of course not unusual in eighteenth-century poetry for a personified abstraction to bear the weight of historical agency and power—I sum up Thomson's deployment of Industry's power to call attention, once again, to the specific historical schema Thomson develops, one whose inherent "progressivism" underlies Britain's claim to global dominance. And even before Thomson describes the riches of the harvest (lines 151–76), which is the certain subject of a georgic poem on autumn, he makes clear that Britain's wealth lies not only in its agriculture at home but in its commerce overseas.

However committed Thomson might have been to these Whiggish themes of progress, his poetic purposes did not allow him to remain content with this saga of historical advance. As John Barrell has pointed out, Thomson's "heroic portraiture," his need to include flattering portraits of patrons and other great men, led to an interesting contradiction in his accounts of British history or of the state of the nation. Since each hero was to be defined as a patriot who exercised his zeal on behalf of his country, it was necessary that the nation be portrayed as needing such intervention, as perhaps "divided and corrupt, and not as it appears in this economic account, as unified and blessed by industry."[44] This is why, in lines 910 to

928, Thomson reverts to a vision of Britain embattled at home and abroad and asks if there is a patriot able to

> cheer dejected Industry, to give
> A double harvest to the pining swain,
> And teach the labouring hand the sweets of toil?
> . . . .
>   nor look on,
> Shamefully passive, while Batavian fleets
> Defraud us of the glittering finny swarms
> That heave our firths and crowd upon our shores;
> How all-enlivening trade to rouse, and wing
> The prosperous sail from every growing port,
> Uninjured, round the sea-encircled globe;
> And thus, in soul united as in name,
> Bid Britain reign the mistress of the deep?

Thomson's answer is a resounding yes, and he invokes the duke of Argyle (Britain's "hope, her stay, her darling, and her boast") and Duncan Forbes ("whom every worth attends") as two men equal to the task (lines 929–49).

The expectations of heroic portraiture are not the only source of the occasional less-than-celebratory accounts of life in Britain. Later in *Autumn*, Thomson's revival of the Horatian theme of rural retirement (lines 1234–351) imposes its own conventional oppositions, many of which counter the force of the mercantile and imperial argument in lines 43–143. The *beatus vir*, the happy man, is conventionally retired from the "public rage" and corruptions of the city, which are here indelibly associated with adventuring abroad:

> What though, from utmost land and sea purveyed,
> For him each rarer tributary life
> Bleeds not, and his insatiate table heaps
> With luxury and death?
>
>   *(lines 1246–49)*

> Let others brave the flood in quest of gain,
> And beat for joyless months the gloomy wave.
> Let such as deem it glory to destroy
> Rush into blood, the sack of cities seek—
> Unpierced, exulting in the widow's wail,
> The virgin's shriek, and infant's trembling cry.
> Let some, far distant from their native soil,
> Urged or by want or hardened avarice,
> Find other lands beneath another sun.
>
>   *(lines 1278–86)*

The ethical imperative of these passages is clear, as is their literary-historical significance. As imperial dreams came to captivate more and more of the public imagination in Britain, it became less and less feasible for commentators to find a contemporary idiom free of the vocabulary of empire, even when they were rewriting the most traditional of artistic forms. Thus, a complex and historically specific picture of the "country" and the "city" emerges in this rewriting: the city is corrupt because it is marked by mercantile commodities and imperial violence.[45] This praise of rural retirement and of the power of "all-sufficient" nature to teach and inspire closes *Autumn*. Yet we cannot read this closure as a final movement away from the more aggressive public posture of the opening of the poem, for such a linear reading is at odds with the repetitive, nonteleological form and method of the poem. While the theme of country privacy and retirement allows for a certain moral cachet to be gained from the disavowal of violence and frenzied gain, it by no means overrides the poem's repeated commitment to a powerful Britain. If anything, it allows the poet to eat his moral cake and have his empire, too, or (to shift to a less mangled metaphor) to inhabit ideological and thematic contradictions without needing to bring these contradictions to crisis or resolution.

Paying close attention to such ideological contradictions in the poem also allows us to better come to terms with the formal characteristics of *The Seasons*, especially its encyclopedic elasticity. The poem incorporates rather than excludes, assembling an eclectic mix of recognizable generic codes and tropes, providing credible transitions between ideas and passages of description on occasion, subsuming such transitions to more pressing considerations at others. To say this is not to exempt the poem from Johnson's well-known strictures against it: "The great defect of *The Seasons* is want of method. . . . Of many appearances subsisting all at once, no rule can be given why one should be mentioned before another; yet memory wants the help of order, and the curiosity is not excited by suspense or expectation."[46] For Johnson, himself immersed in the sea of political ideas that Thomson's poem is awash in, the poet's lack of systematicity is primarily a formal problem, a lack of poetic organization or decorum. We can see, however, that Thomson's method (and we should call it that) allowed him to articulate very different, even opposed, ideas and positions into a series of arguments for a particular ordering of British power. Thomson wrote and revised this poem for more than two decades, and engaged with ideas, values, and discussions current in that time; that themes and analyses are repeated or developed into near-autonomous units within the overall four-part structure is thus the result of the poet's distinct project, which is to participate in a variety of public debates on the shape and purposes of the nation-state. The lack of poetic order might well be considered a formal weakness, but it is also the source of the poem's extraordinary range and ideological weight.

Thomson's political conception of poetic performance is both qualified and borne out by the poem, which at once claims higher—that is, metaphysical— motivations for the poet *and* finds ways of emphasizing his necessary connection with historical processes. If we keep in mind that *Winter* was the first part of *The Seasons* to be written, we realize that it constructs a template of poetic ambition and purpose: the poet, in "deep retirement," but in the company of friends, proposes to contemplate "nature's boundless frame, / . . . / Its life, its laws, its progress, and its end." Contemplation will first lead to theodicean revelation, to the awareness that a "diffusive harmony" unites "the beauteous whole," and that even in "the moral world," all that seems "embroiled" actually moves in "higher order" and toward the "general good" (lines 575–87). The vocabulary here is of spiritual and moral discovery; to scan the world is to see divine purpose writ large. Equally however, this scanning of the "beauteous whole" leads to a new historical and geographical consciousness, one that follows seamlessly on these metaphysical and theological insights:

> The sage historic muse
> Should next conduct us through the deeps of time,
> Show us how empire grew, declined and fell
> In scattered states; what makes the nations smile,
> Improves the soil, and gives them double suns;
> And why they pine beneath the brightest skies
> In nature's richest lap.
>
> *(lines 587–93)*

From this combination of meditation and discovery will emerge the exaltation of poetry and of the poet—of consequence is the particularly *public* and *nationalist* form of the exaltation:

> As thus we talked,
> Our hearts would burn within us, would inhale
> That portion of divinity, that ray
> Of purest heaven, which lights the public soul
> Of patriots and of heroes.
>
> *(lines 593–97)*

Thomson's priorities are clear here, as is his conception of poetry and a poet's fondly imagined rewards.[47] Poetry on important public themes, whether on the divinely inspired harmonies of nature and morality, or on the attributes of empire, will lead to that special animation that makes patriots and heroes of poets.

The connection between patriotism and poetry in *The Seasons* needs again to be emphasized if only because Thomson is understood essentially, and sometimes exclusively, as a poet of nature. In his preface to the second edition of *Winter*, Thomson suggests that the revival of poetry demands "the choosing of great and serious subjects, such as at once amuse the fancy, enlighten the head, and warm the heart. These give a weight and dignity to the poem." While these generalizations might apply to any or all of the subjects and digressive meditations contained within the poem, Thomson himself goes on to specify that he knows "no subject more elevating, more amusing; more ready to awake the poetical enthusiasm, the philosophical reflection, and the moral sentiment, than the works of Nature. . . . What more inspiring than a calm, wide survey of them?" The preferred poetical posture is thus of "retirement, and solitude," from which the best ancient and modern poets, "lost in unfrequented fields, far from the little busy world," meditated at leisure on the "Works of Nature."[48] Thomson claims the "rural Virgil," the poet of the *Georgics*, as his model, but there is little question that Virgil's other persona, that of the preeminent classical poet of empire, figures increasingly in the British poet's understanding of his vocation. For when the poet, in *Winter*, retreats to a "rural, sheltered, solitary scene," he contemplates not nature but Greek and Roman statesmen, military leaders and heroes:

> There studious let me sit,
> And hold high converse with the mighty dead—
> Sages of ancient time, as gods revered,
> As gods beneficent, who blessed mankind
> With arts and arms, and humanised a world.
>
> *(lines 429–35)*

Thomson expanded his catalog of heroes in various editions of the poem, till it came to include, among others, Socrates, Solon, Leonidas, Lycurgus, Aristides, Cimon, Timoleon, Pelopidas and Epaminondas, Numa, Servius, Camillus, Fabricius, Cincinnatus, Scipio, Cato, and Brutus. As a poet, Thomson will learn from this eclectic history of patriots and patricians, and follow the example of others in this pantheon: Virgil, Homer, and walking "equal by his side, / The British Muse" (lines 530–35). In his rural solitude, Thomson's historical sense predominates; he seeks the heroic or epic temper, and sublime flights of verse:

> First of your kind! society divine!
> Still visit thus my nights, for you reserved,
> And mount my soaring soul to thoughts like yours.
>
> *(lines 541–43)*

Thomson, like so many contemporary poets, argues that it is the coincidence of "arts and arms" that made possible and defined empires. Both heroes and the poets who sing their heroism are required for national greatness. It is thus perhaps fitting to close this reading of *The Seasons* with Thomson's lines on the hero of *Winter*, Peter the Great, who modernized Russia and brought it closer to the major European cultures of the early eighteenth century.[49] "Charged with the stores of Europe," Peter goes home to build navies and raise armies and expand the borders of Russia; under him (as under the poet?)

> Sloth flies the land, and ignorance and vice,
> Of old dishonour proud: it glows around,
> Taught by the royal hand that roused the whole,
> One scene of arts, of arms, of rising trade.
>
> *(lines 972–85)*

The Translations of Empire: *Liberty*

That Thomson took seriously the idea of one "scene of arts, of arms, of rising trade" can be seen from the length and detail in which they are worked out in *Liberty* (1735–36), which, like Addison's *Letter from Italy* (1704), begins in a meditation upon Roman ruins and moves on to provide an extended account of historical and cultural transitions in Europe ("to the death of mighty nations turn / My strain"—1.13–14). In each case, the poet thinks about the history of European empires in order to make some sense of the imperial destiny of Britain. The five-part structure of the poem—Ancient and Modern Italy Compared, Greece, Rome, Britain, The Prospect—and the prose summaries, indexed to line numbers, that preface each section, provide a quick and for the most part reliable guide to the thematic and ideological concerns of the poem. Readers and critics of the poem in fact have to fight off the temptation to let the prose summaries stand in for the poem itself. Indeed, in the analysis that follows it has proved impossible to make critical progress without summarizing large chunks of the poem. Johnson's comment ("*Liberty*, when it first appeared, I tried to read, and soon desisted. I have never tried again") continues to be persuasive.[50] But it is worthwhile, before beginning an extended reading of the poem, to quote one instance of these summary contents (of part 4, in this case) to note how they compress cultural, political, and historical theories into a narrative of civilizational transition:

Differences betwixt the Ancients and Moderns slightly touched upon, *to verse* 29. Description of the Dark Ages. The Goddess of Liberty, who during these times is supposed to have left earth, returns, attended with Arts and Science, *to verse* 99. . . . Sculpture, Painting and Architecture fix at Rome, to revive their several arts by the great models of antiquity there. . . . That sometimes arts may flourish for a while under despotic governments, though never the natural and genuine production of them, *to verse* 253. Learning begins to dawn. The Muse and Science attend Liberty, who in her progress towards Great Britain raises several free states and cities . . . *to verse* 380. . . . The Genius of the Deep appears, and addressing Liberty, associates Great Britain into his dominion, *to verse* 450. Liberty received and congratulated by Britannia . . . *to verse* 623. Concludes with an abstract of the English history, marking the several advances of Liberty, down to her complete establishment at the Revolution.

Liberty makes its arguments via repetition, which means that the same themes can be illustrated from various passages in the poem. But the repetition also indicates a deeper concern, one that animates much of Thomson's poetry, which is his need to establish for Britain parallels with classical Roman and Greek nations and city-states, such that Britain can be seen as the legitimate inheritor of their cultural and economic successes. As we have seen, however, it is important for him to demonstrate that Britain does not simply reiterate the form of once-great, now ruined, empires, as that would condemn it to the same historical temporality. The progress of Liberty to the island is thus an intellectual and poetic balancing act between the creation of a convincing imperial genealogy and an equally persuasive demonstration of crucial sociopolitical differences.[51]

In part 1, ancient and modern Italy are described and compared by Liberty, whose influence enabled the achievements of the former ("mine are these wonders"—1.40), and whose absence contributes to the desolation of the latter. Republican Rome was rich, for "nature then smiled on her free-born sons" (1.51); this plenty was also a feature of imperial Rome. Nature itself becomes a metaphor for the wealth of empire: "'See distant mountains leave their valleys dry / And o'er the proud arcade their tribute pour / To lave imperial Rome'" (1.67–69). Many well-laid roads, by "various nations trod and suppliant kings," (1.72) lead to Rome in her glory, but her most glorious feature is the senate, where "fervent eloquence, unbribed, and bold" (1.79) protects the interests of the "commonweal." Thomson here offers two lessons to Britain: that it was a *republican* Rome that was a powerful empire, and that power must be shared within the senate, not usurped by one master (1.75–88). The second point was directed against Walpole's control of the machinery of state and governance, and we have Johnson's wry dismissal of Thomson's position to confirm that Thomson's readers recognized the political parallels he was drawing: "At this time a long course of opposition to Sir Robert Walpole had filled the nation with clamours for liberty, of which no man felt the want, and with care for liberty, which was not in danger."[52]

The bulk of part 1 is made up of long descriptions of the differences between ancient and contemporary Italy, particularly Rome, with Liberty preferring the ruins of the old (and the testimonials to power that they offer) to the degraded present (1.228–49). The decline of Rome began, we are told, "First from your flattered Caesars," till Rome was "doomed to tyrants an eternal prey" (line 286–87). The contrast between republican Rome and the nation ruled by the caesars is used by Liberty to drive home a warning for the British:

> "Hence, Britain, learn—my best established, last,
> And, more than Greece and Rome, my steady reign;
> The land where, king and people equal bound
> By guardian laws, my fullest blessings flow,
> . . . .
> Learn hence, if such the miserable fate
> Of an heroic race, the masters once
> Of humankind, what, when deprived of me,
> How grievous must be thine?"
>
> *(1.316–25)*

This is the "care for liberty" that Johnson found tedious. However, for Thomson, the song of Liberty is the key voice in the imperial chorus the poet conducts. Thus, Liberty's account of Rome then and now addresses not only Walpole and the pacifist overseas policies of his administration, but the expansionist future of Britain, and the rewards that will bring.

But before Liberty gets to Britain, she provides, in part 2 ("Greece"), a long account of her itinerary from the "dawn of time," when she lived with "eastern swains" (2.3). What follows is far from logical in its explanations of either social transitions or in its understanding of the motors of cultural and economic change. Liberty abandons the swains when violence comes to their life of pastoral poverty and peace, but we are not told of the sources of this violence, except for the presence of "Lewd lazy rapine" (2.29), which personifies the problem rather than explains it. In making her way to Greece, she abandons in turn "my sons of Egypt," to whom she had taught "science, virtue, wisdom, arts" (2.47–71); Persia, which "frugal state" reverses into "luxurious waste" (2.71–74); and Phoenicia, to whom Liberty

> first disclosed mechanic arts
> The winds to conquer, to subdue the waves,

> With all the peaceful power of ruling trade,
> Earnest of Britain.
>
> *(2.79–82)*

Phoenicia is a precursor of Britain not only because it is a seafaring and trading nation, but also because it was "first for letters famed / . . . / Of arts prime source, and guardian" (2.75–77). However, Greece, the "promised land of arts," lies ahead, and urges Liberty's flight thither (2.85).

This story of (more-or-less) westward flight does little except provide an unsystematic list of "civilizations" before the Greek, and emphasize once more the indices that Thomson uses to explain the devolution of empires: tyranny, luxury, the absence of arts. Similarly, in explaining the rise and achievements of Sparta and Athens, which is what part 2 of *Liberty* largely does, Thomson emphasizes the obverse of these problems: Sparta, for instance, knew no "shock of faction or of party rage"; since it possessed no wealth, it suffered no corruption (2.120–22). It lacked fine arts, but was "the calm abode / Of wisdom, virtue, philosophic ease" (2.125–27). Athens, too, was "intense / To seize the palm of empire," and was the "hive of science" and home "Of active arts and animated arms" (2.135–44). Liberty's benign influence encourages not only military victories abroad but also the development of philosophy and culture. In a long apostrophe to Greece, Thomson writes in praise of Socrates, Plato, Xenophon, Aristotle, Epicurus, and Homer, and of sculpture, painting, and architecture (2.205–390). All these wonders disappear once internecine warfare allows Xerxes and his Persian forces to overrun Greece; from this, Liberty draws a predictable moral: corruption and vice and "vice-created wants" are responsible for sinking the whole state into slavery (2.490–500).

Thomson's concern, as this account of the first two books of *Liberty* might suggest, is not so much to provide specific histories as to narrate a historical progress that will illustrate themes and issues of consequence for contemporary Britain. Military prowess, naval and mercantile strength, a state administration that is not too centralized or authoritarian, patronage of the arts—these are the features of a successful nation that Thomson illustrates in his history of precursor imperial states. Thus, part 3 ("Rome") repeats themes familiar from part 1: Greek colonies in Italy extend the Grecian model of arts and arms and thus prepare the ground for Liberty to travel to Rome. In this section, Thomson's explanation of the rise of Rome, includes the imperial alibi par excellence, which is that the Roman Empire came into being to counter tyrannies elsewhere and to "set nations free" (3.82–87). Liberty describes the vast territories of the Roman Empire, and Thomson's verse swells to an awestruck crescendo:

> In this vast space what various tongues and states!
> What bounding rocks and mountains, floods and seas!
> What purple tyrants quelled, and nations freed!
>
> (3.254–56)

As an instance of the granting of Roman "freedom" to subject states, Thomson points to the Greek states set free of the Macedonian yoke by Flaminius. The Greeks are amazed that a conqueror would restore their liberty:

> how to generous ends
> To turn success and conquest, rarer still—
> That the great gods and Romans only know.
>
> (3.309–11)

Thomson's vision of an enlightened empire that extends its freedoms and protection to its vassal states was prescient; this, after all, was the political argument most useful to British imperialism in its domination of the globe, particularly in the nineteenth century. The story of Rome, of its rise and power, thus offers a fine didactic text for Thomson, and his version of the decline of Rome holds political and moral lessons for Britain, too.[53] Pride, Usury, and Luxury (here both moral and civic failings) play their parts, as do the downfall of the republic and the advent of the caesars. As other British "neoclassical" supporters of the Roman republic had needed to do, Thomson explains the efflorescence of creative artists, philosophers, and historians in Augustan Rome as a cruel trick played by the caesars. This is Liberty again:

> "What though the first smooth Caesars arts caressed,
> Merit, and virtue, simulating me?
> Severely tender, cruelly humane
> The chain to clinch, and make it softer sit
> On the new-broken still ferocious state!"
>
> (3.484–88)

Liberty is clear that the caesars are in fact "imperial monsters . . . / Vindictive sent, the scourge of humankind" (3.490–91). Thomson's description of the emperors, particularly the repetition of the word "imperial," which he uses nonpejoratively in so many other contexts, carries an uncanny charge—as if the sins of empire must come home to roost, and in its monstrous return, the imperial repressed spells psychosocial vengeance and dissolution.[54]

Part 4 ("Britain") brings Liberty home, but only after an account of Liberty's disappearance during the "Dark Ages," when Contention, Rapine, Scholastic Discord, Superstition, and Ignorance (the familiar horrors invoked in anti-

Papist invective) ruled in her stead. There is no attempt at any kind of historical specificity, and this parade of personifications helps to make medieval Europe appear an allegory of the collapse of reason (4.98–99). Liberty returns, however, by divine command, and brings the arts and science in her train, to foster the Italian renaissance. Sculpture, Painting, and Architecture learn from the ruins of classical practice, and the zig-zagging, westward movement of the arts, and of Liberty, begins anew. She raises "small republics" (4.269; in his notes Thomson tells us that these are Florence, Pisa, Lucca, and Siena), the seafaring states of Genoa and Venice, the Swiss cantons, and Geneva (the civic incorruptibility of whose citizens Thomson calls to the attention of every Briton). She goes by the hardy Scandinavian north but does not stay long (4.370–80) and turns her face south. As she does so, her narrative is interrupted by the poet, who cannot restrain himself from a paroxysm of nationalist joy:

> "O the dear prospect! O majestic view!
> See Britain's empire! lo! the watery vast
> . . . .
> Goddess, forgive!—My heart, surprised, o'erflows
> With filial fondness for the land you bless."
>
> *(4.382–90)*

Liberty's coming to Britain enables the poet's prospect of the British Empire, which vision is really the point of this entire exercise. Thus Liberty is welcomed by the Genius of the Deep, who promises his "sister-goddess" that Britons will have freedom of the seas: to them will belong all the waters that flow by the equator, the Poles, and "The vast Pacific—that on other worlds, / Their future conquest, rolls resounding tides" (4.407–18).

The Genius of the Deep goes on to emphasize the scope of the British Empire: Alexander and the caesars were limited to conquest on land, but Britons, "with star-directed prow," will "drive assured / To distant nations through the pathless main" (4.419–26). But Britain's oceangoing empire will not be based on violence; Britons will earn their triumphs by "deep invention," courage, and the "hand of toil":

> Each conquered ocean staining with their blood,
> Instead of treasure robbed by ruffian war,
> Round social earth to circle fair exchange
> And bind the nations in a golden chain.
>
> *(4.432–38)*[55]

In this version, Britons will in fact sacrifice themselves to further the cause of international commerce. But just in case the nature of this sacrifice is misunderstood, and before he returns to the ocean depths, the Genius of the

Deep underlines his partisan loyalties by using his "loud thunder" to shake "opponent Gallia's shore" (4.449–50). He departs, and Liberty approaches land and is received by Britannia and her "native genii": Virtue, Sincerity, Retirement, Independence, rough Labor, manly Indignation, and Religion ("rational and free") (4.458–573)—all national attributes that will flourish in the years to come.

Once Liberty comes to Britain, part 4 becomes a narrative of British history that begins with its movement away from "Celtic night" (4.624) and continues to 1688 and the Glorious Revolution, which is the "period destined to confine / The surge of wild prerogative" (4.1135–36) and thus to put in place the political balance of power that, in Thomson's argument, crucially marks Britain off from other past or contemporary European states. Liberty claims to have begun the process of limiting royal prerogative early and calls attention to the parliamentary representation of the "commons" (line 796), which Thomson dates to 1264. This raising of "democracy" resulted in the "perfect plan" of

> Britain's matchless constitution, mixed
> Of mutual checking and supporting powers,
> King, lords, and commons.
>
> *(4.791–816)*

So important is this constitutional "liberty" to Thomson that even his celebration of Elizabeth's reign, with its projection of "British thunder," its expansion of trade, and its "peace, plenty, justice, science, arts," is qualified by his sense that royal power was "uncircumscribed," and that "wild and vague prerogative remained" (4.939–50). Weaving through the synoptic history of Britain that Thomson writes is the story of the interrupted and contested, but nevertheless successful, march toward constitutional freedoms. The importance of other events, monarchs, and leaders is often gauged from their roles in making possible, or retarding, this forward movement. Liberty knows her fullest manifestation in Britain, which is "the palace of the laws," where kings and hearty peasants mix, and

> though to different ranks
> Responsive place belongs, yet equal spreads
> The sheltering roof o'er all.
>
> *(4.1180–85)*

Britain thus has nothing to fear externally, not "corrosive time" itself, but must beware internal enemies, the "felon undermining hand / Of dark corruption" (4.1188–90).

This story of Liberty is the prelude to part 5 ("The Prospect"), in which Britain's blessings are compared with those of countries and regions around the globe, and found superior to them. The poet, who speaks while Liberty pauses for a moment, testifies to the fact that in Britain even

> toil, by thee protected, feels no pain,
> The poor man's lot with milk and honey flows,
> And, gilded with thy rays, even death looks gay.
>
> *(5.5–7)*

At the end of that vote of confidence, and in the manner of *The Seasons*, the poet compares Britain with lands that "potent blessings boast / Of more exalting suns." Asia may have silk, jewels and "more delicious fruits"; Gallic vineyards may burst with "floods of joy," as does Tuscany with its olives; Arabia may have spices; "southern rivers" may have their pearls, Africa its treasures, and Peru its gold; the "new discovered world" to the west might have its "wealth and praise"—but all of this will never compare with the "matchless charms" of a Britain blessed by Liberty (5.9–31). As against this list of imported commodities, Thomson enumerates Britain's native charms: farms, the flocks that support the wool trade, cities and towns, oaks and rivers, capacious ports, and, above all, naval prowess: "All ocean is her own, and every land / To whom her rolling thunder ocean bears" (5.34–65). Britain is now the "Great nurse of fruits, of flocks, of commerce," as she is the "Great nurse of men!"—Thomson's song here is contemporary and urgent, a "strain the muses never touched before" (5.81–85).

Yet, in a pattern we have traced before, Thomson's celebration of British strength and power does not cease on this high note, for such celebration always brings with it reminders of the mutability of nation-states and allows disruptive questions to surface. This is the question that the poet addresses to Liberty: "'But how shall this thy mighty kingdom stand? / On what unyielding base? how finished shine?'" (5.86–87). Liberty's answer emphasizes civic virtues (5.121–23), and warns at length against "corruption's soul-dejecting arts" (5.307). This said, Liberty launches into what might be the most interesting digression in the poem, which under the guise of talking about the civic necessity of supporting "science, arts, and public works" includes a vision of the nation diseased from the corrupting flood of commerce and "saved" only in that it has been memorialized in its public works, its architecture, and sculpture:

> However puffed with power and gorged with wealth
> A nation be; let trade enormous rise,
> Let East and South their mingled treasure pour
> Till, swelled impetuous, the corrupting flood
> Burst o'er the city and devour the land—
> Yet, these neglected, these recording arts,

> Wealth rots, a nuisance; and oblivious sunk,
> That nation must another Carthage lie.
>
> *(5.375–88)*

How are we to understand this apocalyptic vision, where trade does not enrich as much as corrupt and devour, and the only recourse is to memorialize the achievements of the culture "on monumental brass, / On sculptured marble, on the deathless page" (5.389–90)? While Thomson might have been looking out for the professional interests of his fellow artists here, the impact of these lines, and of the comparison of Britain with Carthage, is at odds with so much of the breathless jingoism of the poem and its prospect for Britain.

What follows is a continued lament for patronage, in which the "finer arts" are described as neglected and public works as reduced to mere ornaments to "private gain." Britons are asked if they will yield in these matters to France (5.436–46), and Liberty points out again that the arts flourish best under her aegis. She closes her appeal on a note of promise though: when "imperial bounty" joins with her—presumably in promoting the public arts—then Britain will benefit from "every harvest" of every land, from "whate'er invention, art, / Creating toil, and nature can produce" (5.544–48). Cheered by this, the poet prays for, and is granted, a vision of the future, and a mighty vision of British power and social and cultural achievement it is, too: a time comes when "with Rome / Might vie our grandeur, and with Greece our art!" (5.572–73). Princes and kings will maintain the kingdom for "public glory," clear scholarship will produce "Men, patriots, chiefs, and citizens," justice will shine on all, "social labour" will flourish and "beauteous order" will reign (5.574–625). All this domestic strength will go hand in hand with domination abroad:

> The winds and seas are Britain's wide domain,
> And not a sail but by permission spreads.
>   "Lo! swarming southward on rejoicing suns
> Gay colonies extend."
>
> *(5.636–39)*

These colonies, the poet tells us, are not "built on rapine, servitude, and woe" but are meant as refuges for people escaping bigotry, and as an instance he offers Oglethorpe's founding of the colony of Georgia. More of the beatific vision of domestic concord follows, including accounts of the harmonious dance of the sister arts and of the building of many public works. The poet's prophecy ends in a testimonial to the impregnability of the island-nation, as even the "baffled storm," repelled by the "broad imperious mole," roars indignantly (5.647–716).

And yet that is not how the poem ends. It closes not on this note of redoubtable triumph but with the cessation of the poet's vision and his return to the broken monuments that first occasioned his meditation on empire:

> As thick to view these varied wonders rose,
> Shook all my soul with transport, unassured
> The Vision broke; and on my waking eye
> Rushed the still ruins of dejected Rome.
>
> *(5.717–20)*

Once again, doubly ironic in that it closes the poem, the poet's dynamic vision of British glory fragments into an awareness of the mutability of empires, and of the still ruins they leave behind. If *Liberty* is a monument to the dream of empire that so energized Thomson and his contemporaries, both poets and seafarers, painters and merchants, sculptors and politicians, writers and citizens, it is also a reminder that this dream was far from seamless or consistent (or even comforting), and that it included many reminders of the costs and hesitations of overseas triumph. *Liberty* is, for the most part, Thomson's voyage through history and geography to find a convincing historical narrative whose cultural and temporal logic would guarantee, in perpetuity, the progress of the British empire. It is also, as I have pointed out here, a record of the difficulty of sustaining such narratives. Thomson's hesitations are of course overdetermined: the uncertainty underscoring "Thomson's prophecy of British cultural supremacy" in *Liberty* may in fact stem from the poet's uncertainty about appropriate monarchical patronage and encouragement.[56] The poet's vocational anxiety is confirmed by his choice of historical and prophetic themes, and compounded by his equation of British cultural supremacy with imperial power; for, as we have seen, the imaginative celebration of imperial culture is a complex and inconsistent process, one forever haunted by a sense of the rise and fall of prior empires.

Back to the Future: Revivalism and *The Castle of Indolence*

The frame of classical reference that motivates Thomson's understanding of British history and culture is found in *The Castle of Indolence*, too, where Greece, Athens, and Rome are invoked as the artistic and political models for a Britain fired by the spirit of Industry: Homer (whose song "fired the breast / To thirst of glory and heroic deeds") and Virgil show the way to Spenser, Shakespeare, and Milton (canto 2, stanza 52). Thomson's new national hero, Sir Industry (a wonderful fusion of the fanciful apparatus of late medieval chivalry and the more utilitarian poetic enthusiasm of the eighteenth century), has kept alive—and this is as important as the classical inspiration mentioned above—a species of poetry very important to Thomson (cf. *Winter*, lines 587–93, discussed above): but for the influence of Industry, "Dumb, too, had been the sage historic muse, / And perished all the sons of ancient fame" (2.53). Sir Industry, Knight of Arts and Industry, is himself the one who civilizes the "barbarous world," and a figure for cultural and imperial translation, for the westward progress of empire:

> Still, as he passed, the nations he sublimes,
> And calls forth arts and virtue with his ray:
> Then Egypt, Greece and Rome their golden times
> Successive had; but now in ruins gray
> They lie, to slavish sloth and tyranny a prey.
>
> To crown his toils, Sir Industry then spread
> The swelling sail, and made for Britain's coast.
>
> *(2.16–17)*

Once in Britain, Industry likes its soil and climate and the impregnability of the island, and decides to stay:

> "Be this my great, my chosen isle! (he cries)
> This—whilst my labours liberty sustains—
> This Queen of Ocean all assault disdains."
>
> *(2.18)*

The future that Industry orchestrates for Britain is the present as Thomson usually represents it: agrarian and commercial prosperity, British merchants traveling the globe without doing violence, and naval power that can, however, be projected far overseas:

> Then towns he quickened with mechanic arts,
> And bade the fervent city glow with toil;
> Bade social commerce raise reknownèd marts,
> Join land to land, and marry soil to soil,
> Unite the poles, and without bloody spoil
> Bring home of either Ind the gorgeous stores;
> Or, should despotic rage the world embroil,
> Bade tyrants tremble on remotest shores,
> While o'er the encircling deep Britannia's thunder roars.
>
> *(2.20)*

Following upon this westward movement of power are the arts, invited once again by the knight: "The drooping Muses then he westward called" from their home in Greece (2.21). However, a familiar caveat is entered into this account of the knight's successful translation of the arts to Britain: "Yet the fine arts were what he finished least," and this because they require

> The growth of labouring time, and slow increast;
> Unless, as seldom chances, it should fall
> That mighty patrons the coy sisters call
> Up to the sunshine of uncumbered ease.
>
> *(2.22)*

Thomson's professional realism here continues into a complaint about the lack of patronage in contemporary Britain (2.23), but even this topical complaint is not allowed to mar the nationalist pieties being detailed in this account of the coming of arms and arts to Britain. For if there is no authentic Maecenas available, there is, for poets, a loftier (if less material) inspiration: "The eternal patron, Liberty; whose flame, / While she protects, inspires the noblest strains" (2.23). This is particularly apposite, we are told, for the knight had "framed in Britain-land / A matchless form of glorious government," in which "sovereign laws" and the "free consent" of the people lent the monarchy its majesty. Once this is done, the knight moves to a life of rural retirement, where he "Commixed the chief, the patriot, and the swain" (2.25), till he is requested to combat the Wizard of Indolence, whose seductive spell threatens Britain.[57]

All this is familiar from Thomson's oeuvre, and perhaps little commentary is needed. However, it does seem oddly appropriate to find, in the last poem that Thomson wrote, and one with which he tinkered for "fourteen or fifteen years" that two versions of Britain are represented in competition.[58] Canto 1 embodies the luxuriantly pastoral, work-less bliss provided by the Wizard of Indolence, while canto 2 describes the country as it should be, provided citizens play their assigned roles: some in courts, some in camps, some in the senates,

> To high discovery some, that new creates
> The face of earth; some to the thriving mart;
> Some to the rural reign, and softer fates;
> To the sweet muses some, who raise the heart:
> All glory shall be yours, all nature, and all art.
>
> *(2.60)*

The moral and didactic weight of the poem is of course on the side of the Knight of Arts and Industry, and of the Britain he builds, but most readers of *The Castle of Indolence* have felt, as Douglas Grant does, that the first canto is "by far the finer of the two."[59] It may well be that the Spenserian stanza Thomson writes is best suited to the slow and rich development of image and mood that is the subject of the first canto, and that the lingering alexandrine (if nothing else) undermines the resolute postures and action demanded by the second.[60] But there are also other factors at play here, some of which correspond to those elements in Thomson's poetic and cultural vocabulary that we have examined so far.

The wizard outlines his world of indolence in two parts; the first, which describes the landscape around his castle, also includes the song he sings to seduce people into living the life he offers (1.2–19). The representation of the landscape is straightforwardly that of pastoral, full with "images of rest / Sleep-soothing groves and quiet lawns between," "glittering streamlets," "vacant shepherds," "sweet Philomel," and "stock-doves." The landscape inspires "perfect ease," as does the surprisingly persuasive song of the wizard, who argues (as pastoral or the poetry of rural retirement often did) that an ethical exit from the venal cares of the world is entirely appropriate: "For interest, envy, pride, and strife are banished hence" (1.15). The wizard offers a virtuous "repose of mind" (1.16) and argues that it is "grievous folly! to heap up estate" (1.19) when one can live "Above the reach of wild ambition's wind, / Above those passions that this world deform" (1.16). The second part of the world of indolence is the much more problematic life of the castle, where the interior of the castle comes to stand for a luxurious and morally enfeebled life that is at odds with the pastoral simplicities promised earlier. This happens because the castle is the repository of riches and commodities from all over the world, so much so that its "luxurious state" resembles that of the caliph's palace (1.42), rather than the more austere, if labor-free, life of rural retirement. The castle is described in terms of an orientalist fantasy of "quilts on quilts, on carpets spread"; the "pride of Turkey and of Persia land" are so thickly strewn about "that each spacious room was one full-swelling bed" (1.33). Everywhere there are tables loaded with wine and "rich viands" imported from around the world:

> Whatever sprightly juice or tastful food
> On the green bosom of this Earth are found,
> And all old Ocean genders in his round—
> Some hand unseen these silently displayed.
>
> *(1.34)*

The poet, himself in thrall to the wizard, is clear about the source of castle's power and its seductions. He tries to disengage his muse from the "artful phantoms" of the castle, who

> thus in dreams voluptuous, soft, and bland,
> Poured all the Arabian heaven upon our nights,
> And blessed them oft besides with more refined delights.
>
> *(1.45)*

In order to overcome from the cloying bliss of indolence, he prays to "the sacred shades of Greece and Rome," who "virtue with a look impart" (1.47). This opposition between the "Arabian" and the Graeco-Roman, the former a figure for corruption and the latter for virtue, has been prepared for earlier, when the poet, fearful of being forever immured in indolent luxury, promises his muse ("Thou imp of Jove, touched by celestial fire!") that it will sing a more martial and heroic song:

> Thou yet shalt sing of war, and actions fair,
> Which the bold sons of Britain will inspire;
> Of ancient bards thou yet shalt sweep the lyre.
>
> *(1.32)*

In canto 2, after indolence has spread "luxurious vices" over the land (2.29), the bard sings precisely such a nationalist strain. In order to rouse those who are under the wizard's spell, he plays upon his "British harp" (2.46), reminding them of a lineage that fuses the English achievements of Milton, Shakespeare, and Spenser (2.52) with classical precursors:

> "It was not by vile loitering in ease
> That Greece obtained the brighter palm of art;
> That soft yet ardent Athens learned to please,
> . . . .
> It was not thence majestic Rome arose,
> And o'er the nations shook her conquering dart."
>
> *(2.50)*

Thus, even if the world of indolence is the world of pastoral felicity corrupted by the importation of foreign, particularly "oriental" commodities, the poem guards against any suggestion that the fear of luxurious consumption should force Britain to give up its dreams of overseas trade and empire. The cure for indolence is allegiance to the more Spartan tradition that Britain inherits, a tradition that in fact encourages expansionist visions. In his other poems, we have seen how Thomson constantly worries that the same machinery that makes overseas power possible also brings home moral blight, and that all his historical investigations into past empires, including those of Greece and Rome, emphasize the role played by "luxury" in hastening their decline. In *The Castle of Indolence,* however, the allegory he produces inoculates the Graeco-Roman model represented by the Knight of Arts and Industry from such contagion, which is now identified with the Wizard of Indolence and his "orientalized" castle. The knight, exemplar of global discovery (2.11), the mechanic arts and naval sciences (2.12), trained in the sculpture and poetry of Greece (2.13), knows the proper way "a barbarous world to civilize" (2.14). Canto 2, of course, shows us the knight winning the battle for the soul of Britain, but it is instructive to note, once more, that the poem ends with a punitive vision of the sufferings of those who, because they will not follow his lead, are transformed into the equivalent of a pack of snuffling swine in an English village (2.77–81).

In a comment on the "confidence of James Thomson and the mid-eighteenth-century 'Georgic' poets," John Lucas writes that their "praise of 'rich industry' makes for an absolute coincidence of self- and national interest. 'Industry' here is both those who labor and those who direct labor. All are rich. Work for one is wealth for all. Wealth for one is work for all."[61] In my analysis, I have also paid attention to the *difficulty* Thomson has in composing what Lucas calls his "culture of conformity."[62] Since this harmonious order and perfect simultaneity of national interests did not exist in the life of Britain, Thomson's poetry can be read, as John Barrell suggests, as structured around ambiguities that "proceed from the nature of the task that Thomson has set himself, of justifying the fruits of social division, while denying at the same time that any serious social divisions exist."[63] In each case, as in the case of most materialist criticism of Thomson, the poet's social views, cultural concerns, and aesthetic productivity are seen to follow from his investment in particular arrangements of domestic power. My reading of Thomson's major poems has argued that his contribution to the imagining of the British nation can be fully understood only when we realize that his canvas depicted both Britain at home—landscapes of peace, equity, and plenty—and Britain abroad, a Britain that was inevitably a product of its mercantile adventuring and colonial ambitions overseas.

To that extent, Thomson the opposition poet is also Thomson the poet of a nation ambitiously larger than the sum of its domestic politics. To see him as an exemplar of the making of colonial discourse in this period is perhaps to recall his poetic craft and oeuvre to a new centrality in our narratives of the literary history of the eighteenth century. This is the poet industrious in the service of the new national aspiration for power across the globe, a figure whose importance has still to receive appropriate critical or literary-historical attention. Nor is this simply the poetry of seamless and arrogant chauvinism, for I have argued that such poems are more often than not also witness to the anxieties and hesitations of nationalist aspiration even as they celebrate imperial expansion. The twists and turns of form and argument in Thomson's poems, I have shown, chart for us the desires and the difficulties of the eighteenth-century poet in his search for a place in the sun, particularly when that search had expanded to include unknown geographies and new possibilities:

> Should fate command me to the farthest verge
> Of the green earth, to distant barbarous climes,
> Rivers unknown to song, where first the sun
> Gilds Indian mountains, or his setting beam
> Flames on the Atlantic isles, 'tis nought to me.[64]

These lines (100–104) from "A Hymn on the Seasons" suggest once more both the expansive movement of, and the fears that follow upon, the poetic imagination as it ranges across the globe. If "Indian mountains" and the "Atlantic isles" mark the limits of the contemporary imagination, they do so because they are also markers of Britain's holdings and presence abroad. There is no question of the poet's aspiration, even if he claims that his imagination is directed by divine fate rather than poetic desire; but these lines also make clear the unsettling force of the little-known and the unknown. Thomson invokes "fate" to explain the movement of his verse, a trope that functions as an individualized form of the more powerful compulsions of manifest destiny, the divine force that directs nations and offers comfort ("'tis nought to me") via the idea of a guiding and protective divine presence everywhere. Here, Thomson's "Hymn" enshrines this faith that contact with even the furthest, most hostile, reaches of the globe will yield proofs of God's benevolence. At other moments, as we have seen, such wish fulfillment did not come easily to Thomson, whose poems remain, for that reason, compendious examples of the contours and contortions of the imperial imagination.

4

THE MYTHOPOETICS OF
COMMERCIAL EXPANSION

Were we not ourselves made and not born civil in our progenitors days? And were not Caesar's Britaines as brutish as Virginians? The Roman swords were best teachers of civility to this and other countries near us.

—*William Strachey,* True Reportory of the Wracke

THOROWGOOD: Methinks I would not have you learn the method of merchandise and practise it hereafter, merely as a means of getting wealth; 'twill be well worth your pains to study it as a science, to see how it is founded in reason and the nature of things; how it promotes humanity, as it has opened and yet keeps up an intercourse between nations far remote from one another in situation, customs and religion; promoting arts, industry, peace and plenty; by mutual benefits diffusing mutual love from pole to pole.

TRUEMAN: Something of this I have considered, and hope, by your assistance, to extend my thoughts much farther. I have observed those countries where trade is promoted and encouraged do not make discoveries to destroy, but to improve, mankind; by love and friendship to tame the fierce and polish the most savage; to teach them the advantages of honest traffic by taking from them, with their own consent, their useless superfluities, and giving them in return what, from their ignorance in manual arts, their situation, or some other accident, they stand in need of.

THOROWGOOD: 'Tis justly observed. The populous East, luxuriant, abounds with glittering gems, bright pearls, aromatic spices, and health-restoring drugs. The late found western world's rich earth glows with unnumbered veins of gold and silver ore. On every climate and every country heaven has bestowed some good peculiar to itself. It is the industrious merchant's business to collect the various blessings of each soil and climate, and, with the product of the whole, to enrich his native country. (Lillo, *The London Merchant*, 3.1.1–33)

In this exchange between London merchant and apprentice, George Lillo produces the exemplary scene of eighteenth-century mercantilist education. Thorowgood propagates the doctrine of *doux* commerce in its fullest form:

the "method of merchandise" promotes "arts, industry, peace and plenty," enables culture, unites nations. It also encourages the "most savage" to hand over their "useless superfluities" to those who will, in return, "tame" and "polish" them: the industrious merchant is the globalizing agent of "civilization" here, as he is the one who enriches his native country. Lillo designed *The London Merchant* (1731) to be the didactic text par excellence, which is why it so unselfconsciously retails this compendium of contemporary mercantilist clichés. It is another matter that, in the rest of the play, the expansive calm and assurance of such beliefs is destroyed by the actions of the other apprentice, George Barnwell, and the peace of the merchant is transformed into a Gothic nightmare, featuring seduction, blackmail, thievery, murder, and a double hanging. The transition features the tension between Thorowgood's beatific worldview and the much more predatory practices embodied in Millwood, who says of herself, "I would have my conquests complete, like those of the Spaniards of the New World, who first plundered the natives of all the wealth they had, and then condemned the wretches to the mines for life to work for more" (1.2.26–30).[1]

Lillo's play reminds us that one of the crucial problems facing the proponent of commercial and national expansion in this period was the gap between theory and practice, between the dreams of global bounty available to the adventuring trader and the harsher realities of commercial and colonial contact overseas. It was not just that "savages" often resisted handing over their useless superfluities without coercion, but that the process itself—the raising of capital to outfit a ship, the voyages, transactions overseas—was unstable and uncertain. Further, as we have seen, many social theorists, including poets, were fearful (notwithstanding Thorowgood's certainty that the importation of the world's "blessings" is good for Britain) of the impact that increased volumes of overseas trade, and an increased commitment to distant colonies, would have on the political economy and social organization of their nation. I now attend to some of the characteristic ways in which eighteenth-century poets responded to the debilitating weight of historical or contemporary evidence that the spread of commercial and national power was a more uncertain business than might seem to be the case.

I begin with Henry Needler's "A Sea-Piece" (1711), whose view of the ocean as pastoral space is traumatically disrupted by an enormous and destructive storm, to show how even the celebratory poetic imagination was disturbed by the chancy and unsafe life of the ocean. Needler's fear of the unpredictable ocean is a local episode, I suggest, in the attempts of poets to produce credible visions of naval power not subject to the vicissitudes of stormy times. The burden of past empires, as we have seen, troubled all those who would find in contemporary Britain the lineaments of a future empire: here, we will see how even avowed panegyrics to manifest destiny like Edward Young's *Ocean: An Ode* (1728) and *Imperium Pelagi* (1729)—both poems that celebrate British dominion over the oceans—are qualified by the need to develop an ethics of mercantilism, one that will differentiate the British Empire from past, debilitating, precedents. The last section of this chapter suggests, via Richard Glover's *London: or, The Progress of Commerce* (1737) and Dyer's *The Fleece* (1757) some other ways in which poets crafted mythologies of national origin and identity, as also comparative models of the different geographical and cultural regions of the globe, precisely to articulate their visions of Britain as a commercial empire in the face of historical evidence that suggested the inevitability of decline and dissolution.

Stormy Seas and Cloudy Futures

Henry Needler's "A Sea-Piece. Sent in a Letter from Portsmouth, in October, 1711" is a good instance of the many genteel poems, now sunk into the unruffled depths of literary oblivion, that celebrate British navigation and nation, commerce, and culture.[2] (This is an enormous literary graveyard, for we should keep in mind Dobrée's claim that poems on no other topics in fashion could compare "in volume, in depth, in vigour of expression, in width of imagination, with the full diapason of commerce.") Needler's poem is of specific interest here because it, like Defoe's *The True-Born Englishman*, incorporates into its historical argument a memory of Roman Britain, and ingeniously credits the Romans with bringing navigational skills to Britain:

> The *British* Race, 'till by the *Romans* led
> They first the flutt'ring Canvas learn'd to spread,
> Savage and wild, by Commerce unrefin'd,
> Differ'd but little from the Brutal Kind;
> Uncultivated, ignorant and rude,
> A painted Herd, they rang'd the Plains and Wood,
> And prey'd upon their Fellow Brutes for Food:
> With Terror often from the neighb'ring Shore
> They view'd the stormy Waves, and heard them roar,
> But never durst a Thought to entertain,
> Of vent'ring on the Surface of the Main;
> Beyond the Sea they sought no Lands unknown,
> Nor dream'd of other Climes besides their own.
>
> *(lines 77–89)*

Needler's representation of the British as "Savage and wild" before the coming of the Romans is, importantly, part of a more general argument (here more assumed than specified) about the civilizing effects of *doux* commerce (line 79). As the Roman garrisons and colonists were to Britain, so, in this logic, might the British be to those other "Climes" they now dream of: the spread of commerce leads the way, expanding national horizons and refining social practices. Needler's poem is in no doubt about the material and cultural advantages—the historical progress—enabled by Britain's contemporary maritime prowess. In a passage whose crossings and benign world picture could be read as a manifesto of contemporary mercantilist thought, the poet describes Britain's "domestic Poverty" as now enriched by "Foreign Traffick":

> To ev'ry Part of the whole Globe we roam,
> And bring the Riches of each Climate home;
> With Northern Furrs we're clad and Eastern Gold
> Yet know not *India*'s Heat, nor *Russia*'s Cold;
> We taste the Wines, that sultry Soils produce,
> Free from the scorching Beams, which raise the noble Juice;
> Knowledge and Plenty fetch from ev'ry Shore,
> With Arts our Minds, with Wealth our Coffers store.
>
> *(lines 67–76)*

However, Needler's "A Sea-Piece" differs in one key detail from those contemporary poems that celebrated commodity trade or equated the spread of seaborne commerce with culture and refinement: the bulk of the poem enacts the fear that the "pastoral" space of the ocean is but a facade for the stormy death that awaits sailors and merchants. The first twenty-eight lines of the poem approximate a "prospect" poem, in which the poet looks out of Portsmouth onto the ocean in the same way that a poet of rural landscape might look out onto the land, and what he sees is more or less what the landlocked poet might record. That is, Needler's metaphors and similes are all derived from the beatitudes of landscape poetry. In the absence of "stormy Winds" and "tempestuous Blasts," a "smooth unwrinkled Plain accosts the Eye,"

> One Even, Uniform, Unvari'd Scene
> On ev'ry Side extends its wat'ry Green,
> A spacious Field, . . .
> . . . .
> The winding Shore a level Prospect yields
> Of verdant Meadows and of fruitful Fields.
>
> *(lines 1–12)*

The lines that follow describe, in buoyant detail ("gaudy streamers" and all), the fine figure cut by a ship, "that Monster of the Flood" (line 13) as it rides "in Triumph o'er the Main" (line 21). The "chearful Sailor" now sees only the "smiling Aspect of the Seas and Skies," and the "skilful Pilot" has no fears as he "the Helm securely steers" (lines 25–28).

The next line brings a storm sweeping in, the lack of transition emphasizing the suddenness and destructive unpredictability of the "furious Blast." Night falls ("Save where more horrid Day the Lightning lends") and the ship is tossed about in the "wat'ry Mountains" and "dreadful, gaping" valleys formed by the "rolling Waves." The horror mounts as the storm mocks the sailors' pleas for divine intervention:

> The trembling Sailor now of Life despairs,
> And flies to his last Refuge, Vows and Pray'rs,
> . . . .
> In rattling Thunder, Heav'n his Pray'r returns,
> And with red Lightning all the Welkin burns;
> Each glaring Flash the Wretch with Horror views,
> And with repeated Cries for Mercy sues.
>
> *(lines 30–44)*

The winds are too "boist'rous" for the "Strength and Skill" of the sailors and the ship is tossed about till she founders on a rock: "Th' impetuous Shock her Hull in Pieces breaks, / And fills her hollow Womb with doleful Shrieks" (line 50–54). Sailors leap into the "raging Sea"; some, supported by timbers, reach the beach, while "The rest, by the contending Billows tost, / At length are in the swelling Ocean lost" (lines 57–62).

I have quoted Needler's description of death at sea at some length in order to show how completely this near Gothic tone of horror and violence replaces the calm prospect with which the poem begins. To that extent, these lines reject the vision (and the poetry) of settled order and orchestrated nautical progress encoded in the opening and closing of the poem. The description of the storm, that is, disrupts the formal and ideological continuity between the poetry of prospect that begins "A Sea-Piece" and the progress poem that closes it. The "prosp'rous Winds" (line 24) that lead sailors forth turn out to be untrustworthy and ruinous: they make possible the commerce that Britain gains from (and in fact is civilized by), but the poem's emphasis on their destructive changeability is at odds with its larger vision of a Britain committed to seaborne expansion. The storm in this poem thus expresses, in dramatic fashion, a reservation about any complacent understanding of the costs or ease of commercial expansion. While lines 67 to 76 explain the benefits of commerce for contemporary Britain, and the last dozen lines expand that explanation to account for the historical emergence of the nation and the "race," these arguments are made in the face of the storm, as it were. Needler's contribution to the debates and the self-conception of a seafaring commercial nation, then, is a vivid picture of the fraught nature of the enterprise, and of the human costs involved.

This sense of fragility is doubly confirmed by the fact that no divine intervention is available to the storm-wracked sailors. Nor does the poem offer any quasi-deist (or any other such) explanations for their deaths, as poets of nature like Thomson did when they portrayed natural disasters on land.[3] In fact, the placement of the storm sequence in the poem makes clear that the sailors are sacrificed to the economic and commercial good of the nation. This accounting of vulnerability and suffering as inevitable to the power of an island-nation is not unlike, it seems to me, the central irony that surfaces in Defoe's *True-Born Englishman* (its brief history of England is a history of repeated colonization) and is of a piece with the historical ironies traced by a number of contemporary poems, in which England's success as a mercantile and colonial nation comes at a price. Sailors and merchants go to stormy death, international competition leads to war and invasion, and as the nation grows wealthy it becomes prey to moral, social, and economic weaknesses. In Needler's poem, however, the critique of the trading nation, its genealogy, and its ambitions works largely by indirection, in that the primary emphasis of the poem lies elsewhere. If there is resistance to the overall celebration of international commerce and national advancement in "A Sea Piece," it surfaces in the representation of the storm— not, that is, in any conscious or rationalized form, or as a theme. This is no doubt a form of symptomatic critique, a displaced enactment of contemporary material and cultural anxieties, and this is the manner in which many poems that exhort England to greater efforts overseas, predicting its colonial ascendancy and its trading wealth, register such concerns (we might remember here the trapped partridges and the hunted pheasants, woodchucks, and lapwings of *Windsor-Forest*, their deaths an analogue of the "amazed, defenceless prize[s]" taken "When Albion sends her eager sons to war"— lines 98–134).

The search for answers to the instabilities seen to accompany national expansion and the search for riches led to the development of another consequential style of eighteenth-century English poetry on public issues, one that celebrated particular merchants or kinds of trade and elevated commercial personnel and themes to the status of national icons. The foremost instance of such poetry is Dyer's *The Fleece* (1757), but before I get to it I will examine poems by Edward Young, and one by Richard Glover, that weave together a celebration of British commercial and naval power with their search for a nationalist poetics. Of interest in each poem are the new models of, and foundations for, poetic productivity they feature, including the historical tasks they specify for contemporary British poets. These poems also demonstrate some of the ways in which eighteenth-century poets understood the pressures of the "new," and how this understanding motivated their (explanations of) choice of form, theme, and subject, modes of address, and self-representation. Of course, part of the articulation of the historically new involved the strategic or polemical renewal of older (particularly classical) poetic forms and genres, tropes, and topoi in order that the manifest cultural capital inhering in them accrue to the project each poet claims as his own. The claim to poetic originality, then, is in fact mediated in form and practice; as poets explore contemporary themes, they often do so in conventional vocabularies whose very poetic and ethical conventionality molds, limits, or undermines their concerns.

The following analyses call attention to the forms and functions of poetic aspiration in this period, particularly the apostrophe, in order also to reflect upon the claims made by deconstructive critics of poetic voice such as Jonathan Culler and Paul Fry. Fry's account of the ode, for instance, is highly suggestive; it emphasizes the poetic desire for presence or voice as it does the ironic dissolution of that aspiration. For him, "in the considerable odes of every era, a burden of doubt subverts the assertion of knowledge," a formulation whose terms leave out (as pedestrian or as nonreflexive) the bulk of odes produced in the eighteenth century.[4] Certainly Fry does not see fit to include into his analysis the odes I examine here, but that may be because they feature more historical reference and political argument than the odes that he prefers, and are almost by definition excluded from his account of the "considerable" ode. However, I, too, will attend to the prominent rise and fall of poetic aspiration in these poems, but my argument sees the poet's engagement with historical reflection or with the contradictions between social or ethical and commercial practices as responsible for the dissolution of poetic vision or power. In some cases, of course, the ode does not enact such dissolution, and finds a vocabulary or theme that sustains its poetic overreach, thereby confirming the power of the poet's calling, or at least displacing any anxieties about such a calling onto figures of national and civilizational authority.

Forms and Function: The Case of Young

Young's *Ocean: An Ode*, with its self-explanatory subtitle "Occasioned by His Majesty's Royal Encouragement of the Sea Service. To Which is Prefixed an Ode to the King; and a Discourse on Ode," makes no bones about its formal and ideological imperatives.[5] It is written to thank George II for his interest in the Greenwich Hospital for old and infirm seamen and quotes from a speech made by the king to encourage the development of schemes for "the increase and encouragement of our seamen in general; that they

may be invited, rather than compelled by force or violence, to enter into
the service of their country, as oft as occasion shall require it: a consideration
worthy the representatives of a people great and flourishing in trade and
navigation." The ode "To the King" is precise about its objectives:

> Old ocean's praise
>> Demands my lays;
> A truly British theme I sing;
>> A theme so great,
>> I dare complete
> And join with ocean, ocean's king.
>
>> *(lines 1–6)*

    Young's panegyric begins by invoking antiquity, but also insists on the
Britishness of his theme and form; in the next two stanzas, the Roman and
the Pindaric ode (here the Theban) are described—the first "divinely clear,
and strong," the second a torrent that "roar'd, and foam'd along" (lines 9–
12). And then, in phrasing that makes poetic form identical with the nation,
and the ambitions of one coextensive with the other, Young suggests that
Britain inherits and will supplant these models of arts and arms:

> Let Thebes, nor Rome
>> So fam'd, presume
> To triumph o'er a northern isle;
>> Late times shall know
>> The north can glow,
> If dread Augustus deign to smile.
>
> The naval crown
>> Is all his own!
> Our fleet, if war, or commerce, call,
>> His will performs
>> Through waves and storms,
> And rides in triumph round the ball.
>
>> *(lines 13–24)*

    If George Augustus has his imperial destiny mapped out for him in these
lines, it is because poetry has the right and the ability to confer a different
sort of "empire":

> Parent of actions, good and brave!
>> How vice it tames!
>> And worth inflames!
> And holds proud empire o'er the grave.
>
>> *(lines 39–42)*

Poets commemorate national heroes and confer immortality, and in this discover their own heroism:

> Our strains divide
> The laurel's pride;
> With those we lift to life, we live;
> By fame enroll'd
> With heroes bold,
> And share the blessings which we give.
>
> *(lines 61–66)*

The next seven stanzas develop the praise of the British hero, George II, elevating him, the state, and the seaborne power he represents into the overlordship of "foreign kings" (line 95) and Europe. These stanzas are repetitive in tone and image: the monarch as ideal inspiration for the lyricist; the monarch's throne as the sun upon which "The nations gaze"; the monarch, like British oak, as unbending in the face of storms; the monarch as ruler over the seas (from which follows "wealth and state, / And power and fate"); the monarch as a leader of men who is also adored by the gods. This is the routine, hyperbolic vocabulary of panegyric, and there is little here that distinguishes these sentiments from those contained in the enormous volume of songs of praise and flattery that accompanied any royal (or indeed aristocratic) action in this period.

This lack of distinction might be the motivation behind the prose treatise "On Lyric Poetry" that Young sandwiches between the ode "To the King" and "Ocean. An Ode." Young argues the need for his return to lyric poetry, to the ode, and suggests the literary-historical and contemporary reasons why this form is most appropriate for nationalist themes in Britain. As far as he is concerned, then, his treatise sets the critical stage for the performances mounted by his companion odes, the whole adding up to a topical and urgent contribution to the civic discourse of the nation. As we will see, in "Ocean," Young claims not simply newness but also singularity—no one else comes forward to sing the themes he believes require attention, so he must take up the challenge and write the ode. Young's concern with definitions of appropriate poetry and, even more importantly perhaps, appropriate poets, is not new and circulates through much of his work.[6] "On Lyric Poetry" begins in like vein, with a long discussion of the "idea of perfection" that poets have, which is so "rarely attained" that bad poets are inevitably vain about their verse, and good poets, humble. This useful reminder of the gap between aspiration and performance precedes his extended definition of the ode:

as it is the eldest kind of poetry, so it is more spiritous, and more remote from prose than any other, in sense, sound, expression, and conduct. Its thoughts should be uncommon, sublime, and moral; its numbers full, easy, and most harmonious; its expression pure, strong, delicate, yet unaffected; and of a curious felicity beyond other poems; its conduct should be rapturous, somewhat abrupt, and immethodical to a vulgar eye. . . . Fire, elevation, and select thought, are indispensable; an humble, tame, and vulgar ode is the most pitiful error a pen can commit. (148)

So concerned is Young about the pitfalls of poetic performance, and the ease with which this discourse of poetic elevation can turn into a parody of itself, that he concludes this discussion with a warning: "As its subjects are sublime, its writer's genius should be so too; otherwise it becomes the meanest thing in writing, viz. an involuntary burlesque" (148).

Young returns to his definition of the ode after brief comments on "the great masters of lyric poetry among Heathen writers"—Pindar, Anacreon, Sappho, and Horace—and on Dryden's "Ode on St. Cecilia's Day" (148–51): "To sum up the whole: ode should be peculiar, but not strained; moral, but not flat; natural, but not obvious; delicate, but not affected; noble, but not ambitious; full, but not obscure; fiery, but not mad; thick, but not loaded with numbers; which should be most harmonious, without the least sacrifice of expression, or of sense" (152). In this formulation, Young's antitheses follow the rhetoric and syntax bequeathed to the poetics of nationalist commemoration by Denham's lines from *Cooper's Hill* that are quoted as the epigraph to chapter 2. Denham's definition of his poetic hopes uses the Thames as a model; he wishes to write verse that is "Though deep, yet clear, though gentle, yet not dull, / Strong without rage, without ore-flowing full" (lines 191–92). Denham invokes the Thames as the prime figure and agent of English mercantile expansion and thus firmly links poetic aspiration ("O could I flow like thee") with commercial and nationalist ambition. The antitheses Young now offers tap into this history (he is, after all, extending Denham's celebration of the Thames into an account of Britain's control over the oceans), but they also offer a model of decorous, considered balance that addresses the slippery formal problem he wrote of earlier: poetic elevation should be sublime, not burlesque.[7]

The real guarantee of the sublimity of his ode is his choice of theme: "The ancients had a particular regard to the choice of their subjects; which were generally national and great. My subject is, in its own nature, noble; most proper for an Englishman; never more proper than on this occasion; and (what is strange) hitherto unsung" (153). Worth noting are the grounds upon which Young bases his claims to poetic originality and power: he will return to the weighty subjects preferred by the ancients, but this return will feature a subject whose compelling urgency derives from Britain's interests in the present moment. Typically with Young, the claim to literary authority combines a genuflection to classical cultural practices with a precise sense of what matters in the here and now. The "ancients" are invoked as unimpeachable preceptors, but also as a hard act to follow: thus, Young can only hope that the "smaller faults" of his poem "will meet indulgence for the sake of the design, which is the glory of my country and my king" (153).[8]

The first two stanzas of "Ocean. An Ode" mediate the distance between the pastoral poem and the new oceangoing poem quite seamlessly, as the "prospect" of the poet recumbent under the pines in a "Sweet rural scene! / Of flocks and green!" now extends beyond its usual landlocked boundaries to take in "The boundless tide!" The dancing seas invite the measures of the ode, but they also signify a poetic duty:

> Who sings the source
> Of wealth and force?
> Vast field of commerce, and big war!
>
> *(lines 13–15)*

Since Young cannot find any poets touched by "Pæan's ray," he rushes in:

> What! none aspire?
> I snatch the lyre,
> And plunge into the foaming wave.
>
> *(lines 22–24)*

The animation of poetic spirit here is enhanced in the two stanzas that follow, as the poet's song is echoed by the waves, rocks, and nereids, who use "voice and shell, to lift it high" (line 30). The sea breeze does its bit, too:

> The billows beat
> With nimble feet,
> With notes triumphant swell the wind.
>
> *(lines 34–36)*

In these opening stanzas, as Young extends the conventions of pastoral and prospect poetry (the poet in contemplative ease, looking out over an expanse of landscape that can be allegorized into a commentary on socioeconomic relations or the state of the estate or the nation) into the new fields of "commerce, and big war," his verse enacts an unusual confidence of voice and metaphor. It possesses a certainty of tone and purpose that is unembarrassed by choppy repetitions of idea and sentiment; in fact, these are precisely the (wave-like?) mechanisms that the poem relies on to achieve its formal and ideological effects:

> The main! The main!
> Is Britain's reign;
> Her strength, her glory, is her fleet:

> The main! the main!
> Be Britain's strain;
> As Tritons strong, as Syrens sweet.
>
> *(lines 43–48)*

This picture of the fleet glorious in its control of the waves is followed by an extended description (lines 54–102) of a storm (a pattern that we also saw in Needler's "A Sea Piece"). These vignettes of destructive storms, in poems that celebrate a nation's control of the oceans, reflect more than the awareness that sailors face many dangers at sea. Insofar as the poetic voice in these poems is closely identified with national expansion, the enactment of storm-tossed danger plays out the tempestuous emotions required of the ode (which must be "fiery, but not mad"), even as it registers the more material difficulties to be faced by those who sail in the national interest. Equally, these passages stage the poet's mastery over his medium, his ability to navigate through to the calm after the storm, and thus to conduct the ship of state through perilous waters to its true course, to confirm to it its manifest national destiny. The storms that are staged, then, do not destabilize narratives of national and poetic ambition as much as confirm their difficult necessity. Thus, after the storm comes the reaffirmation of purpose:

> Let others fear;
> To Britain dear
> Whate'er promotes her daring claim;
> Those terrors charm,
> Which keep her warm
> In chase of honest gain, or fame.
>
> *(lines 103–8)*

In these lines, the terrors of the deep are translated into spurs to "honest gain" or to the quest for fame (both, as we have seen in Dyer's *The Ruins of Rome*, morally appropriate inducements to the spread of empire, at least till they are corrupted by luxury, indolence, and vanity). But this sense of dangers surmounted is only temporary, for Young's verse is unable to shake off the specter of unbridled desire and its fatal consequences that haunts the antimercantilist moralists of the age.[9] Storms are described again, this time as agents of moral retribution, which "seize the prize," the golden ore, which the merchant, "with proud designs," has dug from Indian mines. His son weeps for his father, complains against the "cruel thirst of gold," but himself "Then ploughs the main, / In zeal for gain" (lines 145–56). "Rage of gold," the poet intones editorially, "disdains a shore" (line 162). The slippery distinction between "honest gain" and the "rage for gold," between storms that offer civic lessons for Britain's merchants and sailors and storms that rise up to emphasize the destructiveness of mercantile greed, is obviously hard to maintain; accordingly, the next five stanzas expatiate on the time-worn opposition between gold (which "pleasure buys; / But pleasure dies"—163–64) and virtue (which "kindles living joys"—line 168). Virtue is understood here in political terms specific to the arguments that record Britain's constitutional difference from other mercantile and colonial powers: the virtuous mind is thus one that fears neither storms nor "civil rage, nor tyrant's frown" (line 183):

> This Britain knows,
> And therefore glows
> With gen'rous passions, and expends
> Her wealth and zeal
> On public weal,
> And brightens both by god-like ends.
>
> *(lines 187–92)*

As evidence of this zeal for the public weal, the poem offers the fund for the Greenwich hospital, and goes on to imagine retired sailors at their ease in this hospital, telling their sea stories, which are "the lenitives of age!" (line 225). In their sociability, the sailors are turned into moral exemplars of a type well known from the poetry of rural retirement, their well-earned repose a contrast to the ceaseless rage for gold. Young has a word of remembrance also for those "warlike slain" whose sacrifices enable Britain's dominance of the seas: their deaths in fact fulfill a divine mandate to shape "a master to mankind" (line 270) from British "hearts and oak" (line 269). Britain's forests are celebrated for much the same reason: they produce the ships ("big with war") that subdue rebel realms so that the

> sumptuous spoils
> Of foreign soils
> Pours in the bosom of our land.
>
> *(lines 277–82)*

Finally, Britain's power to weigh "The fate of kingdoms, and of kings" is compared to the power of the ocean to swell those "streams and rills" that connect to it or to leave "their famish'd channels dry" (lines 283–94).

This comparison, however, seems to unsettle the nationalist certitudes of the poem, turning it from an ode to national power into a meditation on mortality, transience, empty ambition, the rectitudes of life in the countryside, and many of the other topoi of the poems of rural retirement, particularly those that stage the contrast between country and city as a contrast in ethical value systems. The speed of the transition is startling, almost as if the idea of ebb and flow, of rise and fall, contained in the image of the ocean (feeding or depleting streams) disrupts so completely the more linear account of national power and progress that refuge can be sought only in a return to the tried and tested poetic discourse of ethical universals. (As we will see, this retreat is in fact also represented as a failure of poetic nerve—as a seduction into "scenes untried.") The ocean no longer remains the medium most appropriate to the contemporary song of nation but becomes a figure for the "mixt," "frail," and "sure to fail" pleasures "of mankind":

> For who can gaze
> On restless seas,
> Unstruck with life's more restless state?
>
> *(lines 301–3)*

This slide into existential and moral doubt blights the prospect and project of the ode itself:

> A damp destroys
> My blooming joys,
> While Britain's glory fires my mind.
>
> *(lines 295–300)*

The next nineteen stanzas, almost one-third of the poem, expand on these familiar themes, with the poet (and "good men" in general) in retreat from the stormy world:

> The world's the main,
> How vext! how vain!
> Ambition swells, and anger foams.
>
> *(lines 307–9)*

Safe harbor is to be found in a "noiseless shore, unruffled homes!" (line 312); the poet's retreat is so complete that he now asks to be taught "to despise" the "public scene / Of hardened men," a "world few know / But to their woe" (lines 313–18). "True bliss" and "innocence" are seen only in "landscapes green," for "wealthy towns" are marked by the frowns of "Proud labour" and courts by the smiles of "painted sorrow" (lines 325–30). As the swelling tones and topoi of ode eddy into the quieter, more domestic "streams and rills" of the poetry of rural retirement, the poet renounces as misguided the very desires that made him "snatch the lyre, / And plunge into the foaming wave" (lines 22–24):

These scenes untried
Seduc'd my pride.
To fortune's arrows bar'd my breast;
Till wisdom came,
A hoary dame!
And told me pleasure was in rest.

(lines 331–36)

The voice of Dame Wisdom (ventriloquized as the poet's own, within quotation marks) reiterates the sentiments and sociability appropriate to such retirement: the desire for a "friend sincere" (line 340), for the "sylvan chase" (line 370), for the "genial bowl, / Where mirth, good nature, spirit flow!" (lines 374–75). More pointedly, the idiom of commerce and the quest for wealth that energized the earlier sections of the poem are here subsumed into the vocabulary of genial benevolence, as we are told that the

"nobly soul'd
Their commerce hold
With words of truth and looks of love!"

(lines 388–90)

and that their "glorious aim" and "wealth supreme" is simply the "Divine benevolence of soul!" (lines 391–93). Thus, the poet casts away "Prophetic schemes, / And golden dreams" (lines 397–98), his "chief revenue in content!" (line 405). The "honest gain, or fame" (line 108), the twin motivations claimed earlier for Britain's mercantile prowess, are now collapsed into the single pious wish of the poet to leave behind "one beam / Of honest fame," a small memorial that will last unhurt till that time when "mighty nature's self shall die!" The image of the apocalypse that closes the poem is, appropriately enough, one that features the ocean, but in a form far removed from the one that enabled, indeed encouraged, Britain's domination over the globe: Time itself will

"cease to glide,
With human pride,
Sunk in the ocean of eternity."

(lines 412–14)

How do we understand the formal, ethical, and ideological variations in Young's poem, its repeated use of elements from the pastoral and the prospect poem to frame its forays into the world of oceanborne trade and warfare, and its turn away from the confident forward progression and hyperbole of nationalist ode to the decorous, even self-effacing pieties characteristic of the moral communities represented in the poetry of rural retirement? There is of course no reason why the discourse of empire should not contain within its expansive scope idealized descriptions of more domestic arrangements: there is, for instance, no contradiction between the imperial themes Pope celebrates in *Windsor-Forest* (1713) and the portrait of the Man of Ross as a rural moralist and initiator of good works that he offers in *An Epistle to Allen Lord Bathurst* (1733).[10] In fact, as Laura Brown has shown, the combination of imperial enthusiasm and moral rectitude is precisely constitutive of the neoclassical humanism of Pope's poetry.[11] Young's *Ocean: An Ode*, however, stages a retiring sociability as a reminder of the inflated, illusory claims of national expansion, and rewrites the central image of the poem—the ocean as medium for such expansion—into one that embodies the dangerous instability of ambition (including poetic ambition) and the final, watery home of "human pride" and history. Is this a failure of poetic nerve, a recognition, in the face of the restless ocean, of the pretension involved in any attempt to chart its immensity? In that, does it suggest to us a variation of the burden of the past (here the challenge of the present) on the English poet?

As we have seen in a number of poems examined so far, some of this retreat from the themes and images of national expansion can be explained by the perception of historical transience generated by any meditation on the rise and fall of empires and states. The weight of such histories is not carried easily by the poets of a British empire, whose propagandist desires are sometimes blunted by their historical insight. At other times, a poet's "patriotism" takes the form of a survey of the domestic impact of mercantile and colonial success and leads to a more circumspect review of, or even a critique of, the commitment of state resources to shipping and trade. In each case, though, poets struggle to find a form and an idiom appropriate to their ideas of contemporary need, to the exploration of particular themes and issues that they believe distinguish their historical moment and thus energize their poetry. Young's poem follows this pattern, arguing for a revival of the ode because the time and his theme are ripe, but he anchors this claim in a prose treatise, arguing his case rather than enacting it in his poem. And when he does incorporate this literary-historical ("revivalist") energy into the poem, in tropes of poetic and national challenge, he ends up turning away from such inflation and sets aside the very projects and heroism with which he began. Further, throughout *Ocean: An Ode*, Young finds psychic and poetic mooring in the imagery of pastoral and rural spaces, invoking them as safe havens from the stormy and vast possibilities opened up by his ode to seaborne expansion.

What the poem cannot seem to do, then, is to find in the ode—the form Young creates here or the examples he invokes in his discussion of

classical odists and Dryden—both a poetics and an ethics for his vision of
the expansionist nation.[12] Young seems confident that the ode provides formal
and thematic authority for a celebration of ocean as "Vast field of commerce,
and big war," that it provides a model for nationalist poetic ambition ("I
snatch the lyre, / And plunge into the foaming wave"), and that it is fit
instrument for songs of praise for the king, for Britannia, as well as for
sailors and merchants. However, the poem is less certain about the projection
of power or the search for treasures and wealth abroad, about the nature of
the men who venture forth (the merchant "swoln" with desire for gold),
and about the life their pursuits symbolize ("Gold pleasure buys, / But
pleasure dies"). In the poem, resistance to the excitement of empire is
expressed in the vocabulary of prudence and genteel sociability characteristic
of the poem of rural retirement; another way to put this is to say that, in
poetic and ideological terms, Young wishes to be buoyed by his exciting
("Whiggish") ocean, but to retain his settled ("Tory") countryside moorings,
too. Not that this dual desire is unusual in this period; if anything, such a
combination of elements defines the imaginative matrix of these poems
and reveals to us their mediation between older (literary) histories and newer
(cultural) geographies.[13]

   There is another way to understand this interplay between the differing
civic conceptions and vocabularies in this poem—one defined, in part, by the
work of J. G. A. Pocock on the "establishment of the eighteenth-century
Whig commercial regime and the reaction against it in the name of virtue."
Pocock suggests that the "appearance of a new ruling elite (or 'monied interest')
of stockholders and officeholders, whose relations with government were those
of mutual dependence, was countered by a renewed . . . assertion of the ideal
of the citizen, virtuous in his devotion to the public good and in his
engagement in relations of equality and ruling-and-being-ruled, but virtuous
also in his independence of any relation which might render him corrupt."
Since the "ideals of commerce and virtue could not . . . be reconciled to one
another, so long as 'virtue' was employed in the austerely civic, Roman" sense,
Pocock argues that the term *virtue* itself was redefined, "with the aid of a
concept of 'manners.'" In this conception, as the individual moved from the
"farmer-warrior world of ancient citizenship or Gothic *libertas*, he entered an
increasingly transactional world of 'commerce and the arts'" in which his
multiplying "encounters with things and people evoked passions and refined
them into manners," such that it was "preeminently the function of commerce
to refine the passions and polish the manners."[14] Pocock, sensitive as always to
the language of political thought and debate, points out that both the "defence
of commercial society" and the "vindication of classical virtue" was carried
out "with the weapons of humanism," and that one product of the eighteenth

century was a "commercial humanism," with its own vital ideas about the social ethos necessary to the practice of virtue.[15]

Within the sociohistoric and discursive dynamic summarized here, Young's *Ocean: An Ode* might exemplify the difficult negotiation, at least within the formal practice of poetry, between the "independence," public virtue, and citizenship suggested by landowners (and the genteel communities made possible by their patronage) and the more recent and energetic models of national and civic progress suggested by commercial society. There are paradoxes to be noted here: the Pindaric (or the ode in general) is revived as the form most appropriate to these new energies, yet its classical practice featured a personalized celebration of the athlete-hero (and of his family, who often commissioned the poem, and whose reciprocal generosity to the poet completed the circuit of prestige that distinguished all of them).[16] Young's Pindaric seeks, at different moments, to elevate faceless communities or abstractions (merchants or sailors, the nation, Trade and Commerce, Ocean), which, even when personified, can scarcely provide the models of civic virtue traditionally developed in the song of the epinician. In fact, as I have suggested, Young reaches into a different figural heritage (if we can call it that) for the language of ethical and civic responsibility in the poem, and indeed for his final account of the poet's social and literary ambitions and duties. If there is (as indeed there is) a "commercial humanism" being constructed in *Ocean: An Ode*, it is one that does not so much successfully fuse the "commercial" and the "civic" (which is the opening claim of the poem) as shift between poetic representations of these terms, not quite certain how to reconcile poetic ambition with poetic duty. But *Ocean: An Ode* was not the only poem Young wrote on such themes. In fact, in many ways it was a prelude, a preparatory exercise to his long poem on the empire of the sea, *Imperium Pelagi* (1729), to which I now turn.

Young's subtitle describes the poem as a "Naval Lyric" written in "Imitation of Pindar's Spirit," and his prefatory paragraphs once again explain his return to the Pindaric: "Trade is a very noble subject in itself, more proper than any for an Englishman, and particularly seasonable at this juncture." He offers his poem as an attempt at the poetry of the "sublime," which few English poets ("our two famous epic poets excepted") have written. In keeping with that attempt, he hopes only that the reader of his ode will gain "a fuller idea of the real interest or possible glory of his country than before, or a stronger impression from it, or a warmer concern for it." If that happens, then he gives up to "the critic any farther reputation." Having stated, briefly and simply, his nationalist poetic ambitions, Young addresses the more vexed question of the Pindaric once again, this time arguing that his poem is not a copy but an "original, though it professes imitation," for he imitates Pindar's "genius and spirit" rather than his form. He insists that the length of his poem is not a problem in Pindaric terms, since Pindar does have "an unbroken ode of six hundred lines," but goes on to suggest that each section of his poem (he calls them strains) can be thought of as a separate ode, "if you please." In conclusion, he reminds his reader of the tone his poem is striving for: the "Ode is the most spirited kind of poetry, and the Pindaric is the most spirited kind of ode."

I quote Young's comments to emphasize his constant attention to the interplay between ideology and poetic form, his argument that the celebration of trade and glory makes for the most energetic kind of poetry. This is a revisionary claim for Young, particularly when we contextualize his effort within the more "traditional" and aristocratic equation represented, for instance, in Dryden's simple statement "Heroique Poesie has always been sacred to Princes and Heroes." Hence, as Dryden argues, heroic poetry—which is also the poetry of civic and moral instruction—should derive its subjects from "the greatest men."[17] Young couples trade and national heroism here, and even if we do not take his prefatory comments at face value (particularly in that his confident claims seems so little borne out by the dynamic of the poems themselves) we should notice Young's sense of contemporary poetic vocation and voice. "Prelude" (the opening section of the poem) is in fact an extended moment of poetic self-presentation. The poet lies on the shore, under a "naval oak," as inspiration comes to him ("The god descends, and transports warm my soul"—lines 1–6). The occasion for this is the return of the king from overseas, his ship, the *Pine*, bringing the warmth that revives the poet's "strains," which have been much "damp'd" by age (lines 13–18). At this point, the poet's inspiration becomes indistinguishable from the "sacred gales" that fill the sails of the *Pine*, and his poem becomes the prime mover of the ship of state:

> The sea she scorns, and now shall bound
> On lofty billows of sweet sound;
> I am her pilot, and her port the skies.
>
> *(lines 34–36)*

The poet is sure of vocation and voice here, and claims both ecstatic transport ("I glow! I burn!") and ease of composition ("The numbers pure / . . . / Spontaneous stream from my unlabour'd breast"—lines 49–51).

This surge of confidence continues into "Strain the First," in which the poet ("By Pindar led") turns prophet (1.1–6) and offers a glowing vision of Britain's future. This prophecy derives its vocabulary from contemporary religious, commercial, and political discourses, as Young provides elaborate,

quasi-philosophical explanations of how the climate and geography of the
world are ordained to provide Britain mastery of its products and services.
He invokes, near ritually, the divine figures of Industry, Trade, and Peace,
each of which is at home in Britain. He begins with "Bless'd Industry,"
who enables agricultural prosperity (1.16–18) and also naval strength:

> From thee mast, cable, anchor, oar,
> From thee the cannon and his roar;
> On oaks nursed, rear'd by thee, wealth, empire grows.
>
> *(1.19–21)*

The roar of cannon plays no further role in this strain, which expatiates on
the economic, political-philosophical, and cultural benefits of the global spread
of Trade and her sister Peace; after, however, claiming Britain as the birthplace
and future home of Trade (1.45–46). Trade is a powerful, benign force for
change: it "levies gain on every place, / Religion, habit, custom, tongue, and
name," and "draws a golden zone / Round earth and main" (1.56–59), but
there is no doubt which nation is the prime mover behind and beneficiary of
such change. Sloth disappears as British ships and seamen set sail, and faraway
rivers—the "Po, Ganges, Danube, Nile"—smile at their presence:

> Their urns inverted prodigally pour
> Streams charged with wealth, and vow to buy
> Britannia for their great ally.
>
> *(1.69–71)*

Wealth that is prodigal elsewhere (too easily produced? wastefully
consumed?) is now used to buy Britain's favor and commercial attention:
furs from Russia, painted jars from China, wine from France, incense from
Arabia, and "her richest ore" from "distant Ind" (1.73–78). There are many
similar catalogs of commodities in contemporary poems, and in each case
the syntax emphasizes a willing, indeed exuberant, giving up of these spoils
by different parts of the globe to the glory of Britain. What is less common
is Young's audacious extension of this rhetorical pattern to suggest Britain's
ownership of nature and of natural forms globally:

> what tide that flows
> Or stream that glides, or wind that blows,
> Or genial sun that shines, or shower that pours,
> But flows, glides, breathes, shines, pours for thee?
>
> *(1.79–82)*

Britain as final destination of the natural treasures of the world, the ocean
its "servant," the gifts of many nations and regions flowing smoothly as

"boundless dower" to "mighty George's growing power"—these are the chief elements of the spirited song of empire Young writes here.

But Young does more than marshal the rhetoric of national power and entitlement here, persuasive as that might be; he in fact crafts an ethics of mercantilism (a subset of the commercial humanism Pocock writes of) in a way that he could not manage to do (as I have argued earlier) in *Ocean: An Ode*. He is, once again, interested in the enlarged subject of Commerce, that citizen of new wealth and riches who had been treated with suspicion by moralists and was now an even greater challenge for those whose entrenched interests in land and social hierarchy he seemed to stand against. Young's method is to mold, as much as possible, moral and ethical categories that conventionally exclude the language of riches into categories that are themselves enriched by the new wealth, particularly since this wealth belongs to the nation ("All these one British harvest make!" 1.85). Riches, in fact, make possible divinely ordained circuits of benevolence:

> Commerce brings riches; riches crown
> Fair virtue with the first renown.
> A large revenue, and a large expense,
>   When hearts for others' welfare glow,
>   And spend as free as gods bestow,
> Gives the full bloom to mortal excellence.
>
> *(1.91–96)*

The moral man is now the rich trader, who becomes the prime agent of welfare expenditure and social redistribution and thus completes the global circuit that brings the world's wealth to Britain. In the new world fashioned by mercantilism, wealth, not poverty, is the basis of moral standing, for riches, like all other "blessings" (1.102), teach their own lessons: "The truly great find morals in the mine" (1.108).

Young's redefinition of wealth as enabling the moral being encourages him to rewrite the central topos of the Horatian *beatus vir* theme, which had, via the pastoral, become an enormously powerful poetic representation of contemplative, moral man at his ease in the world. Early modern English poetry is replete with images of the "Happy man" but in a very different incarnation from the one Young offers: "Happy the man who, large of heart, / Has learnt the rare, illustrious art / Of being rich" (1.109–11).[18] Whereas earlier poets had emphasized the simple, even austere, life of rural retirement chosen by the patron or hero, here Young claims wealth as the basis of moral authority. Plenty is now "a means, and joy her end" (1.115), and the duke of Chandos (to whom this ode is dedicated) is the model of such a rich and happy man. But the poem does not anchor its claims to cultural

authority solely in the celebration of a patron. It is very much a song of
nation, and Britain is invoked as the guarantor of the morality of the "wealth
and peace" that the divine "Donor" bestows: "Who now His whole creation
drains, / To pour into thy tumid veins / That blood of nations,—Commerce
and Increase" (1.121–26).

In this first strain, Young is at his most compelling ideologically as he
orchestrates his grand symphony of trade and empire. The wide natural
variety of the globe (here represented by its commodities: grain, silk, wine,
"harvests," gold, 1.127–32) is part of a divine masterplan for commerce:
"Heaven different growths to different lands imparts, / That all may stand
in need of all" (1.135–36). This divine sanction also manifests itself in
socioeconomic and social-psychological motivation, such that individual
"Interest" draws "all human hearts" into a common net.[19] In historical terms,
it leads to the emergence of Britain as the mart and arbiter of nations: "All
nations range / A narrow spot,—our throng'd Exchange; / And send the
streams of plenty from their spring." Young's celebration of the "Exchange"
features an intriguing chiasmus, one representative perhaps of the way such
poetry articulates the circuits of commerce within the conventional rhetoric
of nature and natural processes: the power of commerce converts all of
nature into commodities and poetry reimagines all commodities in metaphors
of nature (as in the easy-flowing streams and springs above). This is poetry
reinventing the world in mercantilist terms: nature is represented as coming
to its divinely sanctioned fruition in commerce, and the flow and effect of
commerce are represented in the conventional vocabulary of natural event
and process. The still point of these chiastic turns is of course the nation,
for whom, and from which, all things proceed: "Nor Earth alone, all Nature
bends / In aid to Britain's glorious ends" (1.157–58).

The ethics of mercantilism that Young drafts here are thus predicated
on a reimagining of the world and its material treasures as being at the
service of Britain. The merchant is prime agent of God, nature, and nation,
and this is, as Young wrote in the preface to *Imperium Pelagi*, the argument
of his poem. Interestingly though, this strain does not close with this
emphasis on commodities and riches, but closes in a deep genuflection
(held for all of seven stanzas) at the altar of "godlike Reason." The ode now
shifts away from its engagement with wealth and commerce to more
otherworldly concerns, or rather, it reminds its readers that brief indeed
are the glories of this world. It does so by invoking Reason, which as "the
golden chain 'twixt God and men" (1.169) raises men from their status as
"emmets." It also allows them to weather "Fortune's nod" (1.163–76), an
important detail in a poem on the moral heroism of merchants. Reason is
the human faculty that allows men to remember the "slender worth of

men and things" (1.186) and to recognize the transience of human vanities
and pleasures:

> Life, fame, friends, freedom, empire, all,
> Peace, commerce, freedom, nobly fall
> To launch us on the flood of endless bliss.
>
> *(1.190–92)*

And yet strain 1 has been about everything but transience: expansion, accumulation, and power have been its operative terms. If there is a contradiction
here, it is quickly effaced in the last stanza, in which Reason turns into a
teacher of more than spiritual values: Reason is instructor to "Trade's swarming throng" and "gay Freedom's smile," to "Armies" and to "Peace" and the
"Arts." Reason is also, finally, exalter and defender of Britain (1.199–204).

I have examined strain 1 at some length both because I presume that
even specialist readers of eighteenth-century English verse are not likely to
remember *Imperium Pelagi* in any detail and because it allows a full sense of
the characteristic concerns and vocabulary of the entire poem. In that, it
provides a fine instance of what David Shields has called the "Literary
Topology of Mercantilism"—that iconography and rhetoric produced by
poets and other propagandists to make compelling the argument, post Bacon's
Advancement of Learning, that "trade rather than territory constituted the more
peaceful and economical way to national prosperity." Shields lists the key
elements of this argument: that providence had ordained the spread of
commodities all over the globe so that commerce would provide the link
between regions; that England should control such maritime activity and
thus rule the world; that such rule could be justified by "declaring the
benefits of 'the Arts of Peace' resulting from British superintendence of
world trade" (in the same way as the Roman Empire had justified its rule
"by promoting the benefits of the Pax Romana").[20] Shields's work emphasizes
the ideological potency of the formulae of *translatio studii* and *translatio imperii*,
particularly in that the model of the westward movement of arts and arms
was crucial to the claim of Britain as the inheritor of the traditions of the
Roman Empire. However, as we have seen in our analysis of poems on
imperial themes, historical retrospection of any kind, even if it is designed
to establish flattering correspondences, contains within itself grave pitfalls,
for history is a record of transience as much as of achievement.

Strain 2 of *Imperium Pelagi* addresses one such model of rise and fall in
an effort to inoculate its vision of Britain-triumphant from the contagion
of decline. It describes in great and sumptuous detail the imports and wealth
(the noble "harvest of the seas") of Tyre, an island-state that was the "Ancient
of empires!" (2.36–39). The end comes suddenly; Tyre was the "Great mart

of nations—But she fell" (2.43). Young offers a reason (if we can call it that) for this fall, one that features a generalized corruption: "The Queen of Trade is *bought! Once wise and just, / Now venal is her council's tongue" (2.57–58). The rest of the strain is an unrelenting account of all that goes wrong—politically, economically, socially, culturally, and morally—because of venality, "fatal pride" (2.129) and "luxury" (2.154). Young's verse is particularly energetic in imagining the forms of decline. All the commodities that had once offered testimonial of Tyrian greatness are now reduced to "vain . . . boasts" (line 109); her naval might is abased (2.121–26); her kings groan in despair, haunted as they are by the specter of past glory:

> "How art thou fallen, down, down, down!
> Wide Waste, and Night, and Horror frown,
> Where Empire flamed in gold, and balanced states."
>
> *(2.160–62)*

The ideological payoff of such a Gothic rendering of decline comes in the beginning of strain 3, when Tyre is offered as a moral and civilizational lesson for Britain:

> Hence learn, as hearts are foul or pure,
> Our fortunes wither or endure:
> Nations may thrive, or perish by the wave.
> . . . .
> Ocean's the *womb* of riches, and the *grave*.
>
> *(3.1–6)*

Britain is reminded once again that "Virtues should rise, as fortunes swell," particularly as "large property" is meant to be the "sign of good, / Of worth superior" (3.8–10). Young anchors this moral reminder within a political claim of national difference and greatness. Compared with the "vassals prisoned in the continent," Britons are "High-flushed with wealth, and Freedom's smile" (3.14–15). There are no tyrants here to trample upon "Genius" or "Virtue"—Britain respects property and Freedom equally (3.19–24). Young claims that such freedom is particularly moving for the writer of odes ("I feel her now, and rouse, and rise, and rave")—and then moves on to a set of images and references that suggest just how haunted the poetic discourse of British liberty and freedom was by the existence of the slave trade:

> Verse is gay Freedom's gift divine:
> The man who can think greatly is no slave.
>
> Others may traffic if they please.
>
> *(3.29–31)*

Britain was of course very much trafficking in slaves at this time; here the slave is the repressed other of the poet of freedom and national virtue.[21] The surfacing of the slave trade in these lines threatens the moral empire of the seas that Young claims for Britain and leads to a startling shift in metaphor. Maritime activity is rewritten in the vocabulary of the georgic, and British trade becomes an extension of agricultural practice: Britain "Is born for trade, to plough her field, the wave, / And reap the growth of every coast" (3.33–34).

This is not the only time the poem mentions the slave trade. In strain 5, as Young repeats his explanation that trade is at the root of national greatness and power, he suggests both "Tartar Grand" and "Mogul Great" as examples (line 115). In contrast, he offers Africa, and argues that slavery is the product of the lack of trading skills among Africans:

> While Afric's black, lascivious, slothful breed,
>   To clasp their ruin, fly from toil,
>   That meanest product of their soil,
> Their people, sell; one half on t' other feed.
>
>   Of Nature's wealth from Commerce rent,
>   Afric's a glaring monument:
> 'Mid citron forests and pomegranate groves
>   (Cursed in a Paradise!) she pines;
>   O'er generous glebe, o'er golden mines,
> Her beggar'd, famish'd, tradeless native roves.
>
> *(5.117–26)*

Africa is Edenic, but in ruin, except that the ruin has more to do with the nonexploitation of its natural resources than it has to do with moral failings (though Young does not fail to list some of the common eighteenth-century racist conceptions of Africans: slothful, licentious, even cannibalistic). The argument for moral mercantilism that Young develops in *Imperium Pelagi* requires some acknowledgment of the slave trade, if only because of its great scale and visibility, and Young's answer is to displace agency away from European slave traders and ships onto internecine conflicts in Africa. Further, Africans are condemned for their inability to transform pastoral bounty into the stuff of international trade: the only commodities they produce are slave bodies.

And yet one of the characteristic poetic flourishes of this poem is to convert the language of commodities and commerce back into tropes of pastoral and georgic. Ironically, for Young, Africa may be imagined as a pastoral space that resists the transformative effects of commerce (and thus generates the pathology of slavery), but these transformative effects are themselves constantly rewritten as fundamental natural processes. This is how Young explains the animating spirit of Commerce: "So fall from heaven the vernal showers, / To cheer the glebe, and wake the flowers." Flowers bloom, birds sing, and "Industrious bees ply every wing, / Distend their cells, and urge their golden trade" (4.25–30). In passages like these, we can see a curious logic at play: Young, like any other eighteenth-century poet, is aware that poets of pastoral and georgic had crafted a compelling poetics of labor that fused nature and work, or found in nature analogies for the representation of work as painless and easeful. Here Young wishes to extend that poetic logic or power in a somewhat different exercise, which is to create a similar magical poetics for trade and commerce. Thus, the industry of bees in pursuit of their "golden trade" or the life-quickening touch of spring rain both provide acceptable analogies for a different sort of circulation, that of commodities and commercial goods around the globe. The hold of such conventions over the poetic imagination (especially one that announces itself as reviving older forms in pursuit of new ends) can scarcely be underestimated. In fact, it shapes the form of inspiration itself; when Young calls on the "Dircæan swan" (Pindar), his terms and icons are pastoral:

> like vernal showers;
> My verse shall burst out with the flowers,
> While Britain's trade advances with the sun.
> *(4.10–12)*

    Such shifts in vocabulary or tropology need not be explained solely as a response to contradictions in arguments or values. The formal counterpart of Young's global vision is an encyclopedia of poetic conventions: this ode to Britain and to Commerce contains within itself tropes and topoi identified with the pastoral, the georgic, the progress poem, the Pindaric. It mines, in an entirely eclectic fashion, a variety of poetic forms and practices in order to fashion and enrich its iconography and rhetoric. Indeed, that may well be the signature of this, and other such contemporary poems, on similar themes. They work by repetition and accretion, covering much the same ground but doing so with minor variations in poetic argument, incorporating separate poetic conventions and practices in order to produce an overwhelming and, ideally, seamless account of how providential and historical processes (including the history of poetry) all lead to the elevation of Britain as master of the empire of the seas. Thus, contradictions in argument or vocabulary are not so much reconciled as repressed under the weight of further assertion or celebration. At times the poetry of manifest destiny (which is the genre *Imperium Pelagi* belongs to) seems a melange of providentialist, moral, ethical, sociocultural, natural, climatic, geographical, and historical references, except that the poet attempts to weave these elements into a thickly textured nationalist narrative. If we believe that it is only modern readers, no longer spellbound by such imperialist nationalism, who pay attention to the twists and turns, the warp and the woof, the loose threads, of such poetic construction, we need only remember Johnson's Tory resistance to such whiggish patriotism.

Strain 3, then, contains passages on Britain's scientific genius (Newton is mentioned, as astronomer—lines 61–72), on the fact that no nation is equipped to rival Britain's control of the seas (lines 78–132), and on merchants as national heroes (139–68). Merchants "o'er proudest heroes reign / Those trade in blessing, these in pain" (lines 145–46); they vie with "purple monarchs" and with priests (who only "pray for blessings; merchants pour them down"—lines 148–50). The crescendo of praise for merchants ends, quite literally, in a cosmic theory of commercial value:

> Planets are merchants; take, return,
> Lustre and heat; by traffic burn:
> The whole creation is one vast Exchange.
>
> *(lines 154–56)*

The two last stanzas address the traditional divide between men of letters and merchants, challenging the former to look beyond their cloisters and recognize that in "open life" and amidst "throngs of men, / Experience, Arts, and solid Wisdom dwells" (lines 157–62). Trade aids art and science and studies at first hand the "sites, tongues, interests" of the globe. It follows then that he "Who studies Trade, he studies all; / Accomplish'd merchants are accomplish'd men" (lines 163–68). From the stars to the more mundane, all creation is the type of commercial man, a lesson that is reworked throughout the poem.[22]

All creation, all time, and all history tell the same tale: "Time's whole plain chronicle is all / One bright encomium, undesign'd, on Trade" (5.149–50). The last strain, and the two sections that follow ("The Moral" and "The Close") repeat and embellish the motifs that we have examined so far:

> Trade springs from Peace, and Wealth from Trade,
> And Power from Wealth; of Power is made
> The god on earth.
>
> *(5.151–53)*

Merchants are Britain's ambassadors, statesmen, and scholars (5.175–86), and above all are the agents of national power. In that, they are like the poet who sings their praise, who can, like them, conduct all of nature in the concert of empire:

Roll to my measures, O ye starry throng!
    Ye winds, in concert breathe around;
    Ye navies, to the concert bound
From pole to pole! To Britain all belong.
                                        (5.201–4)

In "The Close," this momentum of nationalist exaltation and triumph extends to the poet, who is now certain that he has found old and new British heroes adequate to the "ancient art and ancient praise" on which he modeled his lays. Indeed, so powerful, worthy, and vast has been the subject of *Imperium Pelagi* that the poet's achievement supersedes that of his master:

Not Pindar's theme with mine compares,
    As far surpassed as useful cares
Transcend diversion light and glory vain:
    The wreath fantastic, shouting throng,
    And panting steed to him belong,—
The charioteer's, not Empire's golden, reign.
                                        (lines 19–24)

This is the telos of the "new, bold, moral, patriot strain" (line 32) that Young writes: the magnification of poetic and national ambition in the anthem of empire. The classical poet is invoked not as awe-inspiring forbear whose long shadow stunts later odists but as a lesser celebrant of populist diversions, whose short-lived and lightweight glories suffer in comparison to Young's historic achievement. Pindar is here a mercenary poet of aristocratic athleticism, Young the puissant poet of nation.[23] As the empire comes of age, so does this poet. If there is any self-consciousness about such a claim, it does not surface in the great wash of patriotic sound and imagery that *Imperium Pelagi* generates.[24]

What we have here is far from the tone of evacuation and retreat that some critics of eighteenth-century poetry have described as the defining temper of the period.[25] If anything, poems like *Imperium Pelagi* suggest to us the obverse of such a cultural logic. Here, poetic vocabulary and method are defined by the poet's identification with broad and weighty themes: history, nation, empire. These poems feature a formal expansiveness, an inflation of poetic prospect and retrospect. They are eclectic compendiums of poetic practice, poems in search of a near-encyclopedic, synthetic idiom adequate to the articulation of complex and wide-ranging ideas, themes, and values. This is not, however, said to claim that such identification always results in a poem that is able to lionize contemporary Britain as the telos of providentialist or more secular historical processes; as seen in our readings of several poems in the preceding chapter, historical analysis itself often occludes the prophetic vision sought by the poet. This occlusion takes many forms: fears that commercial and colonial developments will disrupt domestic social and cultural arrangements; the sense that the lessons of history, particularly the history of empires, do not allow the votary of a British global dominance to remain sanguine about its prospects; nagging doubts about the ethical or moral norms encouraged, at home and abroad, by the practices and methods of contemporary mercantilism and colonization. Often the poems enact the failure of the poet to speak with confidence of empire, but, in each case, such failure is precipitated only after (and perhaps by) the sustained effort to forge a compelling iconography and argument for Britain's rise to commercial and colonial greatness.

In each of the poems discussed so far, I have called attention to the connections between poetic subjectivity and the project and form of the poem itself; that is, to the way in which the poem knits its representation of poetic vocation and power to tropes of nationalist ambition and achievement. For the most part, this is a connection repeatedly made explicit in the poems: as Addison, Lyttelton, Dyer, or Young sing of liberty or trade or Britain or the muse, they incorporate into their poems an account of the poetic self, its aspirations and its fears, its hubris and its humility. But also, as they sing *to* liberty, trade, Britain, or the muse, they put into play in such apostrophes the dynamic circuit of the constitution of poetic-self that Jonathan Culler has defined as the "pure embodiment of poetic pretension: of the subject's claim that in his verse he is not merely an empirical poet, a writer of verse, but the embodiment of poetic tradition and of the spirit of poesy."[26] In his essay, Culler argues that apostrophe must not be passed over simply by seeing it "as a poetic convention" or as a "relic of archaic beliefs" in the calling of spirits; he offers instead a powerful reading of apostrophe as the lyrical impulse itself, as figure of the new temporality, the new "fictive, discursive event" that a poem inaugurates.[27] I wish here to follow upon Culler's lead, but to alter his emphases, for the apostrophes that populate eighteenth-century poems have a referential character that complicates our understanding of their efficiency and utility in bringing about the kind of discursive event Culler defines.

These poems, I suggest, certainly enact for us the constitution of the poetic self, but the personified other—Liberty, Commerce, even the (nationalist) Muse—is such that a historically specific incarnation of poetic aspiration results. Apostrophe here is thus part of a complex of rhetorical techniques that stage the drama of the poet's mind as part of the drama of nation and empire. I am arguing, then, that the fact that the terms personified circulated simultaneously in contemporary discussions of politics, economics, and imperialism should make a difference to our understanding of the enactment of poetic subjectivity. Thus, we do not deal with apostrophe solely as the quintessential poetic act, the vocative that is the "image of voice," the "pure O of undifferentiated voicing," but recognize that such apostrophic addresses, like other tropes of literary authority, derive their discursive and ideological authority from the idiom of nationalism, in particular the iconography of Britain as arbiter of trade and empire.[28] In much eighteenth-century poetry, that is, the aspiration that forms the vocative O derives its vitality, and finds its object, in the imagined life of the nation.[29] As we have seen above, this iconography of Britain is not, of course, a purely and simply British iconography since its historical (retrospective and prospective) power and its global ambitions encourage a range of references and images. In each case, however, the logic of apostrophe and personification follow the arguments of national power, and the apotheosis of the nation (or of its distinctive energies) is the project of the poem, and the making of the poet.

A Mythology for Commerce: Glover's *London*

I move now to a poem whose iconic apparatus is of interest precisely because it fuses apostrophe and apotheosis in its account of the origins of national greatness. Of the poets in this period who imagined Commerce as an itinerant goddess, one whose benign presence enabled the transition between prehistory and civilization in different parts of the world, Richard Glover forged a potent union of mythology and more materialist observations in order to energize his vision of a powerful Britain, the contemporary (and ideally final) home of Commerce. In *London: or, the Progress of Commerce* (1737/38), Glover develops a theory of history not unlike those we have considered earlier, except that he grounds the power of commerce in a myth of divine origins. Glover's crafting of a commercial and nationalist mythopoetics had a local motivation: his poem is one of the many pieces of propaganda (including those that followed upon Robert Jenkins's presentation of his ear before the House of Commons in 1738 as an instance of Spanish brutality) that argued the need for war against Spain, war that was finally announced, to the pealing of bells, on October 19, 1739. The public agitation in favor of war was egged on by the South Sea Company and orchestrated, in part, by the anti-Walpole opposition, including Lyttelton.

"Argument," the prose preamble that leads into the poem, specifies his genealogical objectives:

The following poem represents Commerce as the child of Neptune, and born on the coast of Libya in an island, celebrated in fabulous antiquity for its fruitfulness and plenty during the first uncultivated ages, whence the new divinity is supposed to convey these blessings round the world. Her birth is attended by many of the Gods, who endow her with their several gifts: among the rest Apollo appoints her to be the inventress of letters; Sir Isaac Newton's opinion being here alluded to, that merchandize gave rise to this wonderful discovery.

A fabulous origin, perhaps, but one whose mythical coordinates (Neptune as father, for instance) enable the poem's celebration of the ocean-based commerce that it sees as the engine of civilization: "Commerce is then described as making her first appearance to the world among the Phœnicians, the earliest people, who exercis'd an extensive trade. From thence she proceeds to visit other parts of the globe, . . . [first Carthage in Libya, then from place to place till] allured by the vigour and singular resolution of the Dutch in throwing off the Spanish yoke, she takes up her residence with that indefatigable people."

As we have noticed, the movement from antiquity to the present moment is also a movement from mythology into history, such that it is the political resolution of the Dutch that makes them a people fit to receive the goddess. This political particularity is further sharpened in Glover's account of why Britain is now recipient of the goddess's attentions: "Lastly, by the good laws, which have been made from time to time for the encouragement of trade among us, especially by the act of navigation, which has transferred a great part of the Dutch traffik to ourselves, she is suppos'd on our invitation to choose England for her chief abode, more particularly London, our principal emporium, as well as capital city." However, Glover's sense of the progress of Commerce to London is less sanguine than might initially appear, as his "Argument" closes with the familiar fear that an itinerant goddess might not stay home—that she may, in due course, wander away from Britain. Thus the poem will also be an occasion for an enquiry into the rise and fall of trading states and nations, into "how it has come to pass, that, notwithstanding the great wealth and power attending Commerce, the course of trade should so often have shifted its seat." "Argument" will end, Glover promises, on a pragmatic note: "the means, conceived most effectual to fix this wanderer here, are pointed out."

As with Young's poems, the opening of *London* makes clear the power that can be claimed by the poet of nation. His theme demands the "loftiest strain," (line 13) and his Muse soars like the Pindaric eagle, disdaining "all objects but the golden sun" (line 15):

> So, while her wing attempts the boldest flight,
> Rejecting each inferior theme of praise,
> Thee, ornament of Europe, Albion's pride,
> Fair seat of wealth and freedom, thee my Muse
> Shall celebrate, O LONDON: thee she hails,
> Thou lov'd abode of Commerce.
>
> *(lines 18–23)*

If the poem meditates upon the origins and travels of Commerce, it does so only because it can credibly imagine her now at home in London. And yet Commerce comes to London in "retreat," searching for explanations of her "various wanderings" (lines 23–25), a tone that is at odds with the celebratory power of the opening of the poem.

This sense of forced wandering, and even of defeat, lingers throughout the poem, and manifests itself in different ways. Perhaps it surfaces most obviously in the violence that leads to the birth of Commerce; as in so many Greek and Roman myths of origin, Commerce is born out of rape—that of Phœnicé (who lends her name to her pastoral and fertile land) by Neptune, who rushes "from the deep" and "clasps th' affrighted virgin" (lines 35–37). For the next nine months, Phœnicé is transformed into a "solitary mourner," who

> led
> By shame, once more the sea-worn margin sought,
> There pac'd with painful steps the barren sands.
>
> *(lines 40–43)*

She decides to forsake her native land and asks Neptune, as a "suppliant," for death, but Neptune transports her instead to the equally pastoral Libyan isle of Nysa, where in "the infancy of time" (line 84) Eucarpè (Fruitfulness) and Dapsilèa (Plenty) dwell (line 86). Nysa is bountiful with natural treasures— flowers, groves, minerals, fruit—and this is where Commerce is delivered. Ammon, a neighboring god, makes a prophecy at her birth that identifies Commerce as the power who will complete "God's imperfect labour," people the "barren sea," cause cities to rise in deserts, "enlighten man's unlettered race," and unite remote nations: "The graces, joys, emoluments of life / From her exhaustless bounty all shall flow" (lines 125–41).

Neptune attends to name his child Commerce and to offer her "the empire of the main" (line 148), Minerva blesses her with wisdom, Mercury with art, Vulcan with industry, and "Majestic Phœbus" with a "matchless boon" (lines 153–58):

> Thee with divine invention I endow,
> That secret wonder, goddess, to disclose,
> By which the wise, the virtuous, and the brave,
> The heav'n taught poet, and exploring sage
> Shall pass recorded to the verge of time.
>
> *(lines 159–63)*

Thus blessed with the power of writing, Commerce charms "forlorn and wild" man from his "cheerless caves" and "solitary woods" into "sweet society." She casts the foundations of future cities, produces oceangoing ships ("The surge-dividing keel, and stately mast"—line 187), develops astronomy ("The danger-braving mariner to guide"—line 195), and mathematics. Commerce gives man "letters" and "all, / Which lifts th' ennobled spirit near to heav'n, / Laws, learning, wisdom," "all Minerva's arts," the "philosophic page," and the "poet's song" (lines 200–206).

Even as these lines mythologize the power of Commerce, and make of it the single principle of social and cultural change, the entry of Commerce into history, as it were, is of particular importance to the ideological schema encoded in *London*. Commerce turns out to be sensitive to political arrangements, and her first travels are dictated by her objections to the loss of political "freedom" as a tyrant takes over Phoenician Tyre:

> Indignant Commerce, turning from the walls,
> Herself had rais'd, her welcome sway enlarg'd
> Among the nations, spreading around the globe
> The fruits of all its climes.
>
> *(lines 223–26)*

The next sixty-five lines provide an eccentric list of city-states and nations that came to commercial power and wealth but then lost them as Commerce moved on, prompted occasionally by wars. Finally, as "Argument" suggested, she comes to Holland, to support the "bold Batavian in his glorious toil / For liberty, or death" (lines 282–83) against Spain.

This is the moment when Glover sets the stage for the poem's enactment of the drama of modern mercantilism and colonialism. In the contrast between the "bold Batavian," who fights for "liberty," and the Spaniard, who exports only destruction—both in the name of commerce and trade—Glover charts the ideological ground made particularly their own by so many propagandists of English expansion in the eighteenth century. Holland represents the benign form of trade, Spain its obverse, as Commerce roundly denounces Spain as the "shame of polish'd lands," whose colonial actions have corrupted

> With more than savage thirst of blood the arts,
> By me for gentlest intercourse ordain'd,
> For mutual aids, and hospitable ties
> From shore to shore?
>
> *(lines 299–302)*

Spain exterminated the "immense Peruvian empire" and "lordly Montezuma" (lines 305–6) and now brings this same gold-crazed disregard for liberty to the "smiling fields of Europe" (line 309), which leads Commerce to condemn it to future political and economic disaster, and to a time when only its "insolence and cruelty remain" (lines 321–22).

There is no doubt about the polemical force of Commerce's remarks, and yet a figural irony surfaces, as the Spanish are denounced for the same acts of violence and rapine that Glover imagined at the birth of Commerce. In fact, the "gentlest intercourse" Commerce ordains does not even extend to the spread of Dutch trading across the globe, as it is Mars who raises their standard everywhere:

> On tributary Java, and the shores
> Of huge Borneo; thou, Sumatra, heards't
> Her naval thunder, Ceylon's trembling sons
> Their fragrant stores of cinnamon resign'd,
> And odour-breathing Ternate and Tidore
> Their spicy groves.
>
> *(lines 332–37)*

Even as the ostensibly opposed ways of Spain and Batavia are meant to describe the two poles of modern European expansion, it is clear that military might is the basis for commercial control, and this is indeed the lesson that England, historically the next home of Commerce, must learn. Commerce will move now to Britain:

> Albion sea-embrac'd,
> The joy of Freedom, dread of treach'rous kings,
> The destin'd mistress of the subject main,
> And arbitress of Europe, now demands
> Thy presence, Goddess.
>
> *(lines 386–90)*

Glover identifies Elizabeth's reign as the moment when Commerce comes to England, where she chooses London "for her chief abode" (line 409).

Having brought Commerce home, the poet writes at some length (lines 430–55) about the inspiration he derives from Commerce and pledges to sing her praise. He then asks the crucial question, one that has haunted this entire poem: why has Commerce ("though rever'd / Among the nations") "never yet from eldest times . . . found / One permanent abode" (lines 455–58)? His answer is succinct—at her birth, "the pow'r / Of war was absent." This meant that, "unbless'd by Mars," the "sons" of Commerce

> relinquish'd arms, on other arts
> Intent, and still to mercenary hands
> The sword entrusting, vainly deem'd, that wealth
> Could purchase lasting safety, and protect
> Unwarlike freedom.
>
> *(lines 467–72)*

However, the histories of Carthage and Rome prove that it is heaven's will "that empire shall attend / The sword, and steel shall ever conquer gold (lines 482–84). This is the local political moral *London* is designed to teach, a lesson about the need for war against Spain. More generally, the poem also indicates the role of purposive violence in the expansion of commerce, and the divine sanction for "the sword" that translates trade into empire (and thus creates a fit home for Commerce).

At this point in the poem, Glover's overt commitment to military power begins to rewrite the more ambivalent play of vulnerability and domination figured in Neptune's rape of Phœnicé, and its allegorical suggestion of the encounter between sea-based power and fertile lands and places. Indeed, that figure of vulnerable woman allowed Glover to imagine a scene of domination that might otherwise have found no place in the logic of aggressive militarism that the poem now develops. In the poem, then, both the conception of Commerce and the representation of Phœnicé as ashamed, solitary, and mournful are at odds with the explicit political agenda elaborated in its close. Commerce is now instructed to learn from her "suff'rings" and to understand that Britain is fully prepared for its military and commercial destiny. Britain's "wary magistrates" have armed "thousands and then thousands," who, ranged in "bright battalions," are ready for national and international service (lines 482–92). As Glover warms to his vision of British military preparedness, the tone of the poem changes, and it becomes a song of war, an exhortation to conquest. The earlier account of a *doux* Commerce, spreading civilization across the globe, removing herself in the face of tyranny and warfare, is supplanted by an aggressive militarism, and Commerce is reminded that it is for her that Britons sail and go to war:

> The naval tow'r to vindicate thy rights
> Will sweep the curling foam, the thund'ring bomb
> Will roar.
>
> *(lines 520–22)*

This imposes a reciprocal obligation on the goddess and requires her to change her aspect and incorporate into her blessings "the pow'r of war" that was absent at her birth: "Arm all thy sons, thy vassals, ev'ry heart / Inflame" (lines 527–29). Her inspiration will translate into a people and a nation ready for war:

> and you, ye fear-disclaiming race,
> Ye mariners of Britain, chosen train
> Of Liberty and Commerce, now no more
> Secrete your gen'rous valour; hear the call

Of injur'd Albion;

. . . .

Then bid the furies of Bellona wake,
And silver-mantled Peace with welcome steps
Anon shall visit your triumphant isle.
And that perpetual safety may possess
Our joyous fields, thou, genius, who presid'st
O'er this illustrious city, teach her sons
To wield the noble instruments of war;
And let the great example soon extend
Through ev'ry province, till Britannia sees
Her docile millions fill the martial plain.

(lines 529–54)

I quote this passage at length to show how completely the military imagination rewrites the poem: it is the "furies of Bellona" that bring in their wake "silver-mantled Peace," and "Liberty and Commerce" can only be protected by "the noble instruments of war." The last thirty-five lines of the poem continue in this bellicose vein, imagining alliances of potential invaders ("Mahomet could league / His pow'rful crescent with the hostile Gaul"—lines 560–61), who are destroyed by Britain's "warlike youth" (lines 571–74). This imagined defense of Britain by its newly mobilized armies is once again only the prelude to the projection of power overseas. Conversely, the ability to deploy such power abroad is understood as necessary for peace at home:

Gigantic Terrour, striding round our coast,
Shall shake his gorgon aegis, and the hearts
Of proudest kings apall; to other shores
Our angry fleets, when insolence and wrongs
To arms awaken our vindictive pow'r,
Shall bear the hideous waste of ruthless war;
But liberty, security, and fame
Shall dwell for ever on our chosen plains.

(lines 565–89)

London is of course part of the general run of patriotic eighteenth-century poems that feature a Britain dominant over its European competitors. In many ways, Glover's poem is derivative and predictable, repeating themes and motifs made familiar by a host of poets and other propagandists of mercantile and colonial expansion. *London* develops the idea of a benign, peripatetic commerce that brings civilization in its wake that was, a decade later, to be articulated most forcefully by Montesquieu in his *L'Esprit des Loix* (1748). Glover links it to ideas of the westward "progress" of culture and empire in the myth of

Commerce he crafts in the poem, working the whole into a more polemical, urgent argument for Britain's military and naval preparedness; or rather, into an argument about the centrality of warfare to any scenario of overseas commercial expansion and domestic economic prosperity. Thus the idiosyncratic originality of *London* might in fact lie in its fashioning of a formal myth, and doing it in some detail, to establish a legitimizing prehistory for contemporary *military* competition for trade routes and colonies.

In a brief comment on this poem, Bertrand Goldgar calls it "virtually unreadable" and sums up the belligerence of the poem by quoting lines 584–89 (as I do in my reading above).[30] Although I do not particularly disagree with Goldgar's aesthetic evaluation of the poem (if that is what makes it "unreadable"), I have here demonstrated the necessity of *reading* it, precisely because such thematic and rhetorical critical work will show us how a poem like this one should not be dismissed simply as a product of domestic politics (the opposition clamor for war in 1739), to be understood and dismissed as such, but indicates to us the larger, more historically compelling myths of the bellicose commercial and colonial nation that poets in the eighteenth century produced. And the myth making in the poem does not address only this larger political purpose; it is also part of the literary-historical claim that the poem makes for the seriousness and cultural legitimacy of its concerns. As we have seen, the opening lines of the poem enact the "boldest flight" that is required of the poet of commerce, a strain that is confirmed in the classical apparatus invoked in the Phoenician and Roman origins of the goddess. This apparatus lends a fullness of form, and a dignity, to the contemporary song of commerce and warfare: the apotheosis of Commerce is also the elevation of the poetry that sings her praise. Apostrophic address and odic celebration are expanded into a myth of genesis and providential history. Equally, the poet who sings Commerce into mythic being lays claim to being the poet of epic themes, temporality, and geographical sweep.

Singing the National Commodity: Dyer's *The Fleece*

This argument about epic motifs, time schemes, and geography and the role they play in the eighteenth-century British poetry of nation and empire can best be extended via an analysis of John Dyer's *The Fleece*. I will suggest some ways—the large ambit and ambition, a strong will to forge into conscious being entire communities—in which poems on national and historical themes aspire to the condition of epic. I emphasize these elements of *The Fleece* (which is, in form and conception, primarily a georgic poem) in order to suggest that it is a georgic that understands the production of national wealth as a project that links different subnational communities, particularly those whose vitality is necessary to Britain's mercantile and colonial power. (We must remember that in this period, wool and woollen cloth accounted for almost 40 percent of the value of Britain's exports to the Continent). Since the poem's concern is with a nation made strong by more than its domestic husbandry, it expands its georgic canvas to feature historical and geographical concerns more typically those of the epic. *The Fleece* is, then, not simply about the management and care of sheep and wool, but follows the spinning of this wool into yarn (the pun is hard to resist), the knitting of garments from the yarn, and the export of these garments to Britain's colonies and other captive markets in the temperate regions of the globe. It also explores the social and civic values, the technology (light industrial and naval), and the mercantile and political will that will allow sheep's fleece to become a vibrant symbol of national health. The georgic elements of this poem are the foundation for a complex ideological edifice, and the poem in its entirety is a monument to the more plastic generic and formal practices encouraged by the imagining of trade and colonization. And finally, there is the enticing suggestion that contemporary British shepherds are not simply the humble protagonists of pastoral but in a line with those other nation builders and international adventurers, the Argonauts, who sailed after the Golden Fleece.

Accordingly, the poem opens by defining the different constituencies Dyer wishes to incorporate as the collective subject of the poem. His list is not extensive or indiscriminate; he speaks of and to shepherds (or those involved in the care of sheep or wool), merchants, politically powerful people, and, importantly, to the poor and distressed of the nation, to whom the poem will teach "the wide felicities of labour":

> The care of sheep, the labours of the loom,
> And arts of trade, I sing. Ye rural nymphs,
> Ye swains, and princely merchants, aid the verse.
> And ye, high trusted guardians of our isle,
> Whom public voice approves, or lot of birth
> To the great charge assigns: ye good, of all
> Degrees, all sects, be present to my song.
> So may distress, and wretchedness, and want,
> The wide felicities of labour learn.
>
> *(1.1–9)*

The surprising unselfconsciousness of this opening invocation—it seems so little threatened by any fear of burlesque—might itself be proof of Dyer's faith in the new national subjectivity his poem crafts, one based on a commonality of economic interest and on well-superintended forms of labor, trade, and public governance.[31] This proof of orchestrated and hierarchical national power is meant to teach important lessons at home and abroad. The British poor will learn the necessity of labor (and Dyer goes on to argue for poorhouses where such lessons are institutionalized—3.234–302) and the "restless Gaul" will realize that he cannot subvert Britain's borders (1.10–12).

For Dyer, the care of sheep and the wool trade are particularly British pastimes—sheep thrive in Britain (as they do not in Scandinavia or Libya) because of the temperate climate and the rainfall (1.125–51). They are thus emblems of the natural features that make Britain what it is; before they are commodities and the basis of wealth, they are nature's gifts to Britain. And yet, in the vision of the global marketplace that energizes this poem, nature's gifts are in fact commodities, and as commodities, markers of national difference:

> Hail, noble Albion; where no golden mines,
> No soft perfumes, nor oils, nor myrtle bowers,
> The vigorous frame and lofty heart of man
> Enervate.
> . . . .
> See the Sun gleams; the living pastures rise,
> After the nurture of the fallen shower,
> How beautiful! how blue th' ethereal vault,
> How verdurous the lawns, how clear the brooks!
> Such noble warlike steeds, such herds of kine,
> So sleek, so vast; such spacious flocks of sheep,
> Like flakes of gold illumining the green,
> What other Paradise adorn but thine,
> Britannia?
>
> *(1.152–71)*

In this contrast between commodities that cause national degeneration and natural features that ensure a God-given national strength, sheep play a dual role: as "flakes of gold" they compensate for the lack of "golden mines" in Britain, but their pastoral location (they, along with horses and cows, are as natural as the sky, streams, or pastures) inoculates them from the pernicious taint of commodity, and shows why the wealth they produce will be moral, and not be a blight on the nation.

This distinction is very important for Dyer, but it proves impossible for his poem to keep sheep separate from their value in a near-global system of exchange. This is in part because *The Fleece* is committed to an argument about national difference that is based on "natural" variation: that of climate, landscape, and products (1.226–51). Thus, even when Dyer explores the reasons why some lands support sheep and others do not, he comes up with a list of commodities imported by Britain, against which he proffers (the value of) sheep:

No fleeces wave in torrid climes,
Which verdure boast of trees and shrubs alone,
Shrubs aromatic, caufee wild, or thea,
Nutmeg, or cinnamon, or fiery clove,
Unapt to feed the fleece. The food of wool
Is glass or herbage soft, that ever blooms
In temperate air, in the delicious downs
Of Albion, on the banks of all her streams.

$(1.244–51)^{32}$

While the bulk of book 1 is given over to georgic instruction about the proper conditions of raising and shearing sheep, this advice is always framed within an argument that sees sheep herding and the wool trade as a central factor in defining and creating the international prominence of Britain. The Muse itself thus "strays" to the "frequent towns superb of busy trade," especially London, where it looks upon "groves immense of masts; / 'Mong crowds, bales, cars, the wealth of either Ind" (1.172–85), and every shepherd (whose dedication, labor, and forbearing nature are celebrated) is reminded of the "arts of trade" that convert sheep and their fleece into national wealth.[33]

But the desire to find in the industrious care of sheep a model of rural *simplicitas* that will safeguard Britain from a combination of urban and mercantilist ills lingers. In formal terms, this means the recurrence of pastoral images and personnel in the nationalist georgic that Dyer writes, and book 1 closes with a long description of a festive shearing in which "Hoar-headed Damon, venerable swain, / The soothest shepherd of the flowery vale" sings in dialogue with Colin (1.613–732). Their songs offer conventional pastoral contrasts: the canopy provided by "aged oaks" is no less than any palace roof with "polished pillars"; the pleasing weariness and easy sleep that comes from honest labor is preferable to the life of cities, "where, poets tell,"

The cries of sorrow sadden all the streets,
And the diseases of intemperate wealth.
Alas, that any ills from wealth should rise!

$(1.655–58)$

Colin goes on to describe what he has seen at a distance from the summit of "Huge Brearden": "gardens black with smoke in dusty towns" and crowds of "greedy wretch[es]" rushing "for tardy-rising wealth" (that "nauseates with distempers") (1.666–78). Colin's view inverts the expansionist priorities typical to the prospect: it would have been more in keeping with the ideological priorities of the poem if Colin had seen, as the Muse did, the "frequent towns superb of busy trade" (1.173), but in his vision Colin preserves the ethico-moral schemas of the pastoral, particularly its opposition between the country and the city.[34] At the heart of Dyer's poem, then, is a dialectic of conservation and of expansion, expressed in a number of contrasts: sheep as emblems of a local culture and economy *and* as the basis of international exchange; Britain as both home to pastoral simplicities and aggressive overseas trader in wealth-producing commodities; *The Fleece* as both a poem that celebrates the ancient British self-image of a simple and hardy rural people and one that crafts a more contemporary biography of productive, adventurous mercantilists. The *and* in each case suggests continuity as much as contrast— the link between past and future, the complication of forward-looking poetic desire by forms of historical nostalgia.

While the bulk of the poem, then, is concerned with the care of sheep, Dyer's project is much larger, and engages with (as we have seen in all the poems discussed in this chapter) the cultural and social topography of the nation, its mythology and history, its prospects and his fears for its success. He thus comments on some crucial socioeconomic developments that changed the face of eighteenth-century England: enclosure, for instance, of which he is entirely in favor. Here Dyer does not address "improving" landlords but shepherds themselves, reminding them that the "lightest wool" is to be found on sheep who "poorly toil" in "unimproving farms / Of common-fields" and exhorting them to "enclose, enclose, ye swains; / Why will ye joy in common field?" He has an agricultural reason for disliking unenclosed fields (they run fallow), but his choice of idiom is revealing: "in fields / Promiscuous held, all culture languishes." "Nature frowns" and beggary and thievery increase because of unguarded fields and flocks (2.107–33). This sense of social dissolution is particularly interesting because it is the prelude to a longer foray into the anchoring role played by sheep and the wool trade in the movement of "civilization," a kind of translatio ovium. He begins with a warning against complacency, against taking the centrality of Britain to the wool trade for granted, for there

> was a time,
> When other regions were the swains' delight,
> And shepherdless Britannia's rushy vales,
> Inglorious, neither trade nor labour knew.
> *(2.191–94)*

At this point, Dyer develops a "historical" account of sheep rearing and the wool trade (in keeping with the genealogies of commerce offered by other poems). Britain, we are told, came late to the cultivation of sheep and wool, which in "eldest times, when kings and hardy chiefs / In bleating sheepfolds met" was practiced in Phoenicia, Syria, Judaea: "hence their gorgeous wealth; And hence arose the wall of ancient Tyre" (2.204–11).

Industry and wealth moved next to Colchis, and this is the occasion for Dyer to interpolate the founding myth of fleece and nation: Jason and the Argonauts. They assemble because "rising Greece" looks upon Colchis with "indignation" and seeks to wrest from it the Golden Fleece. As Jason plans his fleet and voyage, Dyer emphasizes the technological and navigational advances spurred by the desire for the Fleece. And when Jason actually gets to "golden Phasis," he finds it easy to steal the Fleece (via Medea's charms, of course) because Phasis is sunk in "luxury" and "riot." Phasis falls because of its moral failings: the chief of shepherds, proud Aëtes, "'gan to slight / The shepherd's trade, and turn to song and dance"(2.218–90). The familiar fear of the corrupting effects of wealth surfaces here, as does the model of decline and fall that we have seen in *The Ruins of Rome* or in Young's poems. The Fleece is a metonym for commerce, and its loss is apocalyptic:

> Thus Phasis lost his pride,
> . . . .
> The tradeship left his streams, the merchant shunn'd
> His desert borders; each ingenious art,
> Trade, Liberty and Affluence, all retir'd,
> And left to Want and Servitude their seats.
>
> *(2.303–8)*

The wool trade then moves on to "Grecian colonies" (at a time when "only tin / To late improv'd Britannia gave renown"). It moves on again, to Rome, where it declines with the city, and then is revived by Venetian trade. In Dyer's time, wool is cultivated in different parts of the world, including northern India, Libya, Iberia, and of course "beauteous Albion" (2.312–71), a cause for celebration, but also of concern, in that British wool will face competition form a variety of new sources, including those in the "new Columbian world" (2.422–43).

Dyer's history of fleece is haunted by the constant fear that the world of trading and the wealth it generates will be fatal for the nation. In a mercantilist and nationalist variation on the Horatian *beatus vir,* Dyer writes:

> Happy the patriot, who can teach the means
> To check his friends, and yet untroubled leave
> Trade's open channels.
>
> *(2.457–59)*

The "honest toil" of shepherds, and the fact that "their airy fields / Far from infectious luxury arise" (2.462–63), is offered as ethical ballast against those "worms of pride" who, for their "repast alone, / . . . claim all Nature's stores, wood, waters, meads, / All her profusion"; those who "in the sepulchre of the Self entomb / Whate'er ye can, whate'er ye cannot use" (2.476–81). This call for an ethical commercial and public practice is echoed in Dyer's description of the poet who, "sedulous of public weal," attends both merchants and the "shepherd's hut" and combines, in his poetry, the "pure simplicity" of the latter with attention to the historical achievements of the former ("the high effects of civilizing trade"). Hence, when the poet describes "yearly festals" that celebrate the invention of the loom, he reminds his readers that the labor of dyeing and finishing wool and woolen cloth involves products imported from different parts of the globe, for which thanks are due to "Trade," that "attentive voyager." But traders are not to be thought of in purely instrumental terms, either: as they sail the world they "view the widest prospect of [God's] works" and learn valuable historical lessons. They sail past the ruins of older, once-powerful city-states and nations and learn the lessons that Carthage and Tyre teach, the latter in particular "a monument to those, / Who toil and wealth exchange for sloth and pride" (2.505–658). In their privileged view of the ruins of history (an idea elaborated in 4.53–79), and in their understanding of the importance of production and exchange, they are types of the poet, whose wish it is "to teach th' inactive hand to reap / Kind Nature's bounties, o'er the globe diffus'd" (2.502–3).[35]

If the loom, the trader, and the poet all bring together the bounty of the globe, the loom itself is a model also for the interdependency of different domestic artisans and craftsmen. The carpenter, the ironworker, the turner (lathe worker), the graver (who carves shuttles)—all are involved: "Various professions in the work unite: / For each on each depends" (3.110–20). This account of professional collaboration and productivity is far more credible than Dyer's hyperbolic description of all that happens when workers are distracted from their tasks. As the loom and shuttle are rendered inactive by "wild Intemperance," vagrancy and misery follow. If however, they hum their creative song (especially in workhouses), all is harmonious: storms thunder without wetting any pillows, pure beverages abound, cooked food is made available, physicians wait to heal each sickness, and priests teach the praise of the Maker (3.226–58). Dyer extends his argument for the wool trade by comparing the benefits it offers workers, and Britain, with those offered by other "national" industries elsewhere. If Manchester, Sheffield, and Birmingham are prosperous in the right way, it is because the wool trade is a better source of wealth than the mining of gold, or even the more comparable flax trade in Belgium, the silk trade in Cathay, or the cotton trade in India. Silk and cotton produce but gaudy, "fantastic web[s]" for the luxurious, while "our kinder toils / Give clothing to necessity" (3.337–78). If the argument for national difference as defined by commodity production seems a little thin here (and the moral claims of wool goods a stretch), its necessity becomes obvious from what follows these lines.

For the hardy labor of sheep farming and the production of wool turns out to be a fine training ground for the soldiers and sailors required to make Britain a force overseas. Dyer's claim is couched in the form of a contrast: he tells the "soft sons of Ganges, and of Ind," that life little needs their "feminine toys"; nor does it ask their "nerveless" arms to "cast the strong-flung shuttle, or the spear." They, he suggests, cannot defend their country from invasion or sail the wild oceans, nor can they lead "to distant colonies" their brethren who are driven away by religious or political persecution. "These are deeds / To which their hardy labours well prepare / The sinewy arm of Albion's sons," Dyer writes, and then launches into an account of the waves of immigrants (especially from the Dutch provinces) who have brought their weaving skills to Britain and have made it the entrepôt of the world (3.379–530). Dyer's contrast between an India static and unable to respond to historical need and challenge and a Britain at the center of vital and active social, political, commercial, and colonial processes allows him to emphasize the single most important feature of his argument about the providential movement of history, trade, and exchange—that the country that controls the sea will, as it were, be in command of history:

> Why to the narrow circle of our coast
> Should we submit our limits, while each wind
> Assists the stream and sail, and the wide main
> Wooes us in every port?
> . . . .
>   Thus our isle,
> Thus only may Britannia be enlarg'd.
>   *(3.546–53)*

This hope of enlargement leads to an encomium on British rivers, whose union allows for the easy transportation of goods to "great Augusta's mart," where "lofty Trade / . . . / Gives audience to the world" (3.565–629). Book 3 closes with a vivid impression of London and its trading glory: Dyer's breathless last couplet enacts his excitement: "What bales, what wealth, what industry, what fleets! / Lo, from the simple fleece how much proceeds!" (3.631–32).

The "how much" is spelled out at length in book 4, as the poem abandons its georgic priorities and indulges in the vision of mercantilist nation (and world) that has energized it all along. Once the "woolly treasures" are "amply stor'd" in ships, the poem follows their progress into different parts of the globe. A global trading map unfolds here as Dyer charts both a history and geography of trade. The ships sail past a panorama

of fallen empires and ruined cities (4.53–79)—past, that is, an unfolding
history of mercantile success and failure, and toward the brave new worlds—
east and west—of contemporary trade. Dyer weaves a wondrous tapestry
of places, people, and products; following Vasco da Gama and Columbus,
"The whole globe / Is now, of commerce, made the scene immense"
(4.167–68).[36] The varied figures and landscapes that populate this tapestry
are the products of historical lore, quasi-ethnographic "observations" about
culture and manners, geographical ignorance, and an overwhelming desire
to read the world as requiring, and as receptive to, the emblems of
Britishness. In America, for instance,

> The Iroquese, Cheroques, and Oubacks . . .
>   quit their feathery ornaments uncouth,
> For woolly garments: and the cheers of life,
> The cheers, but not the vices, learn to taste.
>
> *(4.539–42)*

But Dyer does record competition with the French for markets, as he does,
in a description of Admiral Anson's battles with "the Iberian," the naval and
military realities of mercantile and colonial expansion (4.600–53).

The overriding assertion is of a world made one (and in Britain's image)
by trade:

> Rejoice, ye nations, vindicate the sway
> Ordain'd for common happiness. Wide, o'er
> The globe terraqueous, let Britannia pour
> The fruits of plenty from her copious horn.
>
> *(4.654–57)*

If the globe is to be suckled on a British cornucopia, it is because Britain
(and this claim is ironic given that it follows so closely upon Dyer's
description of Anson's naval exploits) is not interested in "The armed host
and murdering sword of war, / And conquest o'er her neighbours." Britain
is described as never breaking

> solemn compacts in the lust of rule:
> Studious of arts and sciences, she ne'er disturbs
> The holy peace of states.
>
> *(lines 662–64)*

and as being interested only in spreading "harmony" and the "various wealth
of toil" (4.665–67). Peace abroad accompanies increase at home: the swains
are promised (as long as they do not drink of the cup of luxury) that they
will one day clothe California, Japan, and lands yet unknown, and will supply

the wool that will allow even the colonizing of the Antarctic. In anticipation of that exultant moment, the "now weary" Muse returns to the pastoral sheepfolds of Siluria, from which humble space arises the trade that now spreads as wide as the Atlantic and the Pacific and spreads "as air's vital fluid o'er the globe" (4.669–96).

Dyer's translation of the humble fleece into an emblem of national economic and moral strength and into the motor force of a global mercantile system is part of what David Shields has called the poem's "theology of trade."[37] Although there is no denying the importance in *The Fleece* of providentialist explanations of climatic and natural features and products, and of global trade, I have sought to call attention to the more secular mythologies that the poem draws upon and crafts in its account of Britain's place in the world. *The Fleece* is a georgic that aspires to the status of national epic, both in terms of its formal inclusiveness and ambit and its ideological ambition. This aspiration marks it, no less than Thomson's *Seasons* or Young's *Imperium Pelagi*, as a poem of its time and place; each poem speaks to and of a Britain being redefined by mercantilist and colonial ventures.[38] Domestic concerns, that is—anxieties about the forms of economic, social, and political development that were reshaping Britain into its commercial and colonial modernity, dislocating some communities and cultures and empowering others, are framed in these poems by the powerful sense that this modernity was produced by Britain's place within an increasingly global system of circulation and control. Each poem projects a map of vast sections of the world to be harvested, traded with, or repopulated and dominated by Britishers (or by Europeans who functioned under British control). And in each case, the poetic projection of British power is haunted by the specter of past successes and failures, of city-states and nations whose rise and fall defined the dynamic of empires and civilizations that competed with, and supplanted, each other.

History, in this regard, proved a difficult text for these poets—it provided ample foundation for their fantasies, for their fusion of models of *translatio imperii* and *translatio studii* into a preamble for a British empire, but it also reminded them of translation, of the transience of national prestige and power. Their poems both acknowledge and repress this contradiction by concentrating on the ethical, political, and commercial initiatives that Britons must perform in order to make possible their rise to wealth and power and to safeguard against its loss. Also, in each case, discussions of international trade and hegemony are couched in poetic forms and idioms not conventionally utilized for such matters, which makes it possible to chart fissures and shifts in the progress of the poem that correspond to unease about the historical or conceptual viability of the ideas it explores. These are the loose and baggy monsters of British poetry, and as such they are wonderful guides to the grotesque and misshapen elements of nationalist culture. As we have seen, the poems this chapter deals with are, for the most part, exercises in the projection of power, but they are also troubled by their perception of inequities of various kinds, at home or abroad. They are preludes to imperialism, but less certain of that (inter)national project than we might imagine, and they make us aware of just how *constructed* its vocabulary and iconography were—of how hard poets and polemicists had to work to naturalize the expectations and worldview of the phenomenon of modern empire.

There are also, of course, good literary-historical reasons to reread these poems now, to remind ourselves of the very public and nationalist intervention these poets imagined themselves making. Their practices and priorities point us toward a somewhat different understanding of the poetry of eighteenth-century Britain than that made available by criticism that concentrates only on poetic forms insulated from, or in ostensible retreat from, the grand narratives of nation and state. For these poets, and a great many others like them, there was no separation of aesthetics and politics, poetic forms and ideological functions, poetic voice and nationalist aspiration. They were not embarrassed, or even made particularly self-conscious by such overlaps; indeed, they were proud of the identification of poet with nation, of the possibility that poets could enunciate weighty matters of national import. For them, the poetry of landscape and nature, or that of exploration and trade, or that of ruin and memorial, or that of heroes and of plebeians, aristocrats and peasants, or that of historical meditation and providential explanation all were grist to the national and increasingly imperial mill. This is not to claim that they were invariably successful in their efforts, or that these poets are the unrecognized authors of the discourse of modern imperialism. They did their bit, no more and no less, and they are of interest today, in the aftermath of formal decolonization, for that reason. They played larger roles in the *literary* history of mercantilist, nationalist, and imperial discourse, however, and their several voices swelled the chorus of empire. As I have argued, they scripted, and spoke feelingly, prologues to the drama of nation and empire. Perhaps it is fitting then, that they should now, in such reading, also speak its lingering epilogues.

5

THE WORLD OF ANTISLAVERY POETRY

A sight like this, who can unmov'd survey?
Impartial Muse, cans't thou with-hold thy Lay?
See the freed Captives hail their native Shore,
And tread the Land of Liberty once more:
See, as they pass, the crouding People press,
Joy in their Joy, and their Deliv'rer bless.

Now, Slavery! no more thy rigid Hand
Shall drag the Trader to thy fatal Strand:
No more in Iron Bonds the Wretched groan;
Secur'd, Britannia, by thy Guardian Throne.

 —Mary Barber, "On Seeing the Captives . . ."

Let, by my specious name, no tyrants rise,
And cry, while they enslave, they civilize!
Know, Liberty and I are still the same,
Congenial!—ever mingling flame with flame!
Why must I Afric's sable children see
Vended for slaves, tho' form'd by nature free,
The nameless tortures cruel minds invent,
Those to subject, whom nature equal meant?
If these you dare (albeit unjust success
Empow'rs you now unpunish'd to oppress)
Revolving empire you and yours may doom,
(Rome all subdu'd, yet Vandals vanquish'd Rome,)
Yes, empire may revolve, give them the day,
And yoke may yoke, and blood may blood repay.

 —Richard Savage, "Of Public Spirit . . ."

In the late eighteenth century, one cause that greatly energized poets, both men and women, to write feelingly about Britain's place in the world was that of antislavery.[1] As I have argued so far, most British poets in the long century under consideration here engaged with ideas and issues that they believed important to the cause of their nation, particularly those ideas whose novelty and urgency derived from Britain's growing mercantile power and colonial ascendancy across the globe. This engagement shapes eighteenth-century British poetry and gives it its distinctive cultural and ideological character. The horizons of British poetry were widened to a point that almost every poet wrote a poem or two on the interplay between Britain and its competitor European nations, or on Britain and its successes (or defeats) overseas, and some poets made such topics central to their self-conception and to their sense of the vocation of the poet in the age of navigational, commercial, and colonial modernity. Historical retrospection went hand in hand with a poetry of global prospect, leading to reconceptions of the role of the poet and of the poetry of public themes.

As we have seen, many self-conscious innovations in form derived from the desire to create poems adequate to the new heroism, as merchants joined naval officers and statesmen in the British pantheon. A poetry of apostrophe, slogans, and icons resulted, but also poetry expansive enough to register and examine at length the world of British expansion. Equally, the development of British constituencies committed to the various forms of overseas expansion, and the reactions of those who were appalled at their impact at home, meant that few poems on such themes were not partisan in argument or choice of hero. Some of the repetitions of pattern or theme in this poetic nationalism might be read as enacting occasional agreements about national priorities, but for the most part, each poem we have examined suggests not the achievement of, but the desire for, such consensus.

In this chapter, I wish to consider the world of some antislavery poems, or, more particularly, the way these poems represent the world as an arena ripe for the operations of British reform. These poems are the products of reformist and humanitarian thought, and were often written on commission to encourage the efforts of people who mobilized against slavery and the slave trade (David Dabydeen does point out, though, that the deluge of antislavery poetry from the 1770s onward suggests a less idealistic set of motives: it is probable, he says, that the theme of slavery provided "an opportunity for grubs and hacks to indulge in sentiment, to try out verse techniques, and to make some money by either capitalizing on popular feeling or else by cashing in on the latest sensational revelation in the newspapers of West Indian brutalities.")[2] The poems that I consider here were all written in the late eighteenth century, and thus they often commemorate the defeat of parliamentary bills lobbied for by the Committee for the Abolition of the Slave Trade, rather than the successes, in the first three decades of the nineteenth century, of antislavery activists and abolitionists on both sides of the Atlantic.

In spite of these parliamentary disappointments, these poems are for the most part marked by a certainty of tone, one that derives from ethical and religious convictions, but also from the fact that these poems are committed to a vision of Britain stronger and even more powerful globally once it successfully spearheads the abolition of the slave trade and slavery.[3] The vocabulary of "progress" was central to these poems (and to abolitionist thinking generally), and to that extent antislavery discourse drew sustenance from, and contributed to, the development of the larger eighteenth-century European discourse of social and human improvability. Theorists of society and culture generated supple schemas showing that human groupings evolved in distinct stages, from hunting and gathering to agriculture to commerce, and this model of development was used to explain not just the evolution of European societies (including their internal disparities) but was extended to explain the superiority of European economies and cultures over the rest of the world.

Such "enlightenment" vision saw large parts of the globe lying in darkness, awaiting the rays of the northern sun to liberate them from their economic, cultural, and religious shackles (as we will see, this is an image utilized often in antislavery poetry). In the specific case of slavery, the shackles were manufactured in Europe, but this fact enabled British antislavery propagandists to argue that Britain could assume moral and political authority by being the first to act conclusively against the slave trade. The dismantling of the traffic in slaves, and their eventual liberation, would extend the British mandate (and that of "civilization" in general) to those parts of Africa now savaged by British and European slave traders. As historians of antislavery have shown, the success of antislavery activists was quite remarkable: in a few decades after 1760 they were able to mold public opinion against a form of economic organization that had scarcely been questioned before, and whose successful deployment in the New World had contributed immeasurably to the coffers of European states, merchants, and colonists.[4] In the case of Britain, a number of factors made the spread of antislavery sentiment possible, and I here quote Howard Temperley's judicious list: first, economic developments, especially the equation of free labor with greater productivity and efficiency, "encouraged a progressive view of history." Secondly, "social changes associated with that development helped to create a belief that there were universal laws governing human progress." Thirdly, both secular and religious reformers linked "these laws to what they took to be the essential values of Western culture. . . . and finally, we may note how these beliefs were strengthened by the advent of modern nationalism."[5]

In what follows, I will read late-eighteenth-century antislavery poems by William Cowper, Hannah More, Elizabeth Bentley (briefly), and Anna Letitia Barbauld, in particular to examine their account of the place of Britain in the world of the slave trade (and elsewhere). Since I will also develop an argument that antislavery poets constructed the imposing edifice of antislavery on equally elaborate nationalist foundations, my analyses will foreground the celebration (and occasional castigation) of the nation featured in their poems. I arrive at my discussion of antislavery poems via a detour into the world of empire, exploration, and cultural difference as it is represented in several of Cowper's poems other than those written explicitly to further antislavery agendas. I take this route in order to show that this story of antislavery can be understood only within larger narratives of nation and empire, whose imperatives inform the argument of all these poems. I do not attempt to write a history of antislavery poetry here (my endnotes will show that much of this history is now available to us): for instance, I do not examine any poems written in the early decades of the nineteenth century, which is when abolitionists came into their own; nor have I listed the many other antislavery poems written in the last decades of the eighteenth century. This chapter is structured by concerns articulated in the rest of this book; those concerns have determined my choice of poems, as I am sure they have my readings of them.

One last framing observation before I move to a discussion of Cowper: in Britain, the projection of an enlightened nationalism—that is, the argument that abolition would allow Britain to reassert its leadership of European powers in their expansion across the globe—was in part a defensive, rearguard response to events that led up to the U.S. Declaration of Independence in 1776. This major crisis in the political and moral legitimacy of the British Empire generalized the lexicon of natural rights and political self-determination into unexpected quarters, and even though most of the proponents of U.S. independence had no qualms about slaveholding or slavery per se, some like Tom Paine did write against slavery, too. The politics of British America in these years provided an unexpected gloss to Thomson's claim that Britons never would be slaves, and in this case the Americans had established that claim in revolt and via force of arms. There were also instances of British-American Royalists offering freedom to slaves who would desert, and slaves who did so were armed against their former masters (just as some slaves were enlisted on the side of the Revolution). However, Robin Blackburn's comment on this state of affairs is to the point: neither side could "afford to challenge slavery, but as the Revolution unfolded new opportunities were created for making a breach in the slave regime."[6]

Cowper's "World"

In "The Sofa," book 1 of William Cowper's *The Task* (1785), the poet, as part of a Horatian commentary on the man who is truly blessed, suggests that such a man has learned the "manners and arts of civil life" and has needs that are easily supplied by "temperate wishes and industrious hands"

(1.592–99).[7] Such temperance and productivity are not available to "the shiv'ring natives of the north" or to the "rangers of the western world," or even to those who inhabit the newly "discovered" South Sea islands, even though the "constant sun" does "Cheer all their seasons with a grateful smile." These smiling seasons are a mixed blessing, for the lives of the islanders "boast but little virtue," being "inert / Through plenty." The constant sun converts them into "victims of luxurious ease" (1.620–25). Worse, they are

> placed remote
> From all that science traces, art invents,
> Or inspiration teaches

—too far for even the British ships that first sailed there to go by again (1.626–31). The progression in Cowper's definition of the *beatus vir*, the movement of his vision from the centrality of the British countryside (well supplied with the many needs of such a man) to the deficient outer ranges of geography, culture, and morality, describes what becomes, by the late eighteenth century, a familiar poetic mode of organizing the world. It also shows us how a familiar topos ("Blessed the man") was reinscribed into the expanding and global views available to the British poet: where once simpler, more local, contrasts might have served, now both the exemplary citizen (and the poet) are defined via summary comparisons with cultures and peoples across the globe.

Cowper's meditation on the beatific or ideal life is part of a "train of thought" that includes consideration of life on the islands of the South Pacific (the Society Islands and the Friendly Islands), in particular themes suggested by the return to Tahiti of Omai, a native of those islands who had been taken to England by a ship's captain in 1774.[8] Omai returned to Huaheine with Captain Cook in 1776 and was the object of considerable public interest, both while in England and upon his return home.[9] Cowper's Omai (called Omia, "gentle savage," in the poem) is a man caught between cultures, a man who knows the simple joys of a pastoral and naturally fecund life in the South Pacific but who now, after time spent in England, recognizes the "forlorn and abject state" ("from which no power of thine can raise her up") of that life (1.659–60). But Cowper's portrait of Omai is more complex than is suggested by this distinction between the simple and primitive life of the islands and the rich and complex civil society of England—

> our state,
> Our palaces, our ladies, and our pomp
> Of equipage, our gardens, and our sports,
> . . . our music.

> *(1.642–45)*

As this somewhat swollen list indicates, Cowper is, at the very least, ambivalent about the trappings of "civilization" and about its effects on people like Omai,

> whom no love of thee
> Or thine, but curiosity perhaps,
> Or else vainglory, prompted us to draw
> Forth from they native bow'rs, to show thee here
> With what superior skill we can abuse
> The gifts of providence, and squander life.
> *(1.633–39)*

Omai becomes a version of the foreign traveler to Britain, through whose eyes Britons can see their own excesses. In the poem, he is doubly victimized, brought to England in response to British curiosity or "vainglory" and then abandoned to his South Sea island home, without hope of further contact with Britain because his lands have nothing to offer British seamen and traders:

> We found no bait
> To tempt us in thy country. Doing good,
> Disinterested good, is not our trade.
> We travel far 'tis true, but not for nought;
> And must be brib'd to compass earth again
> By other hopes and richer fruits than yours.
> *(1.672–77)*

Cowper of course had no reason to think that Omai thought himself abandoned (and admits as much when he writes: "Thus fancy paints thee, and though apt to err, / Perhaps errs little, when she paints thee thus"— 1.661–62). But this feeling of loss is crucial to the vignette of the nation and its international boundaries that Cowper develops here. The perception of Omai's loss of Britain and its comforts in effect balances the poem's critique of British mercantilism—its reminder that Britain's voyages are motivated by materialist concerns and not by any logic of "disinterested good" (we should also remember that the initial expeditions to the South Pacific claimed to be driven by scientific interests). This critique is set against Omai's sense that Britain has achieved a great deal not available to his countrymen. In Cowper's scheme of things, then, the greed of British traders and the urban lives of those who are enriched by them need to be reproved— particularly as doing so will preserve the genuine superiority of English culture and morality.

For Cowper, of course, such superiority is located in the genteel life and values of the country. His moral schema is built firmly across the divide between country and city (most famously, "God made the country and man made the town"—1.749), and his denunciation of British commercial practices foregrounds the city. Quite remarkably, in doing so, he rewrites the central topos of British mercantilism, the vision of London ("Augusta") as entrepôt to the world, into which goods and commodities stream as effortlessly (and as naturally) as the Thames or its subsidiary rivers:

> In proud and gay
> And gain-devoted cities; thither flow,
> As to a common and most noisome sewer,
> The dregs and fæculence of ev'ry land.
>
> *(1.681–84)*

Cowper writes with an uncharacteristic Swiftian (excremental) edge here, and the tone continues into his more conventional representation of the immorality of abundance, which breeds in "gross and pamper'd cities sloth and lust, / And wantoness and gluttonous excess" (1.686–88).

He does allow London its status as nursery of the arts (1.693–725), but he complicates the comparison by invoking Babylon as a historical model (1.719–24) and then goes on to attack further (this time on a Shakespearean note) "this queen of cities, that so fair / May yet be foul, so witty, yet not wise" (1.727–28). That Cowper's account of public or national degeneration is fueled by his anxieties about the immorality encouraged by empire is clear from his example of "peculators of the public gold." He invokes one of the large company of 'Indian Nabobs' (those administrators of the East India Company who returned to Britain with extraordinary fortunes) then coming into prominence in Britain:

> thieves at home must hang; but he that puts
> Into his overgorged and bloated purse
> The wealth of Indian provinces, escapes.
>
> *(1.736–38)10*

Cowper's fear of empire as a source of domestic corruption is shared by much of the poetry we have considered so far, but "The Sofa" closes with the idea that such corruption will lead not only to the degeneration of public or civic life and values at home but also to the collapse of the empire abroad. This is how Cowper ends his attack on the city (and its indolent and fashionable citizens):

> There is a public mischief in your mirth,
> It plagues your country. Folly such as yours
> Graced with a sword, and worthier of a fan,
> Has made, which enemies could ne'er have done,

> Our arch of empire, stedfast but for you,
> A mutilated structure, soon to fall.
>
> *(1.769–74)*

The poem's closing vision returns us to the models of the rise and fall of empire, and the emphasis on moral degeneracy as the cause of ruin, that we have been tracking in eighteenth-century poetry.

In pointing to those moments in "The Sofa" in which a poetic exercise on mundane, everyday themes and objects ("I sing the SOFA") inevitably turns into an exploration of the wide world of exploration and empire, I wish to suggest the ineluctable redefinition of the "everyday" by the latter.[11] The critique of commodity, or the condemnation of the city, are both energized by a simultaneous, contradictory, fear (and this is a duality that this chapter will explore): that of empire as a source of immoral wealth and luxury, and of a time when "Our arch of empire" will collapse. It is not as if poets before Cowper were unconcerned with the material or moral effects of mercantilist or colonial expansion; indeed, as we have seen, much of the debate about the state of the nation in eighteenth-century Britain took very seriously the role of trade and empire in the forging of the nation. Such concerns were addressed even by those poets fully prepared to celebrate overseas expansion in its several forms. In their own convoluted way, each of them worried about the domestic lessons taught by the conspicuous success of those whom Cowper calls "peculators of the public gold," and about the moral legitimacy of British trading practices, colonial plantations, and military conquest in faraway lands.

But the poetry of the later eighteenth century does register a shift, a variation, on these themes, in which the discussion of the wrongs of overseas trading practices or of colonies, and of the threat they pose to the vitality of the empire, drifts away from its moorings in the classical past, in the history of prior empires, and finds new anchor in the condemnation of specific contemporary instances of wrongdoing. The emphasis is no longer on a comparison with past empires, where Rome or Carthage or Tyre are invoked as models (however abstract or lacking in detail) to emulate and to fear, and whose rise and fall are seen as historically and morally emblematic for the British Empire.[12] The specter of the past loosens its hold on the poetic imagination of empire and a more certain sense of the rights and wrongs of trade and colonization emerges. This vocabulary is of course never given up and continues to inform the discussion; but poets do begin (for a number of reasons, some of which we will examine here) to argue that one way in which empire can be maintained is to cleanse it of its illegitimacies and immorality, and thus to make it appear less questionable, more the sphere of good intentions and values and less that of goods and money. This argument pays systematic attention to egregious instances of public corruption and immorality in order to suggest that a British Empire cleansed of such trading or colonial practices will be an empire living up to its primary, indeed its *real,* purpose, which is the communication of British ethics and culture to those parts of the world mapped by its ships, traders, and colonists. This poetic project provided poets with fine occasions in which to exercise their moral imaginations, and to do so in ways that would assert the continuing and future legitimacy and importance of the British Empire.[13]

Antislavery and Empire in Cowper

But before I move to that discussion, I would like to pay more attention to Cowper's *Task*—to those sections in which we see the emergence of the poetic discourse of antislavery in the context of a more general anxiety about the morality of empire. Of interest are also the formal expressions and tones of sympathy that frame, and indeed demand, the representation of the suffering of slaves: moral indignation develops from fellow feeling for enslaved Africans, and such feelings become the emotional staple of antislavery poetry.[14] "The Time-Piece" (book 2 of *The Task*) begins with the poet seeking a haven from a world of "oppression and deceit," his soul "sick" with reports of war and the "wrong and outrage with which earth is fill'd" (2.1–7). This more general account of human iniquity is sharpened into a condemnation of the man who, when he "finds his fellow guilty of a skin / Not colour'd like his own" enslaves him: "Chains him, and tasks him, and exacts his sweat / With stripes." Noteworthy here is the personalized form of denunciation—the poet would not have a slave to till his ground or "To carry me, to fan me while I sleep" for all the wealth that the slave trade and slave labor have "ever earn'd" (2.12–32). The ironic turn of the last observation extends the personal disavowal of slave labor into an understanding of the great role played by slavery in the making of wealth in general: no one in Britain is free of the circuit of riches generated by the slave trade and slave labor. This connection between British practices abroad and lives at home is developed further in the lines that follow, which contrast the constitutional liberty guaranteed to Britons with that denied to the people they enslave abroad (2.37–44).

Cowper's reminder that "Slaves cannot breathe in England; if their lungs / Receive our air, that moment they are free," plays on the arguments and language used at the precedent-setting 1772 trial of James Somerset, whose master wished to return him to slavery by removing him from England, but was prevented from doing so by a habeas corpus appeal to the Court of King's Bench.[15] For Cowper, this proof that there can be no slaves in Britain "bespeaks a nation proud / And jealous of the blessing" of liberty, a national pride that needs to be translated into action abroad. But the antislavery and slave-trade measures advocated are not meant to counter the broader thrust of empire; they in fact reshape it into a more humane and justifiable enterprise. "Spread [freedom] then," the poet writes,

> And let it circulate through ev'ry vein
> Of all your empire. That where Britain's power
> Is felt, mankind may feel her mercy too.
>
> *(2.44–47)*

The new, British Empire, post-dating the slave trade, is to be defined by its power *and* its mercy, a winning combination of military and moral authority that (and this is important for Cowper's religious vocabulary) serves also to stave off the divine retribution that threatens the misdeeds of a guilty England (2.154–60).[16]

I do not wish to suggest that such a poetic search for moral legitimacy for the expanding British Empire is simply devious or underhanded, but I do wish to show how the language of guilt or sympathy or morality or reform in this period is inevitably caught up in the larger cause of the nation, stable at home and powerful, in control, abroad. To expect otherwise would be anachronistic; equally, we need to recognize just how fully the sentiments of antislavery (and other reformist causes) were accommodated within the plastic and mutable discourses of empire. Thus, when Cowper asks,

> Is India free? and does she still wear her plumed
> And jewelled turban with a smile of peace,
> Or do we grind her still?
>
> *(4.28–30)*

he is not advocating that the East India Company cease its activities in India as much as supporting parliamentary efforts to streamline, and make less corrupt, its administration. His imaginative world of sympathy and reformist sentiment is not fundamentally at odds with the globe as it is rendered by "discovery," colonization, and trading; ideally, though, there should be a less visible gap between poetic ideal and political action. Hence, there are occasions when Cowper uses the language of disease, of "public plague," to suggest the effects of those East India Company nabobs who buy themselves rotten boroughs and are elected to Parliament (4.670–75). Equally sharp is his denunciation of those merchants who, "disclaiming all regard

> For mercy and the common rights of man,
> Build factories with blood, conducting trade
> At the sword's point, and dying the white robe
> Of innocent commercial justice red.
>
> *(4.679–83)*

This language of infection or of bloody commercial exploitation is of a piece with Cowper's condemnation of other forms of national corruption, which feature the emasculation emphasized by Dyer (and by Anna Barbauld, as we will see below). Cowper frowns disdainfully "at effeminates, whose very looks / Reflect dishonour on the land I love." How, "in the name of soldiership and sense," he asks,

> Should England prosper, when such things, as smooth
> And tender as a girl, all essenced o'er
> With odors, and as profligate as sweet,
> Who sell their laurel for a myrtle wreath,
> And love when they should fight; when such as these
> Presume to lay their hands upon the ark
> Of her magnificent and awful cause?
>
> *(2.222–32)*

I quote these lines to show how Cowper, understood often as the poet of personal and psychic retreat, is equally a poet who has strong opinions about the state of the nation, and whose commentary derives its images and energies from precursor poets who fear a falloff in the national will to go to war. Cowper contrasts these "effeminates" with the military and parliamentary exploits of General James Wolfe and the earl of Chatham (whose war policies enabled British gains in North America), and worries that the present moment can offer only "empty talk / Of old atchievements, and despair of new" (2.254–55). All this is understood with reference to the loss of an empire—the American colonies—and the urgent need to consolidate British power again (4.263–84).

While thinking about Cowper's engagement with his world, or his retreat from its urgencies, we must remember that his choice of poetic topics varied greatly, often in response to his mental and emotional instability. He wrote many "political" poems in the late 1770s and in the early '80s; indeed, his editors describe him, in this period, as "responding vigorously, often combatively, to his world; both to immediate personal experience of an everyday sort, and to the vicarious experience offered by the newspapers—politics, war, the atrocities of the London mob."[17] He wrote several anti-French poems, an exhortation "To Sir Joshua Reynolds" to paint Britain's triumphs over France, Spain, and Holland (to show how "Britannia gives the World Repose"), and an ode to Boadicea that is inspired by Thomas Gray's "The Bard" and promises future national greatness in keeping with a model of *translatio imperii*. The Roman triumph in England is short-lived, insists a defeated and dying Boadicea, and her last words confirm a druidical prophecy that the ruffianly Romans will suffer divine revenge, and that Britain will ascend to imperial power ("Empire is on us bestow'd"). Vincent Newey, too, has provided a precise account of Cowper's engagement with national political issues; he argues that "Cowper's retreat" can also be understood in political terms and as connected to "England's 'defeat'" (the loss of the American colonies, the Treaty of Versailles—all of which Cowper found "humiliating").[18]

The Task may begin as a poem of retirement and seclusion, but it is consistently worldly in its concerns, such that the otherworldliness it finally invokes, its religious framework, often reads like a retreat from ideological contradictions and difficulties.[19] Thus, Cowper's final word on the slave trade, or indeed on the future of "England's glory," which now "wax[es] pale / And sickly," comes from the consolations of religion. At the end of a long, despondent passage on the inevitable decline of Britain ("The deep foundations that we lay / Time ploughs them up, and not a trace remains"), a passage whose images and tone are almost identical with the "ruins of empire" sentiment that we have traced, Cowper promises a "liberty" beyond that sung by poets or sanctioned by senators or monarchs, which is a "liberty of heart, derived from heav'n" (5.509–45).[20] In keeping with this otherworldly promise, he suggests that it is "Grace that makes the slave a freeman" (5.688), which is at once a reminder of the immorality of slavery and a retreat from the poet's heartfelt condemnation of its cultural and economic role in the making of the British Empire. The thousand-odd lines of the last book ("The Winter Walk at Noon") of *The Task* are dedicated to the celebration of divine power and beneficence, and all good on an often corrupt earth is seen as inspired by, or a prelude to, the greater good of the hereafter. There is only one real empire, then, only one sovereign with absolute power, and only one law, "the law of universal love" (6.352–60).

Cowper had explored many of these issues and ideas in "Charity" (1782?), a poem marked by his heartfelt denunciation of the slave trade:

> But ah! what wish can prosper, or what pray'r,
> For merchants rich in cargoes of despair,
> Who drive a loathsome traffic, gage and span,
> And buy the muscles and the bones of man?
> *(lines 137–40)*

Cowper's method (if we can call it that) in this poem is informed by the humanitarian values of late-eighteenth-century antislavery discourse. He writes of families torn apart, "bonds of nature" destroyed (line 142), lovers separated (lines 145–50), and, perhaps most tellingly and polemically, of the brutalizing process by which an African ("sable warrior") is transformed into a slave:

> Yes, to deep sadness sullenly resign'd,
> He feels his body's bondage in his mind,
> Puts off his gen'rous nature, and to suit
> His manners with his fate, puts on the brute.
>
> *(lines 151–54)*

As analysts of antislavery discourse have pointed out, such insistence on the essential humanity of Africans, and on their affectional and kinship relationships, worked to counter the claims made by proponents of the slave trade that Africans were a different and lesser species, one that possessed few of the psychological or somatic sensitivities of Europeans.[21] To write of them in the vocabulary of poetic tragedy and romance was to claim for them a dignity and to demand for them the public sympathy that underlay all arguments for the cessation of the slave trade, or at least of British involvement in its cruelties.

Apart from such humanitarian argument, Cowper also condemns those who "Trade in the blood of innocence" and "buy what is woman-born" as unChristian (lines 180–83). Cowper's Christian polemic here takes on a nationalistic force, for

> A Briton knows, or if he knows it not,
> The Scripture plac'd within his reach, he ought,
> That souls have no discriminating hue,
> Alike important in their Maker's view.
>
> *(lines 200–203)*

Early in the poem, Cowper had insisted on the common Adamic origins of all humanity (lines 15–22), and this pointed reference to souls having no "discriminating hue" extends Cowper's dismissal of the racial basis of proslavery arguments. The poem's antislavery positions are imbued with this combination of Evangelical and humanitarian commitment and argue systematically that abolition must necessarily be a part of the self-image and cultural vocabulary of the Christian and the Briton. This last element, the appeal to national self-definition, is of great consequence throughout the poem and is part of a wider scheme of reference that includes accounts of the divinely orchestrated political economy of the globe, the place of Britain within such an economy, and the necessity of abolitionism to establish British moral and material authority over those overseas regions it trades with or colonizes. All these arguments are developed, we must remember, under the aegis of "Charity or love, / Chief grace below, and all in all above" (lines 3–

4), and explicitly argue for the moral and humanitarian basis of British dominance abroad.

The route to this argument is of course the commonplace claim that "the band of commerce was design'd / T' associate all the branches of mankind," that "each climate needs what other climes produce, / And offers something to the gen'ral use," and that such "genial intercourse and mutual aid" "softens human rockwork into men" (lines 84–96). The magical, transformatory force of this last metaphor confirms the power of "Ingenious Art" ("which thrives most / Where commerce has enrich'd the busy coast") to "refine the race," to protect against the specious demands of "luxury," and to guide architects, painters, and poets (lines 97–112). This interplay between a feminine Art and a virile Commerce leads to a moment of visionary sublimity, in which "Providence enjoins to ev'ry soul / An union with the vast terraqueous globe," a moment whose Blakean intensity dissolves into a more conventional, Christianized account of divine blessings that speed onward the "canvass gallantly unfurl'd" on its voyage to knit "th' unsocial climates into one." Indeed, in this extended passage, mercantilist exploration and commercial transactions are rewritten in a vocabulary whose combination of missionary and humanitarian zeal looks forward to nineteenth-century apologia for British imperialism. In this dispensation, fleets sail "to save, / To succour wasted regions, and replace / The smile of opulence in sorrow's face." On such missions, a ship is

> Charg'd with a freight transcending in its worth
> The gems of India, nature's rarest birth,
> That flies like Gabriel on his Lord's commands,
> An herald of God's love, to pagan lands.
>
> *(lines 113–36)*

But it is not only the doctrine of *doux* commerce or missionary idealism that is meant to characterize the British form of exploration and contact; Cowper, like many late-eighteenth-century poets, claims that his nation is distinguished from competing European imperialisms because it is the home of Liberty (and thus in a position to export its values across the globe) and home to an explorer like Cook, who is represented as the very type of culturally sensitive benevolist and democrat. The poem appeals to Liberty (who came from "Sparta hither, and art here at home") to intervene and to "Teach mercy to ten thousand hearts that share / The fears and hopes of a commercial care" and to "Chain up the wolves and tigers of mankind" (lines 270–87). Cook is a patriot (he in "his country's glory sought his own") who is "loved for savage lives he saved," in contrast to the exemplar of Spanish colonialism, Cortez, who was "odious for a world enslaved!" (lines 23–40). Cowper develops the contrast between Cook and Cortez into an extended meditation upon colonial cruelty, which (in contrast to British commerce) worships the "Mammon" that "makes the world his legatee / Through fear not love," and which thus inevitably leads to the corrosion of public values and the state, each "Starved by that indolence their mines create." The dialectic of empire is important here, and the fall of the Spanish Empire is seen through the eyes of the defeated and enslaved Incas, who speak of their joy to see Spanish glory brought low by Spanish avarice (lines 45–82). Thus, the discourse of antislavery in "Charity" is framed within, and plays a crucial role in enabling, the definition of a nation determined to be free of the moral and materialistic weaknesses that cause equivalent empires to rot (in lines 62 and 63, Cowper uses the phrases "fretting plague" and "canker'd spoil" to describe the decline of the Spanish Empire).

Perhaps the best indicator of the precision with which Cowper's abolitionist imagination, his Evangelical commitment, and his nationalist yearnings for British success overseas dovetail[22] is provided by his vignette of the future after slavery is abolished by right-minded Britishers. The freedom they offer includes Christian revelation; slaves "by truth enlarg'd, are doubly freed." The mediation of religion causes the slave to see his master as his "dear deliv'rer out of hopeless night," but also to see his own origins in a new light: "I was a bondman on my native plain, / Sin forg'd, and ignorance made fast the chain." (Slavery is here the product of *African* moral and religious depravity, not of the actions of British slave traders.) Moved by his double manumission, the slave realizes that his greatest freedom lies in remaining at his deliverer's feet:

> Farewell my former joys! I sigh no more
> For Africa's once lov'd, benighted shore,
> Serving a benefactor I am free,
> At my best home if not exiled from thee.
>
> *(lines 228–43)*

David Brion Davis calls this conclusion an act of "psychological imperialism": emancipation is represented "as a conversion to voluntary servitude," and Charity redeems "the fruits of trade as well as the existing social order."[23] The postabolition world does not look very different from the world at present made available by British merchants, slave traders, and colonizers; in fact, British dominance is now based on ethical and "civilizational" superiority, and internalized as such by those they dominate.

In tracing the place of antislavery discourse in Cowper's worldview, or rather, in detailing the way in which such emancipationist sentiments enabled a renewed and legitimized view of British dominance overseas, I have so far examined what we might think of as his "discursive verse," the poems he wrote as his meditations on consequential public affairs, each written within a recognizable high-cultural, "poetic" idiom—all of which presume upon a literate and even literary audience. I have argued that such poetry allows us to see how ideological and philosophical coherence is crafted out of the often recalcitrant, contradictory materials and positions available to a poet who comments on public issues, national priorities, and historical practices. Both in *The Task* and in "Charity," we have noted that Cowper's concerns were wide, as wide as the globe being mapped by British sailors and merchants, and that he had a consistent sense of how the British colonial and mercantile empire should be developed and enhanced, including by the abolition of the slave trade and the emancipation of slaves. However, as the abolitionist movement developed in the 1780s in Britain, and refined its techniques to focus on lobbying Parliament, the creation of abolitionist groups in towns and cities, and the education of large masses of people, it sought alternative ways in which to address its nonbourgeois constituencies, including illiterate peasants and urban workers.[24] It was in this context that, in mid March 1788, Cowper's friend and patron John Newton passed on a letter from Lady Balgonie asking if Cowper might write some "ballads to be sung about the streets to assist the movement to abolish the slave-trade."[25] Cowper responded with "The Negro's Complaint" and went on to write "Sweet Meat has Sour Sauce: Or: The Slave-Trader in the Dumps," "The Morning Dream," and "Pity for the Poor Africans." In their forced simplicity, in their odd tones and even more odd ventriloquism of speaking and singing voices, in the unexpected jauntiness of refrain in one case, and the measured ironies of another, these poems encourage us to think of antislavery sentiment in ways different from the more "elevated" poems that we have read so far. In many ways, they are better guides to the possibilities and contradictions of antislavery poetry, as they suggest the exhilaration of those convinced of the humanitarian urgency of emancipation and embody the rhetorical difficulties of political understanding and psychological sympathy across great divides of culture and power.

There is first the question of ventriloquism—of speaking in the voice of the slave, or rather, giving the slave a voice considered appropriate to his (or her) station. The well-circulated emblem of slavery, a chained and kneeling African asking "Am I not a Man and a Brother?" did precisely that. In effect these can be construed as attempts to confer a rhetorical dignity, the status of a protagonist even, to someone ordinarily considered outside of polite discourse or indeed of language (that it might lead to some unexpected, perhaps contradictory, results will be the subject of later discussion).[26] Thus, in "The Negro's Complaint" the speaker begins by offering a capsule history of his enslavement, his alienation from Africa's coast, from "Home and all its pleasures" (all "To encrease a stranger's treasures"). He speaks of the culpability of the Englishmen who bought and sold him, but also of his refusal to let his mind be enslaved as his body has been (lines 1–8). So while the ballad takes the form of a complaint, its tone is not peevish or pathetic, but gains strength from its moral and emotional certainty of the wrong that has been done. This is the tone fundamental to the antislavery movement, of course, and the political emphasis of the poem is made clear in the second stanza, which shifts away from individual culpability or evil: "What are England's rights, I ask / . . . / Me to torture, me to task?" Once again, the racial distinctions that were often invoked to legitimize slavery are rejected ("Skins may differ, but Affection / Dwells in White and Black the same"). The third stanza asks "all-creating Nature" why it created the sugarcane that is the basis of plantation slavery, but this is not a philosophical question as much as a reminder to consumers in England of the human suffering that produces sugar: "many backs have smarted / For the sweets your Cane affords" (lines 17–24).

To speak this poem, or to sing it as a ballad, is to assume the position of the slave, a rhetorical identity that puts into play precisely the circuit of sympathy and identification that the antislavery movement sought to inculcate in the British public. This "subject-position," as it were, is the basis of the ironic character of the ballad, a character that is emphasized by the format of questions addressed to British slave traders, policymakers, consumers of sugar, and, in the fourth stanza, to those who would offer slaves a vision of a benevolent Christian God: "Has he bid you buy and sell us / Speaking from his throne, the sky?" The fifth stanza provides an answer to this query— tornadoes, shipwrecks, wasted towns and plantations, whirlwinds—all indicate divine displeasure. The poem closes with an appeal to Britishers to consider the miseries inflicted upon slaves, with the reminder that those who enslave Africans on account of their color lack the very humanity that they claim Africans do not possess:

> Slaves of Gold! Whose sordid dealings
> Tarnish all your boasted powr's
> Prove that *You* have Human Feelings
> 'Ere ye proudly question *Ours.*
>
> *(lines 53–56)*

In this ballad, then, the slave-speaker's values, ironies, and polemical questions are identical with the positions and arguments taken by antislavery advocates like Cowper, such that the poem's critiques of British slave-trading practices and policies, and the domestic economic and moral effects of overseas plantations, all stake the moral and patriotic high ground taken by abolitionists in the late eighteenth century.

There is another important way in which this ballad takes its place within the discourse of moral patriotism being defined by antislavery. It is set to the tune of "Hosier's Ghost,' or As near Porto Bello lying," a political ballad composed in 1740 by Richard Glover to attack Walpole's government for its incompetence in waging the War of Jenkin's Ear. Admiral Hosier's ghost appears to Admiral Vernon's fleet, at rest after taking Porto Bello, to complain about how Walpole's lack of aggressive governmental support had condemned him and four thousand men to dishonorable death by fever while they lay about blockading ports in the Spanish Main in 1726–27.[27] Admiral Vernon's recent successful naval action is thus contrasted with an earlier instance of military-political failure, and the lesson to be drawn is clear—Glover wished to encourage the administration toward an aggressive political and naval foreign policy. Cowper's poem is of course not militaristic in its tone or concerns, but his choice of precursor ballad suggests that his abolitionist, poetic, and nationalist ambitions are no less militant. "The Negro's Complaint" may be written in the voice of a slave, but its singers are meant to be British, as is its audience, and the claim it makes upon the nation is in consonance with Cowper's agenda for a postslavery future, for a Britain whose moral leadership, confirmed by abolition, will translate into a newly legitimized global leadership.

The poem that Cowper wrote a few days after "The Negro's Complaint" also experiments with the speaking or singing voice: it is written from the point of view of a slave trader "in the dumps" because of the success of the abolitionists. If the voice of the slave in the earlier poem enabled Cowper to develop a variety of moral and political ironies, in "Sweet Meat has Sour Sauce: or, the Slave Trader in the Dumps," the persona of the slave trader leads to an unlikely jauntiness of tone and refrain whose ironies are less easily subsumed to the ethical project of the poem. He identifies himself as "A trader . . . to the African shore," one whose "trading is like to be oe'r," and who is thus selling off his stock (lines 1–7). The stock turns out to be instruments of torture used in the slave trade: "Fine chains for the neck, and a cat with nine tails," canes, "padlocks and bolts, and screws for the thumbs / That squeeze them so lovingly till the blood comes," and a "notable engine" that pries apart the jaws of any slave who, on the voyage from Africa, refuses to eat (lines 9–23). He calls these "a curious assortment of daily regales, / To tickle the Negroes with when the ship sails" (lines 9–10), and all designed to produce "A pretty black cargo of African ware" (line 26), a line whose simplicity emphasizes the dehumanization of the slave trader as much as the commodification of the enslaved Africans. As do the other lines quoted above—except that the unselfconscious contrast between the jocularity of utterance and the brutality of all that is being described, the repetitive order imposed by the rhymes within each three-line stanza (regales/sails/tales, for instance, or withdraws/paws/jaws), the flowing ease with which stanzas follow upon each other, and the short refrain between each stanza ("Which nobody can deny") all create rhetorical and poetic effects that suggest a slave trader far from convinced by the humanitarian arguments of the abolitionists, and unrepentant even as he is forced to wind up his gory business.

The ironic distance between the form of the enunciation (as also the attitudes being enunciated) and the moral aims of the poem is so large that it destablizes the ethical polarities that were the foundation of antislavery discourse. Thus, when the trader invites his audience to see how precisely and efficiently he lays out the slave bodies in transit in his ship ("'Twould do your heart good to see 'em below, / Lie flat on their backs all the way as we go"), or demands their sympathy for the loss of his living ("Which nobody can deny"), the poem complicates its circuit of address to a point where a reader might be justifiably confused about the ease with which an abolitionist poem ventriloquizes proslavery speech, especially its most vicious commonplaces. The poem is so unembarrassed about the instruments, details, and effects of torture that it lists, that even as it makes for good drama (the slave-trading protagonist is fleshed out), it also seems to enjoy its own proslavery soliloquy too much. Further, since the poem does not enact the conversion of the slave trader, or register, via a change in idiom or tone, any recognition of appropriate abolitionist values, it is hardly surprising that the Committee for the Abolition of the Slave Trade did not make use of this ballad. It remains for us then a poetic oddity, an unusual instance of how the poetry of antislavery explored voices antithetical to its own positions and found their idiom seductive in some unpredictable ways. The very idea that Cowper would have abandoned the earnestness of tone that characterized both his other antislavery writing, and abolitionist discourse in general, in favor of this ventriloquist's act is surprising, but he clearly found such creative playfulness attractive, for he performed another version of it in the last of the four antislavery ballads he wrote, "Pity for the Poor Africans."

In this poem, Cowper writes in the voice of a British "pragmatist" (which is what I will call the opening speaker of the poem) who argues that unilateral withdrawal from the slave trade will do no more than open it to French, Dutch, or Danish control, and lead to the atrophy of British colonial and mercantile interests in the Caribbean and elsewhere. The speaker registers his shock at "this Traffick in Slaves," his distaste for slave traders, his pity for the slaves' "Hardships, their Tortures and Groans," but quickly states his position: "I pity them greatly, but I must be mum; / For how could we do without Sugar and Rum?" (lines 1–6). Further, if competing European powers take control of the slave trade instead of Britain, slaves will be worse off and their "Tortures and Groans will be multiply'd still" (lines 9–12). Since "Foreigners" have no intentions of giving up the riches they gain "by purchasing Blacks / Pray tell me, why we may not also go Snacks [share in the proceeds]?" (lines 13–16).

At this point, the poem shifts to the telling of a moral tale that offers lessons to the slave trader, but the syntax does not quite make clear who is telling the story. The presence of an antislavery interlocutor is clear—either he tells this cautionary tale to show the "pragmatist" the error of his ways, or (though this is the less credible possibility) the opening speaker of the poem tells it himself to show how he has accommodated his moral scruples about, and sympathy for, African slaves to the realities of international commerce. The story is simple, and tells of Tom, a schoolboy, who is horrified when his compatriots seek to rob apples from an orchard, and argues that the orchard provides bread for the poor owner and his family.[28] His friends will have none of this and say that they will rob the orchard with or without him; if he comes along he will get his share. This convinces Tom, who joins in the raid: "He blam'd, and protested, but join'd in the Plan; / He shar'd in the Plunder, but pity'd the Man" (lines 43–44). This debunking of the "pragmatist's" claim to sympathize with those he must plunder is the polemical point of the poem, and is enabled by the counterpoint of voices and stories in the poem. Unlike in "Sweet Meat has Sour Sauce," the proslavery argument is not allowed to go unchallenged, and the "pragmatist" is not indulged beyond a point, unlike the slave trader in the earlier poem, whose voice (however ironized) has full play throughout the ballad.

Perhaps the poem most representative of Cowper's antislavery sentiments and values is the one that he wrote in the last week of March 1788, shortly after he had composed the first two ballads. Unlike the various forms of poetic ventriloquism that shape the other poems (the voice of the slave in "The Negro's Complaint," that of the slave trader in "Sweet Meat has Sour Sauce," and that of the proslavery pragmatist in "Pity for the Poor Africans"), the "The Morning Dream" is written in the persona of the poet: the "I" that dreams and wakes to learn that his dream-vision is coming to life is identified unequivocally with the poet. As in "The Negro's Complaint," ideas and sentiments are developed across eight-line stanzas and have a dignity and completeness lacking in the four-line stanzas of the other two poems, as also a finished, formal quality that the other two dispense with (perhaps to imply that they mimic untutored, even illiterate, voices). And, as in "The Negro's Complaint," but even more so, the real object of address is the nation, and the vision of abolition is seen as one more step in the greater overseas glory of

Britain. The poet describes his dream in terms of lightness and ease, a "pleasant" sense of sailing buoyantly westward, "While the billows high-lifted the boat, / And the fresh-blowing breeze never fail'd" (lines 7–8). In this dream-voyage, the poet sees an awe-inspiringly beautiful woman sitting in the steerage, and the shield at her side sheds "light like a sun on the waves." She turns out to be Liberty, embarked on this westward voyage "to make Freemen of Slaves," and the poet listens entranced to her song (lines 9–16). Cowper's images and motifs are here derived from the paraphernalia of the quest fable and romance, and this extends into an account of the "slave-cultur'd island" they come to, where "a daemon, her enemy, stood,"

> Oppression his terrible name.
> In his hand, as the sign of his sway,
>   A scourge hung with lashes he bore,
> And stood looking out for his prey,
>   From Africa's sorrowful shore.
>
> *(lines 26–32)*

However, in a moment of magical victory, as soon as the monster sees the "goddess-like Woman," the scourge ("with blood of his subjects imbued") falls out of his hand, and he sickens and dies. He expires, and ecstatic shouts ascend "the sky / From thousands with rapture inspired" (lines 33–40). At this, the poet awakens, and muses on "what such a Dream might betide?" The answer follows soon, in the form of "the glad news" that he hears:

> That Britannia, renown'd o'er the waves
>   For the hatred she ever has shown
> To the black-sceptered rulers of Slaves—
>   Resolves to have *none of her own*.
>
> *(lines 45–48)*

The abolitionist dream Cowper writes here is premised, once again, on a political understanding of contemporary Britain, on an argument that it is distinguished from other European (slave-trading) powers as the constitutional home of liberty, and as the humanitarian enforcer of its values in colonial spaces abroad. That Cowper's poetic appeal on behalf of such action takes the form of a romance fantasy suggests both the centrality of icons like that of a goddesslike Liberty/Britannia to the nationalist imagination of eighteenth-century Britain and also perhaps the poet's recognition that the mundane and difficult political processes that abolitionists were involved with would offer no equally magical resolutions. The fantasy of Liberty triumphant cathects the burdens of slavery even as it imagines a "westward" colonial future safely British. Such agendas, of course, were very important in making antislavery palatable to most Britishers: its ethical and altruistic appeals to a universal humanitarianism were woven into an attractive fabric of nationalist arguments. These new (and some refurbished) motifs in the banner of late-eighteenth-century British imperialism emphasized the supremacy of British cultural, ideological, and religious values in the colonizing and commercial encounters between Europe and the Caribbean, the Americas, Africa, India, and lands further east, and suggested the grounds upon which ideologues of empire in the nineteenth century would insist upon its global utility and necessity. The discourse of antislavery was forward-looking in many ways, not least of which was its argument on behalf of the civilizational burden to be carried by Britain in its military and mercantile expansion across the globe.

However, in the late 1780s and early 1790s, political and parliamentary developments did not suggest an easy path to ending the slave trade. While a number of antislavery campaigners argued for the end of slavery itself, in 1787 the Committee for the Abolition of the Slave Trade took a strategic decision to press only for the abolition of the slave trade. This meant that they could petition Parliament to regulate the slave trade since it had the right to regulate all trade, and also to protect themselves from the claim that they were interfering in property rights by demanding that slave owners give up slaves. There were successes, particularly in mobilizing petitions to Parliament, but both in April 1791 and in April 1792, crucial parliamentary bills to abolish British participation in the slave trade were effectively defeated.[29] In the latter debate, Wilberforce had asked the Commons to vote (they did, 230 to 95) that the slave trade ought to be abolished, but the force of that motion was effectively scotched by Henry Dundas, who inserted a clause for "gradual" abolition (by which he meant "postponement to a specified date: Dundas urged the year 1800, but the House finally agreed on 1796.")[30]

This was the first parliamentary vote against the slave trade; it was not, however, what Wilberforce and his allies had hoped for. Cowper's sonnet "To William Wilberforce, Esq." suggests some of the characteristic ways in which antislavery poets addressed parliamentary disappointments and converted them into occasions for a restatement of principles and ideals. Cowper published this poem in the *Northampton Mercury* on April 21, 1792, along with a letter that quashed "rumors" that he had abandoned his antislavery beliefs.[31] Cowper's address to Wilberforce begins in the name of his "Country," and the first sestet states Wilberforce's embattled position as leader of the abolitionist cause. A distinction is made between the country and those "cruel" and "impious" men who oppose Wilberforce, a distinction that is important for the second sestet, which offers consolation for lack of parliamentary success. Wilberforce has at least "gain'd the ear / Of Britain's Senate." Thus

> Hope smiles, Joy springs, and though cold Caution pause
> And weave delay, the better hour is near
> That shall remunerate thy toils severe
> By Peace for Afric, fenced with British laws.

> *(lines 9–12)*

This last image sums up the twin objectives of British antislavery campaigners: the "fence" built to keep slave traders out of Africa promises control over Africa itself. The British laws meant to regulate or abolish the slave trade will legitimize, in fact make humanitarian and necessary, imperial control over the continent, or at least those parts of it freed from the depredations of the slave trade.[32]

Nationalist Sentimentality: Some Antislavery Poems by Women

As I have argued in this analysis of Cowper's poems, antislavery discourse played an important role in the evolution of British nationalist and imperialist discourse, even as it questioned—or rather, precisely because it questioned—Britain's involvement in the slave trade. As Moira Ferguson has suggested, in many ways, the precursor text for the literary and ideological formulae that I have been tracing is the Oroonoko story (both in its telling in Behn's novella and in its redaction in Southerne's staging).[33] Both Behn's and Southerne's texts demonize slavery and the slave trade (even as they include a worldly-wise awareness of the economic bases of slavery) and ratify largely conservative class, racial, and gender hierarchies (while rejecting some of their most egregious and dehumanizing attributes). They provide exemplary instances of the ways in which a text can register myriad domestic and colonial anxieties while finding, in a language of benevolence and sensitivity, a narrative power that seems both morally purposive and political.[34] The Oroonoko "model," if we can call it that, refers to a text that represents colonial slavery from a more or less abolitionist perspective, while being concerned with issues that are important to the evolving conception of a Britain "Great" at home and abroad.[35]

Behn's novella also depicts horrific sequences of the torture of slaves, in particular that of Oroonoko (who of course suffers his torments in noble silence), thus providing a precedent for the occasionally extended descriptions of torture in some poems, passages that are necessarily at variance with the polite sentimentality of the rest of the text. A good instance of this is Ann Yearsley's description of the torture and death of the slave Luco in *A Poem on the Inhumanity of the Slave-Trade* (1788). Luco retaliates against an overseer who blinds him with a whip; he then tries to escape but is captured, and his end parallels that of Oroonoko: they are burned to death, but slowly. Yearsley tells other tales of torture, including of the amputation of the leg of a runaway slave, and in each case emphasizes what she calls the "fortitude" of these slaves in their refusal to stay alive at any cost. Although Yearsley does invoke British codes of justice and Christian morality in her poem, it is on the whole much less chauvinist and nationalist in its antislavery argument than the other poems I consider here, a fact that probably derives from her social vision as a working-class poet.[36]

Behn's *Oroonoko*, on the other hand, features a woman narrator who constantly calls attention to her gentility and femininity, not least to explain why she is especially moved at the plight of the royal captives and slaves Oroonoko and Imoinda. In Surinam, her colonial and racial status radically differentiate her from Oroonoko and Imoinda, but her gender makes her susceptible both to his charms and to his enslavement. Her antislavery emotions, and occasional feeble actions, are born out of the exercise of sympathy, which (and not only in this instance) is seen as the particular prerogative of women. This cultural and gender logic was of course replicated in a variety of eighteenth-century literary, religious, and educational texts, such that the very language of sympathy took on a feminine aspect: to be a woman was to feel; to feel (too much?) was to be womanly. As Clare Midgley and Moira Ferguson have demonstrated, women's mobilization in the cause of antislavery was often predicated upon, and legitimized, by this emphasis on feeling.[37] Some expressions of sympathy for those enslaved drew upon a dissenting tradition of women writing about their own oppression within the family or other social structures as a form of enslavement, but for the most part, such potentially radical identifications were avoided in favor of a religious or ethical vocabulary—slavery was inhuman and unChristian; slaves were to be pitied, and thus were to be saved. Indeed, the conservative idiom of most of the women poets who wrote antislavery poetry is striking; even more than male poets like Cowper, they were careful to distance themselves from the taint of Jacobin or revolutionary humanist values. The result is a set of poems that are powerful testaments to the fervor and strength of the abolitionist cause in the late eighteenth century, but also to the necessity of articulating this fervor in the service of a larger ambition—that of the nation. In its poetic manifestations, antislavery promises the moral redemption of the nation, the consolidation of its class relations, governing institutions, and cultural codes, and emphasizes a new ethicopolitical basis for its prestige and power abroad.

I will substantiate this large claim via analyses of some antislavery poems by women poets: Hannah More's "The Slave Trade" (1787) and Anna Letitia Barbauld's, "Epistle to William Wilberforce, Esq. On the Rejection of the

Bill for Abolishing the Slave Trade, 1791," among others. These poems share some of the motifs and values we have examined in Cowper's poems; More's poem, too, was commissioned by the Committee for the Abolition of the Slave Trade, with the difference that it was designed to influence leaders of public opinion rather than the less-educated constituencies addressed by Cowper's ballads. Accordingly, its idiom reflects that of Cowper's *Task* and "Charity," and invokes the same goddess whom poems like Thomson's *Liberty* and Dyer's "The Ruins of Rome" had raised to the status of national deity.[38] In these earlier poems, as we have seen, liberty (loosely understood, when it was defined in political terms, as the absence of an autocratic monarchy or as the constitutional balance of power that was represented by the revolution of 1688) was what distinguished Britain from contemporary empires on the Continent, or indeed from analogous empires in history like Rome or Carthage, and it is liberty that provides the moral-humanist sanction for Britain's drive to compete for, and to colonize, the globe. More's Liberty is figured as the "Bright intellectual sun" (line 3) designed by heaven to "irradiate all the earth" (line 18) (an image echoed by lines 13 and 14 of Copwer's "The Morning Dream").[39] Even as Liberty is here a figure for the 'natural' universality of freedom, the specifically political and nationalist resonance established by the work of the earlier poets is not lost: both Thomson and Dyer had invoked Liberty in order to enable a particular vision of the British nation, both at home and abroad.

Hence, just after More's poem asks the question, "While Britain basks in thy full blaze of light, / Why lies sad Afric quench'd in total night?" (lines 19–20), the poet's concern with a more restricted and less universal definition of liberty—a more immediately political and *domestic* definition—surfaces. The liberty to be exported is addressed as a "sober goddess," different from "that mad liberty, in whose wild praise / Too oft he [the bard] trims his prostituted bays" (lines 24–25). More has a specific series of events in mind here: the Gordon Riots that agitated London in 1780 and climaxed in a crowd attacking the Bank of England. The verse in these thirty lines is choppy and energetic, its rhythms and images exercised by the actions of

> that unlicensed monster of the crowd,
> . . . .
> fierce faction's tool,
> Of rash sedition born, and mad misrule.
>
> *(lines 27–30)*

Those in the crowd spurn order and outrage law, they "tread on grave authority and power, / And shake the work of ages in an hour." The general political horror of mobilized crowds is expressed as an inappropriate collective articulation of freedom: the "roar terrific" of the crowd deafens the "ear of peace" (lines 28–29), its "stubborn mouth . . . / No strength can govern, and no skill restrain" (lines 31–32). The crowd is led on by its goddess ("Convulsed her voice, and pestilent her breath") who spreads "Red conflagration o'er the astonished land" (lines 37–40).

More's need to define an appropriate language of liberty and freedom is of course consistent with her conservative domestic morality and politics.[40] Her conservatism is in keeping with David Brion Davis's observation that most "abolitionists were far less concerned with extending the potential impact of their ideology than with the need to prevent a direct challenge to property rights in human beings from undermining the sanctions for property rights in general."[41] But the Gordon Riots were of particular concern for abolitionists, as they offered, as Glyn Williams and John Ramsden suggest, "a sombre warning of the danger of summoning popular support through the organising of petitions, marches and demonstrations," which were some of the mobilizing methods favored by advocates of antislavery, too.[42] The description of "mad liberty" in More's poem is thus key to its ideological concerns, less a digression than a necessary response to a recent socially traumatic series of events and the universalizing, leveling, possibility of antislavery rhetoric. In seeking to inoculate the term *liberty* against any populist infection, the poem makes clear that Britain is not the proper political or social space for those who would claim to act against oppression: "Such have we seen on freedom's genuine coast, / Bellowing for blessings which were never lost" (lines 45–46). Britain's "genuine" freedom guarantees that there are no lost "blessings" to be recovered, and that there are no political parallels between riots at home and insurrections overseas. This point made, the poem goes on to develop its antislavery polemic.

My argument that More's "The Slave Trade" is about much more than the slave trade does not deny the emancipatory potential of her text as much as read it within the historical context it defines for itself. In fact, the poem is written with the awareness that slavery is an issue with moral, religious, political, social, and economic determinants and consequences, and that these have to be addressed if the antislavery position is to achieve any legitimacy or force. Indeed, More also writes with a strong sense of the role played by literary texts in generating an antislavery consensus, and invokes "plaintive Southerne" (a footnote describes him as the "Author of the tragedy of Oroonoko") as her inspiration. But her primary motivation is the "millions" like Oroonoko who were "by rapine dragg'd from Afric's coast" and whose misery makes her "bosom melt" (lines 73–75). She rebukes the "illiberal thought" that claims that Africans lack "the powers of equal thought" and offers in its stead a portrait of a people possessed "Of high-soul'd passion and ingenuous shame," whose "Strong but luxuriant virtues boldly shoot /

From the wild vigour of a savage root" (lines 89–91). More's representation of Oroonoko-style Africans, possessed of natural strengths and virtues, sits oddly with her later account of them as "dark and savage, ignorant and blind" (yet worthy of enlightenment because they, too, are made in Christ's image—lines 165–67). However, this focus on the nobility of Africans and on their need for (British) education is in fact not contradictory:

> A sense of worth, a conscience of desert,
> A high, unbroken hautiness of heart;
> That self-same stuff which erst proud empires sway'd,
> Of which the conquerors of the world were made.
> Capricious fate of men! that very pride
> In Afric scourged, in Rome was deified.
>
> *(lines 94–99)*

Both Behn's *Oroonoko* and Addison's *Cato* had suggested a similar parallel between African chieftains and Roman patricians: Oroonoko looks like a Roman and the Numidian prince Juba is the noblest of Cato's followers. Even as More writes of millions of enslaved Africans, her imagination is molded by such prior literary models, which could only "humanize" Africans by portraying their nobility as European in nature and carriage.

The vast mass of non-aristocratic slaves do make an entry as More depicts "the burning village and the blazing town," the "dire victim torn from social life, / The shrieking babe, the agonizing wife." In an appeal to slave traders, More emphasizes the destruction of families and kinship structures: the "fond links of feeling nature" are broken as slaves are carried off (lines 116–25). She reminds them of their own loved ones at home, of their "British feelings" for liberty, hoping that this combination of "love of home and freedom" will change their ways (lines 128–53). Mindful of warnings, pro slave trade, about the economic losses that will follow upon abolition, More responds with free-trade logic:

> Does thirst of empire, does desire of fame,
> (For these are specious crimes,) our rage inflame?
> No: sordid lust of gold their fate controls,
> The basest appetite of basest souls:
> Gold, better gain'd by what their ripening sky,
> Their fertile fields, their arts and mines supply.
>
> *(lines 154–59)*

In these lines, even as she argues the benefits of peaceful trade, More seems to recognize that such mercantile activity does not and will not fully define the British presence abroad. Hence her attempt to maintain the untenable, or hardly tenable, distinction between "specious" ("Thirst for empire" or "desire for fame") and "sordid" ("lust for gold") desires (untenable if only because the lure of specie is central to the etymology of the earlier adjective). Even as she attacks the slave trade and slavery as corrupt and debased, More retains some acceptable motivations for adventuring abroad—after all, the colonies or markets are not to be given up, and the poem does work toward defining a more persuasive idea of the British presence overseas.

The poem balances its categoric and extended denunciation of slavery and the British slave trade with a celebration of the civilizational virtues of British overseas exploration and commerce; it also suggests (in a thinly veiled historical irony) that slaves can now look forward to a double liberation—into freedom and Christianity. Thus James Cook is heralded as the type of principled explorer who is the benevolent antitheses of the rapacious "white savage," whose "lust for gold / Or lust for conquest" (lines 250–51) make "the sum of human happiness less" (line 269):

> Had these [other voyagers] possess'd, O Cook! thy gentle mind,
> Thy love of arts, thy love of human kind;
> Had these pursued thy mild and liberal plan,
> Discoverers had not been a curse to man!
> Then, bless'd philanthropy! thy social hands
> Had link'd dissever'd worlds in brothers' bands;
> Careless if colour or if clime divide;
> . . . .
> Then with pernicious skill we had not known
> To bring their vices back, and leave our own.
>
> *(lines 278–87)*

This vision of personal benevolence and philanthropy is finally the ideological center of the poem, when, raised to its nationalist power, it appears as the "cherub Mercy," who "Breathes manumission o'er the rescued land" (line 337). As in Cowper's later "The Morning Dream," the coming of Liberty to "the burning shore" (line 216) causes the instant death of the giant, "pale oppression," and restores "the lustre of the Christian name" by clearing the "foulest blot that dimm'd its fame" (lines 216–45). The poem closes with a vignette of Britain ascendant, no longer because of its mercantile or slave-trading prowess, but because it is the emancipatory, Christianizing power:

> The dusky myriads crowd the sultry plain,
> And hail that mercy long invok'd in vain,
> Victorious pow'r! she bursts their two–fold bands,
> And faith and freedom springs from Britain's hands.
>
> *(lines 346–49)*

In the last eight lines, More imagines a new genesis ("Let there be light!"), a mass conversion of Africans; the freedom she now writes of is that provided by religion. In doing so, she returns to the opening lines of the poem in which liberty was represented as a "bright intellectual sun" that would rid Africa of slavery; however, it is now salvation that will "make them free."

That the humanitarian impulse in antislavery discourse, and especially poetry, took the form of such explicitly nationalist or Evangelical exhortation is scarcely surprising. For women who entered into public debate, there were considerable strategic benefits in balancing what was perceived as their inherently "feminine" (and hence impractical and overly emotional) dramatization of the human devastation caused to slave families with powerful reminders that they were committed to the ideal of Britain as a morally and politically legitimate leader of nations. As I mentioned earlier, the judicial decision in the 1772 James Somerset case had defined slavery as fundamentally unBritish, and this notion (even if it was based, as has been pointed out, on a misreading of the judgment handed down), provided legal sanction to the patriotic poetic rhetoric of British liberty and freedom. So complete and seamless seemed this combination of humanitarian and nationalist appeal that we find its constitutive elements repeated in a great many antislavery poems, as in Elizabeth Bentley's "On the Abolition of the African Slave Trade" (1789). Bentley writes of the "free-born Briton" committed to breaking "Slav'ry's galling chains" and to taking "Freedom's ray" to far-off places (lines 4–10); she has a long and dramatic passage about the loss of "the dearest, tend'rest ties of life" as families are broken up, and she mourns for enslaved Oroonokos and Imoindas: "Perhaps the tender youth thus snatch'd away, / O'er sable nations would have borne the sway!" or "some princess to an empire born" will now be doomed to a different fate (lines 31–33). She meditates on the inhumanity of slave traders, rebuking them with the supreme example of Ignatius Sancho, whose writing so conclusively demonstrates that Africans possess "Affections, feelings, sense, and life like ours" (line 52). Or rather, she argues that Sancho proves that "in their uncultur'd minds are sown / The seeds of knowledge equal with our own" (lines 59–60), thereby retaining a space for the power of British education and culture to make a Sancho of a freed slave.

Bentley exhorts Britons to antislavery action in much the same way as More does, reminding them of their preservation of "glorious Freedom on their native isle" (line 68), calling them the "patriot sons of Liberty" (line 75), and calling upon them to "Go, wrest the scourge from vile Oppression's hand, / Make Britain's name revere'd in ev'ry land" (lines 77–78). The abolition of the slave trade will only enhance British power ("Then shall our land with added greatness rise, / Blest by the mighty Pow'r who rules the skies"—lines 87–88), as such "heav'n-inspir'd Philanthropy" will "through each realm spread Liberty and Peace" (lines 93–94). An unexceptionable sentiment, except that the poem makes quite clear that liberty is a peculiarly British institution, whose translation to all such realms will extend to them British patronage and protection. In all this, Bentley shares a vocabulary with many contemporary poets who wrote on similar themes.[43] Examples can be multiplied, but the point is simply that, in many such poems, it is an eminently nationalist and protoimperialist iconography and rhetoric that provides cultural ballast and ideological weight to the abolitionist argument. I will examine one more poem, though not to show overlaps in image and argument as much as to highlight its variations on the patterns we have traced so far. In all the poems discussed above, however intense the poet's condemnation of the slave trade and of slavery, and however fearful his or her sense of the moral and social damage being done to Britain by plantation slavery, the idiom of the poem has scarcely ever shifted away from polite and civil discourse. This is in keeping with the ethical high ground claimed by these poets and their need to intervene in public and parliamentary debates on state policy in a tone appropriate to such discussion. The only exceptions are the image of national effeminacy in Cowper, mentioned above (*The Task*—2.222–32) and the unusually energetic and fearful passage in More on the "mad liberty" that prompted the Gordon Riots; in the poem that follows, however, we have more pathological and dire definitions of the damage being done to Britain by its colonial conduct abroad.

Barbauld's "Epistle to William Wilberforce, Esq." opens and closes with addresses to Wilberforce, in each case celebrating his antislavery activity and offering moral, religious, and (eventually) historical justification and reward for his abolitionist efforts. The poem takes on a prophetic tone as, while condemning an unheeding Britain, it also offers a comforting vision of a slavery-free future. It includes a vision of British greatness sans the slave trade, a vision offered to "Freedom's eager sons" by the Muse, who,

> with ready tongue
> At Mercy's shrine applausive peans rung;
> And Freedom's eager sons, in vain foretold
> A new Astrean reign, an age of gold:
> She knows and she persists—Still Afric bleeds,
> Unchecked, the human traffic still proceeds.
> *(lines 11–16)[44]*

In the face of parliamentary intransigence, the poem offers Wilberforce and his allies spiritual consolation. But not only spiritual consolation, for the last lines posit a redemptive (if mottled) historical narrative:

> Succeeding times your struggles, and their fate,
> With mingled shame and triumph shall relate;
> While faithful History, in her various page,
> Marking the features of this motley age,
> To shed a glory, and to fix a stain,
> Tells how you strove, and that you strove in vain.
>
> *(lines 118–23)*

The end of the poem looks to the future, its vision resonant with the prophecy that, in the beginning of the poem, was offered to Britain: "And Freedom's eager sons in vain foretold / A new Astrean reign, an age of gold" (lines 13–14).

Marked off from the apostrophic addresses to Wilberforce, and the two accounts of British history-in-the-making, is the body of the poem, which, in tone and idiom, diverges greatly, if symptomatically, from that of the Wilberforce sections. This central section is informed by an account of British corruption, luxury, and degeneracy that is somewhat surprising in a poem devoted to a benevolist ethics and a sentimentalist politics, and needs to be examined at some length. This is not true of the entire section, though; lines 19 to 40 remain well within an ethical-moral discourse, in which the battle between the proslavery and antislavery positions is enacted as an unequal debate between "A Nation's eloquence" and the "seasoned tools of Avarice" (lines 25–26). Divine vengeance threatens those who condemn their fellow men, especially those sophists who pervert the Bible by reading in it precedents for slavery. But it is not heavenly vengeance that turns out to be the source of the horrors described in lines 47 through 105. Retribution comes when "injured Afric, by herself redrest / Darts her own serpents at her Tyrant's breast" (lines 45–46). I quote at some length:

> Each vice, to minds deprav'd by bondage known,
> With sure contagion fastens on his own;
> In sickly langours melts his nerveless frame,
> And blows to rage impetuous Passion's flame:
> Fermenting swift, the fiery venom gains
> The milky innocence of infant veins;
> There swells the stubborn will, damps learning's fire,
> The whirlwind wakes of uncontroul'd desire,
> Sears the young hearts to images of woe,
> And blasts the buds of Virtue as they blow.
>
> Lo! where reclin'd, pale Beauty courts the breeze,
> Diffus'd on sofas of voluptuous ease;
> With anxious awe, her menial train around
> Catch her faint whispers of half-utter'd sound;

> See her, in monstrous fellowship, unite
> At once the Scythian, and the Sybarite;
> Blending repugnant vices, misally'd,
> Which *frugal* nature purpos'd to divide;
> See her, with indolence to fierceness join'd,
> Of body delicate, infirm of mind,
> With languid tones imperious mandates urge;
> And with arm recumbent wield the household scourge;
> And with unruffled mein, and placid sounds,
> Contriving torture, and inflicting wounds.
>
> *(lines 47–70)*

Africa's revenge takes the form of her emasculating those men and minds that are "depraved by bondage known," a phrase that could syntactically apply equally to slave or to slave owner and plantocrat. Moral depravity is figured as a diseased and rampant sexuality, from the "serpents" who strike the tyrant to the "sickly langours" that melt "his nerveless frame." Just how the "fiery venom gains / The milky innocence of infant veins" is not clear, but the specter of miscegenation, and possibly of slave wet-nursing, haunts this entire passage, particularly as the consequences are twofold: the same sexual agent causes both the whirlwind of "uncontrouled desire" to awaken and sears "young hearts" to "images of woe."

This fear of a grotesque intermingling, of the coming together of antithetical terms, also marks the character of the "pale Beauty" in lines 57–70; she is taken to be a portrait of a plantation mistress, who is possibly creole. Paradox marks her form and her functioning: "languid tones" urge "imperious mandates"; her "arm recumbent" wields the "household scourge"; her "unruffled mien, and placid sounds" contrive torture and inflict wounds. But such domestic cruelty is not simply the result of the corruptions of absolute plantocratic power as much as it is the result of the "natural" consequence of an unnatural and "monstrous fellowship" that blends "repugnant vices, misallied / Which frugal nature proposed to divide." This monstrous fellowship unites the "Scythian and the Sybarite," two historically and culturally resonant images of emasculation and effeminacy. It is important to note that in each case these references combine luxury and effeminacy, or, rather, suggest that the latter follows upon the former. The *Oxford English Dictionary* records that Sybaris was an "Ancient Greek city of southern Italy, traditionally noted for its effeminacy and luxury" and that a sybarite is "an effeminate voluptuary or sensualist." That the adjective encodes an ethnography is hardly surprising; nor is the fact that it derives from an imperial history. Similarly, as Ann Rosalind Jones and Peter Stallybrass point out, the term *Scythian* has been in play in English imperialist and colonial discourse since the late twelfth century.[45]

Barbauld's somewhat tautological coupling of the Scythian and the Sybarite to describe the monstrosity of her pale beauty emphasizes the fact that for both Herodotus and Hippocrates—the primary sources for such ethnographic lore—the Scythians are the very type of the process by which virile, warlike, nomadic tribesmen degenerate into effeminate, impotent figures who "put on women's clothes . . . play the woman, and with the women, do the same work that women do." Herodotus's *History* describes the Scythians marching into Egypt, plundering the temple of Aphrodite Urania, and being cursed by the goddess with the "female disease." (Jones and Stallybrass suggest that in Herodotus there is some suggestion that the "female sickness" is pederasty, but also that Hippocrates holds that Scythian horsemanship results in their impotence: "the constant jolting on their horses unfits them for intercourse.")[46] Barbauld's plantation mistress—"blending repugnant vices, misallied, / Which frugal nature purposed to divide"—is an overdetermined figure for the sexual and cultural anxieties attendant upon colonial enterprise: indolent, voluptuous, monstrous woman because (but also) degenerate, enfeebled man.

Barbauld's representation of sexualized monstrosity at the edges of empire is by no means unique in this period. As Felicity Nussbaum has shown, a variety of texts enshrine the imperative toward what might be called "national monogamy"; that is, the representation of British culture as different from, and better than, other cultures because it is defined by "monogamous marriage and motherhood" (as opposed to polygamous relationships and less-than-missionary conceptions of sexual practice evident elsewhere).[47] A great many of these texts were written by women, whose claim to full subjecthood was in part based on their arguments for the social and moral necessity of the norms of bourgeois domesticity then being articulated, in text and in practice. These texts often include pivotal passages, like the lines in Barbauld's poem above, whose details offer testimonial both to the centrality of comparative pseudo-ethnographies to national self-definition, but equally to the febrile excitement and anxieties provoked in the further reaches of the imagination of British writers thinking about miscegenation, polygamy, and sexualities not contained within patriarchal monogamy. The pathologized figure of Barbauld's indolent, imperious "pale Beauty" thus condenses a more generalized awareness and fear of eighteenth-century plantation slavery—both its brutal political economy and its violent sexual economy.

That Barbauld's concerns about the effects of the slave trade on Britain are part of a larger concern about the domestic impact of the expropriation and importation of colonial commodities is clear from lines 86–105:

> Nor less from the gay East, on essenc'd wings,
> Breathing unnam'd perfumes, Contagion springs;
> The soft luxurious plague alike pervades
> The marble palaces, and rural shades.

The nabobs of the East India Company are the targets here, their ostentatious wealth a parallel for the extravagant lives of West Indian plantocrats and absentee owners that Barbauld excoriates earlier. In each case, wealth earned overseas threatens social, cultural, and moral conventions and hierarchies at home:

> The manners melt—One undistinguish'd blaze
> O'erwhelms the sober pomp of elder days;
> Corruption follows with gigantic stride,
> And scarce vouchsafes his shameless front to hide:
> The spreading leprosy taints ev'ry part,
> Infects each limb, and sickens at the heart.
> Simplicity! most dear of rural maids,
> Weeping resigns her violated shades:
> Stern Independence from his glebe retires,
> And anxious Freedom eyes her drooping fires:
> By foreign wealth are British morals chang'd,
> And Afric's sons, and India's, smile aveng'd.

This passage shares with the vignette of African slavery a vocabulary of perfumed disease and contagion, of luxurious plague that causes a meltdown of manners, of a spreading leprosy that corrupts social order. Here, too, the sinister effects of "foreign wealth" are dramatized within a scenario of the revenge of the colonial subject, who emerges as the shadowy, triumphant, agent of British degeneration. If in the Africa section the danger lies in "unnatural" states and contacts abroad, in the India section (if I can call it that) the diseases come home to rot and to sicken.[48]

These elements in Barbauld's poem will remind us that in eighteenth-century English poetry, the morally and socially corrosive effects of imperial expansion were often described in terms that foregrounded an emasculating luxury.[49] As we have seen in chapter 2, John Dyer's "The Ruins of Rome" provides a good instance of such description and analysis. For Dyer, Roman emasculation followed from its imperial power. In his version, the very elements (compare the "essenced wings" and "unnamed perfumes" that carry Eastern "Contagion" in Barbauld's poem) conspire to "dissolve" and enfeeble the once-strong Romans. As an advocate of British power overseas, Dyer believed that there were historical lessons to be learned. Not unlike Dyer's poem, but without its explicit historical argument, Barbauld's poem is similarly concerned with decline and decay (to that extent this poem is the important precursor to her *Eighteen Hundred and Eleven*, which does elaborate a longer-term vision of national ruin). "Epistle to William Wilberforce" is written as a compensatory response to a parliamentary defeat for the abolitionist cause, and some of Barbauld's disappointment and anger no doubt fuels her account of colonial pathologies, especially in contrast to her more conventional picture of the reformist zeal, rectitude, and missionary perseverance demonstrated by Wilberforce and other members of the Committee for Abolition of the Slave Trade. The poem makes its point via such rhetorically heightened contrasts, including that between English pastoral and colonial plantations, a contrast I now examine.

Barbauld's poem contains a passage whose dynamic contrast between English pastoral and the topography and culture of colonial plantations play out a theme—the exile of Poetry in the face of, and as a indicator of, national failure—that we have seen several examples of, including Berkeley's "On the Prospect of Planting Arts and Learning in America" and Goldsmith's *The Deserted Village*. In Goldsmith's poem, as we saw in chapter 2, "sweet Poetry" is driven away from the country once the destructive pleasures that betoken the decay of trading empires become widespread. The poem's account of the miseries of Auburn builds up to his claim that ugly domestic changes in Britain are directly linked to its activities overseas. It is of course also the case that Goldsmith's account of the decline of poetry and the arts—the entire poem enacts a poet's narcissistic and nostalgic longing for the traditional subjects of pastoral poetry—emphasizes once more the poet's vocational authority as commentator on the state of the nation.

Barbauld, too, develops such links, describing the "palmy walks and spicy groves" of the plantations as missing "the form benign of rural Pleasure." "No milk-maid's song, or hum of village talk, / Soothes the lone poet on his evening walk"; no "mixed sounds of cheerful labour" are heard; "no blooming maids and frolic swains are seen / To pay gay homage to their harvest queen" (lines 71–78). This is a surprisingly determined compendium of pastoral clichés, if only because poets from Stephen Duck (*The Thresher's Labour*) to Mary Collier (*The Woman's Labour: An Epistle to Mr. Stephen Duck*) to George Crabbe (his *The Village: A Poem in Two Books* was a direct rebuttal of Goldsmith's representation of rural life in *The Deserted Village*) had systematically demystified the conventions and assumptions of pastoral poetry. Goldsmith's *Deserted Village* had suggested that the figure of the poet exiled from the proper vocabulary and matter of English poetry was an evocative expression of national loss; Barbauld exports, as it were, this figure. The lone poet on his evening walk in an overseas plantation wanders unsupported by the sights and sounds of English pastoral, his (professional) alienation from the plantation landscape a sign of its fundamental unBritishness. Barbauld's recourse to these pastoral images, particularly the cheerful and unwearied labor and play of country maids and swains, also allows her to point a key contrast between such representations of "thriving industry and faithful love" and those that mark the presence of slave labor on the plantation:

> But shrieks and yells disturb the balmy air,
> Dumb sullen looks of woe announce despair,
> And angry eyes thro' dusky features glare.
>
> *(lines 80–83)*

Plantation labor cannot be written into the conventions of English pastoral; this time, poetry flees, not Britain, but its overseas possessions: "Far from the sounding lash the Muses fly, / And sensual riot drowns each finer joy" (lines 84–85).

In the years after Barbauld published her poem, the fervor of British antislavery activism was dampened by the general political reaction to what were seen as the dangers and excesses of the Jacobins, who had taken power after the revolution in France. In 1793, Britain went to war with France, and state priorities shifted, with the loss of many of the gains of the antislavery movement, now tainted by its potential association with radical republicanism. In this decade, in fact, the slave trade grew larger than it had ever been before, and this in spite of war in the Caribbean, some successful slave rebellions in the Antilles, and, most spectacularly, the revolution in Saint-Domingue. By some accounts, these events made sugar produced in the British West Indies even more competitive and lucrative; as J. R. Ward writes, "Parliamentary enthusiasm for abolition waned when the destruction of Saint-Domingue improved the British West Indies' fortunes after 1791." Parliament did not ban British involvement in the slave trade till 1807, and for reasons far more material and complex than the public enthusiasm generated by British abolitionists.[50] However, the Evangelical and nationalist vocabularies featured by abolitionists, including by those poets whose poems I have considered here, continued to strengthen the moral—and, as I have suggested here, the forward-looking and imperial—argument against Britain's involvement in the slave trade and in slavery. An "enlightened" future would be a British future, an idea whose ideological force and significance was central to British expansionism in the nineteenth century.

In this chapter, I have sought to read some examples of late-eighteenth-century antislavery poems in the context of their engaged and contentious place within a masculinist poetic and public culture, whose ideological issues and rhetorical forms shaped poems by women as much as by men. Cowper, More, and Barbauld found in the poetry of British Patriotism (Bonamy

Dobrée's phrase for poems like those by Dyer and Thomson that I have written about in earlier chapters) elements of a colonial and domestic vision that they invoked in their search for an abolitionist iconography and discourse weighty enough to intervene effectively in the antislavery debates of the late eighteenth century. For women abolitionist poets, this ability to tap into a masculine idiom and sphere of interest—the formation of the nation as an international power—was particularly important, if only to suggest that their antislavery positions were not derived simply from an overwrought feminine sympathy or a misguided benevolence. After all, many who found justice in the antislavery cause were less approving of women mobilizing: Wilberforce wrote that even as all "private exertions for such an object become their character . . . for these ladies to meet, to go from house to house stirring up petitions—these appear to me proceedings unsuited to the female character as delineated in scripture."[51]

Clare Midgley's research on women antislavery campaigners has shown that though they rarely wrote tracts or pamphlets, they "found a way to voice social and political criticism through the acceptably 'feminine' means of poetic sentiment and appeals to the emotions."[52] As women mobilized and claimed for themselves an important part in the antislavery campaign, they not only shaped its values, but also gained by their efforts public legitimacy and thus shaped a reformist and less exclusionary public sphere. To that extent they were part of the larger effort made by writers like More and Wollestonecraft (writers with very different political opinions but with a commitment to women's "emancipation") to articulate a credo that would allow women to attain, as Felicity Nussbaum puts it, "the individual autonomy associated with Enlightenment emergence from nonage." Antislavery sentiment and activism— the desire to speak and act on behalf of weaker and enslaved peoples—was part of the larger "civilizing process" and the "revolution in manners" that encouraged British women to public self-confidence, if not (as yet) a full-fledged public citizenship.[53] Their positions thus shared some of the discursive and ideological contradictions (progressive ideas enabled by deeply conservative and even racist structures of thought) that defined their times: Moira Ferguson points to the historical irony that "antislavery colonial discourse . . . played a significant role in generating and consolidating nineteenth-century imperialist and 'domestic-racist' ideology."[54]

My readings have, along similar lines, argued for the importance of the nationalist (sub)text of so much of the antislavery writing of the period under discussion, and for the enabling foundation of the idea of the imperial nation as it had been articulated by poets in the century before antislavery became a public cause. As they voiced opinions on slavery and the slave trade, women activists and poets necessarily took positions on a constellation

of social and political issues that surrounded slavery, defined the British public
sphere, and commented on the legitimacy of British imperialism. They spoke
in the name of an enlightened collectivity and to the nation, a rhetorical
frame that had, since antiquity, been less than welcoming of women's voices.
And in speaking so, these poets contributed an ethical sensibility to the
new languages of nineteenth-century empire, which, as Anthony Pagden
has argued, were "transfigured products of their early-modern forbears." In
his comment on crucial shifts in the self-conception of imperial European
states, Pagden points out, however, that these transfigurations were not of

the languages of empire but instead of the critique which the enemies of imperialism
had levelled against them in the closing years of the eighteenth century. This had
insisted that the inescapable legacy of all forms of colonialism could only be human
and material waste followed by moral degeneracy. Europe's relationship with the
non-European world should, in future, be limited to forms of harmonious exchange.
As commerce had replaced conquest, so enlightenment would replace evangelization
and the crasser forms of cultural domination. . . . The conception of a world imperial
base, generating enlightenment and technology and laced with a certain amount of
Christianity which constituted the 'white man's burden,' was perfectly in keeping
with the late eighteenth-century notions of empire.[55]

    In speaking for enlightenment and empire, antislavery poets, both women
and men, demonstrated that they belonged to the august company of British
poets who tied the fortunes of their trade to those of their trading and
colonizing nation, and whose sense of poetic destiny was inseparable from
their sense of the manifest destiny of Britain as it developed over the long
eighteenth century. The world of eighteenth-century British poets, as I have
argued throughout in this book, is vast and engaged, and our literary history
and criticism must take seriously that ambit, as indeed the vocabulary of
poetic ambition it encouraged. Their imaginations roamed the globe, and
culled from its varied geographies, histories, cultures, and economies themes
to orchestrate into energetic and grandiose symphonies of trade, colonization,
overseas dominance, and empire. These poets worked constantly with a
powerful retrospective understanding of the British literary-historical tradition
that they were also forging, one that derived considerable strength from its
engagement with the affairs of the nation. Equally, they developed a
perceptive sense of a future whose terms (some of which they invented or
popularized) would be rewritten by an imperialism that colonized the globe
in the name of "enlightened" ethical, political, and religious agendas. In
their search for a Britain adequate to their poetic prospects, these poets
argued with, exhorted, or damned their countrymen, worried about the
example of precursor empires or contemporary competitor-nations, wrote

mini-ethnographies and accounts of the people and lands European merchants and colonizers came to dominate, and crafted a literary viewpoint from which the world could be seen as rightfully subordinate to the achievements of British constitutional authority and governance, science and technology, arts and culture, as also Christian values and beliefs. If *Paradise Lost* imagined a universe to be traversed and worlds for the taking, then the poets of the long eighteenth-century rewrote that ambition in more worldly terms. They may not, except in moments of whimsy, have believed that the moon could be colonized, but this globe, including its newly "discovered" and faraway reaches, was theirs for the imagining.[56] This chapter, and this book, has argued that they did just that.

CONCLUSION

The conquest of the earth, which mostly means the taking it away from those who have a different complexion or slightly flatter noses than ourselves, is not a pretty thing when you look at it too much. What redeems it is the idea only. An idea at the back of it; not a sentimental pretence but an idea; and an unselfish belief in the idea--something you can set up, and bow down before, and offer a sacrifice to.

—*Joseph Conrad,* Heart of Darkness

Marlow's musings, precise in their simplicity, here offer (as they do at other moments in Conrad's fiction) coruscating historical and ideological insights into empire. On this occasion, Marlow meditates not only on the making of modern empires, but on processes that are far older. His retrospection takes him back to Roman Britain (and to themes that link *Heart of Darkness* with many of the issues I have explored in the preceding chapters). He thinks of the "feelings of a commander of a fine . . . trireme in the Mediterranean" who is ordered to Britain, at that time "the very end of the world," home to "Sandbanks, marshes, forests, savages,—precious little to eat fit for a civilised man, nothing but Thames water to drink." The commander, and men from Rome like him, did their duty, trapped as they were by the "savagery" and mystery of their surroundings, all of which were "incomprehensible," "detestable," but also, for that very reason, seductive (theirs is the "fascination of the abomination"). That was then: Marlow understands his account of the Romans in Britain to be a description of the psychodynamics of ancient conquest ("robbery with violence, aggravated murder on a great scale"), which is to be differentiated from the colonizing efforts of the British in the present. Theirs is now the "conquest of the earth" in the "unselfish" service of "the idea"—and the "idea" is what "redeems" it all.[1]

In different ways, with multiple local motivations and varying degrees of literary and public success, the poems that I have considered in this book contributed to the forging of eighteenth-century versions of this "idea": of "Great Britain"; of British greatness demonstrated not in dominance of Europe but across the globe; of a self-legitimating British greatness that

exported enlightenment in exchange for the surplus of territories they
controlled as traders or colonists. In order to contribute to this idealized
model of commercial and colonial aggression, these poems were exercises
in persuasion (as indeed the preceding chapters are, though of course with
vastly different objects in view, and equally different intellectual genealogies).
I will comment on my own methods later, but first, a reminder of the key
rhetorical and ideological models these poets took as their own. Their poems
derive energy, inspiration, and working methods from the vocabularies and
cultural assumptions of classical humanism, including the understanding that
there was no disjunction between humanist vocabularies or values and
particular, utilitarian, ends. David Armitage has argued for the importance
of this perception to any account of writing in the early modern period,
and his is a succinct account of the connections between "literary" writing,
commercial expansion, and national well-being:

In particular the classical *ars rhetorica* provided indispensable techniques for those
involved in the promotion of commerce and emigration and the conduct of
government, whether within the Three Kingdoms or further afield. Since from the
very beginning neither the English nor the Scottish Crowns had supplied the financial
resources to support colonization, just as investment in privateering had been personal
rather than state-sponsored, most of the early literature of overseas enterprise was
promotional in intent, and hence persuasive in form. It was therefore a vernacular
branch of classical rhetoric, and revealed its origins in its informing tropes, genres,
and visions of political community.[2]

   The poems of the late seventeenth and eighteenth centuries that I
examine extend this tradition in several ways: the tropology of community
and nation is, for instance, crucial to their political, social, and ethical concerns,
and frames and legitimates their craft. They weave their models of persuasion
in patterns that combine classical and more vernacular motifs, and this
combination of convention and innovation defines poetic form, imagery,
and choice of theme. In seeking to persuade, poets renew models of rhetorical
and civic responsibility and fuse poetic inspiration with national aspiration.
(Our example might come once again from Thomson's and Mallet's *Alfred*,
in which the Hermit exhorts Alfred, who is in retreat from the Danes, to
act and bring about a lustrous future for the nation. "My labouring breast
expands / To give the glorious inspiration room," says the Hermit, and he
offers Alfred the prophetic visions summed up later in the play in the bard's
anthem "Rule, Britannia!")[3] The literary, cultural, and historical past is a
resource to be mined for present creativity, all in the name of a glorious
national future.
   However, as I have shown, the dynamic of these poems suggests that it

is not only poetic breath that is labored: each of the poems offers evidence of the difficulty of crafting seamless narratives of the making of a "Great Britain" in the face of culturally and racially differentiated geographies and histories (both within and without the boundaries of Great Britain). The nationalism forged in these poems is complex and supple: it is compounded of partisan politics enunciated as the transcendental pieties of manifest destiny; of imperial genealogies whose models of the rise of "arts and arms" derive in particular from the classical Roman Empire; of memories of successful nation-states—trading and mercantile powers, both "European" and Mediterranean; of cultural, moral, and religious arguments made for contemporary British superiority to their continental rivals, and of course to those whom they traded with or colonized. Crucial to this nationalist poetics is also the poet's awareness that any discourse of national exaltation within a colonialist or imperialist frame that relies on historical precedent must come to terms with the decline, as well as the rise, of empires. The historical vision and geopolitical schemas these poems encode are often a response to this debilitating sense of the pitfalls of imperial growth. Further, each poem, as I have shown, features rhetorical strategies designed to counter this sense of transience and mutability. Thus, both the ideologically supple and inclusionary, and the aggressive and exclusionary, discursive features of these poems can be understood as rhetorical forms necessitated by both philosophical and material resistance offered, at home and overseas, by opponents of British expansionism.

My readings of these poems, and the larger literary-historical and cultural-ideological narratives to which I return them, and about which I wish to persuade my readers, derives from the critical conviction that attention to the formal practices of poetry (as much as to its themes) allows us to trace the lineaments of social or collective desire at a moment in history, no matter that each poem is a different and individuated articulation of that desire. Here, without subscribing to Northrop Frye's larger claim about the archetypal nature of poetic tropes or forms, we might remember his argument that poetry must be studied "as part of the total human imitation of nature we call civilization. Civilization is not merely an imitation of nature, and it is impelled by the force that we have just called desire. . . . The efficient cause of civilization is work, and poetry in its social aspect has the function of expressing, as a verbal hypothesis, a vision of the goal of work and the forms of desire."[4] Frye's exemplary reminder of the priority of "work" in the making of human societies suggests also that the critical understanding of cultural expression will benefit from analyses of the mediated ways in which texts, in their "social aspect," delineate relationships between human communities and nature, or indeed among different human communities.

Each poem, then, in articulating its vision of the goal of civilizational work, discovers again not just the formulae of collective desire but also the terms in which, in each historical moment, desire is refused or curtailed. This is not a utopian or transcendental poetics; it is an argument that a critic who wishes to locate a poem most compellingly within a particular history and cultural geography must take seriously the poem's formal choices, its innovations, and those moments in its movement that suggest philosophical and argumentational aporia. Doing so allows us to be good literary historians, in that we specify a poem's (and a poet's) difficult or fluent relation to the modes of poetic enunciation understood as conventional or current at the time. Further—and this is of consequence for critics of a materialist temper—such a critical protocol will teach us how the poem defines, and is reciprocally constituted by, specifiable contradictions in structures of thought and affect, which, since they are produced by and definitive of their time and place, are precisely historical.

More specifically, such a critical poetics will emphasize for us that the important work performed by the eighteenth-century poems we have considered here, their persuasive dynamic, is their enunciation of both the energetic possibilities, and the limiting realities, of the idea of a great and imperial nation, all within the formulae and conventions that govern poetic practices at the time (and against which any innovations must be effected). As I have been at pains to argue, this is not to claim that these poems, written over more than a century, are all equivalently enthusiastic or anxious about British mercantile and colonial expansion. Such expansionism might not even be the primary or overt theme of each poem. These poems are written for all the occasional and local reasons that poets in this period wrote poetry—to express an intensity of idea and emotion; to solicit the attention of a patron or friend; to intervene in public debates on weighty ethical, cultural, or political issues, and thus to rebut opposed positions and constituencies; to imagine a future different from the present. They feature themes germane to their cultural and political ends, which ends also suggest (and are defined via) their choice of form, or indeed their mix of formal elements. The idiom of each poem, its characteristic topoi, its dramatization of event and character, its representation of poetic personae, all follow from vocational or creative dilemmas, but—and this has been the consistent argument of this book—the frame within which these choices are made and these dilemmas explored is that of the nation within the international system then in the making. Thus, as I have said before, the horizon of these poems—the range of their desires and the limits of their ambition—is the globe as it was being mapped and made available by European merchant and explorer, slave trader and colonist, soldier and scientist, pirate and administrator.

The critical problem of method here—in general the problem of critical method for cultural and historical materialists who write on the practice of poetry—is how to move from the "sinews of power" (to return to John Brewer's evocative phrase) to the worldview generated by these poems *in particular*.[5] The problem is therefore one of mediation, of taking into account macrophenomena (the shift from feudal to capitalist arrangements in the economy, polity, state apparatuses, and social relations, all of which, at any moment in the late seventeenth and eighteenth centuries, suggest the knotted overlay of competing forms and ideologies rather than the clarities of completed transformation or hegemony) and the microdetails of the organization or imagery or idiom of a poem (such mindfulness being the reason why a critic chooses to write on poetry in the first place). In this period, one of the key ideological forms through which both approval of and resistance to change was voiced was the vocabulary of nationalism, which endlessly figured models of the nation as forcefully incorporative (Great Britain as forged from Ireland, Scotland, and England—the smithy, of course, being English) and as expansionist (in the Caribbean, in North America, in Africa, and in Asia, and indeed wherever ships could sail and traders establish viable beachheads). Both the struggles for state and local power within Britain, and the battles for overseas territories and dominance of trade routes, insisted on the priority of national glory. The discourse of patriotism is thus at its supple and cynical best in this period, informing everything from the fulsome, lacking-in-irony celebrations of the goddess Britannia to the scatological and profane crudities of caricaturists who skewered such national self-aggrandizement and amour propre.

For the analyst of culture, the superabundance of patriotic *sententiae* makes matters worse, not better, if only because the idiom of the nation—of citizenship and subjectivity, of individuality and collectivity—becomes common expression, and saturates, becomes naturalized into, the English language itself. What begins in the aggressive cultural and intellectual drive toward self-determination as a nation and as a "people"—a will to power intensified in a period of international commercial and territorial competition—ends up providing the commonplaces of language and writing, even when such writing might fashion itself in self-conscious opposition to political ideas it considers retrograde (as in the writing of antislavery, for instance). Thus, Walpole's hacks *and* those in opposition to him are certain that Britons never will be slaves, but see no need to extend such a denunciation of dehumanizing subordination to the actual slaves of that moment, the Africans enslaved by Britons in order to ensure the greatness of Britain. The critic of literary language who reads the term *slaves* only as a token of political exchange within the incestuous circuits of Whig and

Tory or "court" and "patriot" power brokers in England remains circumscribed within the conceptual limits imposed by the eighteenth-century performance of "Englishness," a language and an idea that would legislate enslavement as foreign to its privileged subjects but as natural to those outside its charmed collectivity. This version of "English" is indeed one modern "language of empire," and a subset of that collocation of provincial European tongues, each with a competitive universalist ambition, that bespoke the forms of imperial modernity. This is a language whose "fundamental anthropological assumptions," as Anthony Pagden suggests, "persisted from the sixteenth into the nineteenth century, and in many cases into the twentieth."[6]

As I have argued, however, linguistic and cultural performances encode not only the will to power but the discovery of the fissures and limits of such will: as critics of poetry, we tease out that uneven process of discovery, the convolutions of idea and argument, the misfit of image and phrase, that is the movement or the progress of a poem. The analytic model here need not be thought of as derived narrowly from theories of psychic functioning, in which the unconscious operations of desire and the drives offer evidence of conflict and tension, and of irresolution and anxiety, rather than of the coherence and wholeness prescribed for the cogitative and rational subject. There are other formulae, perhaps more amenable to the historical critic, that help us understand the interrogations of linear progress that these poems signal even as they are committed to teleological explanations of event or national progress. The long eighteenth century is the period in which, to quote Pagden again, "the older providentialist languages of imperialism [were] transformed into a pretence to enlightened rationalism" (and this book has tracked, in the practice of poetry, that difficult and uneven transformation).[7] There are binaries we can use to suggest why this process might have been traumatic and always less than complete, less than credible: the shift is from the discursive closures of religious faith to the skeptical awareness of the historically informed imagination, from belief to experience, from insularity to an Enlightenment cosmopolitanism. And yet these binaries are not entirely accurate, for these poems and this cultural history show us how providentialist parables are retold as narratives of manifest destiny; how flexible and mendacious theological conceptions of "man" and "nature" serve collective or individual cupidity and arrogance; how Enlightenment vocabularies in this period, including various forms of cosmopolitanism, are banal justifications of experiences and attitudes derived from forced colonization and the making of modern empires.

The practice of poetry in this period, I have argued, is inseparable from the new sense of British community (the *Imperium britannicum*) being brought into effect by consolidations of power at home and overseas. In these poems, the poet's creative trepidation and ambition is articulated closely with his or her civic concern and responsibility; vocational struggle and success finds its parallel in the ebb and flow of national power. To sing a nation glorious— to specify the terms of its greatness *and* to warn against symptoms of its decline—is to achieve the proper condition of poetry. The apostrophic moment in these poems—the vocative O, the enabling fiction of poetry itself—addresses Muse and Nation, and finds in the suture of nation and muse a historically necessary and ideologically potent figure of poetic vocation. Such sutures are not of course a first for poetry, which is why my readings have followed the historical and cultural retrospection featured in so many of the poems: their search through formal and figural conventions that achieved similar currency and success in other times and places; their inventory of past and present rhetorical techniques for dramatizing the equation of poet, citizen, and prophet. But to suture is not to achieve seamless continuity or identity; these poems enact that lesson as vocational anxiety and as ideological contradiction, as the historical and anthropological incoherences of the imperialist imagination. The progress of the British empires of the long eighteenth century was an uneven business, unsettled by military, commercial, and territorial losses and beleaguered as well by more philosophical doubts about the form that these empires should take. Thus, in their enactment of tension and doubt, and in their varied recovery from such fears, these poems perform the cultural work required by ideologies of empire. The conviction they offer is of a difficult task heroically performed. The persuasive lesson they teach is of the historical necessity of particular forms of aspiration, even when the odds seem stacked against the merchant, the nation, the poet.

In an aside, therefore, on our writing of literary history, I might point out that it is the work of these poets in the long eighteenth century that prefaced (and thus complicates) Shelley's claim that poets are the unacknowledged legislators of the world. In their resolutely "literary" contributions to public debate, these poets demonstrated a simultaneous commitment to specialized creativity and to the "legislation" of collective ideals, and in the process crafted the reams of verse against which some forms of romantic disinterestedness recoiled. In practice and in aspiration, these poets are legislators of nation and empire, and their productivity renders ironic the progressive stance Shelley might have wished to strike in claiming an "unacknowledged" social and political instrumentality for poets and poetry. Indeed, James Chandler's comment that Shelley, Keats, Scott, Hazlitt, and Cobbett were "all arguably, though in different degrees, drawn to letters out of [a] sense that this is where (in every sense) the action was—where the work of cultural specification, historical determination, and national

constitution seemed crucially to be going on," actually describes a state of
poetic affairs in existence for a century before the poets of high romanticism
produced the fictions of originality that marked them out, in part by
translating the embarrassing vocational anxieties of eighteenth-century poets
into the elevations and visionary sublimities of romantic poetic discourse.
As the poems I have considered in this book show, throughout the eighteenth
century the visionary poem was the historical poem, which put on display
its difficult engagement with sociohistorical materials and concerns, at least
until Wordsworth worked out the formulae of poetic sublation, in which, as
Marjorie Levinson puts it, the "success or failure of the visionary poem
turns on its ability to hide its omission of the historical."[8]

Joseph Roach has recently argued, in the context of circum-Atlantic cultural
performances, that texts bear within themselves memories of encounters
particularly "subject to forgetting"—that is, encounters between different
people of different races in the violent theaters of modern conquest, trade,
and colonization. We can expand the scope of his argument--and it is an
argument that can wonderfully bear such generalization--to remark the ways
in which the poems considered here transact, in their memorial and prophetic
functions, similar experiences across the globe. Roach suggests that the
dynamic of such texts requires them to engage with, but marginalize or
repress, the dramatic results of asymmetrical power relations made more
pointed by racial and inter-national difference: representations of such
encounters, he argues, are marked by the selective disappearance of crucial
experiences. Never completely, however, which is why a critic today is able
to mark in the dynamic of a poem its argumentative or agonized negotiation
with the world it brings into being: "Such disappearances are necessary to
ensure the untroubled performance of a dominant trope: that of genealogical
succession, imagined as a stately procession, as an everlasting club whose
members succeed one another as if on parade. In a world constantly
reinvented by intercultural propinquity, however . . . the order of any
procession may be threatened with interruption or usurpation."[9]

The world of the British poet of "Great Britain" was a world under
such dramatic reinvention: this is in fact the shock of the new, of the
modernity brought into being by European colonialism. These poets strove
to produce, for their nation and their people, untroubled accounts of progress;
of genealogical succession (which is what their *translatio* motifs are); of the
religious, ethical, cultural, and political *rightness* of their spread across the
seas. When they admitted to intercultural propinquity, they located such
dubious kinship within a motivated calculus of power and possession (which
we, in our own acts of selective memory, call the Enlightenment). This

calculus proved itself enlightened precisely by emphasizing the need to shift other people in other places out of the trajectory of their own histories and into a needy and subservient relation within the self-aggrandizing narratives of British nationalist and imperialist thought. These are of course acts in self-conception, but the materials with which, and against which, that self was crafted were mined elsewhere, and under conditions whose violent logic inexorably fissures and marks (Roach's "interruption or usurpation") the national autobiographies being written. Given the history of European colonialism in the seventeenth century and after, these rhetorical acts of self-conception also had very material consequences for people in Britain, in Europe, and in those parts of the globe being brought into their ambit. The poems that I have considered here show an awareness of these consequences, and of their ideological underpinning; indeed, the debates they stage, and the uncertainties they display, all work toward a more supple set of legitimations for British dominance. But in doing so, they also generate palimpsestic records of those intellectual, cultural, and material practices—some within Britain, most without—that resisted such dominance. The job of the critic, in particular the postcolonial critic, is thus to pay attention to this record.

And to pay attention by reading these poems not so much against their grain but precisely along with it: thus, I have followed convolutions of thought and argument, noted odd juxtapositions of topoi and images, and marked those moments when narrative coherence is interrogated or refused by some recalcitrant memory, idea, or experience. What I *have* of course read against is the self-conception of these poems, their drive toward explanatory and ideological closure, their will to imagine an imperial telos for the lurching progress that Britain made in its trade and territorial wars. In practice, this has meant reading slowly through long (and wearying!) poems, and making my argument by catalog and accretion, which are, ironically, rhetorical procedures crucial to the poems' own inventories and stocktaking of the fecundity and riches of the globe. Perhaps my readers would have been happier with more summary (to which I have quite often resorted); even eighteenth-century readers, attuned to a more leisurely pace, complained about the ponderous length of some of these poems. Few of those readers, we are assured, read *The Seasons* more than once, but many had their favorite passages, which they savored aloud in company, thereby allowing Thomson to move them into imaginative and historical spaces not their own. It is unlikely (and perhaps not to be wished for) that this book will benefit from such sociality, but if my arguments—or sections of them— cause my reader to accede to their vision of critical work, this book will have done its work of persuasion, and will thus have served its own memorial and forward-looking functions.

NOTES

Introduction

1. Easthope's discussion of the feudal ballad in *Poetry as Discourse* allows us to see some of the formal reasons why "Rule, Britannia!" achieved its popularity. Easthope suggests that intertextuality, incremental repetition, the use of accentual meter and emphatic rhyme, and the coincidence between meaning and stanza unit all work to promote the sense that a ballad is part of the sociolect, the language community in general, rather than a performance of the idiolect, or individualized speech (78–93). Not all these elements are at play in "Rule, Britannia!" (and not always in the way Easthope suggests), but there is little doubt that the ballad-like form of the poem has much to do with its absorption into the cultural fabric of the British Empire.

2. Thomson, "Rule, Britannia!" in *Complete Works*, 422. Unless otherwise indicated, all references to Thomson's poetry are to this edition.

3. Blackburn, *Overthrow of Slavery*, 42. Blackburn offers Locke as an instance of a philosopher of political liberties who argued that slavery was against the very spirit of Englishness, but not inappropriate to the condition of Africans (he did own stock in the Royal Africa Company).

4. See Colley, *Britons*, 11. Mallet Englished his name from the Scots Malloch (a translation that earned him Johnson's ire). Like other Scotsmen who went to London and England in search of literary preferment, Mallet also sought to English his pronunciation and his style: Robert Crawford sees this vocational and cultural phenomenon as crucial to the making of a "national" literature (see note 17 of this introduction). On a more resistant note, Pittock has emphasized the many political and cultural tensions (including Jacobite sympathies) that complicated the incorporation of Ireland and Scotland into Britain in *Inventing and Resisting Britain*.

5. Colley suggests a geographical factor in the consolidation of a "British" national identity: especially in comparison with continental European states whose boundaries constantly fluctuated, the "simple fact that Great Britain was an island" allowed the sea to be imagined as a "telling symbol of identity. . . . British boundaries after 1707 seemed settled once and for all, marked out by the sea, clear, incontrovertible, apparently pre-ordained" (*Britons*, 17). The sense of an island-nation does of course pre-date 1707 (and arguably makes that historical moment possible). Marvell provides a nice instance of this sentiment in "Upon Appleton House: To My Lord Fairfax":

> Thou paradise of four seas,
> Which heavens planted us to please,
> But, to exclude the world, did guard
> With wat'ry if not flaming sword.
>
> *(lines 323–26; Selected Poetry and Prose, 76–77)*

This idea of the island-nation is most famously and lyrically expressed, of course, by John of Gaunt in Shakespeare's *Richard II:*

> This fortress built by Nature for herself
> Against infection and the hand of war,
> This happy breed of men, this little world,
> This precious stone set in a silver sea,
> Which serves it in the office of a wall,
> Or as a moat defensive to a house,
> Against the envy of less happier lands,
> This blessed plot, this earth, this realm, this England.
>
> *(2.1.43–50)*

As McEachern suggests, however, for "all of the immediacy that Gaunt insists upon, the point of his speech is that 'this' England is not present to him." (Gaunt goes on to complain that "That England that was wont to conquer others, / Has made a shameful conquest of itself" [2.1.65–66].) As we will see in the analysis of Thomson's poetry, and that of many of the other poets treated in this book, the imagination of nation—especially when that nation expanded from "England" to "Great Britain"—is all too often at its performative fullest at moments that reflect on, or are fearful of, the decline of the nation. McEachern again: "The nation is an ideal of community that is, by definition, either proleptic or passing, ever just beyond reach" (*Poetics of Nationhood*, 6).

6. Gerrard, *Patriot Opposition*, 3. Burden also details the political circumstances of the play in his study of its staging and its musical arrangements, *Garrick, Arne*.

7. Wilson details the enormous impact of Vernon's victory on public consciousness in her *Sense of the People*, 140–69. She describes Vernon as a naval and imperial hero who became a rallying point for the anti-Walpole opposition, who argued that the prime minister's policies were both a threat to liberty at home and circumscribed "Britain's position in the world. In this way, the Vernon agitation kindled and focused a nascent imperialist sensibility that defined British identity through expansion abroad as well as through birthrights, liberties and constitutional traditions" (164).

8. Gerrard, *Patriot Opposition*, 3–4. Gerrard's book is in part a tribute to the difficult nuances of individual affiliation and party propaganda (which she meticulously unravels) in the poetry of the period under consideration.

9. Thomson and Mallet, *Alfred: A Masque* (1740), rpt. *Plays of David Mallet*, ed. Nussbaum, 43–44. Nussbaum suggests that Mallet's obsequious relation to Frederick, Prince of Wales, might be explained as the effort of a Scottish Roman Catholic (with a Jacobite heritage) to ingratiate himself into Hanoverian England (xi); she also provides a history of the staging and revisions of *Alfred* (xxv–xxxi).

10. Hall, "Signification," 106.

11. In such discussions, it is useful to remember Michael Meehan's argument that in most eighteenth-century usage, the term *liberty* (or *freedom*) "refers to the British achievement of personal, or *civil* liberty—the security that comes with the rule of law—rather than that broader kind of freedom, *political* liberty, which offers democratic participation in government" (*Liberty and Poetics*, 15). Stevenson calls attention to the ideological weight of such ideas in popular definitions of Englishness: "London crowds in the eighteenth century frequently asserted the 'rights' and 'liberties' of Englishmen and that these concepts enshrined an interrelated network of ideas, including popular chauvinism, no-popery, and a belief in the distinctive rights of Englishmen. The beliefs that Englishmen were not 'slaves,' did not wear 'wooden shoes,' and were possessed of a 'birthright' were frequently articulated in slogans, handbills, and popular rhymes, and appear often to have been derived from the religious and constitutional struggles of the seventeenth century" (*Popular Disturbances*, 322).
Stevenson has the work of George Rudé in mind here.

12. I am grateful to Jay Fliegelman for this observation.

13. A quick, well-known reference will serve to gloss the iconographic and ideological place of this symbol. In Pope's *Windsor-Forest* (1713), the arboreal riches of the world are not to be envied so long as "by our Oaks the precious Loads are born, / And Realms commanded which those Trees adorn" (lines 31–32). In the poem, oaks from Windsor rematerialize as warships that "Bear *Britain's* Thunder, and her Cross display, / To the bright Regions of the rising Day" (lines 387–88). Thomson the Whig and Pope the Tory have no problem sharing a symbolic naval platform, as it were, which is a reminder that contemporary domestic political differences (even when they involved differences in overseas economic policy) did not prevent poets and propagandists from celebrating the same national icons. For a less celebratory, more analytical account of the connections between forests and naval might, see Albion, *Forests and Sea Power*.

14. Crider, "Structure and Effect," 64. On the westward movement of the arts and their domestication in Britain, see also Hartman, "Romantic Poetry," 311–36.

15. Crider, "Structure and Effect," 57.

16. This representation of the British "fair" as needing male protection was of course elaborated during the course of the eighteenth century to the point that it became one of the key topoi of the discourse of British imperialism. See, for instance, "The Freeman's Oath," a print produced as anti-invasion propaganda in 1803. Britannia, seated on her lion, looks belligerently abroad, while below her British soldiers wave their swords defiantly. They are framed by a seated mother, nursing her child, and a soldier who carries in his arms a young woman; both of them look to Britannia for succor. The print is reproduced by Colley, *Britons*, 311. For an extended discussion of "the figure of the woman in the colonial text," see Sharpe, *Allegories of Empire*.

17. Crawford, *Devolving English Literature*, 18, but cf. 16–44. Crawford reads the drive toward "improvement" not as an instance of English cultural imperialism, but of the rise of pro-British sentiment among the Scots: "The provincials could win

respect, partake of power, and compete with the men of the capital on the capital's own ground; but only by paying stylistic homage to the capital's standards" (38). In this context, we might note that the *Dictionary of National Biography* (that infallible guide to English values) sees as "remarkable the purity of Thomson's style and its freedom from any admixture of provincial idiom" vol. 19 (1909), 726.

18. Siskin, *Work of Writing*, 88.

19. Goldgar, for instance, has shown the close relations between "men of letters" and "men of power" in this period and has argued that the way of these poets was "not to abjure the rough world of partisan politics but to enter that world and make it the subject of their art" (*Walpole and the Wits*, 221).

20. My use of *conversation* here presupposes a model in which some people talk (typically, male poets) while others are silenced by the force or terms of the conversation. Those silenced are, typically, women poets and those outside the privileged circle. In literary-historical terms, this means that certain genres of poetic practice are elevated while others are taken less seriously, in some cases precisely because women are at home in them. I return to this issue later in the introduction.

21. My argument here is comparable to, and indebted to, Stallybrass and White's insight that the "position of transcendence" so important to the "master-poets" in this period requires acts of "discursive rejection" through which they seek to raise themselves above the "carnival" of poetic productivity: "In each case however, this apparently simple gesture of social superiority and disdain could not be effectively accomplished without revealing the very labour of suppression and sublimation involved. Such a project is constitutive, not contingent" (*Politics and Poetics*, 123–24).

22. Most impressively by Jameson in *Political Unconscious*, esp. 1–110, but the later writings of Raymond Williams are also crucial in this effort.

23. Dryden's editors, Edward N. Hooker and H. T. Swedenborg, argue that the poet is here "engaged in countering the effects of seditious propaganda represented by a group of pamphlets whose very title he employed against them." For an account of the historical circumstances of the writing of *Annus Mirabilis*, see Dryden, *Works*, 1.256–60.

24. However, as Nussbaum shows, in *Pamela* the most compelling and ideologically central details of a Christian monogamy are achieved in contrast with polygamy, the idea of "multiple marriages occasioned by men's explorations of the larger empire" (*Torrid Zones*, 19, and chapter 3, "Polygamy, *Pamela*, and the Prerogative of Empire"). Nussbaum's work makes clear the impact of overseas discovery and "empire" on the eighteenth-century novel. But more on that in the body of this argument.

25. These origins are underlined by Azim, *Colonial Rise*.

26. I should note that Swift, for instance, whose *Gulliver's Travels* is here an example of "colonial" themes and narratives, also produced a body of poems (including his city satires and love poems) that are municipal and "domestic" in concern and orientation. In his prose, especially his commentary on Irish affairs, Swift charts the limitations of the nation, or indeed the inequality of relations between metropolis and colony; his poetry offers scant evidence of such themes.

27. Nussbaum, *Torrid Zones*. For complementary work, see Brown, *Ends of Empire*.

28. Ellis, *Politics of Sensibility*.

29. A good summary of such plays and their themes is provided by Scouten in Loftis et al., *Revels History of Drama,* 256–79.

30. For an illuminating discussion along these lines see Thompson, "Dryden's *Conquest of Granada*, 211–26. Thompson argues that Almanzor "functions as an emblem of the military conquistador who, under the demands of a budding colonial empire, must be replaced with or translated into a new type of hero, a prototype of the colonial administrator" (211).

31. Dryden, "To the Most Excellent . . . Princess Anne" appended in 1667 to the play (*Works*, 9.25).

32. Addison, *Cato*, 480. Further references to the play are to this edition.

33. Michèle Cohen has shown how English masculinity in this period was defined against the effeminacy and "Frenchified" manner represented on the stage by the fop. See *Fashioning Masculinity*, 37–41.

34. Centlivre, *Bold Stroke*, 98.

35. I have discussed this in "Reading Literary Symptoms," 80–96.

36. However, the best-known "personal" letters in the period, Mary Wortley Montagu's *Letters Of the Right Honourable Lady M—y W——y M——u* (written 1716/17 but published after her death in 1762) are full, too, of ethnographic curiosity and libidinal excitement, as is evident from her account of music and dance in a Turkish harem: "Nothing could be more artful, or more proper to raise *certain ideas.* The tunes so soft!—The motions so languishing!—Accompanied with pauses and dying eyes! half-falling back, and then recovering themselves in so artful a manner, that I am very positive, the coldest and most rigid prude upon earth, could not have looked upon them without thinking of *something not to be spoke of*" (letter dated April 18, 1717). The distance between this passage and the tone of distanced, philosophical melancholy that characterizes Johnson's *Rasselas*—whose seraglio sequences feature boredom rather than sexual excitement, and anticipate a convent— is one more example of the way narratives set in foreign places clean up their acts.

37. The full title of this work is *Secret Memoirs and Manners of several Persons of Quality, of Both Sexes. From the New Atalantis, an Island in the Mediterranean. Written Originally in Italian.* For an account of Manley's arrest and trial, see Ros Ballaster's introduction to her edition of Manley's work, xiv–xvi. Warner, in "Elevation of the Novel" (578–81), argues that eighteenth-century novelists and critics distanced themselves from Behn's and Manley's fiction.

38. Siskin, *Work of Writing*, 5–6.

39. It is ironic that the poems in this period most strenuous in their desire to contribute to the discourse of national power found no place in the nineteenth- and twentieth-century British poetic canon (which might be thought of as a systematized instance of such national cultural capital). The irony is rendered more pointed when we consider that it is Gray's *Elegy*, that meditation on the village graveyard, on the endurance of the *local*, that has become the paradigmatic instance of poetic ambition and its vicissitudes in the canon of English poetry.

40. Kroebner marshals evidence from literary and political documents to argue correctly that through the seventeenth century, the "chances of a British Empire remained bound up with the political and constitutional prospects of a kingdom of

Great Britain" (*Empire*, 63). Both Colley and Kathleen Wilson suggest such reciprocity, too, with a greater emphasis on the role played by the making of the British Empire in the consolidation of the island-nation of Great Britain.

41. Anderson, *Imagined Communities*. Of particular relevance is Anderson's argument that all modern—and thus bourgeois—nationalisms are predicated upon and sustained by the sense of nation and community orchestrated through print culture.

42. Colley, "Britishness and Otherness," 66.

43. Brewer, *Sinews; Bayly, Imperial Meridian*. Here, and in the next two footnotes, I mention only a few of the better books from what is by now an extensive and rich bibliography on these issues (some of which will be referred to below).

44. Newman, *Rise of English Nationalism;* Wilson, *Sense of the People*.

45. Greenblatt, *Learning to Curse, Marvelous Possessions*, and *Renaissance Self-Fashioning*; Helgerson, *Forms of Nationhood*.

46. Hulme's discussion of Robinson Crusoe as "a relentlessly 'modern' man" who breaks "the feudal and patriarchal ties that would bind him to a law career in York in favour of the dangerous 'opening' on to the sea offered by Hull" is relevant here. Hulme describes Crusoe's subjectivity as the product of an individualism "which staggers backwards into the future, lacking in self-understanding, full of guilt, self-contradictory, fearful, violent: the modernity of European consciousness shipwrecked in the Caribbean, that very archipelago of its subversion" (*Colonial Encounters*, 214–15).

47. One exception to the rarity of individuation is the Yarico and Inkle story retold in a variety of forms through the eighteenth century (cf. Wechselblatt, "Gender and Race" 197–223). Such characters do show up in antislavery poems, where they are part of a conscious effort to engender sympathy for the victims of the slave trade by providing them with individual histories. These biographical details are, in practice, entirely romanticized and of a type, derived as they are from the conventions of contemporary literary sentimentalism.

48. I would call this the "work of poets" or of the "work of the writing of poetry" in the period, and thus align it with what Siskin has defined as the broader "work of writing" in his *Work of Writing*.

49. Griffin's *Literary Patronage* is the most recent, and perhaps the most revealing, account, but cultural critics beginning with Alexander Pope and Samuel Johnson have emphasized the instrumentality of much poetry written in the late seventeenth and eighteenth centuries. Some other cultural historians and critics who have written on this issue are Beljame, *Men of Letters*; Foss, *Age of Patronage*; Rogers, *Grub Street*.

50. Pocock's writing has convincingly emphasized the continuing "tension between virtue and commerce" in this period. He shows the importance of the contemporary perception that "there were now two ways—an ancient and a modern, a classical and a commercial" in which property could be seen to determine "social and political personality," as also of the "increasing awareness that the latter way furnished the human creature with a history, the former with a means of protesting against it." This dialectic between "progress" and "reaction" is important to all the poems I examine in this book. See "Mobility of Property" in Pocock, *Virtue*, 122.

51. Pope, "An Essay on Criticism," in *Poems*, ed. Butt, 165.

52. Weinbrot, *Augustus Caesar.*

53. Bloom, *The Anxiety of Influence.* Walter Jackson Bate, who does not use a psychoanalytical vocabulary, offers a similar literary-historical model in his *Burden of the Past.*

54. Doody, *Daring Muse,* 84, but cf. all of chapter 4, "The New Augustans and the Roman Poets," which is an illuminating account of the "highly selective" appropriation of Augustan poetic practices by English poets.

55. There are of course many histories of this period, but for our purposes here the opening chapter ("'Imperium': The Roman Heritage") of Kroebner's *Empire* (1–17) is very useful. In his recent *Classical Culture and the Idea of Rome,* Ayres suggests that "for purposes of political self-justification the classical political heritage" served late seventeenth- and eighteenth-century English oligarchs conveniently, but Ayres also holds that such self-conscious opportunism went hand in hand with the belief, among those who invoked Roman precedents, in the "continuing validity of the classical idea of *libertas* or the social virtue obligatory in citizenship or *civitas*" (2). As I show throughout, poems that invoked the rhetoric and iconography of Roman *libertas* and *civitas* did so to bolster claims they made for the coming of age of an imperial Britain, a nation whose civic and political institutions allowed it to assert European primacy and a global destiny.

56. Alpers, *Singer of the Eclogues,* 65–71.

57. Quoted by Weinbrot, *Augustus Caesar,* 50.

58. Weinbrot, *Augustus Caesar,* 108.

59. After Vasco da Gama returned to Portugal in August 1499, King Manuel, who had outfitted the expedition, referred to himself, for the first time, as "Lord of Guinea and the Conquests, Navigations and Commerce of Ethiopia, Arabia, Persia, and India." See Lach, *Asia in the Making of Europe,* vol. 1, bk. 1, 97.

60. For an account of the English context, see Andrews, *Trade, Plunder, and Settlement.*

61. In *Daring Muse,* Margaret Anne Doody quotes this passage from Pope as evidence of the energetic, "appetitive" urge in contemporary poets, the desire to "reach out and grab the world" (8). "The appetite for wealth and glory is an appetite for the great globe itself, for space and all the products of earth and sea," she writes (15).

62. Poetry can thus provide particular insight into the iconography and tropology of British imperialism, which, as Kathleen Wilson has argued, must be understood as a composite of the public "ideologies, values and practices supporting Britain's push for establishing and consolidating an empire" (*Sense of the People,* 23). Wilson adds a useful footnote to explain that her term *empire* here "subsumes the narrower historical form of colonialism (e.g., the West Indies and the North American colonies) as well as the 'informal' empire of trade and arms (India); both, in any case, are contained in the eighteenth-century English notion of the 'Empire of the Sea.'"

63. In "British Politics and the Demise of the Roman Republic," Frank Turner emphasizes the reciprocity between British cultural politics and historical interpretations of the Roman republic. In the early eighteenth century, for instance, the country-party critique of the growth of commercialism (and the new financial

institutions), of the national debt, the standing army, and of centralized executive power (via placemen in Parliament) in Britain exemplified these evils by referring to their role in causing the decline of republican Rome, while a Hanoverian propagandist like Thomas Blackwell refuted this interpretation (in his *Memoirs of the Court of Augustus*) by arguing that modern prosperity would not be corrosive since Britain possessed several "institutional bulwarks of liberty" not available in Rome. See *Contesting Cultural Authority*, 231–61, esp. 231–37.

64. Weinbrot, *Augustus Caesar*, 59–85.

65. For further examples of this "historical sleight-of-hand," see Meehan's discussion in *Liberty and Poetics*, 66–68.

66. Welsted, *Poems on Several Occasions*.

67. Weinbrot's 1993 *Britannia's Issue* highlights the benign form of such comparative thought: "Knowledge of Greece and Rome blends with knowledge of France and then of Germany, and always with Old and New Testament values and literatures. One consequence was writers and readers extraordinarily aware of alien cultures they were asked to assess, adapt, variously enjoy, and incorporate" (3). However, many late-seventeenth- and eighteenth-century texts commented on and assessed a number of "alien cultures" other than those we now call European, and they often did so, as we will see, with a view to "incorporate" them and their products.

68. Spate, "Muse of Mercantilism," 121.

69. Berkeley, "On the Prospect of Planting Arts and Learning," 19.

70. Spate, "Muse of Mercantilism," 123.

71. In a related comment, Marshall Brown suggests that while "generic types are neither rigidly limited in number nor inflexible in definition, they appear, especially in eighteenth-century works, to impart an externally based stability to the flux of literary expression." Brown believes, as I do, that such "stability" does not foreclose innovation within, or the intermingling of, different forms and generic types. *Preromanticism*, 17.

72. Kroebner surveys some of these poems in his *Empire*, 71–94; for Pope, see Laura Brown, *Alexander Pope*. Brown's book was one of the first contemporary critical studies to argue for the importance of the "interconnected developments of capitalism and mercantile imperialism" (3) to any study of eighteenth-century poetry.

73. Kaul, "Why Selima Drowns," 223–32.

74. Leask, *British Romantic Writers and the East*, 19. Leask refers to Schwab's *Oriental Renaissance*. See also Makdisi, *Romantic Imperialism*.

75. As Newman puts it, "The concept of national identity is propagated not only in poetry—though this medium, uniquely given to symbolic representation, is often of major importance—but in an immense variety of literary, artistic and educational processes" (*English Nationalism*, 126). We can add other systems of symbolic education to Newman's list: the rituals of the monarchy, of parliamentary processes, of church practices, of military organization, of pubs and coffeehouses, of the public media.

76. Doody, *Daring Muse*, 17, 18.

77. Zahedieh reminds us that England's transoceanic trade at the end of the

seventeenth century "accounted for about 20 per cent of total overseas commerce," but that it was "the rapidity of its growth rather than its absolute scale which drew fascinated attention from contemporaries and later historians." Zahedieh's article is especially good at pointing out the many and various sectors of English maritime, commercial, artisanal, educational, and cultural life quickened by the rapid expansion of the Atlantic and East Indies trade ("Overseas Expansion," 420).

78. Williams, *Country and City*, 6, 7.

79. Williams, *Country and City*, 2, 51.

80. Williams, *Country and City*, 23, 68–71.

81. Even Richard Feingold, who sees "the pastoral and the georgic" as "forms of social and political understanding" (*Nature and Society*, 2), and thus offers a historically acute and formally sensitive argument about the collapse and virtual disappearance of these two poetic forms by the end of the eighteenth century, does not recognize the importance of passages in which these poets engage with the prospects and problems of overseas expansion.

82. In his "British-American Belles Lettres," Shields points to a number of poems written on the other side of the Atlantic (in particular James Kirkpatrick's *The Sea Piece*, published in London in 1750) that echoed and developed these ideas (309–43; esp. 329–32).

83. In the matter of making such connections, Nicholson is a recent exception: he writes that the "project of *The Spectator*" was to develop the "market forms of sociability, sympathy and honesty" into a redefinition of "citizenship," and extends this argument into readings of early-eighteenth-century poetic satires (*Writing and the Rise of Finance*, 3).

84. Johnson, *The Vanity of Human Wishes* (1749), lines 1–2, lines 176–83. Johnson's particular allusion here is to the duke of Marlborough's victory over the French at Blenheim.

85. Brown, *Preromanticism*, 17. As will be obvious to any reader of Brown's book, my interpretive method is very different from his, but I share his sense that we can learn a great deal by engaging with the "stratified temporality" (19) of a text, the way it constructs its past, present, and future.

86. Kaul, *Thomas Gray and Literary Authority*.

87. Nandy, *The Intimate Enemy*, 32.

88. Cecil's biography of Cowper is entitled *The Stricken Deer*.

1. The Poetry of Nation

1. Corrigan and Sayer, *Great Arch*, 80. They also quote Larner, who calls this shift "'the political dethronement of God.' The Kingdom of God on earth ceased to be a political objective and was replaced by the defence of property, nationalism, and liberty" (Larner, *Thinking Peasant*, 56).

2. Corrigan and Sayer, ibid., 81.

3. Elliott begins his *Old World and the New* with an account of the hesitations of Abbé Raynal and some of his contemporaries "in evaluating the consequences of the discovery and conquest of America," hesitations that "sprang precisely from the

dilemma involved in attempting to reconcile the record of economic and technical progress since the end of the fifteenth century with the record of the sufferings endured by the defeated societies" (4).

4. Hulme, *Colonial Encounters*, 96–97.

5. McKeon, "Pastoralism, Puritanism, Imperialism," 61.

6. This is not only an English conceit: in "The Golden Island or the Darian Song" (1699) by "A Lady of Honour," the poet describes the trees of the "Noble Land" of Darien (Panama) joining hands and bowing low "for Honour of *Scotland*" and lists birds, beasts, and natives who spontaneously offer presents and "Tribute" to the Scottish colonists. See Lady of Honour, "Golden Island." This poem was part of the promotional material that encouraged Scottish public interest in "The Company of Scotland Trading to Africa and the Indies," established in 1695 as a rival to the English East India Company. Unfortunately for the Scots, the Darien scheme failed by 1700.

7. Greene says that the Bible "mentions Lebanon chiefly as a source of timber for large buildings. Solomon's palace and Temple were built with Lebanon cedar (1 Kings 4.33; 7.2; 10.17, 21)" (*Oxford Companion to the Bible*, s.v. Lebanon).

8. Chaudhuri, *Trade and Civilisation*, 85.

9. McKeon, "Pastoralism, Puritanism, Imperialism," 61–62.

10. In May 1655, Jamaica was captured by the English, becoming the first colony they gained by conquest (even though it was an attempt to make up for a failed attack on Hispaniola). Lloyd believes this to be an event of great consequence in that it "indicated another approach to the art of colonization, in which the government took valuable colonies away from Europeans who had reached them first" (*British Empire*, 33). We should keep in mind though that the failure of Penn and Venables to capture Hispaniola was a serious blow to Cromwell's providentialist faith in his "Western design," which itself ended in disappointment.

11. Colley, *Britons*, 8–9. Colley argues that, in the eighteenth century, it was "shared religious allegiance [Protestantism] combined with recurrent wars that permitted a sense of British national identity to emerge alongside of, and not necessarily in competition with older, more organic attachments to England, Wales or Scotland, or to county or village" (18). Her account emphasizes British enmity with Roman Catholic France, but the same role of war and mercantile competition can be seen at play in mid-seventeenth-century relations between England and the United Provinces, which were Protestant in faith.

12. All quotations of Waller's poetry are taken from *Poems*.

13. In *Poetry of Limitation*, Warren L. Cherniak reminds us that Waller had "ample precedent, literary and other, for his characterization of the islands of the Western Hemisphere as an unfallen Eden." Cherniak provides an instance from John Smith's *Generall Historie of Virginia, New England, and the Summer Isles* (1624), and suggests a second work by Smith, *The True Travels, Adventures, and Observations of Captaine John Smith, in Europe, Asia, Affrica, and America* (1630) as the source for Waller's tale of the trapped whales (178–79). Waller's images of natural—labor-free—bounty (as those of Marvell after him) are part of the persuasive iconography delineated by those who celebrated the New World at the expense of the Old, in opposition to those

who condemned the inferiority of Caribbean or American conditions or who emphasized the horrors of the Atlantic crossing. Such representations played some role in shaping patterns of migration. See Zuckerman, "Identity," 117–27.

14. Todd analyzes some of this propaganda in "Equilibrium," 169–91.

15. Appleby suggests that "envy and wonder stimulated a great deal of economic thinking in England in the middle decades of the seventeenth century." In particular, "Dutch commercial prowess acted more forcefully upon the English imagination than any other economic development of the seventeenth century" (*Economic Thought*, 73). See also Edmundson, *Anglo-Dutch Rivalry* and Davis, *English Shipping Industry*, 8–13.

16. Adam Smith describes the provisions of the 1651 Navigation Act as being directed largely against Dutch control of shipping and commerce. He also makes clear that the "national animosity" between the English and the Dutch followed from belligerent economic competition (*Wealth of Nations*, I, 485–86).

17. A comment Appleby makes on English puzzlement at Dutch commercial success helps explain the economic envy that overdetermines Marvell's choice of satiric beginning: "Their innovative methods often involved a denial of conventional wisdom; their departures from traditional expectations compelled analysis. Dutch prosperity, like Dutch land, seemed to have been created out of nothing" (*Economic Thought*, 74).

18. In their work on cultural representation in the early modern period, Stallybrass and White have shown just how powerfully "the grotesque body may become a primary, highly-charged intersection and mediation of social and political forces, a sort of intensifier and displacer in the making of identity" (*Politics and Poetics*, 25).

19. Todd, "Equilibrium," 191.

20. Marvell is not alone is using a specific form of trade and colonization to define national difference and to argue for an exculpatory dimension to British imperialism. For instance, in "Of a War with Spain, and a Fight at Sea," Waller argues that in lands abroad "Our nation's solid virtue did oppose" the "gilded majesty" of the Spanish, "the rich troublers of the world's repose" (lines 13–18).

21. The irony here—the anti-Royalist Cromwell is called "the best of kings"— has caused at least one editor of Marvell's poetry to reject this poem. See *Marvell: Complete Poetry*, ed. George de F. Lord.

22. As McKeon puts it, by "exploiting the conjunction of Puritan historiography with the allegorical resonances of the pastoral mode, Marvell developed the highly characteristic style whereby his subjects are saturated with the suggestive aura and immanence of English politics and sacred history" ("Pastoralism, Puritanism, Imperialism," 50–51). McKeon goes on to suggest that Marvell's engagement with politics in the 1650s can be fruitfully read as responding to two questions: "What precedents may be available for authenticating the apparently unprecedented events of the English revolution? How amenable are those events to the traditional rhetorical figure of the *translatio imperii*?" (51).

23. Nicholas Canny has argued convincingly that the English conquest over and settlement of parts of Ireland provided the pattern of colonization followed in the Atlantic world in the seventeenth century and later; Cromwell's triumphs were a confirmation of those patterns. See, for instance, his *Elizabethan Conquest of Ireland* and "The Permissive Frontier."

24. As is well known to students of Marvell's poetry, the Horatian ode has attracted a great deal of contradictory critical attention. Rather than discuss those debates here, I will call attention to Robert Wilcher's account of them in his edition of Marvell's *Selected Poetry and Prose*, 196–97, 201–4, and to his comment that the "entire ode can be seen as a structure of tensions between apparently irreconcilable principles and contradictory interpretations" (202). Donald M. Friedman also provides a useful summary of these issues in his "Andrew Marvell," in *Cambridge Companion to English Poetry*, 275–82.

25. Armitage, "Cromwellian Protectorate," 533. Armitage's essay is a rich account of the interplay between the vocabularies of providentialist republicanism and those of an equally providentialist imperialism in the conduct of Cromwell's foreign policy, particularly his "Western design." He argues persuasively that "the intellectual history of Britain must attend to the languages of empire as keenly as to the words of republicanism which have effectively drowned them out" (533).

26. See Armitage's discussion of Marchmont Nedham's 1652 translation of John Selden's *Of the Dominion, or Ownership of the Sea*. (Selden's *Mare clausum* was originally written in 1618 to counter Grotius's *Mare liberum*.) Armitage quotes Nedham as arguing that "the sovereignty of the seas flowing about the island hath, in all times . . . been held and acknowledged by all the world, as an inseparable appendant of the British Empire" (Armitage, "Cromwellian Protectorate," 534).

27. In his "Instructions to a Painter, for the Drawing of the Posture and Progress of His Majesty's Forces at Sea, Under the Command of His Highness-Royal; together with the Battle and Victory Obtained over the Dutch, June 3, 1665," Waller offers a concluding apotheosis of Charles II:

> Like young Augustus let his image be,
> Triumphing for that victory at sea,
> Where Egypt's Queen, and Eastern King's overthrown,
> Made the possession of the world his own.
>
> *(lines 301–4)*

In his recuperation of the import of such images, Cherniak argues that when Waller "celebrates British power, he is praising not force, but law; the best conquests are bloodless. The dream of empire shades off into the dream of a golden age. . . . In the *Panegyric* and again in *Instructions to a Painter*, Waller speaks of England as a second Rome. This is no casual metaphor but embodies his central vision, the universal rule of peace, civility, and law" (*Poetry of Limitation*, 19). Neither Rome nor Britain came to their empires bloodlessly, and Waller's poems certainly do not pretend otherwise. Cherniak's comment is born out of the critical desire to rescue art and artists from their participation in political and sociocultural processes, which is ironic particularly in that Cherniak is quite clear about Waller's concern "with the growth of trade and with colonization"; he calls attention to the fact that Waller was "appointed a commissioner of trade by Cromwell in 1655 and after the Restoration served on the Councils of Trade and Foreign Plantations" (18).

28. Gilbert reads this reference to Joseph as being part of Waller's Hobbesian

argument in the poem: Cromwell's rule is legitimized by his powerful exercise of state power, and his Joseph-like qualities as "provider" make him worthy of replacing "an anointed king" (*Edmund Waller*, 80–86).

29. The quotation is from the editor's headnote to sonnet 16 in *Milton: Poetical Works*, ed. Bush, 190.

30. This is not to claim that Milton the poet remained unaffected by developments in English mercantilism and colonial conquest. Evans argues that *Paradise Lost* is, "among other things, a poem about empire" and that the poem plays out Milton's ambivalent feelings about the colonization of America "by reenacting on the cosmic stage many of the central events of the conquest of the New World" ("Imperial Epic," 229, 232, 238). See also *Imperial Epic*.

31. Quint, *Epic and Empire*, 255, 265, 324. Evans disagrees with Quint's reading and argues that, for Milton in *Paradise Lost* and elsewhere, "Imperial expansion . . . is morally neutral. When it is practiced by the virtuous, it is entirely admirable. When it is practiced by the wicked, it is one of the greatest evils that the human race can endure" (*Imperial Epic*, 147).

32. Lloyd, *British Empire*, 30. Quint lists similar crucial changes in foreign policy as part of his discussion of Milton's fear of the "easy transition and slide from republican to Royalist statism," where he emphasizes Milton's concern that such "statism" fostered his "countrymen's hunger for trade" and thus constituted "a threat to their freedom" (*Epic and Empire*, 337–38).

33. The Barbadian plantocracy, under a Cavalier governor, Francis Willoughby, continued to resist parliamentary authority until the island was blockaded for three months by a parliamentary fleet commanded by George Asycue. In January 1652, it agreed to recognize the rule of Parliament in exchange for some autonomy in trade relations.

34. Lloyd, *British Empire*, 30–34. Corrigan and Sayer also emphasize these events as anticipations of "the aggressive commercial foreign policy and wars waged by the English state in the eighteenth century" (*Great Arch*, 83).

35. Zwicker's acute reading of *The First Anniversary* is to be found in his *Lines of Authority*, 87.

36. While reminding us that it would be "a serious mistake to think of English (shortly to be British) naval history" in the mid and late seventeenth century "as an unbroken succession of glorious victories," G. E. Aylmer argues that in this period "a standing navy became much more firmly established and more generally accepted, never being regarded with the same political—indeed ideological—suspicion as a standing army." Parliament supplied money for, and sought some oversight over, the fleet, and Aylmer sees this interest as proof that "trade and empire were seen as matters of national importance" ("Navy, State, Trade, and Empire," 468–69).

37. Additionally, this poem contains a couplet on Cromwell that captures within its antithesis the peculiar combination of imperial authority and domestic constitutionalism that Britain was to claim as characteristic of its administrators overseas: "Abroad a king he seems, and something more, / At home a subject on the equal floor" (lines 389–90). This antithesis was a crucial component of the

ideology of "enlightened," constitutional authority that, in the nineteenth century in particular, legitimized the consolidation of the British Empire.

38. Dryden's lines in the first epigraph to this chapter are from "The Art of Poetry, Written in French by the Sier de Boileau, Made English," in Dryden, *Works*, 2.33. Dryden was responsible for finding English analogies for the poem's references to French writers and events. Here, line 294, in which the Ganges bows to the British monarch, updates Boileau's original, which had the river Scheldt bowing to Louis XIV. When these lines were written, the East India Company had begun to make good profits from its trade in India, but if the Ganges bowed to anyone, it did to Aurangzeb, whose Mughal Empire was then at its zenith. Dryden's Englishing of Boileau's line fuses imperial and poetic agency: here, the writing of an ode makes a subject of the Ganges. For a brief account of the English presence in India in this period, see Lloyd, *British Empire*, 34–36.

39. Some lines from "Astrea Redux" (1660) offer a ready gloss on the connection between empire and civilization made here. When Dryden describes the "lawlessness" that had overtaken England in the period of Charles II's exile, he suggests that his countrymen had reverted to the state of their "painted Ancestours" before "Empires Arts their Breasts had Civiliz'd" (lines 43–48). In this poem, written not long after the "Heroique Stanza's" on Cromwell, Dryden rewrites many key images and ideas from the earlier poem. Antimonarchical political "Freedom" is now equated with a state of "savagery"—with the prehistory of England. The syntax of the lines quoted here does not make clear if it is England's prowess at building empires that has civilized its people, or if it is England as a colony that learned the arts of civilization. In either case, these lines emphasize the conjunction between arts and arms that was offered as the fruit (and sometimes as the justification) of the spread of empire.

40. Dryden's panegyric emphasizes Cromwell's victories, but it is important to remember that Cromwell's successes, both domestic and imperial, had also been evaluated differently. A good instance is provided by Hawkins's *Discourse* (1657), which suggested that the Commonwealth had been debilitated by "ease and vice" after the first Anglo-Dutch war, and so was condemned to be "laid in the dust, with those other glorious States of *Rome, Athens, Sparta,* and *Carthage*" (quoted by Armitage, "Cromwellian Protectorate," 552). This assertion that the fall of empires is caused by the luxurious behavior that follows imperial success becomes increasingly important in eighteenth-century poetry, as we will see in later chapters.

41. MacLean, among others, has argued that among "the most typical gestures of Restoration panegyric is one learned from the oppositional poets of the 1630s and 1640s who, writing against the grain of Stuart absolutism, insisted that the national identity depended upon foreign policy. By associating Charles with the growth of British trade and empire, poets in 1660 continued a line of argument from Cromwellian panegyric which had celebrated mercantile expansion during the 1650s" (*Time's Witness*, 264).

42. This is an irony that has been noted at length by Dryden's biographers and other commentators; perhaps Johnson's well-known comment bears repetition: "When the King was restored, Dryden, like the other panegyrists of usurpation, changed his opinion or his profession, and published *Astrea Redux*. . . . The reproach of inconstancy

was on this occasion shared with such numbers, that it produced neither hatred nor disgrace! If he changed, he changed with the nation" ("John Dryden," in *Lives*, 114).

43. In his account of "Royalist Prophecy," McKeon remarks on the number of contemporary commentators who saw in the Restoration not only a recall of "the bounty of the past" but also a promise of "the greater wealth and glory of an imperial future" (*Politics and Poetry*, 235–36).

44. Another instance of this combination of elements is to be found in a companion poem, "To His Sacred Maiesty, A Panegyrick On His Coronation" (1661):

> It was your Love before made discord cease:
> Your love is destin'd to your Countries peace.
> Both *Indies* (Rivalls in your bed) provide
> With Gold or Jewels to adorn your Bride.
> This to a mighty King presents rich ore,
> While that with Incense does a God implore.
>
> *(lines 121–26)*

45. In a general comment on Dryden's writing in this period, David B. Kramer writes that as "we read the Dryden of the 1660s and 1670s, we are constantly reminded of his reverence for England's military and poetic might. Indeed, English military and poetic greatness are often used to signify one another, and the myth of English poetic and military invincibility is articulated throughout his criticism, poetry, prologues, epilogues, and plays" ("Onely Victory in him: the Imperial Dryden," 56).

46. See Weinbrot, *Augustus Caesar*; Erskine-Hill, *Augustan Idea*. As Levine points out, the interest in classical Rome dovetailed with a renewed antiquarian enthusiasm for Roman Britain, which offered scholars "the intersection of their two chief historical concerns, classical antiquity and the national past—their education emphasized the one, their patriotic feeling the other." The excavation work that accompanied the rebuilding of London after the Great Fire turned up many antiquarian finds, including remnants of Roman London, and provided a fillip to such study (*Woodward's Shield*, 133).

47. For a brief discussion of similar issues, see my *Thomas Gray and Literary Authority*, 170–71, 180–85.

48. This is the full title of the poem as it was printed in Walter Charleton's *Chorea Gigantum* (1663). Cf. Dryden, *Works*, 1.385.

49. Kroll, *Material Word*, 33. Kroll also points to the interweaving of intellectual categories in Dryden's poem: "While for analytical purposes, the modern critic (and even Dryden himself) might treat as distinct the activities of 'science,' 'politics,' 'philosophy,' 'history,' 'literature,' and so forth, they become entirely equivalent discursive activities within the world of the poem" (35).

50. Greenfield also emphasizes the importance of science (which was "first the sign of the cultural specificity of the English," and "soon became the proof of their superiority") in the making of "the English national identity" (*Nationalism*, 80). Greenfield's book contains a very useful account of the changing vocabulary of nation in sixteenth- and seventeenth-century England (29–87).

51. For brief biographical details of the lives and work of these scientists, see the editor's notes to the poem in Dryden, *Works*, 1.252–53.

52. Jones's argument was entitled *The Most Notable Antiquity of Great britain, vulgarly called Stone-Heng on Salisbury Plain. Restored by Inigo Jones* (1655). The context of this debate is recreated by the editors in Dryden, *Works*, 1.248–49. The controversy over the origins of Stonehenge was by no means settled by Charleton's contribution. Others argued that it was a Phoenician, or a Celtic, and later, that it was a Saxon, monument. For an account of these debates, see Atkinson, "Stonehenge," 181–204, and, more briefly, Levine, *Woodward's Shield*, 73–74.

53. Winn argues that Dryden's argument here is part of a larger reassertion of his faith in the powers of poetry against the skepticism about rhetoric encouraged by the new science: poetry can find a metaphoric resolution of the "problem" of Stonehenge by seeing in it a temple and a Danish coronation site (and indeed a royal sanctuary) all at once, a symbolic synthesis that escapes dogmatic scientists who can only claim it as one or the other (*Dryden and His World*, 135).

54. See Weinbrot (*Britannia's Issue*, esp. 154–62) for a review of revisionary attitudes toward Aristotle's scientific and cultural authority in this period.

55. Dryden represents the energy shared by the "discoveries" of modern science and post-Columban trading practices via a common metaphor: Harvey's demonstration of the circulation of blood (lines 29–31) provides an incontrovertible "natural" model for the movement of commodities in *Annus Mirabilis*, where we are told that Trade "like bloud should circularly flow" (line 5). Harvey belonged to a well-known mercantile family, a fact discussed by Keynes in *William Harvey*, 128–33.

56. McKeon, *Politics and Poetry*, 274. My reading of the specifically nationalist elements of the poem presumes upon McKeon's exemplary investigation into the historical and ideological concerns of *Annus Mirabilis*.

57. I say typically because, as Colley reminds us in her study of the "forging of the nation" between 1707 and 1837, the idea of "Great Britain" or of "a single people" emerged "not because of any political or cultural consensus at home, but rather in reaction to the Other beyond their shores" (*Britons*, 6). Colley emphasizes the unifying effects of a century and more of wars against the French, and also of British wars (and of 'peaceful' action) against colonized peoples.

58. A similar connection between commodities and violent death is to be found in Waller's "Of a War with Spain, and a Fight at Sea" (1658) in which the marquis of Badajos, viceroy of Mexico, and his wife perish aboard their flagship as "Spices and gums about them melting fry" (line 83).

59. Adas points to the contribution of advances in ship design and construction, navigational techniques, and naval weaponry in the development of the European sense of their "civilizational" superiority to most of the cultures with which they made contact (*Machines*, 37, 47–49). See also Burke, "*Annus Mirabilis* and New Science," 307–34, for a nuanced account of Dryden's incorporation into his poem of elements of the scientific rationality encouraged by the workings of the Royal Society.

60. McKeon, *Politics and Poetry*, 171.

61. Stevenson has shown that "Elizabethan praise of bourgeois men was expressed

in the rhetoric—and by extension, in terms of social paradigms—of the aristocracy" (*Praise and Paradox*, 6). In *Forms of Nationhood*, Helgerson's discussion of Hakluyt's *Principal Navigations of the English Nation* in the chapter entitled "The Voyages of a Nation" is a reminder that Dryden's use of romance elements and the vocabulary of aristocratic heroism to define the new merchant-champions of the nation follows upon a century of similar complex and conflicted expression.

62. Miner's comment on Dryden's closing images is simple and acute: "English imperialism of the next two centuries has been envisioned and its ideals provided" ("Forms and Motives," 245).

63. Dryden, *Poems and Fables*, 43.

64. For an instance of the problem Dryden addresses, see McKeon's discussion of the composition of the Royal Company of Adventurers Trading into Africa and his description of the mutual distrust that characterized interaction between the gentlemen and traders who had been brought together by Charles II in an effort to strengthen the company (*Politics and Poetry*, 110–13). For a discussion of the competing and complementary roles played by gentlemen and merchants in the early seventeenth century, see Rabb, *Enterprise and Empire*.

65. Helen Burke offers a complementary reading of this passage: she invokes the History of Trades program of the Royal Society, which had as "its goal the acquisition of technological and industrial data in order to render it more useful, a goal that would necessarily involve closer interaction between different social and economic groups." Dryden's learning of a marine vocabulary thus displays "his awareness of contemporary scientific trends" ("*Annus Mirabilis* and New Science," 312). Hunter's account of the Royal Society in *Science and Society* is useful reading here.

66. Dryden, *Poems and Fables*, 46. Johnson's comment on Dryden's desire to write a nautical idiom points out that Dryden's 'realism' did not actually color his description of the naval battles as much as it did his account of the refitting of the fleet: "in the battle, his terms seem to have been blown away; but he deals them liberally in the dock" ("Dryden," 172). (Johnson points to stanzas 146–48 to illustrate the latter.)

67. Dryden's invocation of Virgil ("my Master in this Poem") offers the precursor poet as an instance of someone who was master of both heroic and georgic idioms: "See his Tempest, his Funeral Sports, his combat of *Turnus* and *Aeneas*, and in his *Georgicks*, which I esteem the Divinest part of all his writings, the Plague, the Battle of Bulls, the labour of Bees, and those many other excellent Images of Nature" (47). In this passage Dryden esteems the *Georgics* above the *Aeneid*, a strange choice in the preface to a poem ostensibly about military leadership and the greatness of arms. The choice makes sense if we recognize that *Annus Mirabilis*, even though it features aristocratic and royal leaders in action, is very much a poem about the coming of age of English shipping and commerce.

68. Doody suggests usefully that the *Georgics* "offered not something to be dutifully copied but the deepest encouragement to poetic aspirations . . . a high and congenial example of the possibility of mastery and courageous inclusiveness" (*Daring Muse*, 117–18). See also her chapter "Some Origins of Augustan Practice: Civil War

Verse and its Implications," particularly her comments on the Restoration sensitivity to matters of style or genre (47–56).

69. In Dryden's usage here, Britain is England and more than England, perhaps because Roscommon is from Ireland (though his ancestors were English). Dryden, like all his contemporaries, is aware of the historical tensions involved and touches upon the complex relation between Ireland and England (including a mention of Roscommon's "conquering Ancestors") in lines 41 to 52.

70. It is instructive to compare Dryden's comments on rhyme with those of Milton on the "heroic verse without rhyme, as that of Homer in Greek and of Virgil in Latin" of *Paradise Lost*: rhyme is "no necessary adjunct or true ornament of poem or good verse, in longer works especially, but the invention of a barbarous age, to set off wretched matter and lame meter." Milton argues that his poem is "an example set, the first in English, of ancient liberty recovered to heroic poem from the troublesome and modern bondage of rhyming" (*Poetical Works*, 211). Both Milton's and Dryden's comments suggest the specificity with which aesthetic and formal decisions were related to political and ideological issues. Their positions differ, but both poets are clear, as Helgerson suggests of Milton, that poetry is the vehicle for "statist ideology" and that any argument for a "distinctly English poetry" (with different cultural antecedents, to be sure) would always serve "the interests of a national state" (*Forms of Nationhood*, 61–62).

71. Dryden's brief "Lines on Milton" (1688) echo this sentiment and embody it in the figure of Milton:

> Three *Poets*, in three distant *Ages* born,
> *Greece, Italy*, and *England* did adorn.
> The *First* in loftiness of thought Surpass'd;
> The *Next* in Majesty; in both the *Last*.
> The force of *Nature* cou'd no farther goe:
> To make a *Third* she joynd the former two.

72. For an account of the portrayal of commercial practices and personnel in Dryden's plays, see McVeagh, *Tradefull Merchants*, 34–37. McVeagh suggests that Dryden, as a dramatist, ignored "commercial life in his early and middle years . . . presumably because it appeared hostile to him by its association with his political opponents." When Dryden did directly engage with commerce, "as in the opera 'Albion and Albanus' (1685), he warns firmly against its dangerous spirit, which, he insists, must be regulated for the maintenance of social order; but when that is done he finds he can respond with ardour to its splendour and potency" (34–45).

73. Levine offers a brief discussion of Dryden's *ancienneté*, including his lifelong concern with "the conflicting claims of the ancients and moderns with respect to poetry," in *Battle of the Books*, 272–77. Lucas suggests that Dryden addressed his translations, particularly of Virgil, to those who were "full citizens" of England, looking for a sense of its cultural maturity: the nation was thought of "as modelled on the Graeco-Roman city-state, with free men as those who alone have an interest in the state's welfare, which will include all matters of cultural importance" (*England and Englishness*, 14).

2. The Ebb and Flow of Nations and Empires

1. Denham's *Cooper's Hill* (which supplies one epigraph for this chapter) is part of a long history of patriotic verse, some of whose characteristic features are in fact developed in this poem. This is Dobrée's comment on such poetry: "There seems to have been a definite need for the expression of the emotion [of patriotism], and we find the theme making its way into poems by a variety of doors, marked indifferently Liberty, Trade, Historic Sense or Vision of the Future, Peace, Public Works, Justice, or Pride in Literary Achievement" ("Theme," 52). Dobrée goes on to remark that "None of the other themes, the splendour of liberty, the glory of bygone days, the triumph of arms or arts, nor the enthronement of justice, can compare in volume, in depth, in vigour of expression, in width of imagination, with the full diapason of commerce" (60).

The essays collected in McKendrick, Brewer, and Plumb, *Birth of a Consumer Society* and in Brewer and Porter, *Consumption* are a full guide to these developments and to the various moral, social, and political objections raised against this empire of goods and merchandise.

2. This paragraph, and some of what follows, summaries a complex series of military, political, and economic events that are better described, in a historiographically evenhanded and incisive survey, by O'Gorman, *Long Eighteenth Century*, 51–62.

3. See Jones, *Britain and the World*, 115–16.

4. Defoe, *An Appeal to Honour and Justice* (1715), quoted in the editor's introduction to *True-Born Englishman*, 259.

5. Canny, "Origins of Empire," 7.

6. I should make clear that the shift in power-relations that characterizes this moment is quickly reversed, as members of Behn's party use the magic of their music (their flutes) and of technology (a magnifying glass) to put the Indians in their proper place, as marked by "extream Ignorance and Simplicity" (*Oroonoko*, 48–49).

7. A graphic illustration of this turn is the print entitled *The Third Volume of Mr. T. Brown's Works no. 1*, reprinted in Brewer, *Common People*, 61. In it, the author (Mr. Brown) shows the sights of London to a visibly astonished Indian from the West Indies. The volume itself is a satire of the "sights and manners" of London, and in the print, the Indian functions to defamiliarize the street life of the city.

8. Black, introduction to *Culture and Society in Britain*, 8. Black argues that the ruins visited by travelers "took on much of their appeal from the degree to which past glory contrasted with a setting of present insignificance, poverty and backwardness. The remains thus served to demonstrate the cyclical nature of history: Italy, particularly Rome, was a *memento mori* of civilisation" (10). These claims are elaborated in Black's *British Abroad*.

9. My concerns in this section parallel some of the themes traced in the first two chapters of Janowitz's *England's Ruins* (her introduction, "The Ruin Poem in English," and "Ruinists in Rome"). Janowitz's book shows how the "eighteenth-century 'ruin sentiment' in painting and architecture, variously documented, was what we might think of as a 'cultural affect' attending Britain as the nation moved into its imperial phase" (2).

10. Addison's "A Letter from Italy" (1704), 41–44.

11. Kliger, *Goths in England*, 2.

12. Dowling, *Epistolary Moment*, 59. Dowling offers an interesting argument for the Ciceronian scene of writing (in *De Officiis*) as the "exemplary moment" of literary and philosophical Augustanism: Cicero says he writes (rather than practices his civic craft as an orator) because the republic is no more. Dowling comments: "The Republic had been for its citizens, in short, the polis of the Greeks reborn in Roman actuality, and poetry and philosophy begin only in the moment of its vanishing." For Virgil and for Horace, writing after the accession of Augustus, the republic becomes "a moral resource for poetic expression, [and] the poet is someone with a power to bring it to alternative life within the sphere of language" (57–58).

13. Lyttelton, *An Epistle to Mr. Pope, from a Young Gentleman at Rome* (London: 1730).

14. In *Patriot Opposition*, Gerrard points out that Lyttelton's poem was one of a series of attempts in which he "and the Patriots tried to persuade Pope of both the inadequacy of satire and the superiority of Prince Frederick" (76; see also 77–84 for an account of the decade-long attempt, in correspondence and in verse, to convince Pope to become cultural and "moral tutor" to Frederick).

15. Pope, *Minor Poems*, 202–4. For the complicated history of the composition and publication of this poem, see the editors' notes (205–6). Sections of the poem may have been written in 1713 and revised in 1719 before publication.

16. In his discussion of the major public construction work initiated or furthered by Augustus, Wells notes that much "of this construction work was paid out of war booty," in which "the spoils of Egypt were exceptional" (*Roman Empire*, 89). Wells also points out that Augustus used inscriptions on buildings and monuments, milestones, and coins to remind people of the benefits of the empire made available by his rule (85–90).

17. The editors' notes to lines 26–30 point out that they refer to identifiable coins issued by Roman emperors: for example, no. 26 "Coins of Vespasian and Titus show a seated figure of Judea mourning under a palm tree"; and no. 27 "Triumphal arches appear on the coins of Domitian and Trajan" (Pope, *Minor Poems*, 206).

18. See, for instance, the discussions of key poems by Pope in Brown, *Alexander Pope*.

19. Goldstein, *Ruins and Empire*, 3–4.

20. Janowitz, *England's Ruins*, 2. See also her illuminating reading of *The Ruins of Rome* (30–40).

21. Goldstein, *Ruins and Empire*, 40.

22. Ayres suggests that this idea was "a crucial part of the oligarchy's self-justifying rhetoric" and a slogan used often against Walpole's corrupt England, undermined by the "indecent wealth and tasteless self-indulgence" of commercial magnates (*Classical Culture*, 25, 39–40).

23. Armitage's introduction to Bolingbroke, *Political Writings*, xxiii. The opposition between *libertas* and *imperium* was in fact rarely precise in the many Roman "performances" in this period.

24. In her lucid analysis of the emblem of 'ruins' in Gibbon's *Decline and Fall*,

Craddock argues that, for Gibbon, "each ruin could represent any relationship between past and present except irrelevance." Craddock shows that, for Gibbon, ruins suggested not just the destruction of states but the transfer of power, and that "transformation *is* destruction—and vice versa," which is a lesson in allegorical and historiographical balance that came less easily to Dyer ("Edward Gibbon," 63–64).

25. Goldstein, *Ruins and Empire*, 33. The poem is entitled "To Clio, From Rome."

26. Goldstein, *Ruins and Empire*, 37–39.

27. Cooper's study of sixteenth-century French poems on the ruins of Rome suggests a similar set of responses: Rome is dead, but Rome, it might be argued, lives on in France in the work of the poet ("Poetry in Ruins," 156–66).

28. Goldsmith, *Beauties of English Poesy, in Collected Works*, 5.321.

29. It is of course the case that most historians—amateur or professional—and other commentators on national and public culture wrote in prose, but my concern here is the world that poets made available, particularly in their poems.

30. From *Citizen of the World*, see in particular letters 11 (which argues that the tempered desire for luxury—when "consistent with our own safety, and the prosperity of others"—enables civilizational differences between nations); 25 (on the "natural rise and decline of kingdoms," which argues the position that when a "trading nation begins to act the conqueror, it is then perfectly undone"); 50 (which defines liberty in England and elsewhere); 56 (which offers a comparative commentary on European states); 91 (which offers a climatic explanation of national character), and 121 (on political rationality in England and in Asia) (Goldsmith, *Collected Works*, vol. 2).

31. Ibid., 2.108.

32. Ibid., 2.72–75. A few months earlier (December 1759), in an essay published in the *Weekly Magazine*, "Some Thoughts Preliminary to a General Peace," Goldsmith argued many of the same themes, linking them to his demand for a just and negotiated peace. He argued against British expansion, saying that "an empire, by too great a foreign power may lessen its natural strength . . . dominion often becomes more feeble as it grows more extensive. The ancient Roman empire is a strong instance of the truth of that assertion" (ibid., 3.32).

33. Letter 119, ibid., 2.458–65. Given the great increase in British armies and wars in this period, it is not surprising to find the landscapes of later-eighteenth-century poetry dotted with figures of broken and forlorn former soldiers. Wordsworth sees them on Salisbury Plain and in the *Prelude*, but here I will list a more homely example from a Scottish poet of the country, Joanna Baillie. In her "A Winter's Day," the after-dinner gathering around a farmer's fire includes a soldier who tells tales of "war and blood." His listeners

> gaze upon him,
> And almost weep to see the man so poor,
> So bent and feeble, helpless and forlorn,
> That oft' has stood undaunted in the battle
> Whilst thund'ring cannons shook the quaking earth,
> And showering bullets hiss'd around his head.
>
> *(Poems, 15)*

34. Goldsmith, *Collected Works*, 3.195–98.

35. Ibid., 4.235–69. Further references to this poem are to this edition—the Friedman, ed., *Collected Works*.

36. Lonsdale, *Poems of Gray, Collins, Goldsmith*, 653–54. The relevant passage is in Goldsmith's *History of England* (1771), 4.382.

37. "Some Thoughts Preliminary to a General Peace," (1759) in *Collected Works*, 3.32.

38. Lonsdale, *Poems of Gray, Collins, Goldsmith*, 626. Lonsdale provides these and other instances of approval of *The Traveller*, but particularly of the difference the poem made to Goldsmith's public reputation.

39. Goldsmith, *Collected Works*, 4.285–304. Further references to this poem are to this edition.

40. See Dixon's discussion in *Oliver Goldsmith Revisited*, 107–9.

41. Brown, *Preromanticism*, 124–25.

42. Ibid., 138–39. Brown suggests also that Goldsmith's villages can "legitimately be called the first purely aesthetic fictions in Western literature" because they "never existed" and "offer an ideal image of a space that is connected to past and future only by the tenuous link of a transmitted vision, and not by any developmental sequence or plot" (139). Brown is precise about the idealization at work in the poem, but I would suggest that the "plot" that *The Deserted Village* develops is in fact that of (British) history itself and that the key narrative that it does not develop, but takes absolutely for granted, is that of the rise and fall of nations and empires.

43. Both Johnson's major poems, "London" (1738) and "The Vanity of Human Wishes" (1748), suggest his unease with and anger at the power of capital (the "gen'ral massacre of gold") and overseas expansion ("For such the steady Romans shook the world; / For such in distant lands the Britons shine, / And stain with blood the Danube or the Rhine") to transform his city and nation (if not human nature per se). The quotations are lines 22 and 180–82 from the later poem, in *Poems*. Boire's "'Wide-wasting Pest'" provides a sharp reading of the poem as making available "a poetic grammar for the processes whereby the new capitalism radically altered the ways in which men and women viewed their own lives."

44. Brewer, *Sinews*, 27, 30.

45. Barbauld, "On the Deserted Village," in *Poems*, 33.

46. An insulting anonymous review (which was in fact written by John Wilson Croaker) of Barbauld's poem labeled her "this fatidical spinster," and quarreled with her intervention into political and historical debates. He hoped, he wrote, "the empire might have been saved without the intervention of a lady-author" (*Quarterly Review* 7 [June 1812], 309). Chandler emphasizes Croaker's misogyny and suggests that, for Croaker, *Eighteen Hundred and Eleven* "created a mismatch of gender and genre" (*England in 1819*, 114–15). Although this chapter enacts my disagreement with some of Chandler's claims about the historical origins of historicist consciousness, which he locates substantially in the early nineteenth century, my section on Barbauld is indebted to his compelling comments on her poem.

47. O'Gorman provides a succinct account of these campaigns, of the mobilization, and of their impact on the economy of Britain in *Long Eighteenth Century*, 233–42.

48. McCarthy and Kraft's headnote to the poem describes Barbauld's skepticism and the fact that in 1803 British liberals justified preparations for war by emphasizing a prepared and self-defending citizens militia (Barbauld, *Poems*, 302).

49. Chandler, *England in 1819*, 127, 128.

3. James Thomson and the "Sage Historic Muse"

1. The epigraph to this chapter is from McKillop's *Thomson: Letters and Documents*, as quoted in Sambrook, *Thomson*, 48. Both Mallet and Thomson came to England in pursuit of literary careers and advancement; like other literary Scotsmen who wrote in English, they helped make possible the idea of an inclusive and expansionist "Great Britain." Sambrook points out that though Thomson spoke with a Scots accent all his life, his poetry is largely free of Scotticisms; indeed, Thomson may have believed that Scots "was not a suitable language for serious poetry" (50–51).

2. Thomson dedicated his 1727 "A Poem Sacred to the Memory of Sir Isaac Newton" to Walpole and described him as "balancing the Power of *Europe*" and "informing the whole Body of Society and Commerce" (*Liberty, The Castle of Indolence*, 6). In 1729, when Thomson published the anti-Walpole *Britannia*, he was attacked by supporters of Walpole for his inconstancy (see Sambrook, *Thomson*, 74–76).

3. Goldgar, *Walpole and the Wits*; Gerrard, *Patriot Opposition*.

4. The circumstances surrounding the publication of this poem are detailed by Grant, *James Thomson*, 172–75.

5. As Grant tells us, the poem was published in two newspapers (*Whitehall Evening-Post* and *St. James's Evening-Post*) and Thomson was not pleased that the last line of the poem was printed with a degree of public circumspection (thus: "When *Fr——e* Insults, and *Sp——n* shall Rob, no more!). Thomson wrote to Andrew Millar, who had placed the poem for him, complaining: "I thank you for getting my ode printed. . . . In the meantime, who was so very cautious as to advise France & Spain being printed with a dash? You, I dare say, it was not—you have a superior Spirit to That" (Grant, *James Thomson*, 174–75; see also Sambrook, *Thomson*, 168–70).

6. Grant's account of the publication of the poem includes a description of an anonymous attack on Thomson published in Walpole's mouthpiece, the *Daily Gazetteer*, on October 6, 1737 (*James Thomson*, 175). Such responses, as is well known to students of eighteenth-century English poetry, testify to the topicality and partisan urgency of the contemporary practice of poetry.

7. Barrell and Guest, "Uses of Contradiction," 95–96.

8. Turner, *Politics of Landscape*, 132.

9. There is by now a considerable and varied bibliography on the links between eighteenth-century British writers and the commercial and colonial institutions that shaped their world. A good example is Dabydeen's "Eighteenth-century English Literature," 26–49.

10. Grant, *James Thomson*, 83. See also Goldgar, *Walpole and the Wits*, 85–86.

11. In this passage, Neptune realizes that Aeneas's fleet is being overwhelmed by

storm winds dispatched by Aeolus (on Juno's behest), and intervenes to quiet the winds. He upbraids the winds, reminding them that "Power over the sea and the cruel trident" were his ("by destiny") and did not belong to Aeolus (Virgil, *Aeneid*, trans. Fitzgerald, 1.184–89). Thomson's quotation of this passage from Virgil (1.134 in the original) refers his poem on Britannia's fluctuating imperial and political fortunes back to this precursor national epic. It also emphasizes, via the mythic idiom of Virgil's poem, the great conflicts that go into the shaping of national destinies, especially the founding of powerful states. The *Aeneid* has of course been read as making available both a public celebration of Augustan empire and a more muted, but nevertheless effective, questioning of the scope and nature of that empire (cf. Hardie, introduction to *Aeneid*, xvii–xxi). Such ambivalence, as I will suggest, marks Thomson's poem, too.

12. Sambrook, *Thomson*, 53.

13. For an extended account of country-city oppositions in seventeenth- and eighteenth-century poetry, see Williams, *Country and City*.

14. I know no explanation for these shifts in metaphor, or indeed for Thomson's choice of terms.

15. Barrell, *English Literature in History*, 17–50.

16. Johnson, "James Thomson," in *Lives*, 449.

17. As Sekora has demonstrated, the contemporary attack on luxury expressed not only "a theory of value, an ethic for both individuals and nations," but also "a theory of history, an explanation of both personal and collective decline in the past" (*Luxury*, 67).

18. For a sense of the commercial energies and social changes unleashed by the development of a consumer culture, see McKendrick, Brewer, and Plumb, *Birth of a Consumer Society*.

19. I am not suggesting that these poets and the social and political philosophers who wrote about the place of Greek city-states and Rome (both republican and imperial), or even of Carthage or Tyre, in the history of Europe achieved a consensus about the appropriate values to be derived from, and the historical lessons, to be learned from the rise and decline of these nations. They often held, as we know, sharply differing views of the place and role of "Augustanism" in late-seventeenth-and eighteenth-century English culture, but such a conceptual inheritance was very important to the political and cultural imaginary of Britain.

20. For an account of the "unwieldy mythology" of "sententious national deities" produced by contemporary poets who invoke Liberty, see Meehan, *Liberty and Poetics*, 17.

21. Condensed into this line is the climatic theory of political and civilizational explanation described in Kliger, *Goths in England*. Cf. Montesquieu's *The Spirit of Laws* for a good instance of the form and vocabulary of such sociopolitical theory.

22. Barrell and Guest, "Uses of Contradiction," 89–90.

23. For a theoretical elaboration of the role of literary and cultural texts in the expression of social anxieties and ideological contradictions, see Jameson, *Political Unconscious*, 9–102, esp. 77–83. Jameson's analysis in the latter pages follows upon the work of Claude Lévi-Strauss on Caduveo facial art.

24. Barrell and Guest, "Uses of Contradiction," 89. They suggest further that, in the eighteenth century and after, "the institutions of criticism managed to train readers of poetry in the forms thus invented to read in such a way as ensured that they would overlook the contradictory nature of the ideologies those forms were able to express."

25. Sambrook provides a useful chart of the dates of publication of the various editions and of the differing lengths of both the constituent parts of *The Seasons* and of the complete poem in his edition of *The Seasons and The Castle of Indolence* (xxiii); he also has a more elaborate account of the circumstances of the composition and publication of each of the parts of the poem between 1725 and 1730 in his *Thomson*, 24–105.

26. A comprehensive account is offered by McKillop, *Background of Thomson's "Seasons,"* and more recently by Cohen, *Unfolding of the Seasons*.

27. As we saw in chapter 2, Dyer's *Ruins of Rome* (1740) uses the same historical and literary formula to represent the responsible civic roles played in Roman history by Cinncinatus and Cato the Censor.

28. Sambrook, introduction to *Seasons*, xi.

29. See Landa, "Pope's Belinda," 215–35, for a discussion of Tyre as a symbol of mercantile magnificence.

30. Quoted in J. Logie Robertson's variorum edition of *Poetical Works of James Thomson*, 48–49.

31. The quoted words are from Sambrook, *Seasons*, 218.

32. When, in lines 481 to 493, the poet describes his love Amanda ("pride of my song! / . . . loveliness itself!") he writes of her "downcast eyes, sedate and sweet, / Those looks demure that deeply pierce the soul" and invites her to gather "Fresh-blooming flowers to grace thy braided hair / And thy loved bosom, that improves their sweets." In comparison, this is Thomson's more excited account of the about-to-fall rural virgin:

> Her lips blush deeper sweets; she breathes of youth;
> The shining moisture swells into her eyes
> In brighter flow; her wishing bosom heaves
> With palpitations wild; kind tumults seize
> Her veins, and all her yielding soul is love.
>
> *(lines 966–70)*

At this point, the poet warns the "fair" to be "greatly cautious of your sliding hearts" and to avoid "the infectious sigh; the pleading look, / Downcast and low, in meek submission dressed, / But full of guile" (lines 973–77).

33. In an astute comment on this aspect of Thomson's poetics, Lucas suggests that "Thomson's Miltonics have the effect of trying to 'tame' Milton by adapting his manner to the Georgic vision of *The Seasons*. Language, subject, form: all *conform* to this produced image of an England which is focused on the connections between property and propriety. Liberty is in the possession of those with both" (*England and Englishness*, 38).

34. The elephant—"wisest of brutes"—turns into an odd figure for one who (like the poet?) reviews historical change:

> Here he sees
> Revolving ages sweep the changeful earth,
> And empires rise and fall.
>
> *(lines 721–25)*

Elephants are however also described as vulnerable to poachers and to those who tame them for civil or military purposes.

35. Thomson's concern with the violent history of early modern colonization is a recurrent feature of the poem. For instance, in his account of the lands fed by the Amazon and its tributaries, he writes of

> many a happy isle,
> The seat of blameless Pan, yet undisturbed
> By Christian crimes and Europe's cruel sons.
>
> *(lines 853–55)*

The flexibility of pastoral iconography allows Thomson to represent idyllic, precolonized American lands in some of the same vocabulary that he does the more cultivated British countryside to which he occasionally retreats.

36. McKillop, *Thomson's "Seasons,"* 129–71.

37. It is not strictly correct to sum up Thomson's range of geographical references as "the tropics," but since the presence of the sun is an important link between the different regions he surveys, and because there is no other more accurate or serviceable term, I use *tropical*.

38. I take the phrase "contact zone" from Mary Louise Pratt's *Imperial Eyes*, where she uses it to "refer to the space of colonial encounters, the place in which peoples geographically and historically separated come into contact with each other and establish ongoing relations, usually involving conditions of coercion, radical inequality, and intractable conflict" (6).

39. Ibid., 5.

40. Such fears are a constant feature of *The Seasons*. Whether it is the description of frightful animals in *Summer*—green serpents, tigers, leopards, hyenas, lions (lines 898–938)—or the account of the desert regions and their caravan-burying sandstorms (lines 959–79), foreign climates and lands are full of "monsters" (line 952) and "terrors" (line 959).

41. In his notes to *Summer*, Thomson describes Don Henry's "strong genius" as inspiration that led "to the discovery of new countries" and as "the source of all the modern improvements in navigation" (124).

42. Pratt, *Imperial Eyes*, 5.

43. The first, in which lightning kills Amelia when she is clasped in her lover's arms, is meant to suggest the unknown ways of "Mysterious Heaven" (line 1215) that strike down even those who do not deserve punishment. The latter, in which Damon spies his Musidora bathing naked in the heat, is a fine instance of the

overheated poetic imagination and is the prelude (and the contrast) to the poet once again temperately addressing his beloved, Amanda, which he does only once his tale is told and the "Sun has lost his rage" (line 1371).

44. Barrell, *English Literature in History*, 67.

45. This complex (and in Thomson's case, contradictory) contrast between rural virtue and city riches finds an international equivalent in Thomson's description of Lapland in *Winter*. The Lapps wisely "ask no more than simple Nature gives"; they have "No false desires, no pride-created wants" (lines 845–47). The lack of possessions allows their wives to be described as kind and "unblemished" (line 880), this last word deriving its moral weight from contemporary satiric portraits of female consumers (Pope's Belinda, for instance). The Lapps' poverty is also the guarantee of their freedom: "Thrice happy race! by poverty secured / From legal plunder and rapacious power" (lines 881–82). While Thomson is happy to employ the literary conventions and ethical contrasts of the country versus the city to idealize the Lapps, the pastoral poverty of Lapland in no way provides a model for the development of the British economy or empire.

46. Johnson, "James Thomson," 456.

47. That Thomson, in this passage, charts his poetical and public ambitions is made clear in the lines that follow, where lack of professional advancement is seen to blight the very scope of poetry:

> But, if doomed
> In powerless humble fortune to repress
> These ardent risings of the kindling soul,
> Then, even superior to ambition, we
> Would learn the private virtues.
>
> *(lines 597–601)*

Thomson then provides a compensatory list of rural and moral virtues to be explored. Finally, if for some reason "serious thought is foiled," he suggests (in keeping with the hierarchy of poetic forms he works through here) that the exercise of "frolic fancy" and "lively wit" sustain the poet (lines 601–16).

48. This preface to *Winter* was dropped in 1730, when the first collected edition of *The Seasons* appeared. We can only conjecture whether the decision to drop the Preface reflected Thomson's sense that it no longer provided an accurate introduction to, and defence of, the poem, but that does seem a possibility. The preface is included in Robertson, *Poetical Works of James Thomson*, 239–42 (quotes from 240–41).

49. Fulford reminds us that the portrait of Peter the Great's Russia as a "cultural ideal" is "implicitly a critique of Walpole's Britain." Fulford's reading of *The Seasons* shows persuasively how "Thomson's foreign landscapes" and his "interventions in home politics" make it hard to read landscape (poetry) as if the "disorder and contradiction" it contains are but "signs of nature's and God's law," rather than the manipulations and partiality of the poet (*Landscape*, 36–37, but see also 18–35).

50. Johnson, "James Thomson," 456.

51. These differences are not only established via developed arguments, of course, as Thomson is adept at reworking icons and symbols to suit his polemical purposes. A quick instance is the transformation of Liberty as she appears to the poet:

> Not, as of old,
> Extended in her hand the cap, and rod,
> Whose slave-enlarging touch gave double life:
> But her bright temples bound with British oak,
> And naval honours nodded on her brow.
>
> *(1.26–30)*

Liberty is an "island-goddess now; and her high care / The queen of isles, the mistress of the main" (lines 33–34). This pointed shift in the iconic status of Liberty is representative of Thomson's method—his invocation of the goddess allows him, in the poem in general, to write a theory of history and culture centered around her benign presence, but her representation as an island-goddess crowned with British oak stems form a more local and contemporary commitment to the development of British naval power.

52. Johnson, "James Thomson," 450–51.

53. Gerrard argues correctly that "*Liberty* is not quite the manifesto of an untroubled Whiggish progressivism that many critics seem to assume . . . [and that] much of *Liberty*'s admonitory strength lies in the gloomy possibility that Britain may and perhaps must go the same way as Rome" (*Patriot Opposition*, 132–33).

54. In fact, this vengeful aspect is assumed by Liberty herself as she urges the sack of Rome. Roused by her, the men of the "cold-compressed" north attack the remains of the empire: They

> o'er the banks
> Of yielding empire, only slave-sustained,
> Resistless raged—in vengeance urged by me.
>
> *(3.536–38)*

55. The same claim to "social" commerce is repeated later, when we are told of the expansion of British trade under Elizabeth. Trade

> poured with every tide
> A golden flood. From other worlds were rolled
> The guilty glittering stores, whose fatal charms,
> By the plain Indian happily despised,
> Yet worked his woe.

Liberty blames the Spanish, "zeal-inflamed barbarians," for bringing violence to the pastoral existence of the Indians, and exhorts the British to be different: "Be no such horrid commerce, Britain, thine! / But want for want with mutual aid supply" (4.910–21).

56. Thomson saw in Prince Frederick, then in political opposition to his father

George II and to Walpole, a figure who might preside over a British cultural renaissance; however, events (and the prince's strained finances) in the 1730s did little to encourage such a faith in Frederick's power. Gerrard, *Patriot Opposition*, 50–51.

57. For a reading of this poem as part of "the wave of oppositional Spenserianism" in the 1730s, see Gerrard, *Patriot Opposition*, 180–84. Gerrard sees this Spenserianism as part of an Elizabethan revival whose nostalgia was fueled by historical memories of "the aggressive, expansionist Protestant mercantilism associated with the victories of Cadiz and the Armada, an Elizabethanism shaped above all by pressure for war with Spain" (105).

58. The quoted words appear in a letter from Thomson to William Paterson in April 1748. Quoted by Grant, *James Thomson*, 256. Sambrook comments on the composition and publication of the poem in *Thomson*, 263–65.

59. Grant, *James Thomson*, 256. Robertson comments that there is "poetry in the first canto: the second is mostly didactic" (*Poetical Works of James Thomson*, 307).

60. Hollander offers a lovely reading of the close of the Spenserian stanza, which, he says, "Ends in an alexandrine, gently rocking / The stanza back to sleep, lest the close be too shocking" (*Rhyme's Reason*, 18).

61. Lucas, *England and Englishness*, 4.

62. Ibid., 39.

63. Barrell, *English Literature in History*, 89.

64. Thomson, "A Hymn on the Seasons," 100–105 (editions from 1730–38 used "hostile" in place of "distant" in line 101).

4. The Mythopoetics of Commercial Expansion

1. Lillo, *London Merchant* (1731).

2. Needler, "A Sea-Piece," in *Works*.

3. A classic instance is Thomson's account of a shepherd caught in a snowstorm ("Winter," lines 297–321), in which the shepherd's death only confirms the poem's overarching argument that nature, in all its complexity, is a reflection of divine power. Thus, as Fulford puts it, the description of the shepherd lost in the snowstorm functions as "a spectacle giving an awe-inspiring sense of man's insignificance in comparison with the great objects of nature" and as a "theatre in which moral purpose reinforces social hierarchies" (*Landscape*, 24).

4. Fry, *The Poet's Calling*, 8.

5. Young, *Poetical Works*, 2.141. All page references are to this edition.

6. Young's "Two Epistles to Mr. Pope" ("concerning the authors of the age") (1730) is his most systematic attempt to define and legislate appropriate poetic practices, an effort that continues into his *Conjectures on Original Composition* (1759). For a discussion of Young's embattled sense of cultural location, see my "The World of Letters: the Legitimation and Regulation of Cultural Authority," chapter 1 of *Thomas Gray and Literary Authority*.

7. In *Ode from Milton to Keats*, Schuster saw fit to leave Young's odes out of his analysis. He does however call attention to Young's preface, and in particular to the

passage on the ode that I quote here as echoing Denham. For Schuster, Young's language is "reminiscent of Polonius," which is a fine reminder that Young's fears that poetic elevation might easily be read as burlesque rather than sublime were well founded (189). This may also be an appropriate time to mention that Fry, in his important book on the ode, dismisses Young's odes with the single word "disastrous" (*Poet's Calling*, 131).

8. Not that Young wants to be too exact in his composition, for, as he inimitably puts it, "A poem, like a criminal, under too severe correction, may lose all its spirit, and expire" (153–54).

9. For a short and incisive discussion of these issues, see Hirschman, *Passions*.

10. Perhaps *Windsor-Forest* does provide a model for the turn taken by Young's poem, in that it closes with the poet in retreat into the more circumscribed world of the pastoral:

> My humble Muse, in unambitious strains,
> Paints the green forest and the flowery plains,
> . . . .
> Enough for me, that to the listening swains
> First in these fields I sung the sylvan strains.
>
> *(lines 427–34)*

11. Brown, *Pope*, 46–93.

12. I should make clear that there was no single model (or even well-defined set of models) of poetic practice for the eighteenth-century odist. This problem of definition has not really been solved; Schuster, for instance suggests that by *ode* he means "in general a lyric based either upon the model of some classic poem which bore that designation or upon other English poems which go back, directly or indirectly, to imitations of the bards of Greece and Rome." The Pindaric model was broad enough to include "poems of praise, worship, reflection, commemoration, and patriotic sentiment"; that is, broad enough to allow any English poet who wished to write on public themes to claim it as precedent without feeling constricted by well-defined rules of form or function (*Ode*, 6, 12).

13. Except in particular matters of policy or of personal affiliation, there was often a great overlap between literary "Whigs" and "Tories," especially when it came to sharing visions of national trading and naval prowess. As Gerrard puts it, there are no "easy discriminations to be made on grounds of ideological content between the 'gloom of Tory satire' and the optimistic 'Psychology of Whiggism.' Liberty may be a constant refrain of Patriot Whig verse, but trade, commerce, and empire were never, of course, exclusively 'Whiggish' property, as we can see from the presence of a powerful urban commercial strain in a series of 'royalist' works from Denham's *Coopers-Hill* through to Dryden's *Annus Mirabilis* and Pope's *Windsor-Forest*" (*Patriot Opposition*, 73–74). Griffin suggests that Young chose, in the last years of Anne's reign, "the Tory rather than Addison's Whiggish route" to preferment, but that he kept in "good communication with the Whigs," writing commendatory verses to Addison's *Cato* in 1713 (*Literary Patronage in England*, 155–56).

14. Pocock, "Virtues, Rights, and Manners," in *Virtue*, 48–49.

15. Ibid., 50.

16. For a fine discussion of the social context and rhetorical strategies of the Pindaric, see Nagy, "'Professional Muse,'" 133–43.

17. Dryden, "To His Royal Highness the Duke," dedication to *Conquest of Granada by the Spaniards* (1670), in *Works*, 11.3. Dryden rehearses the commonplaces of Renaissance epic here, but the politics of Restoration culture and aristocratic self-representation sharpen the force of his observations.

18. For a full account of the "Happy man" theme, see Rostvig, *Happy Man.*

19. Hirschman writes that the "by-product of individuals acting predictably in accordance with their economic interests was therefore not an uneasy *balance*, but a strong *web* of interdependent relationships. Thus it was expected that the expansion of domestic trade would create more cohesive communities while foreign trade would help avoid wars between them" (*Passions and Interests*, 51–52, and for the larger argument summarized here, 31–66).

20. Shields, *Oracles of Empire*, 15–16, but see 13–20. Shields's book provides a very valuable account of how England's "commercial empire exerted a substantial informing influence upon Augustan poetry" (3).

21. There is by now an enormous and varied bibliography of the history of the slave trade; Barker's *African Link* is useful for our purposes here.

22. With some exceptions, of course. Africa and *its* slave trade do not count, and women are also, predictably, excluded. In a gratuitous comment (in that it does not follow from or add to any larger argument), Young finds a way of enacting gender difference:

> But, Oh! you practise shameful arts;
> Your own retain, seize others' hearts;
> Pirates, not merchants, are the British fair.
> *(5.46–48)*

23. Weinbrot suggests that Young's originality is to be found in his alteration of the "Pindaric emphasis on the individual's achievement" to that of a collective: "one nation in ongoing historical acts motivated by the vibrant abstraction Trade" (*Britannia's Issue*, 357).

24. Submerged into Young's song of British oceans is the "canonical" (Horatian) description of Pindar's poetry as "a river in full spate." (Young follows this description in line 12 of his ode "To the King" prefixed to *Ocean: An Ode.*) As Fitzgerald points out, Horace's lines on Pindaric power are part of the later poet's anxiety that any attempt to soar like the Theban eagle is prone to Icarian failure. Not so for Young: in this stanza, the Pindaric torrent feeds a British ocean (*Agonistic Poetry*, 82–84).

25. See, for instance, Sitter, *Literary Loneliness.*

26. Culler, "Apostrophe," in *Pursuit of Signs,* 143. Culler's essay is a seminal enquiry into the absence of critical interest in apostrophe, which he identifies as "the figure of all that is most radical, embarrassing, pretentious, and mystificatory in the lyric"

(137). This is because, via apostrophe, a poet produces a temporal and discursive space in which nothing need happen, except the poem itself (149). Culler also points out that "invocation is a figure of vocation"—the vocative translates an inanimate object or idea into a sentient, responsive subject, thus setting up a relationship that helps constitute the poet (142). The romantic poems Culler analyzes, however, suggest that his interest in vocation is limited to the "drama of [poetic] mind" (148). The apostrophic addresses in the poems that I examine here are figures of vocation where the drama of mind is layered over, and perhaps supplanted, by a drama of nation; typically, it is not elements in nature that are personified as much as particular political, philosophical, cultural, or moral attributes of the nation, or indeed the nation itself.

27. Culler, "Apostrophe," 152–53.

28. The phrases quoted are ibid., 142.

29. In saying this, I am drawing upon Fry's critical vocabulary in his *Poet's Calling*, but denying some of its literary-historical implications and conclusions.

30. Goldgar, *Walpole and the Wits*, 184.

31. As to there being little fear of burlesque, the two most famous poems that these lines gesture toward are of course Virgil's *Aeneid* and Milton's *Paradise Lost*, both weighty instances of the power and scope of the epic. It is however possible to argue that Dyer here fuses the syntax and tone of the "Arma virumque cano" opening of the *Aeneid* with the more bucolic and agricultural interests specified by the first lines of the *Georgics*, thus invoking both the seafaring epic of nation formation and the more earthbound georgic (which is itself a celebration of the fecundity of Roman lands) as the progenitors of *The Fleece*.

32. Virgil's *Georgics* also provides an instance of different regions and nations of the world distinguished by their products: "See you not, how Tmolus sends us saffron fragrance, India her ivory, the soft Sabaeans their frankincense; but the naked Chalybes give us iron, Pontus the strong-smelling beaver's oil, and Epirus the Olympian victories of her mares? From the first, Nature laid these laws and eternal covenants on certain lands" (1.56–61, *Georgics*, 85).

33. The centrality of merchants and of the wool trade to British wealth is not of course an idea original to Dyer, though *The Fleece* is the most elaborate account of this centrality. Thus Addison on merchants: "They knot mankind together in a mutual intercourse of good Offices, distribute the Gifts of Nature, find Work for the Poor, add Wealth to the Rich, and Magnificence to the Great. Our *English* Merchant converts the tin of his own country in to Gold, and exchanges his Wooll for Rubies. The *Mahometans* are clothed in our *British* Manufacture, and the Inhabitants of the Frozen Zone warmed with the Fleeces of our Sheep" (*Spectator*, 1.296). And Richard Blackmore in *Eliza, An Epick Poem* (1705):

> Where, for their woolly Riches, every Year
> Ten Thousand Sheep the wealthy Farmers shear.
> Whose Spoils are truly Albion's Golden Fleece,
> Outvying that of Legendary Greece.
> These sent abroad from Britain's noble Loom,

Bring forreign Wealth, and distant Pleasures home.
Silks, Pearl, and Spices, from the wanton East,
Rich Drugs, with Gold and Silver, from the West.
                                                  (4.29–36)

34. It might be argued that this contrast is not necessarily pastoral; the *Georgics*, in its description of the lives the old Sabines once lived, offers a similar opposition between the life of the husbandman and the lives of those who "vex with oars seas unknown, dash upon the sword, or press into courts and the portals of kings" (2.490–532, *Georgics*, 151–52). However, the frame of this opposition in *The Fleece*—a dialogue between Damon and Colin—does suggest that Dyer has the pastoral in mind.

35. The magic of the loom also provides a fine model for the workings of the poet in the poem:

What need we name the several kinds of looms?
Those delicate, to whose fair-colour'd threads
Hang figur'd weights, whose various numbers guide
The artist's hand: he, unseen flowers, and trees,
And vales, and azure hills, unerring works.
Or that, whose numerous needles, glittering bright,
Weave the warm hose to cover tender limbs:
Modern invention: modern is the want.
                                                  (3. 153–60)

This combination of fanciful creativity (with an emphasis on natural beauty) and a more utilitarian sense of contemporary need might well describe the poem Dyer writes.

36. However, it is not only the triumphs of trade and commerce that he charts. He writes briefly of the slave trade, and of Africans whose tribes give them up "for life-long servitude" in "our fertile colonies" and plantations. He reminds traders that they should pursue "gainful commerce" with "just humanity of heart," and wonders if a time will come when slaves will rise in revolt and be revenged on their owners: "there are ills to come for crimes" (4.193–208).

37. Shields, *Oracles of Empire*, 65.

38. John Goodridge has recently argued for a sympathetic treatment of Dyer's "rural idealism," of his "serious, socially conscious rural poetry" (*Rural Life*, 179). Goodridge offers a full account of *The Fleece*, but even though he notices many passages where Dyer defines England, its topography, its climate, and its wool trade, in contrast with those of past and contemporary nations or regions of the globe, he does not emphasize their centrality to the ideological concerns of the poem, as I do.

5. The World of Antislavery Poetry

1. In my discussion of "antislavery" discourse and activities in this chapter, I follow Davis's definition: "'Antislavery' is a vague and flexible concept. It has been used to

describe an organized social force; political activity aimed at eradicating the slave trade or slavery itself; a set of moral and philosophic convictions that might be held with varying intensities; or simply the theoretical belief that Negro slavery is a wasteful, expensive, and dangerous system of labor which tends to corrupt the morals of white Christians." Generalist discussion of "anti-slavery," Davis suggests, might homogenize these meanings, but this risk is balanced by, "at the other extreme, the risk of becoming distracted by an elaborate and artificial taxonomy" (*Slavery in the Age of Revolution*, 164). See also his discussion of the terms *antislavery, abolition*, and *emancipation* on 21–22.

The epigraphs to this chapter are from Barber, "On Seeing the Captives, lately redeemed from Barbary by his Majesty" (1735), in *Poems*, and Savage, "Of Public Spirit in Regard to Public Works" 1739), in *Works*, 1.141–42. Barber's poem celebrates the return of English prisoners (taken by Barbary Coast pirates) to London on November 11, 1734, and helps initiate the sentimental discourse of antislavery. There is of course an irony here—the slaves are English, and the English slave trade finds no mention in the poem. The last four lines of the poem represent Britain as the home of liberty and the emancipator of prisoners, an idea crucial to antislavery discourse later in the century:

> Shall not each free-born *Briton*'s Bosom melt,
> To make the Joys of Liberty more felt?
> So, *Albion*, be it ever giv'n to thee,
> *To break the Bonds, and set the Pris'ners free.*

2. Dabydeen, "Eighteenth-century English Literature," 44. Oldfield emphasizes the importance of print culture and consumer culture—the economy of professional writers (Dabydeen's "grubs and hacks"), publishers, and readers—to the spread of abolitionist sentiment in *Popular Politics*.

3. In a related matter, Viswanathan has pointed to the "key role" played by the Clapham Evangelicals (led by William Wilberforce) "in the drama of consolidation of British interest in India" in that they supplied "British expansionism with an ethics of concern for reform and conversion" and argued that "British domination was robbed of all justification if no efforts were made to reform native morals." This allowed, among other things, the state to intervene in the workings of the East India Company via the Charter Act of 1813 ("Beginnings," 11).

4. Even as we give due credit to the efforts of metropolitan antislavery activists, we must not lose sight of Blackburn's argument that even "a thoroughly satisfactory account of abolitionism as a system of ideas would not add up to an account of the actual forces at work in the overthrow of colonial slavery" (*Overthrow of Slavery*, 61). Blackburn's book shows "how, and by whom, the slave systems were destroyed" and features the material realities of slave societies and plantation economies and the resistance of those enslaved.

5. Temperley, "Anti-slavery," 348.

6. See Blackburn, *Overthrow of Slavery*, 102–4.

7. Cowper, *Poems*, 2.132–34. All references to Cowper's poems are to this edition, ed. Baird and Ryskamp.

8. The phrase "train of thought" is Cowper's; he uses it to describe his method of composition in his "Advertisement"—a preface to the poem: he was commissioned by "A lady" to write a poem in blank verse on "The Sofa," and since he had "much leisure" he "connected another subject with it, and, pursuing the train of thought to which his situation and turn of mind led him" produced at length *The Task* (*Poems*, 2.113). This poem is thus a fine compendium of the world of a contemplative eighteenth-century poet and, in its associations, a reminder of the ineluctable connections between the vocabulary of poetry in this century and the idiom of empire.

9. For a brief account of Omai's presence in England, and Cowper's interest in Cook, see the editors' commentary on lines 633–77 of "The Sofa" (*Poems*, 2.347).

10. The editors of Cowper's poem identify Sir Thomas Rumbold (governor of Madras, February 1778–April 1780) as the target of these lines (*Poems*, 348–49). Rumbold was one of many examples of colonial corruption, the best known of which, in this period, was Warren Hastings.

11. *The Task* includes a passage on newspapers and travelogues that highlights these connections between the intimate spaces of Cowper's home and the world at large. In book 4, "The Winter Evening," the poet finds himself at one with the traveler who, "as the bee" flits between flowers, moves "from land to land" and "sucks intelligence in every clime." "He travels and I too," writes Cowper,

> I tread his deck,
> Ascend his topmast, through his peering eyes
> Discover countries, with a kindred heart
> Suffer his woes and share in his escapes,
> While fancy, like the finger of a clock,
> Runs the great circuit, and is still at home.
>
> *(4. 107–19)*

12. I realize that I am making this claim in the face of Gibbon's *Decline and Fall of the Roman Empire* (1776/1788), but this monumental text is the last (and most full-blown) attempt to write the history of a classical empire for the lessons it might offer contemporary Britain. (For an analysis of similar shifts in Gibbon's philosophical vision and historiographical idiom over the twenty years in which these volumes were written and published, see Womersley, *Transformation*). In the later years of the eighteenth century, the progress, or devolution, of empire becomes a matter of public policy rather than of allegorical or historical enquiry. In this chapter, I argue that poetry in the service of the antislavery campaigns follows this shift toward *managing* empire by debating its constituent features, particularly those that can be reshaped by public and parliamentary opinion.

13. David Brion Davis suggests that an important theme in the discourse of late-eighteenth-century British antislavery was "the preservation of English liberty" and that this theme legitimized the articulation of dissenting, if not always radical, political positions. Davis argues that the ideology of antislavery "emerged from a convergence of complex religious, intellectual, and literary trends—trends which . . . must be understood as part of a larger transformation in attitudes toward labor,

property, and individual responsibility" (*Slavery in the Age of Revolution*, 82). Antislavery discourse, that is, served to consolidate a series of overlapping moral-religious, bourgeois-individualist, free trade, and colonial agendas, only one of which was the abolition of slavery and the slave trade.

14. In *Radical Sensibility*, Jones suggests rightly that the "common mode of sentimental poetry also stresses the capacity of feeling in the poet at the expense of the characters contemplated," such that the contemplation of political or social wrongs leads to a refinement of the poet's sentiment rather than to individuated accounts of the victims of such wrongdoing (67). This is, for the most part, true of Cowper's antislavery poetry, too. However, it is possible to argue that, in the specific case of antislavery, since the call for Britons to "feel" the pain of slaves accompanied more activist efforts to lobby Parliament to abolish the slave trade (and to boycott sugar and other products of slave labor), poetic sentimentality did work toward an end larger than the delineation of the poet's ego.

15. Fryer offers a brief but nuanced account of this case in *Staying Power*, 120–26. Fryer reminds us that this case did not in fact spell the end of black slavery in Britain and that the judgment only prevented slaves from being removed by force from Britain.

16. The passage that precedes these lines describes, at length (2.75–153), the devastation visited upon Sicily by recent earthquakes, which Cowper reads as signs of divine displeasure. His account of fallen palaces, broken columns, and "rude fragments" and of the deaths, by flood, of princes and commoners parallels many of the descriptions of the ruins of empire that we have examined, such that Sicily becomes a contemporary reminder of the decline of states and nations. Cowper then suggests that Britain could easily qualify for such divine attention ("none than we more guilty").

17. *Poems*, 1.xxii.

18. Newey, "Cowper," 129.

19. Fulford suggests that "Cowper, in the end, was unable to generate a vision of personal or social authority not based at least partly upon the subordination whose effects he so frequently regretted in rural and colonial politics." Fulford's account of the effects of such contradictions in Cowper's poetry is precise and rich. *Landscape*, 65–66; see also 38–66. Griffin also ends his essay "Redefining Georgic" with a reminder that Cowper's "world of spiritual labor—despite the universalist claims of his evangelicalism—is limited to the few," and that it is only "the man of 'refinement'—education, leisure, and a comfortable income—who rises through spiritual georgic to an apprehension of divine order" (878).

20. Feingold argues that Cowper's "inconclusive" discussion of political liberty serves to "remove from the poem any further consideration of politics and the state as morally significant aspects of human experience" (*Nature and Society*, 183).

21. In *Slavery in Western Culture*, Davis quotes Janet Schaw (the author of *Journal of a Lady of Quality; Being the Narrative of a Journey from Scotland to the West Indies, North Carolina, and Portugal, in the Years 1774 to 1776*) as writing that the Africans were "brutes" whose "natures seem made to bear it, and whose sufferings are not attended with shame or pain beyond the present moment." Slaves were understood as "indifferent even to the division of their own families in public sales." Davis points out that such opinions were representative, and were shared by Oliver

Goldsmith as much as by the racist Edward Long, both of whom commented on "Negro" physiognomy and character (459–64).

22. In an account of the blessings of charity, Cowper writes of the "Immortal fragrance" that spreads around one who "holds communion with the skies." The fragrance is unmistakable, he suggests, in the same way as the scent of a ship freighted with spices from India, upon return to "some safe haven of our western world," announces its port of call (lines 435–46). Cowper's evangelical vocabulary is not given to rhetorical elaboration; it is therefore even more interesting that this simile should describe the mystery of communion via the aura of the commodities most symbolic of overseas riches.

23. Davis, *Slavery in the Age of Revolution*, 373. Davis argues that "the guilt of commercial exploitation" is exorcised by this "emphasis upon emancipation," an argument that can also be traced in the contours of Cowper's nationalist aspirations. Of interest is also Davis's comment on the "Quaker ethic" that was so important to the leadership of the abolitionist movement: "Liberation from slavery did not mean freedom to live as one chose, but rather freedom to become a diligent, sober, dependable worker who gratefully accepted his position in society. Freedom required the internalization of moral precepts in the place of less subtle forms of external coercion" (254).

24. For a useful account of the development of the movement, see Walvin, "Popular Sentiment," 149–62.

25. These details are provided in the headnote to the poem "The Negro's Complaint" in the editors' "Commentary on the Poems" (*Poems*, 3.283–84).

26. We should remember though that these years also saw the publication in London of Ottobah Cuguano's *Thoughts and Sentiments on the Evil and Wicked Traffic of the Slavery and Commerce of the Human Species* (1787) and *The Interesting Narrative of the Life of Olaudah Equiano, or Gustavus Vassa, the African: Written by Himself* (1789), two important reminders that the humanity and learning of slaves did not have to be vouched for only by white antislavery activists.

27. Cf. *Poems*, 3.284.

28. Macdonald argues that Cowper derives this story from Saint Augustine's *Confessions* and that the robbing of an apple orchard alludes to Adam and Eve. These precursor texts grant Cowper's ballad a density and power in that they "draw a compelling parallel between original sin and slavery" ("Abolitionism," 171–72).

29. For an analysis of these parliamentary debates and of the extraparliamentary issues that shaped them, see Bass, "Efficient Humanitarianism," 152–65.

30. I am here quoting Davis, *Slavery in the Age of Revolution*, 115. The details of these parliamentary and extraparliamentary activities are available in a variety of sources, including Davis, 84–148. Anstey's *Atlantic Slave Trade* is a good guide to relevant issues, events, and personalities.

31. See Cowper, *Poems*, 3.333–34.

32. Cowper's editors suggest that the parliamentary setback recorded by this sonnet was responsible for Cowper's changing of the last two lines from "Then let them scoff—two prizes thou hast won— / Freedom for Captives, and thy God's— WELL DONE" to "Enjoy what thou hast won, esteem and love / From all the Just on earth, and all the Blest above" (*Poems*, 3.183, 334).

33. Ferguson, *Subject to Others*. Ferguson's book is a rich account of the roles women played, as writers and lobbyists, in the antislavery movement. She writes at length about some of the poets and issues I discuss here, but she and I tend to read the same poems very differently.

34. For an elaboration of these issues, see my "Treating Literary Symptoms," 80–96.

35. William Dodd's "The African Prince, when in England, 1749. To Zara at his Father's Court," in *Poems*, features an African prince betrayed by his compatriots into English slavery but freed by royal command once he was brought to Britain ("No more Britannia's cheek the blush of shame / Burns for my wrongs, her king restores her fame"—lines 161–62). In his verse epistle to his beloved Zara, he mentions attending a staging of *Oroonoko*, and a footnote tells us that he was "so affected as to be unable to continue, during its performance, in the house."

36. See, in this regard, Landry's chapter on Yearsley in her admirable *Muses of Resistance*.

37. See Midgley, *Women against Slavery*, 20, passim.

38. The epigraph of More's poem is derived from Thomson's "Liberty":

> O great design!
> Ye sons of mercy! O complete your work;
> Wrench from Oppression's hand the iron rod,
> And bid the cruel feel the pains they give.

39. More, *The Slave Trade: A Poem*.

40. See, for instance, Ford, *Hannah More*, 83–126. For a parallel instance of More's social concerns, see Pedersen's account of More's intervention into the morality and content of popular culture (in particular that of cheap chapbooks) in "Hannah More," 84–113.

41. Davis, *Slavery in the Age of Revolution*, 361.

42. Williams and Ramsden, *Ruling Britannia*, 118. They also point out that the "later days of the disturbances, with Wilkes shooting rioters and Gordon trying to stop looters, showed the sense of shock which united the propertied classes regardless of their political inclinations."

43. There are for instance the poems on slavery by the sisters Maria and Harriet Falconar. Maria's poem begins with an extended flowery apology for having dared to write (her poem is as a daisy to the roses that already adorn the altar of philanthropy), but she goes on to a robust attack on the tyranny of slavery and on Roman Catholic "superstition," all in the name of liberty and Britannia. Harriet's poem is distinguished by a long passage on "the tree of commerce" that grows in "Britain's paradise, by freedom made," on which, however, also grows the poisoned branch of slavery, with its "tempting manna" and beauteous golden blossoms. While the biblical force of the metaphor of forbidden fruit is clear here, what is even more emphatic is the organic connection between British commerce and the slave trade (*Poems of Slavery*).

44. Barbauld, "Epistle to William Wilberforce, Esq.," in *Poems*, 114–18.

45. Jones and Stallybrass, "Dismantling Irena," 157–71.

46. Herodotus, *Histories*, 204, and Hippocrates, *Airs, Waters, Places*, 127–28, both quoted by Jones and Stallybrass, "Dismantling Irena," 162. Jones and Stallybrass's account of the early modern English dread of men rendered effeminate abroad—in this instance Englishmen contaminated by Irish wet-nurses or Irish wives—suggests that Barbauld's anxieties tap into a longer history of colonial fear and loathing (163–64).

47. Nussbaum, *Torrid Zones*, 93.

48. There are other, more explicit, expressions of the revenge of the enslaved subject: Midgely points to Henry Fuseli's painting *The Negro Revenged*, in which an African man and woman seem to invoke lightning to destroy a ship (presumably a slaver). Midgley reproduces an 1807 engraving by Raimbach that glosses the painting with (slightly misquoted) lines from Cowper's "The Negro's Complaint" in which a Christian God responds to a slave's appeal:

> Hark! he answers—Wild tornadoes,
> Strewing yonder seas with wrecks;
> Wasting towns, plantations, meadows,
> Are the voice with which he speaks.
> *(Midgley,* Women against Slavery, *12–13)*

49. Not only in poetry: Edmund Burke's speeches in his prosecution of Warren Hastings call relentless attention to the fact that corrupt fortunes made overseas would suborn British institutions and values: "enormous wealth has poured into this country from India through a thousand channels, public and concealed; and it is no derogation from our honour to suppose a possibility of being corrupted by that by which other empires have been corrupted." Burke's comment, from his "Speech in Opening the Impeachment" (February 15, 1788), was only the most recent, and spectacular, instance of such polemic (*Works*, 9.341).

50. Ward, "British West Indies," 425; see also 424–28.

51. Quoted in Davidoff and Hall, *Family Fortunes*, 429.

52. Midgley, *Women against Slavery*, 34.

53. The quoted phrases are from Nussbaum, *Torrid Zones*, 193.

54. Ferguson, *Subject to Others*, 6.

55. Pagden, *Lords of All the World*, 10.

56. See, for instance, Thomas Gray's tripos verses in Latin, "Luna est habitabilis" (1737). I have argued that such whimsical and occasional poems can also be read as palimpsestic records of the influence of empire on the poetic imagination (*Gray and Literary Authority*, esp. 166–202).

Conclusion

1. Conrad, *Heart of Darkness*, 18–20.

2. Armitage, "Literature and Empire," 104–5. Armitage draws upon Fitzmaurice's essay "Classical Rhetoric."

3. Thomson and Mallet, *Alfred*, 2.iii.

4. Frye, *Anatomy of Criticism*, 105–6.

5. In *Sinews*, Brewer shows how the British Empire required the efforts not only of military and political heroes, but of now-anonymous record keepers, clerks, and those who developed the logistical apparatus necessary to sustain long, brutal campaigns overseas. The work of these faceless men made possible the fiscal-military state, and thus its victories and the empire. This is a useful model for a critic who would study the writing of poets who have dropped out of the celebrations of literary-historical memory, and a reminder that these near-anonymous poets are the faceless men whose rhetorical toil helped produce eighteenth-century literary culture and thus built and sustained the national consciousness necessary to the making of empire.

6. Pagden, *Lords of All the World*, 6.

7. Ibid., 10.

8. Chandler, *England in 1819*, 45–46; Levinson, *Wordsworth's Great Period Poems*, 39.

9. Roach, *Cities of the Dead*, 124.

WORKS CITED

Adas, Michael. *Machines as the Measure of Men: Science, Technology, and Ideologies of Western Dominance.* Delhi: Oxford Univ. Press, 1990.

Addison, Joseph. *Cato.* In *British Dramatists from Dryden to Sheridan*, ed. G. H. Nettleton and A. H. Case, rev. G. W. Stone. Carbondale: Southern Illinois Univ. Press, 1969.

———. "A Letter from Italy, to the Right Honourable Charles Lord Halifax." In *The New Oxford Book of Eighteenth-Century Verse*, ed. Roger Lonsdale. Oxford: Oxford Univ. Press, 1984.

———. *The Spectator.* Ed. Donald F. Bond. 5 vols. Oxford: Oxford Univ. Press, 1965.

Albion, R. G. *Forests and Sea Power: The Timber Problem of the Royal Navy, 1652–1862.* Cambridge: Harvard Univ. Press, 1926.

Alpers, Paul. *The Singer of the Eclogues.* Berkeley: Univ. of California Press, 1979.

Anderson, Benedict. *Imagined Communities: Reflections on the Origin and Spread of Nationalism.* 2nd ed. London: Verso, 1991.

Andrews, Kenneth R. *Trade, Plunder, and Settlement: Maritime Enterprise and the Genesis of the British Empire, 1480–1630.* Cambridge: Cambridge Univ. Press, 1984.

Anstey, Roger. *The Atlantic Slave Trade and British Abolition, 1760–1810.* Atlantic Highlands, N.J.: Humanities Press, 1975.

Appleby, Joyce Oldham. *Economic Thought and Ideology in Seventeenth-Century England.* Princeton: Princeton Univ. Press, 1978.

Armitage, David. "The Cromwellian Protectorate and the Languages of Empire." *Historical Journal* 35, no. 3 (1992): 531–55.

———. "Literature and Empire." In *Origins of Empire*, ed. Nicholas Canny, 104–5.

Atkinson, R. J. C. "Stonehenge and the History of Antiquarian Thought." In *Stonehenge.* London: H. Hamilton, 1956.

Aylmer, G. E. "Navy, State, Trade, and Empire." In *Origins of Empire*, ed. Nicholas Canny, 467–80.

Ayres, Philip. *Classical Culture and the Idea of Rome in Eighteenth-Century England.* Cambridge: Cambridge Univ. Press, 1997.

Azim, Firdaus. *The Colonial Rise of the Novel.* London: Routledge, 1993.

Baillie, Joanna. *Poems.* London, 1790. Rpt. Oxford: Woodstock Books, 1994.

Barbauld, Anna Letitia. *Poems.* Ed. William McCarthy and Elizabeth Kraft. Athens: Univ. of Georgia Press, 1994.

Barber, Mary. *Poems on Several Occasions.* London, 1735.

Barker, Anthony J. *The African Link: British Attitudes to the Negro in the Era of the Atlantic Slave Trade, 1550–1807.* London: Frank Cass, 1978.

Barrell, John, and Harriet Guest. "The Uses of Contradiction: Pope's 'Epistle to Bathurst.'" In John Barrell. *Poetry, Language, and Politics,* 79–99. Manchester: Manchester Univ. Press, 1988.

Barrell, John. *English Literature in History, 1730–80: An Equal, Wide Survey.* London: Hutchinson, 1983.

Bass, Jeff D. "An Efficient Humanitarianism: The British Slave Trade Debates, 1791–92." *Quarterly Journal of Speech,* 75 (1989): 152–65.

Bate, Walter Jackson. *The Burden of the Past and the English Poet.* Cambridge, Mass.: Belknap Press, 1970.

Bayly, C. A. *Imperial Meridian: The British Empire and the World, 1780–1830.* London: Longman, 1989.

Behn, Aphra. *Oroonoko.* Ed. Joanna Lipking. New York: Norton, 1997.

Beljame, Alexandre. *Men of Letters and the English Public in the Eighteenth Century.* Trans. E. O. Lorimer. London: Kegan Paul, Trench, Trubner, 1948.

Berkeley, George. "On the Prospect of Planting Arts and Learning in America." In *The New Oxford Book of Eighteenth-Century Verse,* ed. Roger Lonsdale. Oxford: Oxford Univ. Press, 1984.

Black, Jeremy. *The British Abroad: The Grand Tour in the Eighteenth Century.* London: Stroud, 1992.

———. Introduction to *Culture and Society in Britain, 1660–1800,* ed. Jeremy Black, 1–28. Manchester: Manchester Univ. Press, 1997.

Blackburn, Robin. *The Overthrow of Colonial Slavery, 1776–1848.* London: Verso, 1998.

Blackmore, Richard. *Eliza, An Epick Poem.* London, 1705.

Bloom, Harold. *The Anxiety of Influence.* New York: Oxford Univ. Press, 1973.

Boire, Gary. 'Wide-wasting Pest': Social History in *The Vanity of Human Wishes." Eighteenth Century Life,* 12, no. 1 (1988): 73–85.

Bolingbroke, Henry St. John, Viscount. *Political Writings.* Ed. David Armitage. Cambridge: Cambridge Univ. Press, 1997.

Bolt. Christine, and Seymour Drescher, eds. *Anti-Slavery, Religion, and Reform: Essays in Memory of Roger Anstey.* Hamden, Conn.: Archon Books, 1980.

Brewer, John. *The Common People and Politics, 1750–1790s: The English Satirical Print, 1600–1832.* Cambridge, U.K.: Chadwyck-Healy, 1986.

———. *The Sinews of Power: War, Money and the English State, 1688–1783.* London: Unwin Hyman, 1989.

Brewer, John, and Roy Porter, eds. *Consumption and the World of Goods.* London: Routledge, 1993.

Brown, Laura. *Alexander Pope.* Oxford: Blackwell, 1985.

———. *The Ends of Empire: Women and Ideology in Eighteenth-Century English Literature.* Ithaca: Cornell Univ. Press, 1993.

Brown, Marshall. *Preromanticism.* Stanford: Stanford Univ. Press, 1991.

Burden, Michael. *Garrick, Arne, and the Masque of "Alfred": A Case Study in National, Theatrical and Musical Politics.* Lewiston, N.Y.: Edwin Mellen, 1994.

Burke, Edmund. *The Works of the Right Honourable Edmund Burke.* 12 vols. Boston, Little, Brown, 1866.

Burke, Helen M. "*Annus Mirabilis* and the Ideology of the New Science." *ELH,* 57, no. 2 (1990): 307–34.

Canny, Nicholas. *The Elizabethan Conquest of Ireland: A Pattern Established, 1565–1576.* New York: Barnes & Noble, 1976.

———. "The Origins of Empire," introduction to *The Origins of Empire: British Overseas Enterprise to the Close of the Seventeenth Century,* ed. Nicholas Canny. In vol. 1 of *The Oxford History of the British Empire,* ed. William Roger Louis. Oxford: Oxford Univ. Press, 1998.

———. "The Permissive Frontier: The Problem of Social Control in English Settlements in Ireland and Virginia, 1550–1650." In *The Westward Enterprise: English Activities in Ireland, the Atlantic and America, 1480–1650,* ed. K. R. Andrews, Nicholas Canny, and P. E. H. Hair, 17–44. Liverpool: Liverpool Univ. Press, 1978.

Cecil, David. *The Stricken Deer.* London: Constable, 1933.

Centlivre, Susannah. *A Bold Stroke for a Wife.* Ed. Thalia Stathas. Lincoln: Univ. of Nebraska Press, 1968.

Chandler, James. *England in 1819: The Politics of Literary Culture and the Case of Romantic Historicism.* Chicago: Univ. of Chicago Press, 1998.

Chaudhuri, K. N. *Trade and Civilisation in the Indian Ocean: An Economic History from the Rise of Islam to 1750.* Cambridge: Cambridge Univ. Press, 1985.

Cherniak, Warren L. *The Poetry of Limitation: A Study of Edmund Waller.* New Haven: Yale Univ. Press, 1968.

Cohen, Michèle. *Fashioning Masculinity: National Identity and Language in the Eighteenth Century.* London: Routledge, 1996.

Cohen, Ralph. *The Unfolding of the Seasons.* Baltimore: Johns Hopkins Univ. Press, 1970.

Colley, Linda. "Britishness and Otherness: An Argument." *Nations and Nationalisms: France, Britain, Ireland, and the Eighteenth-century Context.* Oxford: Voltaire Foundation, 1995.

———. *Britons: Forging the Nation 1707–1837.* New Haven: Yale Univ. Press, 1992.

Conrad, Joseph. *Heart of Darkness.* New York, Penguin, 1995.

Cooper, Richard. "Poetry in Ruins: The Literary Context of du Bellay's Cycles on Rome." *Renaissance Studies,* 3, no. 2 (1989): 156–66.

Corrigan, Philip, and Derek Sayer. *The Great Arch: English State Formation as Cultural Revolution.* Oxford: Blackwell, 1985.

Cowper, William. *The Poems of William Cowper.* Ed. John D. Baird and Charles Ryskamp. 3 vols. Oxford: Clarendon, 1995.

Craddock, Patricia B. "Edward Gibbon and the 'Ruins of the Capitol.'" In *Roman Images,* ed. Annabel Patterson, 63–82. Baltimore: Johns Hopkins Univ. Press, 1984.

Crawford, Robert. *Devolving English Literature.* Oxford: Clarendon, 1992.

Crider, John. "Structure and Effect in Collins' Progress Poems." *Studies in Philology,* 60 (1963): 57–72.

Croaker, John Wilson, "Mrs. Barbauld's *Eighteen Hundred and Eleven.*" *Quarterly Review,* 7 (June 1812). Rpt. in *British Romantic Poets,* vol. 1, ed. Caroline Franklin, 377–81. London: Thoemmes, 1998.

Cuguano, Ottobah. *Thoughts and Sentiments on the Evil and Wicked Traffic of the Slavery and Commerce of the Human Species.* London, 1787.

Culler, Jonathan. *Pursuit of Signs: Semiotics, Literature, Deconstruction.* Ithaca: Cornell Univ. Press, 1981.

Dabydeen, David. "Eighteenth-century English Literature on Commerce and Slavery." In *The Black Presence in English Literature,* ed. David Dabydeen, 26–49. Manchester: Manchester Univ. Press, 1985.

Davidoff, Leonore and Catherine Hall. *Family Fortunes: Men and Women of the English Middle Class, 1780–1850.* Chicago: Univ. of Chicago Press, 1987.

Davis, David Brion. *The Problem of Slavery in the Age of Revolution.* Ithaca: Cornell Univ. Press, 1975.

———. *The Problem of Slavery in Western Culture.* Ithaca: Cornell Univ. Press, 1966.

Davis, Ralph. *The Rise of the English Shipping Industry in the Seventeenth and Eighteenth Centuries.* London: Macmillan, 1962.

Defoe, Daniel. *The True-Born Englishman. In Poems on Affairs of State: Augustan Satirical Verse, 1660–1714,* vol. 6, *1697–1704,* ed. Frank H. Ellis. New Haven: Yale Univ. Press, 1970.

Dixon, Peter. *Oliver Goldsmith Revisited.* Boston: Twayne, 1991.

Dobrée, Bonamy. "The Theme of Patriotism in the Poetry of the Earlier Eighteenth Century." *Proceedings of the British Academy,* 35 (1949): 49–65.

Dodd, William. *Poems.* London, 1767.

Doody, Margaret Anne. *The Daring Muse: Augustan Poetry Reconsidered.* Cambridge: Cambridge Univ. Press, 1985.

Dowling, William C. *The Epistolary Moment: The Poetics of the Eighteenth-Century Verse Epistle.* Princeton: Princeton Univ. Press, 1991.

Dryden, John. *The Works of John Dryden.* In 20 vols., ed. Edward N. Hooker, H. T. Swedenberg Jr., and Alan Roper. Berkeley, Univ. of California Press, 1956–.

Easthope, Anthony. *Poetry as Discourse.* London: Methuen, 1983.

Edmundson, G. *Anglo-Dutch Rivalry during the First Half of the Seventeenth Century.* Oxford: Oxford Univ. Press, 1911.

Elliott, J. H.. *The Old World and the New, 1492–1650.* Cambridge: Cambridge Univ. Press, 1970.

Ellis, Markman. *The Politics of Sensibility: Race, Gender, and Commerce in the Sentimental Novel.* Cambridge: Cambridge Univ. Press, 1996.

Equiano, Olaudah. *The Interesting Narrative of the Life of Olaudah Equiano, or Gustavus Vassa, the African, Written by Himself.* London, 1789.

Erskine-Hill, Howard. *The Augustan Idea in English Literature.* London: E. Arnold, 1983.

Evans, J. Martin. "Milton's Imperial Epic." In *Of Poetry and Politics: New Essays on Milton and His World,* ed. P. G. Stanwood, 229–38. Binghampton, N.Y.: Medieval and Renaissance Texts and Studies, 1995.

———. *Milton's Imperial Epic: Paradise Lost and the Discourse of Colonialism.* Ithaca: Cornell Univ. Press, 1996.

Falconar, Maria, and Harriet Falconar. *Poems of Slavery.* London, 1788.

Feingold, Richard. *Nature and Society: Later Eighteenth-Century Uses of the Pastoral and Georgic.* New Brunswick: Rutgers Univ. Press, 1978.

Ferguson, Moira. *Subject to Others: British Women Writers and Colonial Slavery, 1670–1834*. New York: Routledge, 1994.

Fitzgerald, William. *Agonistic Poetry: The Pindaric Mode in Pindar, Horace, Hölderlin, and the English Ode*. Berkeley: Univ. of California Press, 1987.

Fitzmaurice, Andrew. "Classical Rhetoric and the Promotion of the New World." *Journal of the History of Ideas*, 58 (1997): 121–44.

Ford, Charles Howard. *Hannah More: A Critical Biography*. New York: Peter Lang, 1996.

Foss, Michael. *The Age of Patronage*. Ithaca: Cornell Univ. Press, 1971.

Friedman, Donald M. "Andrew Marvell." In *The Cambridge Companion to English Poetry: Donne to Marvell*, ed. Thomas N. Corns. Cambridge: Cambridge Univ. Press, 1993.

Fry, Paul H. *The Poet's Calling in the English Ode*. New Haven: Yale Univ. Press, 1980.

Frye, Northrop. *The Anatomy of Criticism*. Princeton: Princeton Univ. Press, 1957.

Fryer, Peter. *Staying Power: The History of Black People in Britain*. London: Pluto, 1984.

Fulford, Tim. *Landscape, Liberty, and Authority: Poetry, Criticism and Politics from Thomson to Wordsworth*. Cambridge: Cambridge Univ. Press, 1996.

Gerrard, Christine. *The Patriot Opposition to Walpole: Politics, Poetry, and National Myth, 1725–1742*. Oxford: Clarendon, 1994.

Gibbon, Edward. *The History of the Decline and Fall of the Roman Empire*. London: 1776/1788.

Gilbert, Jack G. *Edmund Waller*. Boston: Twayne, 1979.

Glover, Richard. *London: or, the Progress of Commerce. A Poem*. 2nd ed. London, 1739.

Goldgar, Bertrand. *Walpole and the Wits: The Relation of Politics to Literature, 1722–42*. Lincoln: Univ. of Nebraska Press, 1976.

Goldsmith, Oliver. *Collected Works*. Ed. Arthur Friedman. 5 vols. Oxford: Clarendon, 1966.

Goldstein, Laurence. *Ruins and Empire: The Evolution of a Theme in Augustan and Romantic Literature*. Pittsburgh: Univ. of Pittsburgh Press, 1977.

Goodridge, John. *Rural Life in Eighteenth-Century English Poetry*. Cambridge: Cambridge Univ. Press, 1995.

Grant, Douglas. *James Thomson: Poet of the Seasons*. London: Cresset, 1951.

Greenblatt, Stephen. *Learning to Curse: Essays in Early Modern Culture*. New York, Routledge, 1990.

———. *Marvelous Possessions: The Wonder of the New World*. Oxford: Clarendon, 1991.

———. *Renaissance Self-Fashioning: From More to Shakespeare*. Chicago, Univ. of Chicago Press, 1980.

Greene, Joseph A. "Lebanon." In *The Oxford Companion to the Bible*, eds. Bruce M. Metzger and Michael D. Coogan, 428. Oxford: Oxford University Press, 1993.

Greenfield, Liah. *Nationalism: Five Roads to Modernity*. Cambridge: Harvard Univ. Press, 1992.

Griffin, Dustin H. *Literary Patronage In England, 1650–1800*. Cambridge: Cambridge Univ. Press, 1996.

———. "Redefining Georgic: Cowper's *Task*." *ELH*, 57, no. 4 (1990): 865–79.

Hall, Stuart. "Signification, Representation, Ideology: Althusser and the Post-Structuralist Debates." *Critical Studies in Mass Communication*, 2, no. 2 (1985): 91–114.

Hartman, Geoffrey H. "Romantic Poetry and the Genius Loci." In *Beyond Formalism*. New Haven: Yale Univ. Press, 1970.

Hawkins, Richard. *Discourse of the Nationall Excellencies of England*. London: 1658.

Helgerson, Richard. *Forms of Nationhood: The Elizabethan Writing of England*. Chicago: Univ. of Chicago Press, 1992.

Herodotus. *The Histories*. Trans. David Grene. Chicago: Univ. of Chicago Press, 1987.

Hippocrates. *Airs, Waters, Places*. Trans. W. H. S. Jones. London: Heinemann, 1926.

Hirschman, Albert O. *The Passions and the Interests: Political Arguments for Capitalism before its Triumph*. Princeton: Princeton Univ. Press, 1977.

Hollander, John. *Rhyme's Reason*. New Haven: Yale Univ. Press, 1981.

Hulme, Peter. *Colonial Encounters: Europe and the Native Caribbean, 1492–1797*. London: Methuen, 1986.

Hunter, Michael. *Science and Society in Restoration England*. Cambridge: Cambridge Univ. Press, 1981.

Jameson, Frederic. *The Political Unconscious: Narrative as a Socially Symbolic Act*. Ithaca: Cornell Univ. Press, 1981.

Janowitz, Anne. *England's Ruins: Poetic Purpose and the National Landscape*. Oxford Blackwell, 1990.

Johnson, Samuel. *Lives of the English Poets: A Selection*. Ed. John Wain. London: Everyman's, 1975.

———. *Poems*. Ed. E. L. McAdam with George Milne. New Haven: Yale Univ. Press, 1964.

Jones, Ann Rosalind, and Peter Stallybrass. "Dismantling Irena: The Sexualizing of Ireland in Early Modern England." In *Nationalisms and Sexualities*, ed. Andrew Parker, Mary Russo, Doris Sommer, and Patricia Yaeger, 157–71. New York: Routledge, 1992.

Jones, Chris. *Radical Sensibility: Literature and Ideas in the 1790s*. London: Routledge, 1993.

Jones, Inigo. *The Most Notable Antiquity of Great Britain, vulgarly called Stone-Heng on Salisbury Plain. Restored by Inigo Jones*. London, 1655.

Jones, J. R. *Britain and the World, 1649–1815*. Atlantic Heights, N.J.: Harvester Press, 1980.

Kaul, Suvir. "Reading Literary Symptoms: Colonial Pathologies and the *Oroonoko* Fictions of Behn, Southerne, and Hawkesworth." *Eighteenth-Century Life*, 18 (1994): 80–96.

———. *Thomas Gray and Literary Authority: A Study of Ideology and Poetics*. Stanford: Stanford Univ. Press, 1992.

———. "Why Selima Drowns: Thomas Gray and the Domestication of the Imperial Ideal." *PMLA*, 105 (1990): 223–32.

Keynes, Geoffrey. *The Life of William Harvey*. Oxford: Clarendon, 1966.

Kliger, Samuel. *The Goths in England: A Study in Seventeenth and Eighteenth Century Thought*. Cambridge: Harvard Univ. Press, 1952.

Kramer, David B. "Onely Victory in him, the Imperial Dryden." In Jennifer Brady, Greg Clingham, David Kramer, and Earl Miner, *Literary Transmission and Authority: Dryden and other Writers*, ed. Earl Miner and Jennifer Brady, 55–78. Cambridge: Cambridge Univ. Press, 1993.

Kroebner, Richard. *Empire*. Cambridge: Cambridge Univ. Press, 1961.

Kroll, Richard W. F. *The Material Word: Literate Culture in the Restoration and the Early Eighteenth Century*. Baltimore: Johns Hopkins Univ. Press, 1991.

Lach, Donald F. *Asia in the Making of Europe*. Vol. 1, bk. 1. Chicago: Univ. of Chicago Press, 1965.

[Lady of Honour, A] "The Golden Island or the Darian Song." In *Kissing the Rod*, ed. Germaine Greer et al., 439–43. New York: Farrar, Straus, Giroux, 1989.

Landa, Louis. "Pope's Belinda: The General Emporie of the World, and the Wondrous Worm." *South Atlantic Quarterly*, 70 (1971): 215–35.

Landry, Donna. *The Muses of Resistance: Working-Class Women's Poetry in Britain, 1739–1796*. Cambridge: Cambridge Univ. Press, 1990.

Larner, Christina. *The Thinking Peasant: Popular and Educated Belief in Pre-industrial Culture*. Glasgow: Pressgang, 1982.

Leask, Nigel. *British Romantic Writers and the East: Anxieties of Empire*. Cambridge: Cambridge Univ. Press, 1993.

Levine, Joseph M. *Dr. Woodward's Shield: History, Science and Satire in Augustan England*. Ithaca: Cornell Univ. Press, 1991.

———. *The Battle of the Books: History and Literature in the Augustan Age*. Ithaca: Cornell Univ. Press, 1991.

Levinson, Marjorie. *Wordsworth's Great Period Poems: Four Essays*. Cambridge: Cambridge Univ. Press, 1986.

Lillo, George. *The London Merchant*. London: 1731.

Lloyd, T. O. *The British Empire, 1588–1983*. Oxford: Oxford Univ. Press, 1984.

Loftis, John, Richard Southern, Marion Jones, and Arthur Scouten. Vol. 5 (1660–1750) of *The "Revels" History of Drama in English*, ed. T. W. Craik. London: Methuen, 1976.

Lonsdale, Roger, ed. *The Poems of Gray, Collins and Goldsmith*. London: Longman, 1969.

Lucas, John. *England and Englishness: Ideas of Nationhood in English Poetry, 1688–1900*. London: Hogarth, 1990.

Lyttelton, [George]. *An Epistle to Mr. Pope, from a Young Gentleman at Rome*. London, 1730.

Macdonald, D. L. "Pre-Romantic and Romantic Abolitionism: Cowper and Blake." *European Romantic Review*, 4, no. 2 (1994): 163–82.

MacLean, Gerald M. *Time's Witness: Historical Representation in English Poetry, 1603–1660*. Madison: Univ. of Wisconsin Press, 1990.

Makdisi, Saree. *Romantic Imperialism: Universal Empire and the Culture of Modernity*. Cambridge: Cambridge Univ. Press, 1998.

Manley, Delarivier. *Secret Memoirs and Manners of several Persons of Quality, of Both Sexes. From the New Atalantis, an Island in the Mediterranean. Written Originally in Italian*. Ed. Ros Ballaster. London: Pikering & Chatto, 1991.

Marvell, Andrew. *Andrew Marvell: Complete Poetry.* Ed. George de F. Lord. Englewood Cliffs, N.J.: Prentice-Hall, 1968.

———. *Selected Poetry and Prose.* Ed. Robert Wilcher. London: Methuen, 1986.

McEachern, Claire. *The Poetics of English Nationhood, 1519–1612.* Cambridge: Cambridge Univ. Press, 1996.

McKendrick, Neil, John Brewer, and J. H. Plumb, eds. *The Birth of a Consumer Society: The Commercialization of Eighteenth-Century England.* London: Europa, 1982.

McKeon, Michael. "Pastoralism, Puritanism, Imperialism, Scientism: Andrew Marvell and the Problem of Mediation." *Yearbook of English Studies,* 13 (1983): 46–67.

———. *Politics and Poetry in Restoration England: The Case of Dryden's "Annus Mirabilis."* Cambridge: Harvard Univ. Press, 1975.

McKillop, A. D. *The Background of Thomson's "Seasons."* Minneapolis: Univ. of Minnesota Press, 1942.

———, ed. *James Thomson, 1700–1748: Letters and Documents.* Lawrence: Univ. of Kansas Press, 1958.

McVeagh, John. *Tradefull Merchants: The Portrayal of the Capitalist in Literature.* London: Routledge & Kegan Paul, 1981.

Meehan, Michael. *Liberty and Poetics in Eighteenth Century England.* London: Croom Helm, 1986.

Midgley, Clare. *Women against Slavery: the British Campaigns, 1780–1870.* London: Routledge, 1992.

Milton, John. *Poetical Works.* Ed. Douglas Bush. Oxford: Oxford Univ. Press, 1973.

Miner, Earl. "Forms and Motives of Narrative Poetry." In *John Dryden,* ed. Earl Miner, 234–66. Athens, Ohio Univ. Press, 1975.

Montagu, Mary Wortley. *Letters Of the Right Honourable Lady M——y W——y M——u, Written, during Her Travels in Europe, Asia and Africa, To Persons of Distinction.* London, 1762.

Montesquieu, Charles de Secondat, Baron de. *The Spirit of Laws.* Trans. Thomas Nugent. Rev. J. V. Prichard. Chicago: Encyclopedia Britannica, 1955.

More, Hannah. *The Slave Trade: A Poem.* London, 1787.

Nagy, Gregory. "The 'Professional Muse' and Models of Prestige in Ancient Greece." *Cultural Critique,* 12 (1989): 133–43.

Nandy, Ashis. *The Intimate Enemy: Loss and Recovery of Self under Colonialism.* Delhi: Oxford Univ. Press, 1983.

Needler, Henry. *The Works of Mr. Henry Needler.* London, 1724. Rpt. Augustan Reprint Society, no. 90. Introduction by Marcia Allentuck. Los Angeles: Clark Memorial Library, Univ. of California, 1961.

Newey, Vincent. "William Cowper and the Condition of England." In *Literature and Nationalism,* ed. Vincent Newey and Ann Thompson, 12–39. Liverpool: Liverpool Univ. Press, 1991.

Newman, Gerald. *The Rise of English Nationalism: a Cultural History, 1740–1830.* London: Weidenfield & Nicolson, 1987.

Nicholson, Colin. *Writing and the Rise of Finance: Capital Satires of the Early Eighteenth Century.* Cambridge: Cambridge Univ. Press, 1994.

Nussbaum, Felicity. *Torrid Zones: Maternity, Sexuality, and Empire in Eighteenth-Century Narratives.* Baltimore: Johns Hopkins Univ. Press, 1995.

O'Gorman, Frank. *The Long Eighteenth Century: British Political and Social History, 1688–1832.* London: Arnold, 1997.

Oldfield, J. R. *Popular Politics and British Anti-Slavery: The Mobilisation of Public Opinion against the Slave Trade 1787–1807.* Manchester: Manchester Univ. Press, 1995.

Pagden, Anthony. *Lords of All the World: Ideologies of Empire in Spain, Britain, and France, c.1500–c.1800.* New Haven: Yale Univ. Press, 1995.

Pedersen, Susan. "Hannah More Meets Simple Simon: Tracts, Chapbooks, and Popular Culture in Late Eighteenth-Century England." *Journal of British Studies,* 25, no. 1 (1986): 84–113.

Pittock, Murray G. H. *Inventing and Resisting Britain: Cultural Identities in Britain and Ireland, 1685–1789.* London: Macmillan, 1997.

Pocock, J. G. A. *Virtue, Commerce, and History: Essays on Political Thought and History, Chiefly in the Eighteenth Century.* Cambridge: Cambridge Univ. Press, 1985.

Pope, Alexander. *Minor Poems.* Ed. Norman Ault and John Butt. New Haven: Yale Univ. Press, 1954.

———. *The Poems of Alexander Pope.* Ed. John Butt. New Haven, Yale Univ. Press, 1963.

Pratt, Mary Louise. *Imperial Eyes: Travel Writing and Transculturation.* London: Routledge, 1992.

Quint, David. *Epic and Empire: Politics and Generic Form from Virgil to Milton.* Princeton: Princeton Univ. Press, 1993.

Rabb, Theodore K. *Enterprise and Empire: Merchant and Gentry Investment in the Expansion of England, 1575–1630.* Cambridge: Harvard Univ. Press, 1967.

Roach, Joseph. *Cities of the Dead: Circum-Atlantic Performance.* New York: Columbia Univ. Press, 1996.

Robertson, J. Logie, ed. *The Complete Poetical Works of James Thomson.* London: Oxford Univ. Press, 1908.

Rogers, Pat. *Grub Street.* London: Methuen, 1972.

Rostvig, Maren Sofie. *The Happy Man: Studies in the Metamorphoses of a Classical Ideal.* 2nd ed. Oslo: Norwegian Universities Press, 1962.

Sambrook, James. *James Thomson, 1700–1748: A Life.* Oxford: Clarendon, 1991.

———, ed. *"The Seasons" and "The Castle of Indolence."* Oxford: Clarendon, 1972.

Savage, Richard. *The Works of Richard Savage.* 2 vols. London, 1777.

Schuster, George N. *The English Ode from Milton to Keats.* New York: Columbia Univ. Press, 1940.

Schwab, Raymond. *The Oriental Renaissance: Europe's Rediscovery of India and the East, 1680–1880.* Trans. Gene Patterson Black and Victor Reinking. New York: Columbia Univ. Press, 1984.

Sekora, John. *Luxury: The Concept in Western Thought, Eden to Smollett.* Baltimore: Johns Hopkins Univ. Press, 1977.

Sharpe, Jenny. *Allegories of Empire.* Minneapolis: Univ. of Minnesota Press, 1993.

Shields, David S. "British-American Belles Lettres." In *The Cambridge History of*

American Literature, vol. 1, *1590–1820,* ed. Sacvan Berkovitch, 309–43. Cambridge: Cambridge Univ. Press, 1994.

———. *Oracles of Empire: Poetry, Politics, and Commerce in British America, 1690– 1750.* Chicago: Univ. of Chicago Press, 1990.

Siskin, Clifford. *The Work of Writing: Literature and Social Change in Britain, 1700– 1830.* Baltimore: Johns Hopkins Univ. Press, 1998.

Sitter, John. *Literary Loneliness in Mid-Eighteenth-century England.* Ithaca: Cornell Univ. Press, 1982.

Smith, Adam. *The Wealth of Nations.* Ed. Edwin Cannan. Chicago: Univ. of Chicago Press, 1976.

Spate, O. H. K. "The Muse of Mercantilism: Jago, Grainger, and Dyer." In *Studies in the Eighteenth Century,* ed. R. F. Brissenden, 119–31. Canberra: Australian National Univ. Press, 1968.

Stallybrass, Peter, and Allon White. *The Politics and Poetics of Transgression.* Ithaca: Cornell Univ. Press, 1986.

Stevenson, John. *Popular Disturbances in England, 1700–1832.* 2nd ed. London: Longman, 1992.

Stevenson, Laura Caroline. *Praise and Paradox: Merchants and Craftsmen in Elizabethan Popular Literature.* Cambridge: Cambridge Univ. Press, 1984.

Temperley, Howard. "Anti-slavery as a Form of Cultural Imperialism." In *Anti-Slavery, Religion, and Reform,* ed. Christine Bolt and Seymour Drescher, 335–50.

Thompson, James. "Dryden's *Conquest of Granada* and the Dutch Wars." *The Eighteenth Century,* 31, no. 3 (1990): 211–26.

Thomson, James. *The Complete Poetical Works of James Thomson.* Ed. J. Logie Robertson. Oxford, Oxford Univ. Press, 1908.

———. *"Liberty," "The Castle of Indolence," and Other Poems.* Ed. James Sambrook. Oxford, Clarendon, 1986.

Thomson, James, and David Mallet. *Alfred: A Masque.* 1740. Rpt. in *The Plays of David Mallet,* ed. Felicity Nussbaum. New York: Garland, 1980.

Todd, Richard. "Equilibrium and National Stereotyping in 'The Character of Holland.'" In *On the Celebrated and Neglected Poems of Andrew Marvell,* ed. Claude J. Summers and Ted-Larry Pebworth, 169–91. Columbia: Univ. of Missouri Press, 1992.

Turner, Frank. *Contesting Cultural Authority.* New York: Cambridge Univ. Press, 1993.

Turner, James. *The Politics of Landscape: Rural Scenery and Society in English Poetry, 1630–1660.* Cambridge: Harvard Univ. Press, 1979.

Virgil, *The Aeneid.* Trans. Robert Fitzgerald. London: Everyman's, 1992.

———. *Georgics.* Trans. H. Rushton Fairclough. 2 vols. Cambridge: Harvard Univ. Press, 1965.

Viswanathan, Gauri. "The Beginnings of English Literary Study in British India." *Oxford Literary Review,* 9, nos. 1–2 (1987): 2–26.

Waller, Edmund. *The Poems of Edmund Waller.* Ed. G. Thorn Drury. 2 vols. London: Routledge, 1893.

Walvin, James. "The Rise of British Popular Sentiment for Abolition, 1787–1832." In *Anti-Slavery, Religion, and Reform,* ed. Christine Bolt and Seymour Drescher, 149–62.

Ward, J. R. "The British West Indies in the Age of Abolition, 1748–1815." In *The Eighteenth Century*, ed. P. J. Marshall, vol. 2. of *The Oxford History of the British Empire*, ed. William Roger Louis, 415–39. Oxford: Oxford Univ. Press, 1998.

Warner, William. "The Elevation of the Novel in England: Hegemony and Literary History." *ELH* 59, no. 3 (1992): 577–96.

Wechselblatt, Martin. "Gender and Race in Yarico's Epistles to Inkle: Voicing the Feminine/Slave." *Studies in Eighteenth-Century Culture*, 19 (1989): 197–223.

Weinbrot, Howard D. *Augustus Caesar in 'Augustan' England: The Decline of a Classical Norm*. Princeton: Princeton Univ. Press, 1978.

———. *Britannia's Issue: The Rise of British Literature from Dryden to Ossian*. Cambridge: Cambridge Univ. Press, 1993.

Wells, Colin. *The Roman Empire*. Stanford: Stanford Univ. Press, 1984.

Welsted, Leonard. *Poems on Several Occasions*. In *The Works*. London, 1787.

Wilcher, Robert. *Andrew Marvell: Selected Poetry and Prose*. London: Methuen, 1986.

Williams, Glyn, and John Ramsden. *Ruling Britannia: A Political History of Britain, 1688–1988*. London: Longman, 1990.

Williams, Raymond. *The Country and the City*. London: Chatto & Windus, 1973.

Wilson, Kathleen. *The Sense of the People: Politics, Culture, and Imperialism in England, 1715–1785*. Cambridge: Cambridge Univ. Press, 1995.

Winn, James. *John Dryden and His World*. New Haven: Yale Univ. Press, 1987.

Womersley, David. *The Transformation of "The Decline and Fall of the Roman Empire."* Cambridge: Cambridge Univ. Press, 1988.

Young, Edward. *Conjectures on Original Composition*. London: 1759.

———. *The Poetical Works of Edward Young*. 2 vols. London: Bell & Daldy, 1866.

Zahedieh, Nuala. "Overseas Expansion and Trade in the Seventeenth Century." In *The Origins of Empire*, ed. Nicholas Canny, 398–422.

Zuckerman, Michael. "Identity in British America: Unease in Eden." In *Colonial Identity in the Atlantic World, 1500–1800*, ed. Nicholas Canny and Anthony Pagden, 117–27. Princeton: Princeton Univ. Press, 1987.

Zwicker, Steven. *Lines of Authority: Politics and English Literary Culture, 1649–1689*. Ithaca: Cornell Univ. Press, 1993.

INDEX

Winners of the Walker Cowen Memorial Prize

Elizabeth Wanning Harries, *The Unfinished Manner: Essays on the Fragment in the Later Eighteenth Century*

Catherine Cusset
No Tomorrow: The Ethics of Pleasure in the French Enlightenment

Lisa Jane Graham
If the King Only Knew: Seditious Speech in the Reign of Louis XV

Suvir Kaul
Poems of Nation, Anthems of Empire: English Verse in the Long Eighteenth Century